With the Border Ruffians

R.H. Williams, J.P.
ætat 70.

WITH THE
BORDER RUFFIANS

MEMORIES OF THE FAR WEST
1852—1868

BY R. H. WILLIAMS
SOMETIME LIEUTENANT IN THE KANSAS RANGERS
AND AFTERWARDS CAPTAIN IN THE TEXAN RANGERS

EDITED BY E. W. WILLIAMS

With Historical Notes by Arthur J. Mayer
and Joseph W. Snell

University of Nebraska Press
Lincoln and London

First Bison Book printing: November 1982
Most recent printing indicated by the first digit below:
1   2   3   4   5   6   7   8   9   10

Library of Congress Cataloging in Publication Data
Williams, R. H. (Robert Hamilton), b. 1831.
   With the border ruffians.
   Reprint. Originally published: London: J. Murray, 1907.
   1. Williams, R. H. (Robert Hamilton), b. 1831. 2. United States—
History—Civil War, 1861–1865—Personal narratives—Confederate
side. 3. Virginia—Description and travel. 4. Kansas—History—
1854–1861. 5. Texas—History—Civil War, 1861–1865. 6. Sol-
diers—Kansas—Biography. 7. Soldiers—Texas—Biography. I. Wil-
liams, E. W. II. Title.
E605.W72 1982   973.7'82   82-8400
ISBN 0-8032-4721-4   AACR2
ISBN 0-8032-9704-1 (pbk.)

With the Border Ruffians: Memories of the Far West, 1852–1868 was first
published by John Murray, London, in 1907.

PUBLISHER'S PREFACE

Written and published many years after the events described, *With the Border Ruffians: Memories of the Far West, 1852–1868* mentions many names and places that may be unfamiliar to modern readers. To make matters more complex, Williams often changed names, to shield real people or from lapses in memory. To assist readers of the Bison Edition, historical notes have been appended to the text. Notes for the Kansas chapters were prepared by Joseph W. Snell; notes for the Texas chapters were prepared by Arthur J. Mayer. The notes begin on page 473.

CONTENTS

BOOK I

WESTERN VIRGINIA, 1852–54

CONTENTS

BOOK II

KANSAS IN 1855-59

CHAPTER III

The Delaware Reserve Sales—Scenes at the Auction—
Owner of a Gambling Saloon—Claim-making on the
Shawnee Reserve—" Shad " the Frontiersman—Judge
Lecompton—Attempt to Arrest Cline—Fracas at the
Preaching—My Claim is "Jumped."

CHAPTER IV

Settling down on Cedar Creek—Claim-jumpers Again—
Wagon-master with Major & Russell—A Bully at a Dance—
Shawnee Half-breed Girls—Sally Blue-Jacket—A Shawnee
Execution—Member of Johnson County Board—Sunday
at the Ranch—A Fight between Rival Squatter Associa-
tions—Death of Molesby—A well-armed Funeral Party.

CHAPTER V

A Western Tornado—A Lawsuit re Cedar Creek Claim—
A Western Water-wizard—A Cold-blooded Murder—A
Stealthy Ride into Missouri—A Clever Catch—A Trial and
a Fiasco.

CHAPTER VI

Miliner Let Loose—A Trip to Fort Kearney with Forty-
five Wagons—Through the Sioux Country—A Vast Herd of
Buffalo—The Daughter of Tecumseh—Wintering Cattle for
" Billy " Russell—Margaret Hendricks, a Typical Western
Girl—Cline redivivus—His Threats of Vengeance—He
takes out a Warrant, and I leave Kansas.

CHAPTER VII

Kidnapping on the Mississippi—Crossing the Alleghanies—
Changes at Home—I revisit Monticello—Engineering at
Philadelphia—There I meet Thompson—Go to Canada
with him—We decide against Canada, and for Texas—The
Journey thither—Landing at Indianola.

BOOK III

TEXAS, 1860–62

CHAPTER I

CHAPTER II

CHAPTER III

CHAPTER IV

CHAPTER V

CHAPTER VI

CHAPTER VII

BOOK IV

IN THE CONFEDERATE SERVICE

CHAPTER I

CHAPTER II

CHAPTER VII

CHAPTER VIII

CHAPTER IX

CHAPTER X

CHAPTER XI

CONTENTS

Major Hatch wants to Hang Them—My own Boys Support my Refusal—" Now See to it that I haven't to Shoot You "—Fruitless Wanderings after Indians—Sent on Scout with Mexicans—Their Cowardice—We white men hold a Strong Position—No Water and no Tobacco !—Eight of the Deserters Escape.

CHAPTER XII

A Dry March—The First Day without Water—The Major Still Obstinate—The Second Day without Water—The Third Day we can stand it no longer—A Disorganised Rabble—A Drink at Last—The Major and I Part—The Back Trail—A Difficult and Unknown Country—Westfall Brings us Through.

CHAPTER XIII

Magruder and " Commissary " Banks—Colonel Ford and his Merry Men—Resignation of Command and Re-election—The Expedition to Fort Lancaster—Major Hunter's Reconnaissance—The Enemy's False Security—A Night Attack—Surprise and Rout of Californians.

CHAPTER XIV

An Unfortunate Spec.—Comanchés Again—A Race for Cover—We Hold a " Mott "—Jack Hillson's Shot—A Chip of the Old Block—The Fight on the Hondo—Comanchés in Strong Position—I Shoot the Big Buck—A Charge and a Surprise—The Indians Bolt.

CHAPTER XV

Jim and Dick French—The Murder of the Mexicans—French senior Hanged in Front of the Padre's House in San Antonio—The Boys Agree to Bide their Time—Jim and Dick Avenge their Father's Death—I meet them at Atacosa Court House—Their Doings There—Their Search for Asa Minshul.

BOOK V

THE BREAK-UP, AND AFTER

CHAPTER I

CHAPTER II

CHAPTER III

CHAPTER IV

CONTENTS

LIST OF ILLUSTRATIONS

INTRODUCTION

HE whose adventurous story is told in the following pages was born in the summer of 1831, the eldest of a large family, his father being a country clergyman.

His father and mother intended him for the Church ; he himself had aspirations for the Army, or the Indian Service, but neither could be managed for lack of means. Finally he went to sea as a middy on Messrs. Green's East Indiaman the *Madagascar*, sailing from London in February, 1848, when he was nearly seventeen years old. Green's was in those days the best service in England ; but it was too staid, too quiet, for a youth like this, thirsting for adventure, so after one voyage to India he gave it up.

After this he shipped as an ordinary seaman on a Liverpool barque, bound for Callao to load with guano at the Pixo Islands. The ship, having got her evil-smelling cargo on board, returned to Callao, where the boy (he was only eighteen) deserted to escape the brutal ill-treatment of the captain. When the barque had sailed he emerged from his hiding-place in the pampas, and for some months worked as mate on board a small coasting brig.

The gold fever in California was then at its height, and his next idea was to get to the new Eldorado if possible, where fortune awaited the fortunate and adventures were to be met with at every turn. But no passage was obtainable for love or money ; for every ship bound for San Francisco was full of eager gold-seekers and there

was no room for him. So at last, weary of waiting, he
shipped as an A.B. on board a 600-ton barque, bound
for Dundee with a cargo of guano.

It is not proposed to tell his adventures on that leaky
old tub, which took six months to roll herself round the
Horn to the Cove of Cork. Suffice it to say that the
miserable craft, like so many of her class in those bad
days, was short of hands, short of provisions, short of
water, short of everything, in fact, but that awful guano
that pervaded everything on board.

With a dislocated shoulder, and half dead with scurvy,
the lad was discharged at Cork, and sent to hospital,
whence, being then as tough a specimen of humanity as
you could wish to see, he speedily made his way home,
in no way the worse for his rough experiences.

But he wouldn't give up the sea yet, and next went a
voyage to Adelaide in a full-rigged emigrant ship named
the *Andromache*, as third officer. From that port, which
in the year of grace 1850 consisted of a few " frame "
houses and many streets pegged out by speculators, they
sailed for Melbourne, where the young ship's officer went
wallaby-hunting with some friends over country now
covered with villas and parks, and had good sport of its
kind.

When, after a brief holiday at home, the *Andromache*
was due to sail again, he was persuaded to give up the
sea, in the hope that he would settle down in England.
So the good ship, with its full complement of passengers
and crew, sailed from London without him, on what
proved her last voyage, for she was never heard of more,
and must have foundered with all hands somewhere on
the stormy ocean.

But he *couldn't* settle down to life in quiet England ;
the restless craving for adventure was too strong on him,
and if he must leave the sea, he would fare forth to the
West and the backwoods of the Great Republic. So,
after a brief apprenticeship to farming with the Vicarage

tenant, he sailed from Liverpool on a small barque called the *Sutlej*, bound for City Point, Virginia.

Having given this brief sketch of the opening chapters of an adventurous life, the rest of the story shall be told mainly in the words of the actor therein, from his notes and diaries, supplemented by many a yarn told by him to the writer as they smoked their pipes together by the happy fireside of the peaceful English home in which he lived, and in which he ended his days, full of years and full of honour.

A strange, wild story it is too, and perhaps worth the telling, if only for the reason that the stage on which it was enacted has so completely changed that the scenes in which the adventurer took his part, and the life he led in the far West and South, can never recur as long as the world endures. Civilisation, railways, and the advancing tide of population have swept them into the limbo of forgotten things so completely that it is hard to realise that such a state of society could ever really have existed only forty or fifty years ago.

The first act runs its course in Western Virginia amongst the then most primitive, simple, and manly race of farmers to be found in any part of the world. Far from railways, towns and civilisation, these simple folks led their pastoral lives in great content and comfort. All their wants were self-supplied, to their very clothes, which they spun and weaved and made themselves. Work on their farms, hunting and fishing, a visit to the distant " Court House " in the far-away town or village, with now and then a " preaching " or " camp meeting," filled their lives, and they were content.

Act the Second has for its scene the wildest of the Wild West—Kansas—where in 1855-56 was fought the prelude to the great War of Secession, the epoch-making struggle between North and South, which settled once for all the burning question of slavery or freedom for the negro in the United States. In that border region, where each man was a law unto himself, and life was not valued "at a pin's fee," deeds were done, on *both sides*, at which we may well shudder.

The story is a dreadful one, but it is fairly and frankly told by him who took an active part on the pro-slavery side, and who never hesitated to risk his life for the cause he had espoused.

Act the Third, after a brief interlude at home and in Canada, opens in Texas, on a cattle ranch, in the heart of the Comanché (Indian) country.

Cattle raising and desperate fighting with the Comanchés, the most warlike of all the Indian tribes, fill the first scenes.

Then comes the War of the Secession.

Shortly after the end of the war in 1865, the curtain falls, and the story is finished.

BOOK I

WESTERN VIRGINIA

1852–54

CHAPTER I

IT was in the early spring of the year 1852 that I sailed from Liverpool to seek my fortune in the United States.

Those who have not personally watched the growth of that marvellous country cannot realise the changes those fifty years have wrought, so long in a man's life, so short a span in a nation's history. Then there were thirty-one States in the Union with a population of about twenty-five millions ; now there are forty-one States, and the population verges on eighty million souls. Railways were comparatively few ; now there are nearly two hundred thousand miles in operation.

When I first went West, in the early 'fifties, all the region west of the Missouri River to the Rocky Mountains, from about 35° N. to the limits of what are now the States of North Dakota and Montana, was inhabited only by roaming bands of Indians, except in Kansas and Nebraska, where there were a few settlers. Where to-day stand flourishing towns and cities, and over the plains where now is heard the busy hum of the steam reaping and thrashing machines, roamed countless thousands of buffalo ; as extinct to-day in those lands as the dodo is in his.

But the greatest change that Time has brought, since I first knew the States, is the abolition of negro slavery.

In those days the Southern States, with their great " Institution," were at the zenith of their power, and were ambitious of extending it beyond the boundary to

3

which they had been restricted by the Missouri Compromise of 1820.

I fought for that cause in Kansas, in what may be called the prelude to the great struggle between the North and South, and in Texas, and elsewhere, afterwards ; for in those days I believed in slavery, and owned some few negroes myself. Looking back through all these years, whilst I sit by my quiet, happy English fireside, I confess that I was mistaken, and freely admit that it is well the great fight ended as it did. But though I make this admission, I think it is only right to put it on record that, as far as my own personal observation went, the cruelties of slavery have been over-drawn.

The separation of families, by the sale of the father, mother or children, was cruel and detestable. Doubtless there were here and there brutal masters, and worse overseers ; but these were the exception. Negroes, it must be remembered, were *chattels*, and most valuable chattels too, and it was the owner's interest to treat them well. On the great cotton plantations of the South, where the planter lived in patriarchal state, and owned perhaps two or three hundred slaves, or more, the negroes were generally well treated and happy enough, except for the overshadowing fear of separation.

Slavery on the American Continent has vanished into the limbo of almost forgotten things ; the planter, with his opulent, easy-going life and boundless hospitality, is extinct, but the negro remains, and increases and multiplies, after his kind, and, as I gather, becomes a daily more and more difficult problem to deal with.

It was in the month of February, 1852, being then a lad of twenty, but with some rough experiences at sea behind me, that I set sail from Liverpool in the *Sutlej,* a barque bound for City Point, Virginia.

The capital I had at my disposal was £400, which my father had raised for me with some difficulty. Resources

had to be carefully husbanded, so I took a steerage
passage, and shared the discomforts thereof with a party
of emigrants going out to settle on lands in West Virginia.
Most of these had been lured to try their fortunes in that
forest land by the specious tongue of an agent in London,
and had cause to rue the day they met him. I myself
was one of his intended victims, but broke loose from his
toils as soon as I saw the country in which he intended
to bury me.

Amongst many presents given me by kind friends I
had a beautiful liver-coloured setter, bought at a great
price for me by four kind lady friends, who lived together
in my father's parish, and were a centre of peace and
goodness for all the neighbourhood. I called the dog
" Manor " after the house from which he came, and he
was a true friend and companion to me until, to my
great sorrow, I lost him some years after in the West.

Amongst the emigrants I found a typical navvy from
Lancashire, Jack Galliers by name, who for some reason
took to me at once, appointing himself my henchman,
looking after my dog, and my things, with much assiduity.
He was a very fine specimen of that wonderful breed,
the British navvy, which no other country, as far as I
know, can produce. He dressed the part, too, to perfec-
tion, in massive hob-nailed high-lows and moleskin
garments.

His contempt for America, and Americans, and all
their ways and doings, was unbounded, nor did he ever
attempt to disguise his sentiments. Indeed, so much
was this the case that when, in his most candid moods,
he would " dom " America, and all things therein, I often
feared he would be mobbed. But no, the Virginians only
seemed to marvel at him and his ways, as though he had
been some strange denizen of an unknown land. When
he clenched his " fistises " and bragged what he could do
with them, or boasted that " my country," as he always
called it, was far better than theirs, they only laughed,

and treated him to whiskey, of which poor Jack could swallow any quantity. Then they would get him to sing, which he did readily enough in a fine, mellow tenor ; or dance a clog dance in those thundering high-lows, to their intense amusement. So Jack, his eccentricities notwithstanding, became a most popular character wherever he went, and I had no more anxiety on his behalf.

The old *Sutlej* was loaded with pig-iron and made very bad weather of it, so it was six weeks before we dropped anchor in the James River. It was a Sunday morning, and a lovely spring day, so I borrowed a boat and, with a few of my fellow-passengers, pulled ashore.

We found ourselves on a tobacco plantation, and there first saw negro slavery in the States. The planter, who received and welcomed us most hospitably, owned about three hundred negroes, who seemed to be very happy and contented, as far as we could see. He also owned a pack of fox-hounds, of which he was very proud.

Returning to the ship, we found a tug waiting to take us all up the river to Richmond, about twenty miles, for the *Sutlej* could not cross the bar.

Arrived there, Jack and I, and some seven more, who had attached themselves to us, found accommodation in a small hotel. We were, no doubt, a strange enough looking party, and the natives were much puzzled to make us out. When, however, Jack began to show off, and Manor to do his tricks, at which he was very clever, they made up their minds we were showmen on tour, and I did not undeceive them.

I had a letter of credit on a merchant firm in Richmond on whom I called at once. The partners were most friendly and tried to persuade me to remain in the town, instead of going up country. But I had made up my mind to see what it was like at any rate, and told them I would go, but would leave my money with them, except what I wanted for current expenses.

These gentlemen kindly gave me full particulars of the route, which was first by canal passenger-boat to Buchanan, the head of navigation, and some sixty miles above Lynchburg, the great centre of the tobacco trade, and the second largest slave market in the States. From Buchanan we had to make our way across country, some 150 miles on foot, as best we might, to Wyandotte County, West Virginia.

When I told my plans to Jack he " dommed " the country with much emphasis, but said he would go anywhere with me, and five others elected to join the party. So after a brief stay in Richmond we left the quiet town, little thinking that, in ten years' time, the eyes of the world would be anxiously fixed upon it, whilst the Titanic struggle between North and South waxed ever more desperate and bitter.

Canal passenger-boats are things of the past, and pity it is they are so, if one were not in a hurry to finish one's journey. Towed by two horses, we pursued our leisurely way so slowly that passengers wanting exercise could get out and walk, and easily keep up with the conveyance.

The scenery was beautiful, and the weather superb with bright sunshine and cool refreshing airs.

Certainly the domestic arrangements on board our craft were somewhat primitive, though the attendance was good and the cooking excellent. She was much crowded, chiefly with merchants returning up country with their summer goods, and many had their wives and daughters with them. These latter slept, and went through certain only partially concealed ceremonies, behind a curtain stretched across the saloon. In this we all took our meals, and we used it as a sitting-room till 9 p.m., when it at once became the most crowded dormitory I ever saw. The washing had to be done in one or two pewter basins, beside which hung three or four towels, brushes and combs, and *tooth-brushes*, for public use.

I think the use of the latter was " more honoured in the breach than in the observance," but they *were* used by some.

Arrived at Buchanan, our voyage, on which I had made many pleasant friends, was ended, and I was sorry it was.

Having got directions from many friends " on board," the next morning after our arrival saw our queer-looking party on the road, with a weary tramp of about 150 miles before us ; Manor, I believe, being the only one who really enjoyed it. Heavy baggage was left behind, each one carrying only what was necessary. The stalwart Jack insisted on carrying my bundle for me, and cheerfully backed it the whole way.

We proposed to do thirty miles a day, and actually made our first point, Henderson French's plantation, on Brush Creek, Mercer County, a distance of 120 miles, in five days ; not bad going for foot-sore wayfarers, such as we were. How Jack anathematised the country, its roads, its people, and all therein, as he trudged along with his double burden, and how the simple folk in their solitary little farms wondered at him, and all his ways !

French was a well-to-do middle-aged bachelor, a member of the State Senate, and the owner of the lands we had been inveigled out to settle. He was, moreover, a very shrewd Yankee. Approaching his plantation, with weary feet, we trudged, for a mile or so, through a fertile valley which had been heavily timbered, but where now the trees had been deadened by " belting," and stood gaunt and sombre skeletons. The undergrowth had been grubbed up, and the grass was springing in its place. Here and there were bunches of cattle, and a few hundred sheep scattered about.

Wondering what our future would be, and whether it was destined to be fixed in this spot, and what reception we should meet with from the man we had travelled so

far to see, we presently came out on the clearing, in which
stood his homestead, a long, one-storey frame house.

French was very friendly, and called up his manager
and his wife to help look after us, an English couple of
the servant class, who had come out about a year before.
It was pleasant to see cheerful English faces in that distant land, and to receive the kindly greeting of these good
folks, who were as pleased to behold their fellow-country-
men again as we were to find them so unexpectedly.

Besides this excellent couple, French had eight negro
slaves, and was a prosperous man for those parts.

After a day's rest, a Doctor Cook appeared on the
scene to conduct us to French's lands, on which we were
supposed to settle. This man was an English medical
man, who had been trapped into coming out to Western
Virginia, as we had been, by the Yankee's London agent ;
having been an innocent pigeon when first caught, he had
now developed into a rook, and acted as French's agent
and decoy for simple Britishers.

The lands lay in three different counties, the nearest
point being sixty miles distant, so to see them a good
long tramp was necessary. Very early in the morning
we started off on our journey, all but Cook being on foot.
That gentleman knew too much about the country to
walk, so took his horse and saddle-bags.

Our route lay over ridges and hills of moderate height
intersected by valleys, through which ran clear, bright
streams, like English trout brooks, and here and there
from out the hillsides burst springs of cool water. By
bridle-tracks and forest paths we wandered on under
the splendid timber. Glorious oaks were plentiful, of
three different kinds, and the rest of the forest growth
was mainly chestnut, walnut, maple, sugar maple, and
" Wachoo."

The trunks of these often shot up seventy feet, straight
as an arrow, before throwing out a branch : a sight to
gladden the heart of a timber merchant, if only he could

get his wood to market ; but what possibility was there
of making a living, to say nothing of a fortune, by clearing
such land for farming purposes ?   Young as I was, the
impossibility of the thing became more apparent to me
the farther we went into the great depths, though our
friend the Doctor wasted much eloquence in pointing
out the richness of the land and the great advantages
of the country for settlers.

Game abounded in these solitudes, and deer would
jump up close to the path, whilst turkeys and pheasants
would calmly survey us till Manor made a dash and
scattered them ; but unfortunately no one carried a
gun, for we had enough to carry without that.

Settlements were indeed few and far between, and
those only log cabins of the poorest.   After a twenty-five
mile walk we reached one of these, the owner of which
took us in and fed us on bacon and maize corn bread, the
staple food of the country.   The Doctor took the only
bed, and we, his victims, shook down as best we might,
on the floor.

The next morning, after a delightful wash at the
spring, off we set again, for another twenty or thirty
miles' tramp, and, passing through the same lovely
scenery and the same heavily timbered country, at
nightfall reached the cabin of two English brothers,
Walker by name.   These unfortunates had been persuaded by our friend the Doctor into buying some of
French's land.   The cabin, and all its surroundings,
seemed hopeless and wretched, and its owners absolutely
unfitted for roughing it in such a country.

Our arrival only added to their misery, poor fellows,
for I brought with me two of their younger brothers, lads
of sixteen and fourteen respectively.   They had been
sent out by their step-father, who probably didn't care
what became of them so he was rid of them, and had
joined our party for the journey from Buchanan.

I felt sad and sorry for their plight, but could do

nothing to help them. We parted next morning, when we resumed our weary way, and I know not what befell them thereafter. But I know that, within two years from that time, two English settlers in the same district, one a retired sea-captain, found a way out of their miseries by their own hands.

More and more it was growing plain to me that it would never do to buy any of French's lands; for I could not live on scenery, however beautiful, and to clear anything like a farm, of that terribly heavy timber, even with the valiant Jack's assistance, was beyond my strength.

At our next halt my growing resolve to cut loose from the toils of the wily Cook was confirmed by our host, who was a " Major " Amos Walker, Justice of the Peace, and Surveyor of Wyoming County. The old gentleman (he was nearly eighty) was a very fine specimen of the American of almost pre-revolutionary days. His father had been killed in the revolutionary war, fighting under General Washington, and he himself had fought under Andrew Jackson ("Old Hickory") in the War with England of 1812. To me, he was most kind and courteous, and a real friend, as long as I remained in Virginia, but " Britishers," collectively, he abused roundly, and hated with a pious hatred.

I took to the Major at once, for there was that in his personality which invited confidence. I therefore told him frankly how I was situated, what available funds I had, etc., etc., and asked his advice. He at once most strongly recommended me to have nothing to do with French's settlement, but to go on to Princeton, Mercer County, where the country was less mountainous and more settled, and where land, well situated, could be bought for less money than Cook was asking his dupes.

Accordingly, when the Doctor mustered his little party the following morning I told him that neither the land nor the country suited me, and bade him good-bye.

Jack decided to follow my fortunes. Cook was very irate, and blustered a bit, but finding that no good, finally rode off. I watched the little party, which now mustered about twelve, till it disappeared under the grand timber on the mountain side, and never saw any of its members again.

I stayed on with the Major, at his pressing invitation, for a week, and as his mode of life was typical of the best class of backwoodsmen of those far-off days, I propose to describe it more particularly in the following chapter.

CHAPTER II

A BACKWOODSMAN'S HOME

ON the last day's journey with the Doctor, as the sun was sinking in the west, our party, weary, footsore and dejected, followed a narrow bridle-path descending into a dip between the timber-clad ridges. Wider it grew, and more distinct, and then we came suddenly out of the forest shade into a clearing, in which stood a good-sized log house. The owner thereof came out, and welcomed us all most kindly. It was a blessed relief to know our day's tramp was over and that we had found rest and hospitality.

The Major's family consisted of his wife, an elderly lady, two unmarried daughters, and a son of about nineteen years old. These, with a little occasional help, had cleared the land, raised the corn, tended the stock, carded, spun, wove and made up their clothing, and indeed were self-contained and self-supporting. Theirs was perhaps not a very refined life, and certainly it was not luxurious, but it was one of abundance and contentment.

The cabin, built of logs, and chestnut-shingle roofed, was two-storied, and contained only two rooms, each about twenty feet by eighteen feet, with floors of split timber. In the sitting-room was a huge fireplace in which blazed a cheerful fire of hickory logs. Close behind the house stood the kitchen, and a little farther away a milk house, spring house, a small stable and cow-house, all of course of logs.

Round the homestead the great forest trees, such as oaks, chestnuts, hickories and gums, had been left standing in all their beauty, and were then clad in the fresh greenery of spring, but in the little clearing of about fifty acres the timber had all been " deadened," and still stood gaunt and weird, mere ghosts of trees.

The stock the Major owned got a good living in the woods nearly all the year round.

The old lady, as kindly and hospitable as her husband, was very proud of her poultry, of which she had a good show, and of her " bee gums," or hives. These, with her weaving, fully occupied her time.

Such was the Major's establishment, and as it was typical of the best class of forest farms in those days, I have fully described it.

I often wonder how many of such are to be found now, or whether civilisation and progress have stamped them out ? It was a simple, manly, independent life, and pity it is if it has quite vanished.

The domestic arrangements, especially those for sleeping, were decidedly primitive, but they were a matter of course throughout that country, and it never entered into any one's head to think evil of them, though male guests and the unmarried sons and daughters of the house slept in the same room upstairs, whilst the old folk usually, as in this case, slept below. I can aver that in all my experience of Western Virginia I never heard a whisper of impropriety arising from this condition of things.

Anything of the sort would have received sharp and sudden retribution at the hands of father or brother, who were always armed with rifle and six-shooter, and would not have scrupled to use them.

When bed-time came, the boys of the house and the guests lay down, half dressed, in their bunks, on beautifully clean linen, as a rule. Then the girls slipped in, and all was silence.

At the first streak of dawn the girls slipped out, as quietly as they had come. Then after an interval the men turned out, and on the gallery stood cedar buckets of cool, clear water in which one's ablutions were performed. Some one, usually one of the girls, " poured water,"—*i.e.* into one's hands,—and so the washing was done, not always with soap, which in those parts was a scarce commodity.

As soon as the Doctor and his victims had gone, my friend the Major warmly congratulated me on cutting loose from him and his land scheme, and I felt happier than for many a day. I had £400 to my credit, and with youth, health, strength, and boundless possibilities before me, the world looked very bright. Looking back through all these long years of life, with their chequered joys and sorrows, that day seems one of the brightest.

Major Walker pressed me in the kindest way to stay with him as long as I liked, and I, partly because I had taken a great liking for the fine old fellow, and partly because I knew he would be glad of help to get his corn in, accepted for Jack and myself for one week certain.

After the manner of his kind, for no creature on this earth can, or will, work like a British navvy, Jack set to at his task, and fairly astonished the natives with his energy. Buttermilk and coffee were the only drinks available in place of his well-beloved beer. He " dommed " vigorously, but he drank them and worked untiringly.

In his hob-nailed high-lows, the pride of his life, he looked down from a serené height on his host's family, who, for the most part, went bare-footed, and were not ashamed.

Jack's sense of propriety was terribly shocked by this state of things, to which he could not reconcile himself, and ever and anon would burst out with : " What'd they say in my country if farmers and landowners trampled round bare-footed ? Dom such a country, says I."

For myself I worked but little, as Jack worked for both of us. Most of the time I spent in the woods with the Major's old Kentucky rifle, and Manor for a companion, and many a grey squirrel and coon we bagged ; or, when horses could be spared, rode with Walker to some settlement ten or twelve miles away, learning all I could from my old friend about the country and its ways. Always our path lay over lofty ridges and down deep ravines ; and everywhere the same magnificent timber grew and flourished. A most beautiful country to look upon, but hopeless from a settler's point of view.

One night Council Walker, the son, took me to a " deer lick," in a creek about two miles off. A " deer lick " is a saline spring, the flavour of which is irresistible to all the Cervidæ. I was to do the shooting, and he would carry the torch of fat pine wood.

At eight o'clock we set out. There was no moon, and though the stars shone brightly it was pitch dark in the forest, showing up the gleam of the fireflies (called by Council " lightning-bugs ") most brilliantly.

On the bank of the creek, opposite the lick, was a " blind " for concealment, and behind it a hole in the ground to keep a smouldering fire in. When a deer comes to suck, the torch is lighted, and shown for a moment ; the deer raises its head and gives the watcher a shot.

Behind the blind we lay for what seemed to me hours. Only the distant bay of a wolf, the smothered growl of a panther, or the hooting of an owl broke the solemn silence of the forest.

What if " buck ague " should attack me ? This was my first chance at a deer, and the very fear of the attack almost brought it on. Presently Council touched me on the shoulder, and whispered under his breath, " Look out ! "

Down the steep side of the creek I could hear a deer coming—almost my heart stopped beating. On he came, halted and snorted. Did he wind us, and would he go thundering off into the woods with his hinds ? No; he stepped into the creek, and I could hear him suck.

What a moment of excitement! Council laid his torch in the embers and quietly blew it into a flame. My rifle was in the rest, but my hand shook so, I felt sure I should miss my shot.

The bright light shone for an instant above the blind ; the buck raised his head to stare at it. I set my teeth, pulled myself together, and let drive. There was a plunging and a splashing in the pool, and all was still.

We rushed out, and there lay a fine buck of five points, stone dead, with a bullet just behind the shoulder. Many I have shot since at licks, or by stalking, or driven by hounds, but this, my first triumph, I can never forget.

In the evenings we would all sit round the great fire-place, our only light the smouldering hickory logs on the hearth. The Major did most of the talking. He had an inexhaustible store of anecdotes, and recollections of the stirring times in the early part of the century, and talked remarkably well. Andrew Jackson he regarded as the greatest general, hero, and statesman of the age. He had much to say about the "effete" British aristocracy. It was always "Britain" and "British," never England and English, with him.

Though professing great contempt for the worn-out old country, there was evidently behind it all a firm belief in the greatness of the race from which he sprang, and in its lofty destiny. But he always wound up by saying "the Eagle would whip creation."

So passed a most pleasant week away, and then I parted with my kind host, with much shrewd advice from him, and a very warm invitation to stay with him again should I finally elect to settle in Western Virginia. Then Jack shouldered my bundle as usual, and off we set, in very good fettle, as he called it, after our week's rest from walking.

Princeton, our destination, was about forty miles

away ; but time being no object we took it leisurely, and
halted long before sundown at a farm owned by Emmanuel
Jenks, a great character, who kept whiskey and sold it.
Jack, you may be sure bought it, but I don't remember
that he overstepped the bounds of what was moderation
for him.

Jenks had taken a contract to make a " county road "
about fifty miles long, and much coveted Jack to help at
the work. He offered him big wages, but Jack elected to
stick to me, though road-making was an occupation dear
to his heart.

By Jenks's advice we made up our minds to put up
the next day at the house of a friend of his, Absalom
Lusk by name, about ten miles out of Princeton. The
road, or rather track, led us through the same heavily
timbered country, over lofty ridges and into deep valleys.
It was even more stony and rougher than usual ; the
day was hot, and Jack " dommed " the road with an
added energy that surprised even me. However, at
about six o'clock we arrived at Lusk's cabin and clearing,
and received a hearty welcome.

As usual he and his wife, his sons and daughters, did
the work of the farm, including the raising of a small
crop of tobacco.

Absalom was a strong Methodist, so at nine o'clock the
women-folk stopped their wheels, all talking ceased, and
the father read a chapter from the Bible ; a hymn was
sung, a short extemporary prayer said, and the service
was over. Jack probably, in all his experience, had never
been present at the like, and seemed dumfounded at
the proceedings.

Bed-time had come, and we all turned in ; Jack being,
for the first time, admitted to the upper room where, as
usual, the boys and girls slept. Circumstances make us
acquainted, it is said, with strange bedfellows, and that
night Jack and I slept together !

I may say that he did not regard these customary

arrangements with any favour, but loudly asked me next morning what they would say to it in " my country." Indeed it was all I could do to keep him from making unpleasant remarks about it to our kind host.

After breakfast we set off again on our travels, the good folks utterly refusing to accept any payment for our entertainment, and saying they would be glad to see us again if we passed that way.

Presently we began to hear the tinkle of many cow and sheep bells in the woods, and knew we must be nearing the settlement or town. Coming suddenly upon it, after being buried so many days in the interminable woods, it seemed quite a place, though in reality the houses were but few, and they all frame or log built ; not a brick in any of them, except in the chimneys, now and then.

We put up at a " tavern," kept by one Joe Alvis, which was a fairly large frame house, painted white, two stories high, and with a wide gallery, or verandah, round it. The host and his wife were pleasant people, and the terms, $3 a week, all found, reasonable enough ; so I soon made up my mind to stay with them while looking about me.

It was very quickly " orated round " that two strangers, belonging to an emigrant party, were staying at Alvis's, and that one of them was looking out for land. So that same evening, whilst Jack and I smoked the pipe of peace on the gallery, after supper, a party of all sorts and sizes collected to see what kind of people had dropped down upon them.

No wonder they were curious, for in those days for- eigners or emigrants were *raræ aves* indeed, and " store clothes " seldom seen west of the " Blue Ridge."

Amongst our visitors was Ben McNutt, the Sheriff of the County ; Judge Hale, formerly Probate Judge, but now a merchant and practising lawyer, who had the best house in the town, and a merchant who had come up with us on the canal boat to Buchanan, and was most friendly and cordial in his greeting. Whilst I chatted with these, the others had been taking stock of Jack, examining with curiosity and wonder his tremendous navvy boots, the like of which had never been seen in those parts. The kindly, open-handed folks quickly made friends with him, and then took him round to the little bar, where they plied him with whiskey.

Unlimited beer, of the strongest, was Jack's native drink, but he took kindly to the new one, and soon grew very boastful as to his powers, especially with his "fistises." All was taken in good part, however, and I believe he was looked upon as a fine specimen of that strange creature, the "Britisher."

Some one expressed wonder that he could walk at all in such boots. "Walk! Dommee," said Jack, "I'll soon show you," and, a fiddle being brought by a nigger, danced a thundering breakdown, to the huge delight of the spectators. Then he sang song after song to them, only stopping when no longer able to articulate, and finally retired to bed the most popular man in all Princeton!

That night I felt happier than since I had been in Virginia, for I had found friendly and kindly people with whom I could get along, as I thought, and I made up my mind to settle in the neighbourhood, if I could find land to suit me.

I was told by my kind friends in the place, who all invited me, one after the other, to their houses, that the "Court" was held in Princeton Court House, once a month. This answered to our Petty and Quarter Sessions, rolled into one, and all the neighbourhood flocked into the town on the great day, either on business or pleasure bent. As next "Court day" was only ten days off, I determined to hold my hand till then, and make my headquarters at Alvis's house.

Finding I had no use for Jack till I got my land, I paid his bill, gave him a few dollars, and sent him back

to Jenks, who wanted him so badly for road making.
He departed, vowing he would come back directly I
wanted him, and as he disappeared I confess I felt quite
lonely.

Now the desire came upon me to buy a horse. I had
never owned one of my very own since the days of my
early boyhood, when I had had a pony ; and to become
the possessor of a horse is, I believe, the height of every
youngster's ambition. Moreover, a horse was a necessity
to enable me to get about and inspect the country.
Accordingly, hearing of a colt owned by a man named
Carr, which Alvis said was the best in the country, and
could be bought for $60, I determined to purchase it.

I bought a saddle and bridle in Vance's store, and
set out, carrying these, for Carr's place eight miles from
Princeton, where I arrived after a terribly hot walk,
which the thought that I should ride back helped me to
endure.

I must confess that I was green enough in those days,
and being eager to buy, was just such a victim as any
dealer would consider his natural prey. Well, next
morning I bought the colt, and paid my $60, saddled
him, and rode off proud and happy in my new possession. I soon found he was scarcely " bridle-wise,"
and I fancy had never been ridden before ; moreover
he was a terrible slug ; but he was a horse, and he was
mine ! Solemnly I rode into Princeton, and put my
mount up at Joe Alvis's, who praised my judgment and
said I had got a bargain.

Before Court day came I rode my steed many a mile,
and got to know most of the settlers within a radius
of twenty miles of the town. What a hospitable, kindly
folk they were, making you welcome wherever you chose
to go !

One good friend I remember making on one of these
trips—" Squire " White, who lived about ten miles out.
Though his surroundings and mode of life were most

primitive, much like Major Walker's, he had been a member of the State Legislature, and was the Chairman of the County Sessions ; a position analogous to that of our Chairman of Quarter Sessions, only with more power. Life and social customs in that Western land were totally different from those of the old country, and impressed me very much in their favour. Every white man, however poor, if he were honest and decently behaved, was *socially* the equal of those in power and authority ; and to gain power and position it was not necessary to be wealthy, only to be popular ; in fact, to be a *man*. My friend the " Squire," for instance, worked his farm with the assistance of his family, and lived as roughly and plainly as his neighbours, yet was a man of influence in his County. Raw lad that I was, I was at once on terms of equality with him, and felt myself raised to a higher platform by the friendship of such a man.

CHAPTER III

THE FARM ON THE BLUESTONE

"Court day" came, and by 10 a.m. the little town was crowded by the farmers from far and near. Singly, and in parties of three or four, or more, they rode up the straggling main street, and I watched them with great interest, as probable neighbours and friends in the near future.

For the most part they were fine, stalwart men, heavy of bone and light of flesh, with the keen, sharply cut features characteristic of the native-born American. Some were mounted on good horses, and others on wiry Indian ponies, but all, young and old, rich and poor, were clad in homespun ; I don't think there was a suit of " store clothes " in all the crowd. Each man carried his rifle, and could handle it well too.

Presently the Court House, the taverns, of which there were two, and the little stores became crowded by the visitors, and things began to " hum " in quiet little Princeton.

Business in the Court and in the stores finished, the taverns filled, and friends treated each other, all meeting on terms of perfect equality. Judges, magistrates, lawyers, farmers, tavern-keepers, all met as social equals, and there was no such thing as stand-offishness amongst them. Coming freshly from the old country, where social grades were then so much more clearly defined than they are even nowadays, this state of things struck me very forcibly. Evidently it was a country where a

23

man was valued for what he *was*, not for what he *had*, and the more I saw of it, the better I liked it.

Before the Court adjourned, I made my " declaration of intention " to become an American citizen, and in due course, after the necessary interval, became naturalised. As it was known that I was a possible buyer of land, every one who had it to sell sought my acquaintance, pressed me to drink, and to come out and stay with them at their farms. Indeed, my society was in such request, and my health so frequently pledged that, if I had reciprocated in all cases, my own must have been seriously impaired ; as it was, I managed to keep sober, though with some difficulty.

Joe Alvis had mentioned a farm on the Bluestone River, about twelve miles from Princeton, belonging to one Mr. George Baily, as likely to suit me. The old gentleman, he said, was heavily in debt, and anxious to sell out and move West. Baily and his two sons, Thompson and Council, were presently introduced by Alvis, and of course a move was made to the bar, though the old fellow was already, what shall we say—" forrard " ? Next came a most pressing invitation to come out to the farm with them that night, and stay as long as I cared to, which I accepted.

George Baily was a remarkably fine specimen of the Western Virginian farmer, who carried his years (he was about sixty), and his whiskey, wonderfully well. Over six feet in height, spare and straight as a shingle, with finely cut features, dressed in homespun " blue jeans " though he was, he looked a gentleman of Nature's own fashioning.

It was seven o'clock in the evening before the old gentleman could be persuaded to mount, and then, John Gilpin like, he stuffed two bottles of whiskey into his saddle-bags, one on each side ; he must have had at least a quart *inside* him, but seemed none the worse for it. It was a lovely moonlit night, and for six miles we had a fairly good road, which after that dwindled down to a dimly shadowed track between the lofty forest trees.

We started from Princeton quite a large party, though we shed the most of them in a few miles, by narrow tracks leading off to their respective farms. Many a cheery good-night and good-bye were given me by these kindly folks, and many a pressing invitation to come and stay with them, should I settle in those parts. I never met anywhere a more kindly race than these Virginians, and youngster that I was, a stranger in a strange land, their friendliness was very cheering.

One thing struck me as very curious, in that day's experience. Many of my newly found friends asked if I were *really* a Britisher, because I spoke such good English! What could they have expected me to speak ? I never found that out. One fine old fellow, after looking me well over, remarked, " I like your eye, it is blue and clear." Another said, " I see you wrap your fingers in gold," alluding to three rings given me before I left home, and which I then wore.

When we arrived at Baily's log house it was 9.30 p.m., and the old lady was somewhat crusty at first, not being used to such late hours. However, she soon came round and bade me a kindly welcome, the boys took the horses, and I entered what was to be my first very own home.

Let me describe it. On the ground floor, a single room, with unglazed windows, about eighteen feet square, at one end a wide fireplace, and, stuck in the logs by the side of it, a torch of pine splinters for light ; at the other end a staircase leading to the room above. On one side a comfortable-looking bed for the old folks, and on the other a table, and raw-hide-bottomed chairs. Upstairs there were five beds, but no other furniture.

The two girls soon had supper ready, coffee, corn-bread, bacon and eggs, very welcome to hungry mortals. Baily produced one of his bottles and insisted that all should partake, but the ladies declined. Supper over,

Mrs. Baily said, " I reckon you would like to lie down,"
to which I readily agreed ; so Council showed me upstairs, with a pine splinter, by the light of which I saw
girls' raiment hanging on the walls.

That night I slept the sleep of the weary, and heard
no sound till dawn, when I was aware of a light rustling,
and peeping out, saw the girls putting on their frocks.
With their bare feet they noiselessly vanished, and then
the two boys and I followed. It was 5 a.m., and in the
soft bright sunlight the scene was lovely ; for all round
the house was a peach and apple orchard in full bloom,
and through the sunlit vistas between the blossom-laden
trees, glimpses of the sparkling, shining river could be
caught alive with fish, rising for the flies that skimmed
the surface. I stood at the door a brief moment, entranced
and spellbound by the beauty of the scene. It seemed
a veritable paradise, and I resolved to become its Adam,
if possible.

Then the inevitable Eve broke the spell by wishing
me a pleasant good-morning and asking if she could
" pour water " for me. It was Lizzie Baily, the youngest
daughter of the house, barefooted and homespun-clad,
as were her mother and sisters, but full of courtesy, and
of gentle manners. Indeed, all were full of kindly
hospitality, and I felt at once quite at home with them.

Already the day's work had begun ; the cows were
milked, the horses fed, I looking after my own ; and then,
by seven o'clock, we all sat down to breakfast, the bill of
fare the same as at supper. After breakfast old Baily
insisted on a modicum of whiskey, and then started out
with me for a long day's walk round the farm, as fresh
and " fit," his overnight potations notwithstanding, as
though he knew not the flavour of spirits.

The farm, or estate, was nearly a thousand acres in
extent. Below the orchard, sloping down to the river,
was a field of timothy grass, of thirty acres, and beyond
this the clear-running shallow river, thirty yards wide.

On the opposite side of the river the banks rose into per-pendicular cliffs, crowned with magnificent timber, and beyond these were level, fertile fields of about a hundred acres cleared, fenced, and planted with corn. The fencing, which was " worm," was very bad, and on all the farm there were no " slip-bars," or gates.

A quarter of a mile from the house, on the opposite side of the river, a clear mountain stream, called Crane Creek, ran into the Bluestone. This Baily had dammed a short distance from the junction, and put up a log-built mill, with one pair of stones. It was the only corn-mill for miles round, and seemed to be a rather valuable asset. It was worked by George Baily himself, and I found that the running of it was his only contribution to the family resources.

About seven hundred acres of the land lay on Crane Creek, running back on either side to the steep rich ridges covered with heavy timber, amongst which were groves, or " orchards," as they called them, of " sugar trees " and sugar maples. The rest of the farm, about three hundred acres, was in the valley of the Blue-stone, and along it and Crane Creek too there were ancient clearings, probably fifty years old.

There were no outbuildings on the place except a miserable open log shed, in which three horses could stand, and a log pen for fattening hogs. These, in the proper season of the year, were fed on peaches, which would else have rotted and gone to waste ; a diet which would almost commend their flesh to vegetarians, had there been any of that cult in Virginia in those days. Behind the stable was a small garden, or " truck patch," in which the women folk raised what they called " garden sass," no man ever putting hand to such work, which was considered *infra dig.* for them, and only fit for women !

For ten long hours the old man and I walked round the farm, till I think I had seen everything on it that was to be seen. It seemed to me a fine estate, and indeed would have been so regarded in this country, and I made up my mind to buy it, if I could get it at my price, which was $1,500 or £300 in English money.

After supper that evening, as we smoked our long cane-stemmed pipes on the gallery whilst the women were busy with their spinning, the bargaining began. Baily asked me $2,000. I told him I could not pay that, as the condition of the house, mill, and fencing was so bad, but would give $1,500 if the title proved to be good, and pay a deposit now of $20. Probably I would take all the stock he wished to sell. Finding Baily would not give way and that " lying down " time had come, I went to bed, saying I must get back to Princeton in the morning, as I had many other places to look at.

Daylight saw us all astir, and, after " water pouring," Council and I went out into the woods to shoot squirrels for breakfast, Manor of course with us. Poor fellow ! he was not master of the art of " treeing,"—i.e. standing under the tree and barking, when his game had treed, as all the country dogs do. However, Council soon shot a couple with his long flint-and-steel Kentucky rifle, and we returned as fast as we could, as the girls were waiting to cook them. In less than no time they were skinned, cut up, and stewed in cream gravy, and were delicious eating.

After breakfast Baily, finding he could not screw me up to his terms, accepted mine. A piece of paper was found, after considerable search, and I drew up the agreement for sale as well as I could, and paid over my $20, for which I took a receipt.

It was agreed he was to give me possession at Michaelmas, and in the meantime Jack Galliers and I were to board with the family as paying guests. Now I said good-bye, mounted my confounded slug of a colt, and set off for Princeton in high feather with myself and all the world.

You bet, as my Virginian friends would say, I was a
proud and happy youngster that glorious summer day !
Just twenty-one, with health and strength and energy
enough for anything ; the owner of a fine farm, with
money enough to stock it—what more could heart
desire ?

No purchase I have made since, in any part of the
world, has given me the pleasure this did. One drop
of bitterness there was—the thought that settling here
meant long years of separation from friends at home ;
but boy-like I soon brushed the melancholy aside and
was happy again. Youth is selfish ; it is only to the
old that separation is so bitter.

Joe Alvis and his wife highly approved my purchase,
and said, " Now you are a real Virginian."

Next morning I rode off to Emmanuel Jenks to look
up Jack, for I feared he might be flattered and bribed by
that worthy into deserting me for good, and I could not
get on without his help on the farm. Arrived at " Flat
Topped Mountain," I found Jenks and Jack were both
away at the road-making camp. I fed my horse, treated
myself to corn cake and whiskey, and set off on my fifteen-
mile ride to find them.

My way lay by a narrow bridle-path through the forest,
the trees of which stood in their primeval glory, decked
in all their summer beauty of foliage and of flower. No
human being was seen, nor sign of human habitation
met with ; solemn silence reigned, save for the muffled
sound of my horse's feet on the soft earth, and these
forest aisles loomed awe-inspiring in their grandeur ;
temples raised by God Himself, and seeming meet for
His habitation.

It was late when I reached the camp of eight or nine
rough shanties of poles and brush, by the side of the new
road. Jenks and Jack came out and welcomed me
heartily, and soon we were seated on a log enjoying a
good supper of strong coffee, corn-bread, and fried bacon.

When I told my tale, Jenks, who was a good fellow, said Jack was his best hand, but he would not for a moment try to keep him from me. Jack, with many expletives, declared it would be no good if he did, for he meant to work with me anyway. Indeed, I verily believe he was as much pleased as I was to know that I had found a new home for us both.

The road they were making was a simple affair, though it was a County one. The side of the hill was cut down straight with mattocks, the lower side or slope braced with timber cut along it to keep it from washing away, and the surface, about twenty feet wide, ploughed with a wooden plough of local manufacture and then made fairly level with shovels. A soft road indeed, and in wet weather pretty muddy, but much better than none.

After supper, I remember, we sat out on our log, smoking and chatting. Presently Jenks and Jack fell drowsy and I sat on in the soft summer air, under the starlit sky, in a silence only broken, now and then, by the sweet, plaintive cries of the whip-poor-wills, or the distant baying of a wolf in the depths of the surrounding forest.

Next morning, after a sound sleep by Emmanuel's side on a shakedown, a rather scanty " pouring," for water was scarce, and a good breakfast of the usual fare, I arranged with Jack to be at the Bluestone in a fortnight's time, there to await my arrival, if I had not returned from Richmond, where I was going to fetch our things.

Then Jenks and I rode off through the forest, following no path but guided by the sun, to the farm of a man named Salisbury, about four miles away, who was said to have a smart little riding mare, which I wanted to swap my unmannerly colt for. Jenks took us all right through the pathless woods, and we came out straight on Salisbury's clearing. There we were received in the usual hospitable fashion and given an excellent dinner, which besides the inevitable pig meat, I remember, included a dish of venison.

After the meal the mare was driven up, a smart little thing about 14½ hands, well bred, and a good mover. Of course when it came to the deal we both wanted "boots," so finally we left it to Jenks to say who should draw, and what. He decided I was to give $2½, which I did, and I think both Salisbury and I were pleased with our bargains; I know I was, at any rate, for the little mare—I called her "Fiddle"— turned out to be as good as she looked.

One more night I spent in Jenks's camp, rolled up in a blanket, and lulled to sleep by the forest cries of birds and beasts, than which there is no sweeter lullaby for weary mortal.

Jack was pleased to highly approve my swap. He promised again to turn up without fail on the appointed day at the Bluestone, and then with many good-byes I mounted Fiddle and started for Princeton, *en route* for Richmond, a distance of 260 miles there and back; a long and solitary ride, but pleasant enough in those glorious summer mornings and evenings.

CHAPTER IV

THE CAMP MEETING

NOTHING befell me on the journey to Richmond and back worth recording. The canal boat-trip was even more pleasant than the previous one, since the crowd was less and there was more room to stretch one's legs at night. Otherwise everything on board was the same, and I fancied I recognised my old friends the tooth-brushes, hanging in the same old place, but looking rather the worse for wear.

Returning to the Bluestone I was joined in a couple of days by Jack Galliers, and we soon got to work on the farm. I was not to pay for it, or to get possession till Michaelmas, but, as Baily was quite willing to let me do what I liked on the place, if he were not expected to work himself, I settled to pay a very moderate weekly board for Jack and myself, until such time as the Bailys departed.

Nearly all the arable fields were cumbered with deadened and dead trunks of great trees, and the first job we undertook was to log them up and burn them. This was about the heaviest work I have ever done, for the midsummer heat was terrific. Still we stuck to it manfully, Jack working like the British navvy that he was, and by the fall we had made a pretty good clearance, so that the fields looked more shipshape.

Failing his beloved beer, I regret to say Jack took more and more kindly to the " wine of the country," or corn whiskey, which he got at Richard Bailey's still about three miles down the river. He kept sober enough to do his work, but grew quarrelsome in his cups, and the still led at last to our parting, which came about in this way :

As winter came on his vists to the still grew more frequent, and he more morose. I realised I should have to get rid of him sooner or later, and got a man named Bryant and his wife to come to me as helps and to live in the house.

Jack then having left me in a very bad humour, I met him one evening at Thompson Bailey's house, when he challenged me to fight with " fistises," as he called them. I knew I was no match for him, the great burly navvy with muscles like iron, but I could not show the white feather before the natives, for the credit of Old England. So for half an hour we had it up and down, in the front of the house, to the delectation of the spectators. Jack, I am bound to confess, whipped me badly, and for many a day I bore the marks of his " fistises," though I rejoice to remember that he did not escape scathless.

A few weeks after this he came to my house, about ten o'clock at night, mad drunk, and armed with an axe, with which he began to batter in the door, vowing he would kill me. Mrs. Bryant, in terror, begged me not to go out, but I had to, unless I wished to see the infuriated Jack burst in upon us, for the door was giving way. I can't say I liked the position, but, realising that it was safest to take the aggressive, I seized a pair of " pot-hooks," suddenly opened the door, and before Jack could use his axe, felled him to the ground.

We carried him into the house in a pretty bad way, for I had nearly cracked his skull, hard as it was, and it was a week before he was well enough to leave. He had the grace to confess that he had only got his deserts. It was a rough but salutary lesson to him, for he was afraid to molest me any more.

While Jack still abode with us and was fairly decent in his behaviour, we got through a lot of work on the

3

place. Besides clearing the land of logs, we put all the
fencing into good repair, put up a pretty porch over the
door, and windows and partitions in both the rooms, so
that the house, when I sold it in the following summer,
was, for that country, and those times, quite a nice
place.

Till the Bailys left in the fall we got on very well
together, the old lady and the girls doing all they could
to make me comfortable. They were always hard at
work in their kitchen, or at their spinning or weaving;
but Baily himself took things very easy, and did scarcely
any work, so it was not difficult to understand why he
had not made a success of farming. Indeed, his was
no exceptional case, for many of the backwoods farmers
seemed thoroughly lacking in energy and go ; probably
it was the hopelessness of the conditions under which
they lived, in those dense forests, that made them so.

During all this summer of hard work my only recreation
was to ride, with one or other of the girls, to an occasional
preaching, held at some neighbour's farm.

As August drew to an end a great event happened,
and that was the holding of a Methodist Camp Meeting
at Brush Creek, a few miles from the Bluestone. All
the folks I knew in the neighbourhood were going, and
hundreds more from the surrounding counties would
collect for what, to them, was the greatest and most
exciting annual event in their placid lives. Of course I
went too, having received many invitations from friends
living near the spot, and from others who had permanent
camps fixed at the meeting-place.

It was the first function of the kind I had seen, and I
confess it made a great impression on me. Let me try
to describe it in its light, and in its shade ; for like all
things mundane, it was a mixture of good and evil,
though I think the former predominated.

The setting of the picture was some of Nature's most
beautiful handiwork, for all round the little clearing, of

about two acres, stood the primeval forest of oak, hickory, and walnut, and from their giant limbs hung and twined, and twisted and stretched, the all-embracing grape-vines, their leaves just lightly touched with the bronze of the fading summer. Round three sides of the square, under the shade of the overhanging trees, were the permanent cabins of the well-to-do people of the neighbourhood. On the fourth side the preaching house stood open-sided, and seated with rough " puncheon slabs," a passage in the middle dividing the men from the women. In the centre was a platform and rostrum for the preacher, and just below it an open space, about fourteen feet square, enclosed by a rail, called the " Mourners' bench."

Camp guards were appointed to keep order and decorum within the precincts of the meeting-ground, and within its boundaries everything was decorous enough. The stillness and solemnity there were only broken by the preacher's voice, or the singing of popular hymn tunes, with an earnestness and enthusiasm that carried one away, as by a flood, when the congregation had been stirred and moved by some powerful pulpit oration. That singing haunts me now; I never heard its like in any church or cathedral. The dark solemnity of the surrounding woods, contrasted with the flickering gleam of the torches, which half revealed, half hid the intense excitement of the faces upturned in an exaltation of repentance, as the preacher denounced woe and tribulation on unrepentant sinners, made a scene never to be forgotten.

Towards midnight, when the fervour had reached its highest pitch, from the semi-darkness surrounding the preacher would be heard cries and screams and ejaculations. The " Mourners' bench " would fill with penitents, and girls would cry to their lovers, fathers and mothers to their children, to join them there and find salvation.

There was something so weird, so striking, so contagious in this intense exaltation, that the hardest and wildest natures were affected, at least temporarily, and those who elsewhere, and at other times, scarce uttered a prayer, might be seen weeping and lamenting their sins in deep abasement. For my own part, I felt deeply moved, but, though frequently called upon, I did not " go forward to get religion."

This was one phase of camp-meeting life, and its best ; the other side of the picture was of the world, worldly.

In the woods, away from the camp ground, were rows of buggies and light wagons, and pens for horses, kept by negroes, who took in and fed your mount for a dollar a day ; a busy, merry scene of cooking and laughter and picnicing, innocent enough, but somewhat incongruous. Farther away still, about a mile from camp, and kept very quiet, were to be found a few barrels of whiskey by those who knew where to look for them, and a good many apparently did.

Then there were constables collecting debts, horse dealers and " swappers " plying their trades, and crowds of young folks bent solely on amusement, though even these probably would be swept into the vortex of excitement and enthusiasm when the " Mourners' bench " began to fill.

Strolling in the quiet woods, still farther afield from the camp, card parties might be seen, and a good deal of heavy gambling went on amongst them. Indeed, the whole scene was an epitome of the world and life in general, for many good people were there, and many bad.

The negroes, of course, had their own separate preaching stand, and once or twice I was present at their meetings, which were much like those of the whites, only, if possible, marked by wilder and more frantic excitement.

These Camp Meetings were their happiest times, poor fellows, and exactly suited to the negro temperament.

Amongst the first friends I met at the camp were a Mr. and Mrs. Herndon, who had brought their family, two girls of fifteen and sixteen, and two younger boys.

He was a well-to-do planter, and, besides his family, had brought quite a retinue of slaves. I put up with the Herndons and was charmed with their society. Mrs. Herndon was a delightful hostess, cultured and refined, and a thoroughly *good* woman. I remember strolling round the camp with her and one of the girls, and how sorely she was troubled by the mixture of religion and vanity in the scene, and how she begged me to keep away from those only bent on pleasure, to think seriously, and to " get religion."

The husband and herself were typical slave-owners of the best class, and the negroes they owned were fortunate. Of course they were all known to me, and one old negress I remember well, a great favouite of her mistress and a thoroughly good old soul, Aunt Rhoda by name.

She was deeply concerned for my spiritual welfare, and, meeting me one night as I left the preaching, threw her ams round my neck and prayed me, with all her might, to " get religion." Poor old soul ! She could not understand, when I tried to explain why I didn't " come forward," and was much troubled as to my future state.

During my life in the West I was present at many other Camp Meetings, which were conducted in much the same manner as this, but none made such an impression on me ; it was a new experience, and a strange one, utterly unlike anything in the Old Country.

I stayed a whole week at the camp with my kind friends, and then one night, when the preaching was over and the singing nearly done, said good-bye and rode off on my homeward journey. It was a lovely moonlit night, and as I rode through the quiet forest glades, the sound of the last hymn at first rang loud and clear, gradually dying away into silence, and all was still. My first Camp Meeting was over, but not the impression it made upon me.

Soon after the Camp Meeting, I joined with the settlers in the neighbourhood in building a log church, for the

Episcopal Methodists, in a lovely secluded spot on the Bluestone, about two miles below me. Every one worked cheerfully and willingly at it, moved thereto by the wave of enthusiasm started by the Camp Meeting, and the church was quickly built. It was a simple enough affair, but a great benefit to the settlement, for " preachings " were often held there, and generally well attended, settlers and their wives and families riding in ten or fifteen miles to the services.

That summer I made a good crop of corn, and, by the aid of a " raising," built a barn to hold it.

It was a kindly, neighbourly custom in those parts, when help was wanted for such a work, for all one's friends to bear a hand. They came from far and near, and it was quite a holiday gathering. Many hands make light work, and by sundown the barn was built.

With the help of my lady friends, who lent me the table requisites, I provided a good supper, with a sufficiency of whiskey and apple-brandy. Then followed a dance, to the music of a fiddle, and we had what my friends called " a good time."

That winter, as farm work was slack, I did a good deal of hunting, and had some very good sport with Manor, and when " still " hunting without him ; but that, and other events that soon after befell me and caused me much disquietude at the time, must be reserved for another chapter.

CHAPTER V

DURANCE VILE

ABOUT the middle of November, there being little or no
work to be done on the farm, I went on a shooting trip—
" hunting," we always called it—with Burrell Baily, my
old friend's eldest son.

One misty, cold morning we started for our ground,
about twenty miles off in the high ridges, and took with
us corn for our horses, and corn-meal, bacon, and whiskey
for ourselves.

We were " still " hunting, so had to leave poor Manor
behind, much to his disgust.

I remember we killed a doe on the way, and when we
made our camp that night in a sheltered hollow, fared
sumptuously thereon. A chat over our plans for the
next day, a pipe and glass of whiskey therewith, and so
to sleep, rolled in our blankets and our saddles for pillows.
No sleep so sound and refreshing is to be got on any
feather bed as in a hunting-camp, after a good hard day's
work in the open air ; you have earned your rest, and
enjoy it the more.

Many and many a time I have slept out on the open
prairie, when travelling or scouting, wrapped in a blanket,
under the glorious tent of the summer sky, with the cool
night air fanning away the scorching of the day, and that
perhaps is the most delightful sleep of all ; unless you
happen to be in an Indian country, and then, possibly,
you may have uncomfortable dreams about your scalp.

The country we were hunting in this trip was about the wildest I ever saw anywhere in the States ; it was a succession of lofty ridges, deep rocky ravines, and tumbling mountain torrents. No human habitation was within miles of us, and game abounded, especially deer and bear, which we were after. Wolves and foxes were numerous too, and so daring that we had to hoist our kills high up on trees to keep them out of their reach.

All the ridges were covered with the finest timber and were fairly clear of brush, but in the bottoms there was a dense growth of " ivy and laurel," splendid cover for the deer.

We started out of camp early next morning, Baily taking one ridge, and I another, not without some fear on my part of losing myself in those vast woods. That day Baily got a bear and a fine buck, and I a doe and a brace of pheasants, which was pretty good for a beginner, for it was only the second time I had tried my hand with an old Kentucky rifle.

Four days we hunted, working hard each day and seeing an immense quantity of game, and then, having got as much bear and deer meat as our horses could carry, started for home, well pleased with ourselves. Of course we only took the hams of the bears and the loins of the deer, and then were well loaded up.

As I have already said, I sold my farm the following summer, and my friend Herndon was the purchaser at $2,000. He was to take possession at Michaelmas, and in the meantime let me have three of his negroes to work it—Rhoda, a cook, and two boys, Buck and Sam by name—and very useful they were.

By that time I had fifty head of nice young cattle on the place, and tried to sell them at auction, but failing to get my price, kept them, and after a bit drove them to Milam's Ridge, a wild out-of-the-way place fifty miles off. One of the numerous tribe of Baileys lived there, with a large family of daughters, in a rough log cabin, and made his living by hunting. He undertook to winter my cattle for $1 a head, and looked after them very well, though he had not much to do except to round them up every now and then, for of course they got their own living in the woods.

Having sold the farm, and being " foot loose," I made an arrangement with another Bailey, Richard by name, and a J.P., at a place called Rock Settlement, to board with him, whenever I liked, at $2.50 a week, including horse-keep as well. There I made the acquaintance of a man named Burnett, who kept a store in partnership with George Paris of Princeton, one of the few men in the town with whom I was not very friendly. Paris was a well-to-do man, for those parts, but was unscrupulous, overbearing, and harsh in his dealings.

Burnett had recently married a girl from Princeton whom I knew, and we three became great friends ; a most unfortunate friendship it proved to be for me, and eventually landed me in prison, though only for a brief period.

My only excuse for getting into such a mess was that I was very young, and quite without business experience, believed Burnett's assurance that Paris was trying to rob him—which, a priori, was not improbable—and when once in it, thought it my duty to protect his wife's interests at all risks.

Burnett was, as events proved, an unmitigated rascal, and I, in my simplicity, was made a tool of by him. He invited me to join him in a horse-selling trip into Eastern Virginia, and I having some fifty horses for sale, agreed to go with him. If his horses sold well he meant to settle up with all his creditors except Paris, who was trying to rob him, and then go out West.

We started with a bunch of 125 horses, seventy-five of Burnett's and fifty of my own, and did very well with them till we arrived at a place called Charlotte

Court House one Saturday evening, with only about a
dozen unsold.

Whilst I was out in the town Paris appeared on the
scene, and he and Burnett had a very lively time, I
believe. The latter reported that Paris was trying to
rob him not only of the proceeds of his horse sales, but
of two notes for $1,000 each which he held. Would I
hold the notes, which he would endorse to me, for the
benefit of his poor wife, and save her from want ? Of
course I would, egregious ass that I was, and pledged
my word to collect the $2,000 and hand them to his
wife, despite the rapacious Paris and anything he could
do ! Then my friend Burnett rode off with about
$2,500 in his belt, after selling me the four horses he
had left, and I never saw or heard from him again.

Well, I soon sold out the rest of my horses and set off
on my homeward journey in high feather, with $250 in
gold, notes, and silver in a purse in my breeches pocket,
and the balance of about $3,000 in a large pocket-book
carried in my saddle-bag. This may seem foolish, but as
there were no banks in which to deposit it, there was
nothing else to be done.

My first halt was at King Edward's Court House, and
as I walked up the steps of the tavern, I thrust my hand
into my pocket to feel for my purse. It was gone ! In
vain I searched all my pockets. It had vanished.

It was Saturday, and a holiday for most of the niggers
on the plantations, many of whom I had met on the
road, and no doubt some of them had found my treasure ;
I at any rate didn't, though I wasted a whole day
searching for it.

It was now the month of May, and the weather very
warm, so on my last day's ride over the mountains I
halted at midday to rest my horse and myself. Sitting
on a fallen log by the wayside in that solitude, I lit my
pipe and then, having nothing else to do, pulled my
pocket-book out of the saddle-bag to examine its con-

tents. Presently I saddled up and reached home without
further halt, just after dark, but when I unpacked the
saddle-bags, my money was nowhere to be found !

Nothing could be done that night, but next morning
by daybreak I started out with my friend George Dillon
to help me, taking my dog Manor with me. We hunted
every yard of the back trail without success, and as we
neared my yesterday's halting place, hope died within
me. But now, when we were in sight of it, Manor, who
had been on ahead, came galloping back with the pocket-
book in his mouth, highly pleased with his find ! The
contents were intact, and I rode home with a mighty load
off my mind.

Once again, many years after this, I temporarily lost
a pocket-book with a large sum of notes in it—£160, I
think it was—but it was restored to me by a man as
honest and faithful as the dog. I was then staying with
a younger brother, an officer at Aldershot. We drove
over to Guildford, and I put my hand in my pocket,
as soon as we arrived, to get some money out—it was
gone.

I remembered my tribulation of long ago in Virginia,
but never supposed I should be lucky enough to recover
such a loss a second time. However, when we drove up
to my brother's hut, there stood his soldier servant, an
Irishman, who had been with him several years, with my
pocket-book grasped in his hand. I had left it on the
dressing-table, and he found it directly after we started.
I, of course, rewarded him suitably, but I well remember
now what a lecture he gave me for my carelessness !

But we must hark back to Virginia, and my troubles
with Mr. George Paris.

A day or two after my joyful return home I rode out to
the Rock settlement, to put up with Richard Bailey, on
my way to Milam's Ridge, to look after my cattle there.

Mr. Paris very shortly appeared, with two friends, demanding to see me. Of course, I knew what was coming,

and braced myself up for the struggle. I firmly believed I was in the right, and wasn't going to be bullied into giving up my friend's property, so put my Derringer in my pocket, and went out to speak with the enemy in the gate. Probably, if he had quietly explained the true state of affairs, and produced *proof* that Burnett was in his debt, we might have settled matters on the spot. But instead of that he blustered and bullied, after the manner of his kind, threatening what he would do for me, if I did not at once hand over the two notes for $1,000, and other moneys of Burnett's, which he said he knew I had in my possession.

With my hand on my six-shooter, I told him very quietly that I did not admit I had any property of his, and certainly should not hand anything over to him, either now or at any other time. The man was a coward, for finding bullying was no good, he mounted his horse and rode off, vowing he would have me locked up as soon as he returned to Princeton. The folks at the settlement were delighted to see the bully, whom all disliked, so cowed, and I leaped into popularity at once.

But I cannot say I liked the position I had got myself into. Paris was a man of wealth, and I was poor and comparatively friendless, with but small chance of holding my own against him in the Law Courts, if it came to that, as it undoubtedly would. But I had given my word to Burnett not to hand over the bills, or their proceeds, to any one but his wife, so I felt in honour bound to harden my heart and see the matter through.

In this frame of mind, which was rather a reckless one, I set out for Milam's Ridge to look after my cattle, intending to return thence to Princeton to surrender myself to the warrant I knew would be out against me.

The woods were all on fire between me and the Ridge, but I determined to push on, come what might, lest I should be arrested before I had made my arrangements ; for once under lock and key, I didn't know what might

happen to me, or how long I might remain there. Young,
and ignorant of law as I was, it came into my mind
that I might be charged with stealing the notes Burnett
had handed me, and how could I prove my innocence ?
Paris, I knew, would swear to anything, and I might soon
be a convicted felon !

With these distracting, tormenting thoughts surging
through my mind, on I rode through the blazing, roaring
flames that at times almost barred my passage. Reckless and absorbed by my own troubles and fears, I paid
little heed to the magnificent scene around and ahead of
me, though it was awe-inspiring enough to give one
pause. The undergrowth, which was not thick, was
quickly consumed, but the flames shot up the dead
and living forest trees, a full hundred feet or more,
a roaring mass of fire. Then, with an appalling crash,
would fall some giant limb across the track, and it was
only by God's mercy they did not fall on me.

Milam's Ridge was fifty miles ahead of me, and as far
as I could see, when the wind, that followed the raging
fire, lifted the curtain of smoke, the whole country was
on fire. Now, when I at last realised my danger, I would
gladly have turned back, but that was impossible ; the
fire barred my passage, and I must push through, or
perish in the flames.

How I did it I don't know, but at last I emerged from
the fiery furnace, not far from the Ridge. Scorched by
the heat and blackened by the smoke, my horse and I
were sorry objects when we arrived, but I was deeply
grateful to the Providence that had brought me safely
through that and so many other dangers in my short
life.

I found my cattle all right, and stayed on with Reuben
Bailey some days in security, knowing there was no fear
of a warrant being served on me in such a wild country
as that. Then I rode back, through the awful desolation
of the charred and blackened forest, to the Rock settle-

ment, where I picked up my friend George Dillon, and went with him into Princeton to give myself up.

Seated on a verandah, playing backgammon, I saw the Sheriff, Ben McNutt, rode up to him, and announced I had come to give myself up. He shook hands, and said he had a warrant against me right enough, but, hearing I was after my cattle on the Gyandotte, hadn't troubled to go out and serve it there, as he knew that I should turn up at the settlement before long.

I told him I was going to put my horse up at Alvis's tavern, and he could take me there. " Bob, my boy," he said, " we'll have supper together there, but after that I must lock you up, sorry as I am to have to do it." We had a very pleasant supper party, for Ben was as good a fellow as you would wish to meet, and all my friends did their best to cheer me up. Then I wrote to Herndon asking him to stand my bail in $2,000, till next Court day in October, and that being done, we all strolled down to the gaol, where I was duly handed over into the custody of the gaoler by my friend Ben.

I was placed in a cell on the ground-floor about ten feet square, the only furniture a rough bed, with mattress and blankets. The window was well guarded with iron bars, and the outer door, for there were two, of which the inside one stood wide open till locking-up time, was protected in like manner on the upper half, but with sufficient width between the bars to admit a hand and a fair-sized parcel.

When my friends departed, and the heavy lock was turned on me, I confess my spirits fell to zero, and I laid myself down on the bed in a despairing mood.

George Dillon had taken charge of my letter to Herndon, and had vowed he would bring him into Princeton next day. But when he came, if he did come, would he, or any one else, bail me, or must I lie in this miserable den till October ? And in October, what would happen to me ? Horrible thought ! I might be sent to the

Penitentiary as a thief, and probably should be. What
would my friends at home think of me when they knew
of my plight? One, I knew, wouldn't believe I had
done wrong; but the rest?

As all these miserable forebodings coursed through
my mind I felt more and more lonely and sad; then
came a rap at the outer door, and a cheery voice ex-
claimed, "See here, Bob, I've brought you a book to
read, and a flask of whiskey, and a plug of tobacco,
to cheer you up. Don't be down-hearted; you shall be
out to-morrow, never fear. Everybody in Princeton is
sorry for you, and no one believes you have done anything wrong." It was good, kind little Mrs. Alvis, and
as she passed the things in to me, through the window
bars, and grasped my hand, I felt hope revive, and that
I could face the worst with an equal mind. So great is
the power of a little sympathy.

Cheered and comforted by my little friend's visit, I
laid me down and slept fairly well, and so passed my
first night in prison.

CHAPTER VI

A DANCE AND A FIGHT

THE next morning the same kind friend who had so cheered me the previous night sent me an ample breakfast ; and the outside door being open, I had many visitors with whom to talk through the open bars of the inner one. Some came to sympathise, and others to stare at the young Englishman George Paris had got into his clutches, for my case was the talk of the little town, and no doubt pleasantly varied the monotony of existence whilst its novelty lasted. But for me that day in prison dragged its slow length out in utter weariness, and my heart was heavy within me, for no word came from George Dillon or Herndon, and I verily thought I was abandoned as a prey unto mine enemy.

The last visitor I had the second evening was a most unexpected one, Jack Galliers of all people in the world. He said he had only just heard of my trouble, and had come into Princeton to see if he could do anything for me. He thrust his hard paw through the bars, grasped my hand like a vice, " dommed " Paris with a vigour all his own, including the whole country in his anathemas, and vowed that, if I would give the word, he would soon show that gentleman what he could do with his " fistises."

I thanked him very warmly for his kind remembrance of me, told him his beating Paris would not help me, but, if I wanted his services, I would be sure to send him word.

Without any prompting from me, he stood outside by
the bars and sang to me two or three of his favourite
ballads in the deepening twilight; then we shook
hands and parted, and I never saw him again.

That second night I slept but little in my prison cell,
feeling very uneasy at the non-arrival of Herndon and
Dillon.

But about eleven o'clock next morning my kind friend
appeared, in great excitement, grasped both my hands
through the bars, and cried, " Bob, my dear boy, what
have the rascals done to you ? You shan't stop here
another half-hour ! Go your bail ? Of course I will.
I reckon I would, if it were ten times as much." What
an immense relief his cheery presence and kindly words
were can be better imagined than described. He wouldn't
stop to listen to my heartfelt thanks, but posted off
at once to give his bond.

The formalities were quickly completed, the lock
was turned, and I stepped forth into the open air that
lovely summer morning a free and happy youth. I
found quite a gathering of friends and acquaintances
at Alvis's, who warmly congratulated me on my release ;
then, with many handshakes, Herndon and I mounted
our horses and rode out to his place, where I was to
spend the night, he explaining by the way that the
delay in his coming to my help was caused by his absence
from home.

Kind, good Mrs. Herndon and all her family, black
and white, gave me quite an ovation, and treated me
more like a hero than a prisoner out on bail.

But I was still very uneasy about my future ; October
would soon come round, when I should have to stand
my trial, and what should I do ? Mrs. Burnett was
begging me not to give up the notes to Paris, which she
roundly declared were not his property, but her husband's, from whom, by the way, I had heard nothing ;
even if I did give them up, in spite of my pledged word,

Paris could still hold me to my bail if he liked, and I felt I was in a great fix, and could see no clear way out of it. Besides all this, I was in a fever of unrest, and wanted to get away to that unknown land of promise, the Far West, as it then was, and which was drawing so many of my acquaintances, like a loadstone.

So, in despite of the advice of a very clever lawyer, Strauss by name, who lived in Taswell Court House, about sixty miles from Princeton, and who wanted me to fight Paris, I determined to compromise the matter with him, making the best terms I could for Mrs. Burnett. Therefore on my return to Princeton, I talked pretty big of what I would do with Paris by the help of Strauss, and then lay low for the next move of the enemy.

In two days' time he sent his confidential clerk to ask me to meet him, and then I felt sure of victory.

I went to his store, and to cut a long story short, eventually settled with him on the terms that I was to give up the notes on payment of $400 ; he to withdraw all proceedings, and to write me a letter stating that he had no cause of complaint against me. Next day I rode out to Rock Settlement, with a lighter heart than I had had for many a day, and handed over the $400 to Mrs. Burnett.

About this time, Wyoming Court House was to be opened as the seat of government of a new County, just formed on the Gyandotte River. Everybody from Milam's Ridge was going to the function, which would be a great gathering of the neighbourhood for miles around. So, with a party of six or seven friends, I rode the fifty miles to the scene of the festivities, through forest paths of the wildest, and overshadowed by the finest of timber.

About three miles from the Court House we came to a prosperous clearing and farm, with fine peach and apple orchards, and a still for converting the produce of them into brandy. The owner was known to some of our party, and we agreed to return in the evening and put up for the night, more especially as there was to be a big dance, to which we were all invited.

The new Court House was the usual small cluster of log and frame houses, and I remember nothing of the opening ceremonies except that one of them was a " Magic Lantern Show," which was regarded as quite an event in those wild parts.

Late in the evening we rode back to the farm, to find quite a large gathering, most of the folks being strangers to us. A plentiful supper was provided for all comers, and peach and apple brandy at ten cents the half pint was in abundance. In the yard was a blazing fire, round which, by the light of torches, much card-playing was going on, and some heavy gambling. Inside the house dancing was in full swing to the music of a fiddle, and I soon joined in, with consequences I have cause to remember, for I got into one of the stiffest rough-and-tumble fights I ever was in, either there or anywhere else.

After midnight some of the boys began to get noisy and quarrelsome, as a result of too many visits to the peach brandy. I had had no quarrel with any one, and was dancing a cotillon with a very pretty girl, when, without the slightest provocation, a young fellow jumped at me, struck me a heavy blow in the face, and bolted. I left my partner, made for him, and caught him before he could get out of the room. In a blazing rage, I went for him, and was giving him the sound thrashing he richly deserved, when his friends piled on me and beat me most unmercifully.

The dancing of course had stopped ; the girls were screaming, and all was confusion whilst I was the " under dog " of a crowd, each of whom was doing his best to kill me. Probably they would have succeeded had it not been for the plucky girl who had been my partner. She told me afterwards that she had tried her best to

give me a bowie knife, to defend myself with, but failing
to get near me, had run out to my friends, who were
card-playing.   They came promptly to the rescue, and
after a free fight cleared the room and saved my life,
though at the time I was quite unconscious of their
help.

When I came to myself next day, I found I had a
fearful gash on the back of my head, caused by a crashing
blow with a full bottle of whiskey, which had stunned
me, and that my left eye had been cruelly " gouged."
I was in a pretty bad plight, and at first thought I had
lost the sight of the eye, but a week's kind nursing by
my friends at the farm set me up enough to enable me
to ride back to the Bluestone, which I did all by myself,
filled with many thoughts as to the experience I had
gained and a not very exalted opinion of the chivalry
of the youth of Virginia.

Having done so well with my horse trade, I next
undertook to drive a herd of cattle into the Valley of
Virginia, to sell in the towns and on the tobacco plantations, in partnership with Ephraim Bailey.

I had about one hundred head running at Milam's
Ridge, and Bailey had about fifty.   So with this herd
of 150 head we set out, I taking Reuben Bailey and his
two boys to help me drive.   The cattle were wild as
hawks, and though Reuben and his youngsters were as
tough and active as Indians, whom in their buckskin
hunting-shirts and mocassins they much resembled, it
was an awful job to get them along at first.   However,
we did contrive to drive them somehow through Giles,
Munro, and Roanoke Counties, crossing the Roanoke
River by the natural bridge of Virginia, a stupendous
work of Nature herself.   Descending into the Valley of
Virginia, where the people were mostly well-to-do de-
scendants of the Pennsylvanian Dutch, and where there
were plenty of good grazing farms, we soon disposed of
the greater number of our stock at good prices.

By the time we reached Culpepper Court House, famous afterwards in the Great War time, Bailey had sold his fifty head, and I had twenty-five left. These I was lucky enough to sell in one lot to a young fellow named Fletcher, who owned a fine plantation and worked it with about fifty negroes.

Fletcher said he could not pay me till he received a draft from Baltimore in about a fortnight, and in the meantime invited me to stay with him at his place. I accepted his very cordial invitation, and having paid off Reuben and his boys and said good-bye to Ephraim, rode out to the plantation with my host. His house was quite a fine one, and after my West Virginian experiences, seemed a mansion indeed. Built in the old Colonial days of red brick, mellowed in colour by the hundred years of its existence, it looked more like an English country house than anything I had seen on the other side, though of course it lacked the beautiful gardens and trim lawns which are so rarely seen out of the Old Country.

Fletcher, who was a bachelor, lived with his overseer, in much comfort and some state. He had plenty of horses, both saddle and harness, and quite a retinue of servants, all niggers of course.

The shooting in the neighbourhood was very good, partridges and pheasants being plentiful, and my stay with him was most enjoyable ; for everything was placed at my disposal, horses, buggies, guns, etc., and I was made to feel perfectly at home. Fletcher, who was a most pleasant, hospitable man, was also a keen sportsman, and very fond of what he called " gunning," so we had many a good shoot together. After three weeks of this pleasant life, the draft from Baltimore arrived, and I said good-bye to my friend and started, with my horse well rested, for my 250-mile ride back to the Bluestone.

Nothing worth recording happened on the ride except that at Lynchburg, where I put up for Sunday, I was present at a great Baptist christening on the banks of the James River. About a dozen grown men and women were plunged beneath the icy water by three preachers, who stood waist-deep in it to receive their converts. It is to be hoped they were benefited by the ceremony, for I remember that all the party, preachers and converts alike, looked desperately cold and miserable.

I reached home at last well satisfied with my venture, and with a well-filled pocket-book and cash-belt, the proceeds of my cattle trades.

Now I hastened my preparations for the Western migration to Kansas, the land that seemed so fair and full of promise, but which was so soon to be the theatre of partisan strife and of the cruel, bitter struggle between North and South that formed the prelude to the great War of Secession. My days in Western Virginia were numbered, and I was very shortly to bid farewell to many kind friends, and to a simple, easy-going life in those woodland regions, which I suppose the march of civilisation, moving so rapidly as it does in the States, has long since stamped out.

Before I leave the Virginian life, it may be of interest to describe the various kinds of shooting and hunting we so much enjoyed.

Deer, bears, coons, squirrels, partridges so called (really tree-grouse), and pheasants abounded in the woods, whilst, in a good " mast " year, pigeons came in countless thousands, and were slaughtered in their " roosts " by every one who possessed a " scatter gun."

Deer were killed in three ways :

(1) At the " licks " by torch light ; (2) by " still " hunting ; and (3) by driving with hounds, kept specially for the purpose, and allowed to run no other game.

The two first methods I have described, but the third, or driving, was by far the most exciting. Four or five of us would go out by daybreak with, say, three couples of hounds, which were hunted by one of the party on horseback. The rest of us would take post on the river at " stands," where the deer-trails showed the quarry would probably " soil." The huntsman and his little pack would make a wide circuit, perhaps for miles, through the heavily timbered ridges, whilst we waited with what patience we might at our " stands."

Then would be heard the distant music of the hounds as they hit a line. Nearer and nearer it would come, and all were frantic with excitement, each one hoping he would have the chance of a shot, which only one could get.

How well I remember the first buck I got in this way! The deep notes of the hounds, now nearer, now far away, as they drove the deer in fine style through the forest, ring in my ears now. Close down to my hiding-place they come in full cry ; I raise my gun, well loaded with buckshot, and, as the deer with a bound plunges into the stream, I pull the trigger and miss him clean with the first barrel, for " buck-ague " is strong upon me. Across the river he swims at a great pace, for now the leading hound appears on the bank behind him. As he scrambles and staggers up the steep side, I steady myself and let drive. Back into the water he falls dead, shot just behind the shoulder, and before I can realise my happiness and good fortune the hounds are upon him, and I have to beat them off as best I can till the huntsman comes up to help, and to congratulate me on my luck. It was rare sport notwithstanding the some-times weary waiting, and we would often get two or three deer in a day. Bears were always hunted with dogs trained for the sport, and they soon got very clever at it. Their part was to drive the bear out of the thick " ivy brakes " along the river-bottoms, and when they had got him out on to the ridges, to stick close to him but keeping well out of the reach of his clutches. Sooner or later the bear was bound to " set up " against a tree or rock if the hounds stuck close to his hams, and then came the hunter's chance.

It was rarely that a man got mauled by a bear, but I
remember one rather curious instance.

About half-way between the Bluestone and Milam's
Ridge, two brothers named Mills had a log shanty and
made a living by hunting, " bee shining," and feeding
hogs on the " mast " in the woods. When I arrived
at the cabin one day, on my journey to the ridge, I
found one of the brothers with an arm badly broken,
and clawed by a bear. They said that the previous
night, which was pretty dark, they had been aroused
by a terrible squealing amongst their hogs, in the pen
close by. One brother ran out with only a butcher's
knife in his hand, the other stopped to load his rifle.
The first jumped over into the pen, and in the dim light
saw a bear with a hog in his clutch.

He went at the bear with his knife to save his hog,
and was at once seized by the left arm, but made a plucky
fight for it, and cut the bear badly. Meantime the other
brother came on the scene with his rifle, and as soon
as he could distinguish which was which, no easy matter
in a rough-and-tumble like that, put a bullet through the
bear's head.

I once spent three days bear-hunting with a Colonel
George of Tassel County, an ex-Congress man and large
slave-owner. He took several niggers with him, and
wagons and horses, and made a regular camp for a
week's hunting on the Gyandotte River.

The first day, starting out at daybreak, his three
couples of hounds soon found in the ivy brakes, and
quickly drove their bear out on to the ridges. Of course,
we were on foot, as the country was too rough for riding.
What a dance that bear led us ! Up hill and down dale,
over rocks and through thick brush ; sometimes half a
mile ahead of us, at others so far away we could scarce
hear the baying of the hounds.

At last, when I really thought I could run no farther,
they held him up against a great tree-trunk. He stood

on his hind legs, the hounds baying round him in a circle, whilst every now and then he would try to catch one in his hug. The Colonel and I fired together, and the bear, a fine old " he," fell dead. We were seven miles from camp, so the niggers only took the skin and the hams.

We killed two more bears, one each day, much after the same fashion, and then I said good-bye to the Colonel, and left him to finish his week's hunting, as I was obliged to get back to the farm.

The tree-grouse, or " partridges," as the Virginians called them, gave little sport. They are dwellers of the woodlands, and, when put up, invariably " tree." The " partridge dog " is trained to work ahead of his master, and, when he has treed his game, to stand and bark till he comes up. The birds are so stupid that they take no notice of the dog, and but little of the man ; so that one may often shoot a couple of brace out of the tree before the rest of the covey fly away.

Of ducks there was an immense variety in the winter season, and good sport could be had with them along the river-bottoms.

Passenger pigeons, or, as we called them, " wild pigeons," were at times so numerous that one is almost afraid to estimate their numbers, lest it should be thought a " yarn " : but indeed they would congregate in a favourite " roost " till the smaller saplings would break with their weight.

I well remember in the autumn of 1853 that immense flocks were seen passing over my farm. George Dillon located their roost, on Brush Creek, about ten miles away, and four or five of us took all the " scatter guns " we could collect and went out to shoot for the pot.

We camped about half a mile away from the roost, and as twilight came on the pigeons flew in, till the smaller trees and brush literally bent under their weight. As night fell we lighted our torches, and then the slaughter began. No other word can describe it, for it was butchery pure and simple, and our only excuse was that we wanted the meat. By midnight we had killed enough to fill the body of my light wagon ; we might easily have filled two such. When we got back we divided the bag, and everybody in the settlement lived on pigeons for many days.

Turkeys were fairly plentiful, but were rarely shot. They were taken in a rather ingenious fashion. When snow lay deep, and turkey signs were seen, a pen was made about ten feet square and covered with brush. A good long trench was dug leading into this, under the bottom log, and corn laid in it, and scattered round.

The turkeys would follow the corn into the pen, and, once in, had not the sense to get out. We sometimes caught as many as a dozen at a time.

CHAPTER VII

IT was the end of November, in the year 1854, before I could settle up my affairs and make a start, impatient as I was to be on the road to my land of promise. Even then my friend Herndon, to whom I had sold my farm and mill, was not ready with my cash. So to make things easier for him and avoid delay, I agreed to take three young niggers—Ann, a girl of about sixteen, and her two young brothers, Shad and Pete, fourteen and twelve years old—in part payment.

One crisp November morning then, with my not very extensive baggage packed in Squire Eli Bailey's wagon, or "carry all," I mounted my horse, and with Manor by my side started on my long journey Westward. But just as we got under weigh, we heard Reuben Bailey's deer-hounds in full cry across the creek. This was more than Manor could stand, and he bolted off to join the sport, turning the deer, so that the hounds, who were close on his heels, pulled him down before our very eyes. That was the last Virginian buck I saw killed.

I found my friend Herndon waiting for me at Princeton with the three young niggers, for each of whom he gave me a bill of sale at the County Clerk's office. So I became, for the first time in my life, that most wicked, cruel monster, a slave-owner!

Strange as it may seem to those whose ideas of slaves, and slave-owners, have been formed by " Abolition " literature, my young darkies went with me cheerfully and willingly, and were quite as much excited at the prospect of the new life in the West as I was myself. What their ideas on the subject were, or what they expected to find when they reached the goal, I know not ; indeed I hardly know what my own ideas were. A complete change from the past, and new conditions of life, we all looked forward to, I suppose.

New and strange enough conditions I certainly did find at my journey's end, and not altogether pleasant ones. Had I known what a seething cauldron of evil passions and bitter political strife awaited me in Kansas, probably I should have turned my steps elsewhere. However, we heard but little of the outside world and its doings in remote Western Virginia, and little guessed that the storm, which would almost rend the Republic in twain, was even then brewing, and that I was innocently and unconsciously going to walk into the midst of its uprising.

At Princeton I said good-bye to many kind friends who had made the young stranger's life so pleasant to him, and with a " carry all " to convey my chattels, set off on a fifty-mile ride to the nearest station on the railway to Richmond, the name of which I forget. My great friend George Dillon went with me to the station, to bring the conveyance back. There we parted, and I have never seen or heard of him since, but he lives in my memory still as the staunchest friend, finest backwoodsman, and keenest sportsman I have ever met.

Arrived at Lynchburg, where we had to change for Richmond, I left my baggage at the station and took my darkies and Manor to Seth Woodruff, to whom I had a letter of introduction, and who, besides being the largest nigger dealer in the State, kept a barrack, where such chattels were taken care of for their owners.

His calling notwithstanding, he seemed a very pleasant, good sort of fellow, and was highly respected in the town. I spent the evening with him, and he tried very hard to buy my niggers, offering me a price that would have paid me well. But that meant their being separated, most probably, and possibly getting into bad hands. I couldn't harden my heart to that, so refused, and to their huge delight took them along with me to the unknown West.

In those days there were only two classes of tickets on the railways, first for whites, and second for niggers and dogs! I therefore took one first and four second class tickets for Richmond. On the journey my little party and myself were regarded with a good deal of curiosity, and some little suspicion. I was manifestly a " Britisher," and very young. What was I doing with three young niggers, and where was I taking them ?

Anything touching a nigger was keenly interesting to the Southerners, who were suspicious of strangers who meddled with them. Runaways were not uncommon, and possibly they thought I was engaged on what was called the " underground business." When, however, I produced my papers they were satisfied, and became friendly enough.

At Richmond I boarded my young folks at the hotel with the kitchen niggers, and in the evening gave them a permit, countersigned by the landlord, together with the price of tickets for the niggers' gallery at the theatre, which was an amazing event in their lives.

Before I could get tickets for Pittsburg in Pennsylvania, which was a Free State, official sanction had to be given, and proof produced from some undoubted authority that the applicant had proper legal title to his black property. In this fix I bethought me of Napoleon French, member of the State Legislature for Mercer County, who was well known to me. The House was in session, and directly I sent in my name by a liveried usher I was at once shown into the Legislative Hall. It was a handsome, nearly circular room ; desks piled up with stationery and books, before each member, filled the outer circumference. The comfort and convenience of the members appeared well cared for, for there were at least fifty page boys in attendance to look after their wants.

French at once gave the certificate I wanted and I bade him good-bye, little thinking that in a few years' time that hall would be the theatre of such momentous decisions and epoch-making laws as were enacted there in Secession times.

Armed with French's certificate I took tickets to Pittsburg for myself and " chattels," and thence went to Cincinnati by steamboat.   There I took ferry and crossed the Ohio River to Covington in Kentucky, which was a Slave State, in which my property would be safer than in the former town, which is in Ohio, a Free State.

Cincinnati was then considered the metropolis of the West, and even in those days was a large and thriving city, the centre of the pork trade.   The river-banks were thronged with steamboats and the streets with eager, busy folks, the half of whom seemed to be Germans.

The weather had now set in very cold, and great masses of ice were coming down the river.   The rivermen prophesied that navigation would be stopped before we could reach St. Louis, my next point, but I had to push on and risk it.   So next morning we ferried over the Ohio again, and took boat for St. Louis.

It was a terribly hard frost, and when we got out into the mighty Mississippi, the ice was coming down the swift-running stream in huge blocks, so that every hour navigation grew more difficult.   Slowly our ancient stern-wheeler pushed her way through the heavy ice, and when at last we reached St. Genevieve about nightfall, the captain tied her up for the night, to see how things looked in the morning.

The morning brought us little hope, for the frost was harder than ever, and it was clear that if it lasted a day or two longer the river would be completely frozen over. Anxiously we all awaited the captain's decision, and when, after breakfast, he made the announcement that

the old crawler could not move, and might have to be
tied up all winter, were heartily disappointed. We
asked for a return of a fair proportion of our passage
money, but were told that was out of the question,
though we might remain on board till the voyage was
completed.

It was hardly good enough, so four or five of us agreed
to hire the conveyance of our baggage to St. Louis on
a wagon which belonged to an old fellow on board who
was emigrating from Ohio to the great West. The
patriarch had quite a large family, and what with his
wife and children, my nigger girl Ann, and all our
baggage, his poor horses had a pretty good load.

The wagon was landed, and the party ready to start,
all but myself, and I was frantically searching for my
friend and companion, the dog Manor. My boys and
all my acquaintances helped in the quest, but in vain ;
nowhere could he be found ?   Finally I had to leave
without him, after adjuring the captain, who expected
to lay there at least a month, to look out for him
and write me any tidings he might get to the P.O.,
St. Louis.

On board the steamer was a party of itinerant gym-
nasts who had made a great pet of my dog, and they too
promised to look for him and bring him on to St. Louis,
which was their destination, if they were lucky enough
to find him.   I little thought the rascals had stolen and
hidden away my pet, but so it turned out to be.

About midday we got off on our long and toilsome
journey, and a curious party we were !   There was the
rough old Ohian who owned the wagon, with his wife
and numerous progeny ; a Californian, a scene-painter
by calling ; two young actors going to play at St. Louis ;
a young Kentuckian emigrant who had his horse with
him, which, as we had made great friends, he insisted I
should ride in tie with him ; and lastly, myself and my
three young niggers.

Though modesty would prompt me not to mention it, yet, as an illustration of ways of thought and social customs, I must explain that as an owner of niggers I was looked up to as the aristocrat of the party. I might have been as ragged and unkempt as a tramp, and without a dollar in my pocket, yet the fact of possessing niggers would have raised me to at least the fringe of aristocracy. So it was throughout the South in those days.

The cold was intense, and the road, if road it might properly be called, of the roughest, so much so that we all had to keep alongside the wagon to push it up the slippery slopes. Every creek was frozen, but sometimes not hard enough to bear the heavy wagon. Then the ice had to be broken, with infinite labour, and the wagon got over somehow. Under these conditions we managed to travel about fifteen miles a day, halting for the night at some farm or other where we could get shelter.

Rough as the journey was, we all enjoyed it, and were as happy as youth, high hopes, good spirits, the bright sky, and clear frosty air could make us. Generally our lodgings were of the roughest, but one night we halted (it was Christmas Eve) at the farm of a French Missourian, who entertained the whole party most hospitably and got up an impromptu dance for our benefit, which was kept up till a very late hour.

Though I have long since forgotten my host's name, I still remember the courtesy of the polite Frenchman as a most pleasing contrast to the kindly, but rough manners of the native Americans.

Arrived at St. Louis, I put up at a large boarding-house, lodging my darkies in the kitchen with the other niggers, and presently, finding that it was impossible to get on to Kansas, either by river or road, hired them out in the city for $12 a week. I kept an eye on them, and saw they were well treated and not overworked.

My landlord's brother was somewhat of a power in

the city, being Market Master. To him I told the sad loss of my dog, and he promised that he would have a good look-out kept, and felt confident he would get him, if he were brought into the city. He was as good as his word, though it was nearly a month before he discovered Manor for me.

I was walking one day in the market when I saw the Master ahead of me, followed by a dog. It was Manor sure enough, and the moment he saw me he left his friend and jumped about me, and on me, in frantic excitement, and we were mutually overjoyed to meet again.

The Master had seen him on the stage of a " side show," performing tricks, at which he was very expert. My friend went behind the scenes, handed his card to the manager, and demanded the immediate delivery to him of the setter he had got, and which he had stolen from a friend of his at St. Genevieve. Of course, the man protested that he had not stolen the dog, only found him wandering about without his master, whose whereabouts he did not know. Anyhow he promptly handed over the dog, under threat of a prosecution.

Harder and harder grew the frost, till the proverbial " oldest inhabitant " declared such had never been known before in his experience, and a few days after our arrival the Mississippi was frozen so solidly that a constant traffic of heavy wagons and vehicles of all sorts was kept up over the ice, between St. Louis and the Illinois side. Walking along the " Levee " it was a wonderful sight to look upon the lines of steamboats all frozen in, literally miles of them, and one could but wonder what would happen when the ice broke up and came down the mighty river with its irresistible force.

When the temperature had fallen to 15° below zero Fahrenheit, my landlord's wife died, and a numerous concourse of people, of whom I was one, attended the funeral ; but the frost was so intense that no grave could

5

be dug, so the remains were deposited in the mortuary
chapel of the cemetery.

It was weary work waiting in St. Louis, frost-bound,
without the possibility of moving on, and though there
were plenty of amusements in the city, such as theatres
and card and dancing parties, the time hung very heavily
on my hands.

After a time I left the boarding-house and took up my
abode with my Kentucky friend at a hotel in the suburbs,
to which was attached a large livery stable with standing
for perhaps two hundred horses, or more.   Much card-
playing went on there, euchre, poker, and seven-up
being the games.   I played pretty often myself, for lack
of something else to do, and I don't think lost, but
rather the contrary.   At this place I met some curious
characters and some rather risky ones, and perhaps I
may mention one or two incidents connected with
them.

A " Colonel " Watson appeared one day, with a drove
of four hundred fine mules, going South for a market.
With him he had a number of his own niggers.   He was
a pleasant enough old fellow, but his chief characteristic
was his ability to " punish " unlimited quantities of
whiskey.

Seated with him one day in the harness-room of the
stable, to us appeared a city constable with one of the
" Colonel's " niggers in charge, whom he had found,
without a permit, on the ice near the Illinois shore.
Now the capture of a runaway nigger meant $50 to
the constable, which the owner had to pay.   The Colonel
was furious at the prospect of having to pay up this
sum, and went for the unfortunate nigger to flog him
with a chain he happened to have in his hand.   I stepped
between them, to save the poor wretch, who protested
his innocence, and declared he was only taking a walk
on the ice, and had at once given the constable his master's
name and address.   Finding he couldn't get at the

nigger, the " Colonel " cooled down at last, and listened to reason, but he had to pay those $50.

If he had not been checked when he was so " mad," he might have half killed the poor darkey, and nothing would have been thought of it.

Another guest at our hotel was a " Colonel " Howard, whose title seemed to be derived from his commanding a drove of many hundreds of turkeys. It was his annual custom to collect these in Missouri and drive them through St. Louis on his way to the Southern markets. Just before the frost set in, he had arrived with a drove of quite a thousand, which he had driven 250 miles. The severe weather caused heavy mortality amongst his stock, but the old boy, who was a planter in a large way and a well-to-do man, with plenty of niggers, bore it philosophically, consoling himself with the thought that prices would go up.

The " Colonel " and I became quite friendly, and often went to the theatre together. The Batemans were running it, and I had the *entrée* to the pit through my acquaintance with the Californian scene-painter.

The last incident I will recall is rather a gruesome one, and might have had most serious consequences for myself.

One afternoon, when a terrible blizzard was blowing with heavy snow, two men came into the hotel, and, taking off their heavy military cloaks, made themselves comfortable in the public room where a lot of us were seated. One was a remarkably fine-looking man, of good address ; the other seemed of lower stamp, and evidently looked up to the first a good deal. Their account of themselves was that they had been buffalo-hunting, out beyond Fort Leavenworth in Kansas, where they had been very successful. They had ridden in to St. Louis through this awful weather, and had had, as we might guess, a terrible journey.

The leader said he came from Baltimore, and the other from Georgia. Both seemed flush of money, and the

Marylander, I noticed, wore a handsome gold watch and chain ; his name, he said, was Henry McNutt ; the other's William Johnson.

I took quite a liking to McNutt, he seemed such a cheery, pleasant fellow. After having inspected their horses, of which they had three very fine ones, we grew quite friendly, and agreed to sup together and then spend the evening at the theatre, Mr. McNutt insisting on paying for the tickets. After the play we strolled about the city together, visiting various " side shows " and saloons, in one of which latter, towards the early hours of the morning, my friends kicked up a terrible row, and tried to pick a quarrel with me when I interfered to stop the fight.

Either because they knew I was armed, or for some other reason, they thought better of it, and made it up.

I said good-bye to them next morning, when they started in the bitter cold on their journey South, crossing the ice to the Illinois side, and thought but little more of them till, in about ten days, I had a call from the City Marshal. He asked me a good deal about these men, and then requested me to go with him to the office of Major Walker, the manager and engineer of the St. Louis and Jefferson City Railway. The Major asked me many questions about my acquaintances, and, when I told him all I knew, horrified me by saying they were wanted for the murder of his friend and sub-engineer, Mr. Gordon.

It seems Gordon had put up at a farm on the road to St. Louis with these two men ; that they had started thence together, and that Gordon, who had a valuable gold watch and chain, and a large sum of money on him, had not been seen since. The watch I saw McNutt wearing was his, as also one of the horses I had admired so much.

After a long search Gordon's body was found by a dog the searchers had with them, buried in the snow close to the roadside, with a bullet wound in the head.

A reward of $2,000 was offered for the apprehension of McNutt and his companion, and they were caught and brought back to St. Louis. Each tried to fix the guilt on the other, but at the trial, which took place four months later, and to which I was subpœnaed as a witness from Kansas, they were both found guilty, and presently hanged.

McNutt's father was a doctor in large practice in Baltimore, and with him, and with the grief-stricken mother, I had a most painful meeting after the trial.

Till the end of February the cruel frost kept every one, and every thing, fast bound in its fetters of iron, and then it showed signs of yielding. How gladly I hailed the coming change!

Naturally, I was impatient to continue my journey West and begin my new career. To add to this, the Press, and the very air, were full of rumours of a conflict already begun in Kansas, between Southerners and "Free Soilers." Excitement was growing day by day throughout the South, and especially in Missouri, and I was as keen as the rest to take my part on the Southern side.

Hope of release grew as one stood on the Levee and watched hundreds of men sawing the ice round the fleets of steamboats, in preparation for the break-up and to save them, if possible, from threatened destruction.

The actual break-up, when it came, was a sight never to be forgotten. The melting snows and pouring rain brought the mighty Mississippi and Missouri rivers down bank-high in flood, and on that united rushing stream came the upper ice, piled, at times, nearly a hundred feet in height. Before this irresistible force and weight the unbroken ice-floor opposite St. Louis burst and split and rent with reports like thunder, and in the grasp of this hurrying glacier-like stream went nearly all the steamboats to utter wreck and ruin.

Madly they crashed one against the other, and those who vainly tried to save them only lost their lives. The destruction wrought was estimated at $3,000,000, and I don't think it was much exaggerated. It was the grandest and yet most awful sight I ever witnessed, and held me, and vast crowds, spellbound by the riverside whilst it lasted.

BOOK II

KANSAS IN 1855-59

CHAPTER I

THE RIVAL PARTIES

THOUGH by the latter end of February the ice on the river had broken up, no boats were running, or could run, for several weeks. I therefore determined to wait no longer, but to ride to Fort Leavenworth on the Missouri, a distance of 450 miles.

Leaving my niggers with their masters, who treated them well, I mounted a fine young horse I had bought, and set off, one bitterly cold morning, on my long and solitary journey. Roads there were none, except near the widely scattered farms, and then they were more like a series of half-thawed mudholes.

The country was very different from the Virginian forest-lands I knew so well, but the people were the same kindly, hospitable folks, making the weary traveller welcome to the best they had, and seldom accepting payment for their entertainment. So I journeyed on, getting over about thirty-five miles a day on an average, and nothing worth recording occurred till Independence, an important town and Indian trading-post on the frontier of Missouri, was reached. There I found the place crowded with Missourians and a goodly sprinkling of men from the Southern States, all full of excitement over the burning question whether the Territory of Kansas, recently opened up for settlement, should be Slave or Free.

The Free State party in the North, managed and worked from Faneuil Hall, Boston, had been sending up men and arms, and had occupied positions defended by light artillery. The Missourians were crossing the river, and volunteers from all the Southern States were marching up to the conflict, which might break out at any moment.

In this scene of seething unrest and wild passion, a stranger was naturally regarded with suspicion until he declared his sympathies. Mine were strongly on the side of the South, and, as soon as I made this known, I was heartily welcomed amongst the " Border Ruffians," as the pro-Slavery party was nicknamed by the Free Staters.

Strong pro-slavery man as I was, I saw a sight, as I rode out of the town next morning, that opened my eyes to the cruelty and barbarity of the " Institution." A slave-dealer was there, with his drove of niggers, collected for the Southern market, and in it was one who had been sold as a desperate character. Just as I started, the unfortunate creature had broken loose, and passed close by me in his frantic rush for the woods near by. After him came his master and some other men, shouting to him to stop. But he was running for life and liberty, and held on in desperation.

He was rapidly nearing the covert when the master raised his rifle, fired, and the fugitive fell dead in his tracks. It was a brutal deed, done by a brute, but the law sanctioned it. It was almost as much as my life was worth to remonstrate ; so I held my tongue and rode on, sickened and disgusted with this, to me, new aspect of slavery.

That night I put up with " Johnny Cake," the head chief of the Delaware Indians in Kansas, on the Delaware reserve. He was a tame Indian, spoke English well, and was a member of the Methodist Church. He treated me very well, and was most hospitable ; but what I chiefly remember of my visit is that my host gave us a long and very extraordinary grace before and after the corn bread and bacon.

Late the next evening I reached Leavenworth City, and, at a wooden shanty dignified with the name of hotel, got taken in.

The " city " was on the Delaware reserve, and was not open for settlement ; indeed the U.S. Government had warned all squatters off it by proclamation, under heavy penalties. But these were " paper penalties " only, *i.e.* never enforced, and were treated as non-existent ; especially as it was known that nearly the whole of the reserve would be thrown open in the fall.

In 1855 the " city," now a great centre of the rich wheat-growing district in which it stands, consisted of a few frame buildings, two or three small stores, and the " hotel " I put up at. *The Leavenworth Democrat* represented the majesty of the " Fourth Estate," and was edited, printed, and published in a small shanty under a big cottonwood-tree by Major Euston, an out-and-out Southerner, and a typical specimen of the South-western fighting editor. He was the quickest man with his six-shooter I ever saw, even in a country where it behoved every one to be on the alert.

The little place was full of gamblers, as all frontier settlements were in those days.

Their " boss sportsman " was a certain A. B. Miller, who had run up a shanty with a showily fitted-out bar and rooms for the accommodation of the fraternity. There roulette, pharo, and poker were going on from midday all through the night, and large sums changed hands. Now and then some unlucky gambler would end his miseries in the mighty Missouri, and many another was shot in the saloon itself during the constant night rows.

In those early days there was no law in the city, not even a Vigilance Committee, and the sporting fraternity, holding all together, and being well armed, ruled without question. They were all " Sound on the goose," or in other words, strong pro-slavery men, and their misdeeds notwithstanding, were in a measure popular with the rest of the community.

In face of all these drawbacks, and the prevailing ruffianism, I soon made up my mind to risk my fortunes in the Territory. With a man named Moses Young from Kentucky, a carpenter and contractor, I entered into a sort of partnership, with the object of buying up likely " lots " and building thereon shanties for the new arrivals who kept pouring in.

If I only had had the prescience to foresee what that new country would so rapidly grow to, I might now be a millionaire, simply by buying up, and *holding on to*, town lots.

As soon as I had made this agreement with Young, I left my horse and other belongings with him and set off for St. Louis to fetch my darkies, and my cash and Manor. The soft breath of spring was in the air, spring that comes so suddenly and so sweetly in the South-western States of the Union, and my six days' trip down the river was delightful. Ten days I spent in St. Louis, and then started back with my " chattels," my dog, and my capital of $2,000, as well as a wagon and harness for a team I had bought as a spec.

The boat was crowded with pro-slavery men, and some few Free Staters ; but the latter kept very quiet. At Leavenworth the Levee was crowded by the whole population, who had turned out to see that our boat had brought no arms for the Free Staters.

Young had found me room in a boarding-house started in my absence, and we marched there in great state, followed by the darkies ; and their possession gave me quite a status in the city ! The landlady of the house at once hired my girl Ann at $20 a month, and the two boys were as quickly taken for $25 each, and their keep. So I had an income of $70 a month, more than enough for my modest wants, and felt quite independent.

Presently I bought another horse and, with my new

SIOUX INDIANS

p. 76

wagon, began carrying, at good paying rates. Then Moses Young and I bought a lot and built a Californian frame house, in which to live ourselves and board our hands, with stabling behind it for our horses. Moreover we dug a garden, and planted it ; the only one, I think, in all the city.

About two miles from the city was Leavenworth Fort, held by a regiment of U.S. cavalry and two or three companies of infantry. The Sioux Indians, then, and for some years after, a very powerful tribe, had been troublesome, and just before my arrival the troops had had a big fight with them. A good many Indians were killed, and a number of prisoners taken, which was an unusual occurrence in those days, when quarter was rarely given by either side. I well remember seeing quite a bunch of these inside the Fort, crouching on the ground in the bitter cold, wrapped in their coloured blankets, apparently quite indifferent to what Fate might have in store for them. All the captive chiefs I know were shot, but don't remember what was done with the rank and file.

Whilst my house was building, some of the officers at the Fort, whose acquaintance I had made, wanted to be taken to Fort Riley, some 150 miles west, and I contracted to take them in my wagon. It was a most delightful trip across the rolling prairies in that lovely spring-time, and with pleasant companions. We camped out each night except one, when we put up at the Pottawattamy Catholic Mission, where the Sisters entertained us most hospitably and pleasantly. To this day I remember the charm of their courtesy and refinement ; it seemed like a memory of the past.

The prairies in those days, one hundred miles back from the Missouri, were covered with herds of buffalo and antelopes, and, never having seen these before, I was astounded at their numbers. The latter were particularly tame, and, moved by their insatiable curiosity, would come circling up quite close to the wagon, have a good look, and then gallop off again in ever widening circles.

We shot two buffaloes on our way up ; we might have shot hundreds had we cared to do so, but as we only wanted their humps it would have been sheer waste.

After a pleasant stay at the Fort, which, by-the-by, is said to be the centre point of the United States, measuring from east to west, I departed on my beautiful but lonely drive over the vast prairies.

Having a good supply of hump with me, I did not kill any more buffalo, though I passed through many thousands of them ; a sight that no man now can see, for on the prairies where they thronged so thickly they are as extinct as is the dodo in Mauritius.

One night, on my back track, I halted, unwittingly, close to the camp of the Delaware chief Bullbone, the leader of the warriors of that nation. I confess I felt rather uneasy when, just as I had unhooked my horses, the chief walked up with three or four " buck " Indians. However, it turned out that he was in a peaceful mood, and only wanted to trade skins for tobacco and whiskey.

As neither of us could speak a word of the other's language, it was rather difficult to arrange the deal ; but we managed it somehow in dumb show, and he departed in high good humour, to my great relief, for in his presence my scalp seemed to fit rather loosely on my head.

That was my first meeting with a real wild Red Indian : I could heartily wish it had been the last, for I thoroughly endorse Artemus Ward's opinion that " they are pison wherever met " ; and I met a great many of them in after days.

I returned to Leavenworth without adventure of any sort, well pleased with the money I had earned, and with the rich rolling prairies of Kansas.

" What a splendid country is waiting the advent of the white man ! " I thought.

What a marvellous change the fifty years that have passed since then have wrought in it! Ah! if, in Western parlance, "my foresights had been as good as my hindsights," what might I not have done?

I should mention that when I started for Fort Riley I was much perplexed as to how to safely bestow my cash capital of $2,000. I didn't want to take it with me, for the benefit of the Indians who might scalp me, and there was no one to whom I could entrust it in Leavenworth. Finally, in this fix, I made up my mind to trust my nigger girl Ann; and, as it turned out, I was right.

The boarding-house where she was employed was raised on piles, and, in my presence, she buried my bag of money under it at night. On my return we went and dug it up, and not a dollar was missing. I believe Ann, poor girl, was the only honest person in the place!

Even then this blessed money bothered me not a little, for there was no place of safety for it. Generally I carried it about with me, but sometimes buried it, and always kept the fact that I had ready money as secret as I could. However, Miller, the boss gambler, got wind of it, and pressed me to lend him $1,000 on the security of his saloon and its good-will. In the then state of affairs I couldn't well refuse, so let him have it, though with many doubts as to whether I should ever see it again.

The Californian frame house was nearly finished by this time, and Ann, the honest, was installed as cook to cater for our carpenters, who crowded in for board and lodging, at high prices, before even the place was ready.

Meanwhile the political excitement had day by day been growing more intense, and now was at fever heat.

Quietly and calmly looking back on the situation in the United States, one sees quite clearly that the struggle for supremacy between North and South, of which the fighting in Kansas was only the prelude, had to be decided

sooner or later. Further, it is also plain that the two
sections were so diametrically opposed to each other in
political ideas that they must have fought it out before
a peaceful *modus vivendi* could be arrived at. Negro
slavery was not *the* cause of the war, but only one of
many causes ; nor did the North enter on the struggle
with the object of freeing the negro.

The South, broadly speaking, was a landed aristocracy,
whilst the North was trading and commercial.

Since the establishment of the Republic, the South,
with its comparatively sparse white population, had, by
the voting power given by its negroes (though these of
course had no votes themselves), ruled the wealthy and
rapidly growing Northern States, and the yoke had at
last become intolerable.

In Kansas the South fought for the right to add to the
number of Slave States, which was its only hope of re-
taining supremacy in the Union ; the North to restrict
slavery within the limits fixed by the agreement arrived
at in 1820.

The law of 1787 forbade the extension of slavery North
of the Ohio River, whilst it prevailed in all the States and
Territories south of that boundary. Then came the
purchase of Louisiana by the States—an immense accession of territory. The portion round New Orleans was
admitted as a Slave State in 1812, under the name of
Louisiana ; but when, a little later, the country round
St. Louis, on the Missouri, where slavery already prevailed, applied for admission, as another Slave State, the
North strongly opposed the application. Finally a compromise was arrived at, by which it was settled that
Missouri should be a Slave State, but that all the rest
of the Louisiana purchase north of its southern boundary, *i.e.* north of 36° 30', should always be free.

This was known as the Missouri Compromise, and no
doubt it deferred the inevitable conflict for many years.

In 1836 Texas, over which the States had acquired

some vague claim by the Louisiana purchase, revolted from Mexico, and set up as an independent Republic. In 1845 this short-lived independence came to an end, and Texas was annexed by the States, and admitted as a Slave State.

In 1846 war broke out between the Federal Government and Mexico, on questions arising from the boundaries of the new State. By the treaty signed at the conclusion of the war in 1848, Mexico ceded to the States the southern and western portions of Texas, as well as New Mexico, part of Arizona, and California.

Here was an immense accession of strength to the South, and the old disputes broke out afresh between the two sections. These were finally allayed by the expedient of allowing the people of each portion of the territory obtained from Mexico to decide the question of slavery for themselves ; this was afterwards known as " squatter sovereignty."

In 1850 California was admitted as a Free State, to the great disgust of the South, which could not control the vote of the emigrants who rushed thither on the discovery of gold. To pacify this the Fugitive Slave Law was passed, under which the Federal authorities were ordered to return to their owners all slaves escaping to the North. The putting of this in force at once gave a great impetus to the party of Abolition, which had hitherto been comparatively insignificant in numbers.

Now in 1854, just before I arrived on the scene of strife, the South attempted to apply the principle of " squatter sovereignty " to the vast territories of Kansas and Nebraska, lying north of the 36° 30′ line. This was manifestly a breach of the Missouri Compromise, and the North was up in arms at once.

This is a long digression from my story, but it seemed necessary to explain, as shortly as possible, the cause of the bitter strife in which I played a humble part.

The Southerners then, whether they had law and right

on their side or not, were determined to establish " squatter sovereignty " in Kansas, and to carry the vote for
slavery. The Northerners were equally determined they
should not succeed.

South Carolina, Missouri, and Texas especially, raised
war funds and organised companies.

Henry Ward Beecher, the moving spirit of Faneuil
Hall, Boston, and his Abolitionist associates, with any
amount of capital behind them, poured men and arms
into the territory, regardless of expense.

The Government at Washington, controlled by the
Southern Democrats, preserved a benevolent neutrality
for the Southerners' cause, and did not interfere until
compelled to do so by the frightful state of anarchy
which eventually prevailed.

To stop the influx of men and arms from the North
into Leavenworth, which was the only easily accessible
port of entry for them, a " minute company," so called
from its brief period of service, was formed to search every
boat, more especially for arms. I joined this company
directly after my return from Fort Riley, and I remember
we seized a great number of rifles ; some of them
Sharp's breech-loaders, two of which were given to me.

Now the elections for the Territorial Legislature came
on, and, considered as elections, were of course a farce.
In many places the Missourians and other Southerners
seized the polls, and crammed the ballot-boxes. In others
the "Free Soilers" did the same. The result was that two
Legislatures were elected ; the pro-Slavery one making its
capital at Lecompton, and the Free State one at Topeka.

The rival parties met at the polls and elsewhere, and
many lives were lost in the fights that took place. The
excitable Southerners' blood was nearly at boiling-point,
when Sheriff Jones, elected by them, was shot dead by
a " Free Soiler," in the execution of his duty.

Then it boiled over, and the fight became general ; but
what I saw of it must be left for another chapter.

CHAPTER II

FULLY resolved to throw in my lot with the South, I now joined a company of mounted Rangers, raised by A. B. Miller, who, though a professional gambler, had the reputation of a plucky fighting man, and was at once elected orderly sergeant myself. No oath of enlistment was taken, but there was no fear of desertion or insubordination, since death would have been the penalty for either crime.

Our company was the best mounted and equipped in the Southern force, and, as soon as we were mustered, moved into camp at Salt Creek, about three miles from Leavenworth City, where about eight hundred Missouri and Southern volunteers were assembled.

Our commander was " General " Davy Atchison, a well-known and influential character in those parts. When I met him, and served under him, he was about fifty-five years of age, and one of the most popular men in his section of the country ; in fact, a typical Western politician. A lawyer by profession, he was also a planter, and large slave-owner ; consequently thoroughly " Sound on the goose." At this time he was U.S. Senator for the State of Missouri, and had been Vice-President of the United States. As an Indian fighter and hunter he had made himself a great reputation.

With a somewhat rough exterior, he was really a kindly man, and, being " hail-fellow-well-met " with all his supporters, was, as I have said, extremely popular.

Miller introduced me to the "General" soon after I joined the camp. He invited us into his tent, and ordered drinks forthwith. Youngster that I was, the old fellow received me without any "side" or stand-offishness, so that I felt on a friendly footing at once, and, like the rest of his followers, would have gone anywhere with him.

Life in camp was pleasant enough at first, for our "General" didn't go in for much drill, possibly because he didn't know much about it himself, and our principal duty was to keep watch and ward over the river and stop all passing steamboats to search them for Free Soilers and their arms. Those that did not stop when ordered were promptly brought to by a field battery we had posted on the river, commanding the passage. All suspected Free Staters were taken out and kept under guard, and of course all their arms were confiscated.

Our excuse for this rather high-handed proceeding was that "The Massachusetts Emigrants' Aid Society," with great resources at its back, was pouring men and arms into Kansas, with the avowed object of conquering and dominating the Territory, by fair means or foul, for the Free State party.

Our first apparently important movement was now made on Lawrence, the Northern headquarters, which was protected by considerable earthworks and held by a force of some two thousand men under Robinson, the "Free State" governor, and other leaders of the party.

I may say at once that, though we did a deal of marching and counter-marching, and though on several occasions a general engagement between the opposing forces seemed imminent, it never came to a pitched battle; and all the many lives that were lost in this miserable border fighting, were lost in small affairs between scouting parties and outposts. Many men too, on either side, were killed in this way to pay out old scores and gratify private spite and revenge.

So one fine morning we " Border Ruffians," as the enemy called us, struck camp and marched out some fifteen hundred strong, with two 6-pr. field-pieces, to attack Lawrence, my company acting as the advance guard. We halted the first night near Lecompton, our capital, my company being on picket duty, spread out fan-like some two miles round the camp. Next morning Governor Shannon, our own party's governor, paid us a visit of inspection, and was pleased to express his high approval of our discipline and workmanlike appearance.

I can't say much for our discipline myself, but there is no doubt we were a fighting lot, if only the Northerners had given us the chance of proving it.

The morning after the inspection we marched on Lawrence, where we expected a sharp fight, which we were fully confident of winning. My company acted again as the advance guard, and when, about midday, we reached Mount Oread, a strongly fortified position, on which several guns were mounted, covering the approach to the town, great was our surprise to find it had been evacuated. As soon as our general received the report, he ordered our company to make a wide circuit round the town, to seize the fords of the Kansas River and hold the road leading east.

Then he moved the rest of his force to within half a mile of the town, formed square on the open prairie, and sent in a flag of truce, demanding an unconditional surrender of the place. To the no small disgust of the " Border Ruffians," Governor Robinson, without further parley, threw up the sponge, and meekly surrendered the town and the 2,500 men it contained.

No doubt his men were not very keen on fighting, being the riff-raff of the Northern towns enlisted by the Emigrants' Aid Society, and most of them quite unused to bear arms of any kind. Many of them bolted for the Kansas River ford and the Eastern road ; and we of Miller's company took quite three times our own number of these valiant warriors prisoners. I well remember how scared the poor wretches were ! I am glad to say that the prisoners' lives were spared, all but two, and they were hanged by the Provost Marshal for horse-stealing, the penalty for which was invariably death, in that Western country, even in ordinary times.

Though the prisoners were spared, I regret to say the town was not, for Atchison's men got completely out of hand, battered down the " Free State Hotel," and sacked most of the houses. It was a terrible scene of orgy, and I was very glad when, about midnight, we of Miller's company were ordered off to Lecompton to report the day's doings to Governor Shannon. There we were kept several days, scouring the country for Free Soilers, and impressing arms, horses, and corn.

In these operations we occupied Topeka, the pro-Slavery capital, and had a brush with a body of Northerners, under Jim Lane, in which we lost two men killed and six wounded.

Next, at " Lone Jack," we had a skirmish with Captain John Brown's men, but the firing was at long range and no harm was done, for the Free Staters soon retired, and we were not strong enough to follow them up.

On the march, the day after this, to Stranger Creek, and whilst scouting ahead of the company with two other men, I came on the bodies of two young men lying close together, both shot through the head. The murdered men, for it was brutal murder and nothing else, were dressed like Yankee mechanics, and apparently had been done to death the previous night.

I had heard that one of our scouting parties had taken some prisoners, but that they had escaped ; and now it was plain what had been done by some of our ruffians. That night I told Miller that I would be no party to such disgraceful villainy, and that if any more of it went on I would quit the company, for I had no mind to fight with murderers, or with a rope round my neck. He made light of the whole affair ; said the other side had done just the same, and that for his part he did not mean to ask for, or give, quarter.

At Stranger Creek we remained the next day, waiting for orders, and a party of the boys was sent out foraging. Presently they returned with bundles of green corn, some chickens, and a pig or two. The eatables were fairly divided amongst the messes, and soon all were busy cooking the welcome additions to the everlasting bacon. But the supply of corn was scanty, and there was almost a fight amongst us for it, each man being keen to get a bit for his horse.

What now followed shows how cheaply human life was held in those rough times, and how feeble was the discipline the Governor had praised so much.

Amongst the foragers was one Mike Murphy, a barkeeper from Leavenworth ; a very quarrelsome and ill-conditioned fellow. He had taken more than his share of the corn, and Lieutenant Kelly, a Texan, ordered him to hand over part of it for his horse. Murphy refused, swore at him, and dared him to come and take it. The lieutenant took no notice of this, but quietly stepped over and helped himself to the bundle.

Murphy seized his loaded rifle, and Kelly bolted for the only tent we had standing, using it as a screen. Mike thought he saw a chance, took a snap shot, missed, then threw down the empty rifle, and ran for the bush. Kelly then whipped out his six-shooter, fired three times, and missed.

All this time Murphy was running for dear life, and had just reached the edge of the covert, when the lieutenant fired again. This time his aim was true, and the bullet struck the fugitive full in the middle of his back. With a tremendous bound, like a shot buck, and one piercing scream, he fell in his tracks and lay motionless.

We carried him into camp, where he lingered till

next day, in great agony, and then died. Kelly reported
what he had done to our captain, and was placed under
arrest.

Though in the opinion of the company, or the majority
of it, he was justified in killing Murphy, it was thought
best he should resign his position, which he accordingly
did, and I was elected by the unanimous votes of the
men to fill the vacancy. To be chosen second Lieutenant
of such a corps may not be thought a very high honour ;
but my comrades, whatever else they were, were fighting
men, and I was proud that they thought a youngster
like myself fit to fill the billet.

We now moved on to Leavenworth, where our chiefs
were every day expecting an attack from the forces led
by Colonel Jim Lane. This man had made a reputation
in the late Mexican War, and was placed in chief command of the Free State invaders, with all the power and
wealth of the New Englanders at his back. Therefore,
as a measure of precaution, a strong laager was formed
round three sides of the town with chained wagons
belonging to Major & Russell, the great firm of freighters.
The fourth side was a bluff overlooking the Missouri,
and needed no defence.

Two mounted companies, of which mine was one,
were camped on Brush Creek, about a mile from the
Leavenworth line, with pickets spread out in a circle,
some six miles round.

Colonel Lane, however, thought himself not strong
enough to attack us, and drew off to Lawrence, where
he entrenched himself. So the rival forces remained
for some time doing nothing, each waiting the other's
attack.

Meanwhile much "bushwhacking" and murdering
went on on both sides, and in this respect there was
but little to choose between them.

On scouting duty we were supposed to burn and
destroy the houses and property of any Free Staters we

could find, and to kill, or capture, the owners. Hateful enough work that I detested, and avoided whenever I could.

Of course I was often in command of parties sent out on such an errand, but I am glad to think that, in this position, I was now and then able to save homesteads from fire, and their owners from murder. On one such occasion I had been instrumental in saving a large ranch belonging to a prominent Free Stater named Cody ; to this I owe it that I am now alive to tell the story that follows.

One night, whilst on picket duty, I left my party, and taking one man, Missouri Smith by name, rode over to a ranch some six miles away in the hills near Stranger Creek. I fully believed there were none of the enemy's scouts in the neighbourhood, and having a great attraction at the ranch, in the shape of a young lady named Margaret Hendricks, staying there, thought I would risk it. I was only twenty-three, so perhaps I may be excused. Anyway I fancy the same thing has been done often enough before, and for the same reason. Bright eyes are hard to resist in the days of one's youth. The owner of the ranch, Falk by name, was, I knew, in the Free State camp, but his wife and her sister, a " Californian widow," were at home, and my friend Margaret was with them. An hour or two's chat with the ladies would be such a pleasant change from camp life, that go I must !

We reached the ranch about 9 p.m., seeing no sign of the enemy by the way, and hitched our horses to the fence close by.

The only arms Smith and I had were our six-shooters ; mine I carried in my belt.

The ladies welcomed us very kindly, though Margaret warned me I was doing a very risky thing, as some of Lane's scouts had recently been seen in the neighbourhood, and begged me not to stay. If they caught me they would surely kill me, and I mustn't risk my life, but go at once. Boy-like, I laughed at the danger, told her she needn't be afraid for me, and stayed on.

We had supper, and were enjoying ourselves mightily, for Margaret had forgotten her fears, when suddenly, without the slightest warning, four men fully armed burst into the room, a pistol was clapped to my head before I could stir, and I was called on to surrender, " or my d——d head would be blown off." I glanced round ; besides the pistol at my head, I was covered by four carbines, and my man Smith, who had been asleep, was already securely bound. It was hopeless to resist, so of course I caved in, and was at once disarmed.

Sergeant Everard, in charge of the party of eight men, abused me roundly. "We know you well, you d——d villain ; we've been after you a long time, and now we've got you at last, we'll hang you pretty quickly."

A pleasant plight to be in ; even a worse one than I feared, for I had expected to be shot, not to be hanged ! But I was helpless, and could only try to brace myself to bear the dread ordeal like a man.

It was no good to plead for mercy, I knew ; my company, or some of its members, had done too many ruthless deeds, for which no doubt I had the credit ; so I held my tongue.

But if I was silent, the three ladies, and especially Margaret, who knew Everard, and another of the party named Cline, begged hard for my life ; but it seemed to me, made no impression on our captors.

They took us out to an oak-tree close by, and got ready the ropes, fastening them to an overhanging branch. The end seemed very near. I stood stunned and stupefied, and said no word ; only the tears and entreaties of the kind women folks sounded in my ears, as though heard in a dream. During those few moments that I stood waiting for my death, the present seemed to vanish, and my thoughts went rushing through all the events of my short life. So short it seemed, and so sad to end it in this terrible way ; and there was no one to tell my dear ones in the far away vicarage home how I had died. Best after all that they should not know it !

Then some one touched me on the shoulder ; the ropes were ready, and our captors impatient to be done with the hanging. That touch roused me from my stupor, and I bethought me of Cody, and what I had done for him only a few days ago. I spoke at last, and told Everard the story ; asked him to ride over to Cody's (it was only two miles off), and he would learn that I was not the ruffian they supposed.

Margaret averred that my story was true, and that I had saved Cody, and others of their friends, from ruin and worse. She, and the others, begged so hard that he would do this little thing, for their sakes, that at last Everard consented, though with a bad grace, and rode off, leaving Smith and myself safely guarded under that oak-tree with its dangling nooses.

For an hour we stood there, with seven men round us, ready to shoot us down if we tried to escape.

Would Cody come, and would he be true enough to speak in my favour if he did ? Hope and despair alternated in my mind, and in all my long life I have never spent such an hour as that ; the minutes seemed hours, and the hour dragged itself out to years.

Now my straining ears caught the distant sound of galloping hoofs. Was it one horse, or two ? How intently I listened to the dull thud on the soft turf !

Nearer and nearer came the sound ; there were two horsemen, sure enough. Cody had come, and the bitterness of death was passed !

The moment he heard Everard's story, he had saddled his horse ; and there he was, shaking my hand most warmly and assuring me I was safe. A moment's whispered conversation apart, between the two men, and I was allowed to go back into the house again.

Everard announced that on Cody's intercession, and on his statement of how I had befriended him, and other Free Staters, my life, and Smith's, would be spared, but we would have to give up our horses, arms, accoutrements, and any money we had on us. You may be sure we were glad enough to get off even on these terms ; so after most warmly thanking the ladies, and Cody, for saving our lives, and many hearty handshakes, we departed.

To Margaret Hendricks special thanks were due ; for it was her influence with Everard, and her tears and pleadings, that saved me from a shameful death.

I thanked her from my heart of hearts ; and so we parted.

I shall never forget that wretched six-mile tramp across the prairie with Smith, who never spoke a word, and seemed dazed and stupefied by the experience he had gone through. For myself, that hour under the oak-tree and its dangling ropes will never be forgotten.

Arrived at camp, miserable and crestfallen, I got a severe reprimand from Miller, but retained my position as second Lieutenant, and had to provide myself with another horse, accoutrements, etc.

By this time the lawlessness and anarchy prevailing in Kansas had become a scandal to civilisation, and great pressure was brought to bear on the Government at Washington to put a stop to it. The President therefore ordered out two regiments of U.S. cavalry, under Colonel Sumner, to keep the peace, and issued a proclamation directing both parties to disperse ; the troops to march against either side that might disregard it.

Thereupon we were marched into Leavenworth and disbanded, and the so-called Kansas War came to an end.

CHAPTER III

CLAIM-MAKING, AND SQUATTER RIGHTS

THOUGH the rival forces were both disbanded, the Territory remained in a state of lawlessness difficult to realise in these days. To add to the anarchy prevailing, and to make " confusion worse confounded," the Delaware land sales were coming on.

These lands by the westward march of civilisation had become valuable, and, as usual in such cases, the unfortunate Indians had to move on, to make way for the white man. The Washington Government had made a new treaty with the Delawares, under which they surrendered the greater part of their reserve in Kansas, receiving other lands in exchange, still further West, and an annual subsidy of so much per head, payable by the Indian Agent.

These sections of the reserve, duly surveyed and laid out by the Government, were proclaimed for sale (but not at the customary " pre-emption " price) on and after a fixed date, which I believe was October 31, 1855. Instead of throwing the lands open for " pre-emption," the authorities determined to sell them by auction to the highest bidder ; and knowing this, the squatters, long before the time fixed for the sale, seized all the best lands, and most of the valuable sites, and banded together to protect what they called their rights.

The squatters' organisation was a very strong one, and it was made thoroughly well known that any Northerner, or land speculator, who dared to bid against one of the fraternity for any land he had seized, would be promptly shot, or lynched.

Though the city of Leavenworth swarmed with anxious buyers, who had come for the auction with well-lined pockets, so great was the terrorism that not one dared to compete with the squatters, who all got their lands at the Government's upset price of $2.50 an acre.

The auction took place outside the walls of Fort Leavenworth, possibly in the hope that the presence there of the U.S. troops might overawe the squatters.

Surely never did auctioneer in his rostrum face such an audience as this one ! From far and near the squatters had come, all well armed with six-shooters and bowie knives ; and, for the time, pro-Slavery and Free Stater men sank their differences and combined against the eager speculators from the North. Hundreds of them, fully armed, stood round the auctioneer, who, when a squatter's land was put up, vainly strove to get an advance on the upset price. Not one could he get, poor man, till he came to the outlying sections which, though valuable enough, were left to the outsiders.

Three days that auction lasted, and, being a squatter myself, I was in constant attendance. It was as stormy and threatening a scene as ever I witnessed, but, wonderful to say, passed off without bloodshed.

Of course, like the rest, I got my own particular claim of eighty acres, for which I paid $200 and promptly sold for $1,500, as it was adjoining Leavenworth City. I thought myself pretty clever to have made such a quick and good turnover ; but I dare say that land is to-day worth $500,000, for Leavenworth City is now one of the most important commercial centres in the West.

Another claim I had on Salt Creek, some distance out, I sold for $100 and a very fine mare.

Now for a brief space I became a bar-keeper and gambling-saloon owner, and can't say I liked it, though the dollars rolled in freely. Soon after we were dis-

banded, on the termination of the "War," I asked
Miller for the $1,000 I had lent him some months be-
fore. Now Miller, gambler as he was, was an honest
man, and frankly told me he hadn't the money, but
would hand over his bar, saloon and stock, in satisfaction of his debt.

I took them, though somewhat reluctantly, and so
became a gambling-saloon owner! For three weeks
I retained that proud position, doing a roaring trade, in
more senses than one ; for the land sales were on, and
the town was crowded. Night after night, and all night,
I had to look after the place, while the money came
rolling in ; but I admit the business had its drawbacks,
and wasn't quite one that a nervous man would choose ;
my customers were too ready with their six-shooters
for that.

Anyhow I got sick of it by that time, and sold out
for the money it cost me ; so I lost nothing by Miller
after all.

Now shortly after the Delaware land sales were over,
the inevitable policeman, represented by the Government
at Washington, ordered the Shawnee Indians to " move
on." Their reserve, situated on the Kansas River,
had become valuable ; so the usual treaty was made,
and they had to pack up and be gone.

Much as I have suffered at the hands of one of their
tribes, and cruel and merciless as they are by nature,
one cannot but pity the fate of the Red Indians ; ever
moving westward before the march of the white man,
till extermination overtook them, like the buffalo on
which they lived.

It was well known that this reserve would be thrown
open to " pre-emption " in August of the following year,
at the price of $1.25 (five shillings) per acre.

By the law of the United States any one could
establish his right to a claim of 40, 80, or 160 acres
by laying the foundation of a log cabin, 16 feet square,

on such claim, and cutting his name, the date, and number of claim on one of the logs. This " squatter right " held good for six months from the day " pre-emption " was authorised by proclamation ; and it was only *legal* to make your claim on, and after, that day. Thereafter, if you wished to retain your claim, you must break up half an acre of ground, put it into some sort of cultivation, and build a cabin on the foundation.

This, as I have said, was the *law* ; but the custom was to make claims as soon as it was known for certain that a reserve would be thrown open. If any one " jumped " your claim, you had no legal remedy ; it was a case of " the strong man armed keeping his house," or rather his foundation. So you may be sure there were plenty of rows, and not seldom bloodshed, over this claim-making.

I had sold my house in Leavenworth, and my three darkies, being obliged to do so through heavy losses I was let in for by my partner Moses Young. I was truly very sorry to part with the poor creatures, and I think they were attached to me ; but I had no alternative, and I found them good masters, which was all I could do for them.

Being then " foot loose," I got up a party of five, all well mounted and armed, to make claims in the Shawnee country. I provided a wagon and horses, and a team of cattle to haul out the foundations, and the simple provisions we required ; for these capital outlays I was allowed first choice of claims.

It was bitter December weather when we started, and the cold was so intense that we were nearly frozen each night, huddled together though we were in our wagon. Crossing the Kansas River on the ice we were at once in the Shawnee country. However, we were first in the field, which was the great thing ; for we knew that a powerful organisation had been got up in Kansas City to lay claims on the best lands, and to hold them by force of arms if necessary.

It would be tedious to tell of all the claims we made. Suffice it to say we made a great many, for though the law only allowed one man one claim, there were ways of evading it ; the commonest being to put them in the names of nominees. At last we came to Cedar Creek, along which the lands were very fine ; deep alluvial soil, well timbered, but not so heavily as to make the clearing of it difficult. There we camped, sheltered from the piercing cold of the open prairies, in a snug hollow. The river was full of fish and " soft turtle," game was abundant, and we fared sumptuously. So we stayed in this paradise for some time, each man making one, or more, claims.

Mine was close to the river, in a beautiful spot, and we put up on it a substantial cabin to serve as head-quarters for the whole party whilst we were looking after, and guarding, our various claims in the neighbourhood. Then we struck across the prairie to the trail from Santa Fé to Independence, making more claims as we went. Then, having taken up as much land as satisfied even us, if we could only hold on to the half of it, returned to Cedar Creek.

There we left a curious old fellow, who went by the name of " Shad " (if he ever had any other it had been lost), with a generous supply of corn-meal, bacon, and whiskey, to look after our interests, a young fellow volunteering to stay with him. The old fellow (no one knew how old he really was) had spent all his life on the frontier ; Indian fighting, claim-rushing, and such like were commonplace events to him. Tall and spare, with a wrinkled parchment-like face, he must have been sixty, or seventy years old, but was as active as a young man, and as tough as leather.

For Indians, and such " varmin," as he called them, he had a great contempt, and, in his cups, would boast that the Redskin didn't live who could " raise his h'ar." I believe he was right, and that he died with it on his head.

In Shad's efficient guardianship then we left our headquarters, and the rest of us returned to Leavenworth,
crossing the Kansas River on the ice, which by this time
was pretty rotten, and let us all in, wagon included.
It was a terribly freezing bath, I remember, but we
scrambled out somehow in safety.

Though the " war " had been put a stop to for
some time, political excitement ran very high.   The
Southern party, owing to Washington influence, was in
the ascendant still, though the Free State party was
slowly but surely gaining ground.

Throughout the South, where he was well known, few
men were more respected, or more worthy of respect
than Judge Lecompton, who was the head of such
justiciary as existed in those parts.   In the North, such
is the evil power of partisanship, he was denounced
as a second Judge Jeffreys, for whom hanging was
too good.   As a matter of fact he was an able
judge, and an upright, honourable man.   With his
wife and family he lived in a double log cabin near
Leavenworth, and there offered to all his friends, of
whom I was one, a simple and refined hospitality
which was as pleasant as it was rare in that wild
country.

The remainder of that winter I spent in Leavenworth
settling up my affairs, or riding about the Shawnee
country looking after my claims.

Early in the following spring an event happened
which changed all the future course of my life, and
eventually landed me in Texas, nearly as wild a land
as the wild West that I had to leave.

In Kansas in those days, as I have, I think, shown,
every man was a law unto himself ; and if he had
suffered wrong, his own right hand alone could get
him redress.   In the story I am about to tell I came
very near killing a man, and, though I had suffered
much at his hands, and he was a big ruffian and bully

whose death would have saved me great trouble and heavy loss, I do not regret that I spared his life when he was at my mercy.

It was about the beginning of March, I think, that Merril Smith (otherwise Missouri Smith) came and told me that he had sufficient evidence to lay an information against the man Cline for horse-stealing and threatening to kill. Now Cline had been a very active member of the party, under Everard, who had captured Smith and myself at Falk's ranch, when my friend Margaret Hendricks saved our lives. If he had had his way we should no doubt have been hanged pretty promptly ; and it was he who insisted that, if we were let go, our horses, arms, and accoutrements should be taken from us. We therefore had rather a heavy score against him, and I, for one, was not unwilling to be quits with him. So I agreed to lend Smith a hand to arrest him.

A warrant having been issued in Leavenworth, we rode off, armed with our six-shooters, to a small settlement on the Stranger Creek, near which Cline had a farm, to find a constable named Pearson, who was to effect the arrest. It was quite late when we found Pearson, and when we told him our errand he at once declined the business, saying the man was a desperado who had quite recently shot two men, and would certainly shoot him if he tried to capture him. However, we plied our man liberally with whiskey till he became pot-valiant and at last consented to serve the warrant, if we would protect him.

The next day was a Sunday, and it was known that Cline would be present at a " preaching " to be held at a cabin about ten miles up the creek. We got our constable off in pretty good time, but he was evidently in a blue funk, and would have turned tail if he had had a chance. For my own part I confess I did not like the job, but having once started on it, one could not turn back ; even at the risk of being shot, one must in honour go on. Moreover I was pretty certain that if any fighting was to be done the lion's share would fall to my lot, and that was not pleasant.

Smith and Pearson hitched their horses to the snake fence of the cabin, and I dismounted and stood with my reins over my left arm, about twenty paces from the door. Under the cavalry cloak I wore, I held my six-shooter ready for action, and Smith stood near me. Pearson, as agreed, walked into the cabin to tell Cline some one wanted to see him about buying some of his corn. As soon as the door was opened we could see the shanty was full of people. Loud and angry voices were heard, and presently Pearson emerged followed by Cline and three or four of the latter's friends. Directly he saw who wanted him he stopped, and the constable, with trembling hand, pulled out the warrant.

The moment he began to read it, Cline vowed he wouldn't be taken by us, or twenty men like us ; declared, with many oaths, I was everything vile and bad, and ought to have been hanged long ago, and that, if I didn't clear out, he would shoot me like a dog. By this time he had got his six-shooter out, and there was no time to be lost if I wanted first innings. I had him covered at the time, but was loath to fire unless obliged to.

It was now or never I saw, his life or mine, and, as I naturally preferred my own, I let drive two barrels, and hit my man in the right arm and side. Down he fell, and the bullet he had meant for my head whistled high over it. Pearson, who held the man in great dread, shouted to me to fire again, and finish him ; but I couldn't shoot a helpless man on the ground, blackguard as he was.

Now it was high time we were off, for at the sound of the firing some twenty men had rushed out of the cabin, some with shotguns and six-shooters, and others with " rocks " in their hands. Pearson was already up and away ; but Smith's mount, which by-the-bye was a mule, had broken loose, and perforce I had to wait for him. Pulling up by the side of a log, Smith scrambled up behind me, and away we went for dear life, as hard as my good mare could gallop. It was a close shave, for the enemy fired a volley after us, but missed us clean.

At the Stranger Creek settlement Smith got a horse, and we rode on to Leavenworth, where my friends of the pro-Slavery party gave me quite an ovation for shooting Cline, though it was the general opinion that I ought to have finished thoroughly what I had so well begun.

As to our friend the constable, it was said that he never stopped till he had put the Missouri between himself and danger, so terrified was he at what Cline's friends might do to him !

Of the man himself I presently heard that, though very seriously hurt, he might pull through ; next that he was well enough to be sent to his friends in New York, and would certainly recover. I soon found that no steps would be taken against me on account of this little affair, but I made up my mind to leave Leavenworth and settle in Johnson County, across the Kansas River in the Shawnee country, intending to make my claim on Cedar Creek my headquarters. Forth I fared then, with my wagon and pair of horses, my saddle-horse, provisions, whiskey, arms and blankets, taking with me four of my claim-making party. These were named Shoemaker, Mike Macnamara William Hitchcock, and Wash Gobel, who all agreed to stand by me whatever happened. Shad and the young carpenter were already at the camp.

I found that things were moving fast indeed in the reserve, and that joining the claim I had made on the Laramie and Kansas City road, a town had been laid out, which had been named Monticello, and that a tavern, groggery, and several shanties were in course of erection. Furthermore that my claim had been jumped by a party of Missourians, who had put up thereon a little frame cabin, where they sold whiskey, tobacco, etc.

I rode over at once and warned these folks that they were trespassing on my land, and that I meant to maintain my squatter rights at all hazards. They refused to move, but about a month afterwards three of my boys rode over one night from Cedar Creek, and so scared the two men left in charge of the shanty that they moved out the little " plunder " they had, and the boys burnt the cabin and restored my old foundation. So far so good, but hereafter I was to have a tougher job than I thought for to maintain my rights over this desirable property, and it eventually landed me in a lawsuit, of which more anon.

CHAPTER IV

THE FRAY AT MONTICELLO

ALL the early part of that spring and summer I was busy making claims, and disposing of others, for which I got prices varying from $50 to $500. It was a free and easy time, with plenty of hunting and fishing, and the life was pleasant enough.

But now I bethought me it was time to settle down, and make myself a permanent dwelling-place. I was then twenty-seven years of age; getting quite old, and all my life I had been a wanderer on the face of the earth! I would build me a house on my 160-acre claim at Monticello, and wander no more—at least for a time.

At once I set to work to haul out the necessary timber, which my hands cut on Cedar Creek, and in a short time we had a very comfortable one-story log cabin put up, with some chimneys. It was quite a mansion for those parts, with four rooms in it; and behind it good log stables and "corn-cribs." When all was finished, I gave a house-warming party to all the folks in the neighbourhood. About twenty of us danced all night to the music of a couple of violins, and nearly wore out our musicians; for when we did dance out in the West, we kept it up with vigour, and polkas and cotillions followed each other without much pause, except for refreshment.

So that summer passed away without any incident particularly worth recording, and in the autumn, I forget the exact day, the President's proclamation was issued throwing open the Shawnee lands for pre-emption. Though I had already built a substantial house on the claim, I had of course to comply with the requirements of the law, and lay a foundation on it, on the day named ; and that before any one else could do so, or I should lose my right to it. The logs for the foundation were all cut, and laid ready, so all I had to do was to put them together. At daybreak, on the day appointed, I was engaged on this, with my six-shooter in my belt, and had all but finished, when I was aware of quite a party of men marching along bearing four logs between them.

I walked over to them, and told them quietly they were trespassing on my claim, and that if they attempted to lay a foundation I would use what force I could to stop them, as I was first in the field, and had already complied with the requirements of the law.

" You use threats, do you ? " said the leader of the party. " I threaten no one, but I don't think it will be healthy for you to steal my property," I answered.

There was a good deal more wrangling, and at one time it seemed as though they meant to fight—they were five to one—but at last they cleared out, saying they should apply to the U.S. Court for pre-emption, as they had been prevented by my threats from laying their foundation. This they eventually did, and I had to fight them in the Court for the claim.

Later on that fall, I took service with the great freighting firm of Major & Russell, as wagon-master. Major we knew nothing of—probably he was a sleeping-partner—but " Billy " Russell, as he was commonly called, was quite a power in the West, and at Washington too, for the matter of that. He owned some 20,000 working cattle and about 2,000 wagons, or " prairie schooners," and did all the freighting west of the Missouri River to the military posts and forts in the Indian

country. It was he who started the " Pony Express,"
carrying mails, by relays of horses, through the hostile
Indian country to the outlying stations.

It was a risky employment, fit only for a daring and
resourceful man to engage in : for the Indians kept
a sharp look-out for the Express in those days, and
killed many of the men. William Cody, so well known
since as Colonel Cody, or " Buffalo Bill," was one of his
first riders, and perhaps the most successful of all.

My first trip as wagon-master was from " St. Joe,"
where we loaded up, to the forts on the " Big Blue." I
had seventy-five wagons, each drawn by eight yoke
of cattle, a driver to each team, and twelve spare men.
Under me was an assistant wagon-master, and I had
two horses for myself, and about a dozen supernumerary
ones. Each " schooner," which was a lumping great
thing with a body about twenty feet long, carried a
load of four to five tons of goods. The whole train on
the march, in single file, would occupy a length of about
1¾ miles ; more of course if the ground was boggy, and
any of the teams lagged. So it was no easy task to keep
an eye on them all. It meant pretty hard riding from
morning till night.

At or before nightfall we made a laager, or " corral "
as we called it, to guard against Indian attacks. It
was made in this way :

The leading wagon was unyoked, and the fore-carriage
turned at a slight angle inwards ; the next wagon was
drawn up as close as possible to it, with its hind wheels
on a level with the front wheels of the first, till a rough
circle was formed. The cattle-chains were then run
from the wheel of one wagon to the wheel of that in
front of it, and the corral was formed. Inside this the
cattle were unyoked and, if there were no Indian signs
about, turned out to graze under charge of a couple
of herders.

Of course, with a strong party like mine all well armed,

there wasn't much fear that the Indians would attack, as long as proper precautions were taken and a good look-out kept ; the greatest risk was that they might stampede your cattle at night, and leave you stranded on the prairie.

Road, properly speaking, there was none, only a track some quarter of a mile wide, made by successive trains. It was usually easy enough going over the prairie, especially as there was a bitter frost, and the ground was hard frozen. But every now and then a deep creek would have to be crossed, with a muddy bottom, and the whole lot of wagons must be hauled through, one by one, with perhaps three or four teams to each. The long line of cattle would be yoked on, and stretched to right or left ("haw" or "gee," it was called), nearly at right angles to the wagon ; the drivers with their whips then swung the cattle over to left or right, as the case might be, and the wagon was bound to come out by the sheer weight of the teams, unless, as some-times happened, the tongue drew out of the body.

I was absent several weeks on this trip, and enjoyed it much ; the only drawback being the intense cold, which almost froze one at night. My pay was $100 a month, and all found ; so I was well satisfied, and I think Russell was too, for he at once engaged me to look after a big lot of cattle he had wintering at Lone Jack, about sixty miles from my ranch. The distance was nothing, and I gladly accepted the employment at $75 a month.

If there was plenty of hard work, there was plenty of fun going too, and many a good dance we had that winter. We all of us, girls as well as men, had to ride long distances to many of these, through the keen frosty air, and the rides were almost as good fun as the dances. One of these, I particularly remember, was held at Olathy, the county seat of Johnson County, on New Year's Eve. The occasion was the opening of a new hotel at this place, which was about ten miles from Monticello. I got together a party of five girls and seven or eight young fellows, all well mounted.

It was a lovely starlit night, with an intense frost, and six inches of snow on the ground. All were in the wildest of spirits, and the gallop over the level trackless prairie was delightful.

At the hotel we found quite a big gathering, and as soon as the ladies had divested themselves of their wraps we were all hard at work at the cotillions and polkas. Our host had provided an excellent supper, and of course liquid refreshments were in abundance. Everything was going off capitally and, what is more, peacefully, till the bully of the place, a man named Cosgrove, of whom I had often heard, but had never met before, picked a quarrel with me in the most unprovoked manner. Probably he had a cargo of whiskey on board, or wouldn't have done it.

I was standing at the bar downstairs with some friends, when this fellow began, with many very forcible oaths, and in a loud voice, to say there was a man from Monticello he meant to " whip " that night. He fixed his eye on me as he spoke, and I knew I was in for a fight. That being so, the sooner it was over the better ; so I stepped across to him, asking my friends to see fair play, and told him he wanted a lesson in manners, and I would give it him.

He rushed at me to clinch, throw, and probably, after the manner of his kind, to gouge me if he could. Luckily I was too quick for him, met him with a straight left-hander between the eyes, and sent him, with a heavy fall, against the stove at the end of the bar. He cut his head pretty badly against the ironwork, and wanted no more fighting that night. I think every one was pleased that the bully had got his lesson, for he wasn't nearly so quarrelsome after it, and I was looked upon rather as a hero by the girls, for taking the bounce out of him. So easily is fame won !

At many of the dances I have spoken of, I often met
Shawnee half-breed girls, daughters, some of them, of
well-to-do people and fairly well educated, others hardly
" tame." Amongst the first I remember the two Choteau
girls, and Mary Owens and Sally Blue Jacket. They
all dressed like other Western belles, and were good
dancers ; but some of them were prone to take a little
too much whiskey. Once when dancing with Sally Blue
Jacket, who was a remarkably handsome girl, I remember
the lady pulled a flask of whiskey out of her pocket, and
pressed me to join her in a drink. It would have been
rude to refuse so delicate an attention, from so charming
a partner, and I of course accepted the offer.

However much I might be occupied, I never lost sight
of my farm work, and during three months of that winter
kept hands cutting timber, and splitting it for rails.
These either Shoemaker or I hauled across the prairie
about two miles from the Shawnee lands, until I had
enough to build a " worm " fence, eight rails high, round
eighty acres. It was a mighty lot of rails, and the haul-
ing of them alone was heavy work, but the doing of
it was a pleasure, for when the fence was up I felt I
should have made a valuable property of my beautiful
claim, especially when I had ploughed and planted
my eighty acres in the coming spring.

Amongst the curious scenes I witnessed about this
time, the most curious was the hanging, by his own
people, of a Shawnee Indian who was supposed to have
committed a murder. Though his crime was in reality
a mild form of manslaughter, the Shawnee council,
which by U.S. law had the power of life and death
over its own people, wished to maintain and exercise
this right, and so insisted on hanging the poor wretch.
Not that he seemed to mind it in the least, for he was
the least excited of all the performers in the tragedy.
The platform under the gallows, in which was the
drop, was occupied by the chiefs of the tribe and local

preachers, who, for about two hours or so, "improved the occasion," whilst the victim sat in a chair, apparently utterly indifferent to what was going on around him. Round the gallows stood a crowd of white men and some Indians.

The former threatened a rescue, and frequently called upon the doomed man, who sat on his chair unbound, to jump, and they would save him. Though these calls were made in his own tongue, and he must have understood them, he gave them no heed whatever, but sat impassive as a statue.

When the preachers had exhausted their eloquence and came to a pause, the man rose, placed himself on the drop still unbound, and waited for the rope to be adjusted. A white man named Paris married to an Indian squaw, who was the Shawnee sheriff, stepped forward, slipped the rope over his head, drew the bolt, and the Indian was launched into eternity without a cry, or a struggle, or effort to save himself, though his hands were free.

I have seen many exhibitions of Indian stoicism, and many a one make his exit from this world, but I never saw anything like this man's calm indifference to death.

Johnson County began to fill up a bit with immigrants, and the Governor of the Territory now issued a proclamation for the election of County officials. Each "township," or district of six square miles, had to elect three supervisors, one constable, and one overseer of the poor.

The County Board of supervisors was something like our present County Councils, but with greater powers. It consisted of the senior supervisors of each township, who also had magisterial powers in their own locality. I " ran " for supervisor in the Monticello township, and being elected at the head of the poll, became a member of the County Board. We received $3 a day

pay whilst in attendance at the Board, which met at
Olathy once a month.

When my house at Monticello was finished, the " boys "
made it the headquarters of a Squatters' Association,
formed to protect our mutual claim-interests, and elected
me president. We met there regularly once a week for
the transaction of business, and often besides this there
would be quite a gathering at the ranch on a Sunday
for hymn-singing, to the accompaniment of a violin and
accordion. It may seem strange that men so rough and
hardened, so inured to bloodshed that they thought
no more of shooting a man in some trumpery quarrel
than a jack rabbit, should have been amenable to such
influences, which for the moment, at any rate, softened
and subdued their wild natures. But so it was, and
an atmosphere of peace and quietness reigned at those
gatherings that was a complete contrast to our everyday life.

I suppose even the roughest and hardest had a tender
spot somewhere in his nature, and that the hymns
we sang touched chords in our hearts that vibrated to
memories of bygone days and other scenes ; I know
they did in mine.

About this period I was much away from Monticello,
looking after William Russell's cattle ranches, on which
he kept fifteen thousand head of work-cattle, or there-
about. These, of course, were scattered over wide distances, and as I had to look them all up at intervals, I
was almost constantly in the saddle.

On my return from one of these journeys I found my
best hand, poor Shoemaker, in a very serious fix. He
had accidentally shot a German boarding-house keeper
named Schleeman, in a drunken row. It seems they got
quarrelling in their cups, and Schleeman brought out his
shot-gun. My man, after a struggle, disarmed him, but
in the struggle the gun went off, and mortally wounded
the German. He was alive when I arrived, but sinking

fast. I went to see him at once, and he fully exonerated Shoemaker from all blame. Nevertheless his compatriots, who were rather numerous in the place, were in a great state of excitement, and it was all we of the Squatters' Association could do to prevent their lynching Shoemaker, who had been arrested, and was under guard in a room in the hotel. However, the Coroner's Jury brought in a verdict of accidental death, and a strong party of us carried our man safely off to the ranch, where he remained under the ægis of the association till the matter had blown over.

I have dwelt much on the lawlessness and ruffianism prevailing in Kansas in those days, but I suppose much the same state of things existed in other newly settled parts of the States before society became organised and the law had gained sufficient strength to overawe evildoers. We certainly were a law unto ourselves in Monticello, and stood sadly in need of some power to restrain our evil passions, which had been strongly aroused by the conflicting interests of claim making and holding.

Between our Squatters' Association and a rival organisation in Monticello, a very bitter feeling existed, and one felt that, sooner or later, bloodshed would come of it. The leader of our enemies was a hotel-keeper in the town, Miliner by name, who undoubtedly was a bully and ruffian of the first water ; just such a one as generally floats to the surface of such troubled waters. He was backed by people from Kansas City and from Missouri, to whom the desirable claims we held amongst us were as so many Naboth's vineyards. I don't pretend that all the right was on our side, and all the wrong on theirs ; it was a mixed matter, like everything in this world is, but it was their " tall talk " and threats that led to the row I am going to describe.

Two of our " boys " had been distinctly threatened that if they ventured into Monticello they would be shot down. This was too much for my hot-bloods to endure quietly ; so one Sunday morning, stirred up thereto by one Molesby, the most absolutely fearless man I think I ever met, they determined to have it out with Miliner and his crew. I did all I could to dissuade them, but in vain ; so of course I had to go too.

Sunday out West was little observed, unless there was a " preaching " going on, and stores and groggeries generally did a brisker trade on that day than on others. So when we walked across to Monticello there were plenty of loafers about, eager to report to my party of seven the threats Miliner and company had that very day made against us.

We halted behind Riche's store, which stood on one side of the square, opposite Miliner's hotel. Peering cautiously round the corner, we could see the barrels of several shot-guns protruding from an upstairs window of the hotel, which completely commanded the approach. It looked like certain death, for some of us at any rate, to attack such a position, and again I tried to dissuade them from it. But Molesby particularly was " mad," and vowed that, if no one would go with him, he alone and unaided would " clear out the shop." The man's daring was infectious, and, against my better sense, I said, " We have no chance, but you sha'n't go alone." Then three others, of whom Shoemaker was one, ranged themselves by our side.

We five then dashed across the open space, which might be some thirty yards, as hard as we could run, making for the bar-room door below the window where the guns were posted. Once in we would storm the staircase, and make things lively for Miliner and his friends.

Molesby and I led ; close behind ran the other three. We got half-way across, when a volley was fired from the window ; Molesby sprang into the air and fell riddled with slugs, whilst the rest of us dashed into the open door for cover. There for a few minutes we stood irresolute, not knowing what to do. Molesby, poor fellow, who had urged us to the fray, lay motionless in the square, his rifle thrown far from him in his death-spring, but still grasping his six-shooter.

Upstairs all was still ; the enemy didn't seem to relish the idea of coming down to attack us, nor, if the truth must be told, did we, as soon as we had cooled a bit, like the task of storming that stairway. So after a time a truce was made, mainly through the influence of three of Miliner's party to whom I was known, and we were allowed to depart unmolested, and to carry off our dead comrade with us. A blessed relief it was to our embarrassment too, for we were like rats in a hole with no exit, except by way of that staircase !

Poor Molesby had twenty buckshot wounds, and I, who was close to him when the volley was fired, had three shots through the loose dragoon cape I was wearing, so had a very narrow escape.

The dead man owned a prairie claim, about a mile and a half from Monticello, the dispute about which was the chief cause of the quarrel that led to his death. There I had a grave dug for him, though Miliner and his gang swore they would not permit us to bury him in it. Ten of us, however, all well armed, laid him to rest in the place we had chosen for his last home, and I, with a sad enough heart, read the burial service over him.

CHAPTER V

EARLY in the spring of 1858 I started ploughing, or
" breaking," my eighty acres of prairie land. I was
the possessor of two breaking-ploughs, each of which
was worked by three yoke of cattle ; with one I broke
my land myself, and the other I let out at $3 a day.
The ploughs cut a width of thirty inches, and the Indian
corn was sown in the turned-over sod by chopping
a hole and dropping in the grain. By this primitive
culture I got a fine crop of twenty-five bushels of corn
per acre ; and between the rows had a fine lot of water-
melons, pumpkins, and cucumbers.

In June that year I had my first experience of a Western
tornado. It was on a Sunday, and there was a " preaching " at Judge Reid's in Monticello, which I attended.
The heat had been most oppressive all the morning, and
by three o'clock the sky had darkened and it was almost
suffocating, for not a breath of air was stirring. The
people in the town stood about in groups, wondering
what was coming. I had dined with the Judge, and
when it was evident a terrific storm was brewing, I invited
all present to come over to my place, where they would be
safer in my one-storied log cabin than in their flimsy
frame houses. They most of them accepted, and we
hurried across to the ranch and were only just in time.

Down came the rain in bucketfuls, a perfect deluge
of water, the sound of which drowned our voices. Suddenly it ceased, and for a minute or two silence reigned.

114

Then came the wind, with an appalling roar. It seemed to shake the cabin to its very foundations, and for the twenty minutes or so that it lasted, the girls of the party crouched on the floor, and we all expected the roof to fall upon our heads. But the stout cedar logs stood the awful strain, and not one of them was displaced.

Outside in my yard stood two great freighting wagons, or "prairie schooners," and they were carried off, and dropped in shreds, over a distance of about three miles. My log stables were down, and quite a mile of fencing, the logs being scattered about the prairie as though they were straws.

In the calm that followed the tornado we all walked back to the town, to find it more or less in ruins. Fortunately the casualties were few, and only one child was actually killed. Curiously enough one small frame house was carried out of the town rather more than a mile, and was little the worse for the trip.

The tornado had swept a belt of country forty-three miles long by about four wide, and in its course had uprooted every tree it encountered, as though they had been reeds.

In the month of August the Land Court, presided over by the U.S. Receiver and Registrar, would be held at Lecompton, to decide the conflicting pre-emption claims on the Shawnee reserve, and I therefore sent in notice of my intention to pre-empt my Monticello claim.

Soon I received notice from the Court that a merchant of Kansas City, named Nash, had filed a claim to the same land, and that the case would be heard early in August. This man was leader of the party I had warned off my claim, as related in the previous chapter, and as he was much incensed against me, it was clear I was in for a big lawsuit.

Though my title to pre-empt the claim, according to "squatter right," and universal custom in the West, was undoubted, for I had not only built a house thereon and lived in it, but had complied with the letter of the law by laying my foundation on the day proclaimed, I felt very uneasy as to the result of the case. My opponent was a wealthy man for those parts, and, what was more, a man of influence with the Free State party, and that counted for much ; for these cases went by favour, as much as by right. However, it had to be fought out ; so I got together my witnesses, six in number, all squatters, and we started in good time for Lecompton from my ranch.

One of my friends and I rode ; the rest went in my smart two-horse wagon, well " fixed " for a week's camping out. It was glorious weather, and the outing would have been delightful if one had not been so anxious. Our first camp was on a lagoon, off the Kansas River, and we caught enough fish for our supper in half an hour, with very primitive tackle. The next night we camped in a beautifully wooded dell, with plenty of grass and water, about half a mile from Lecompton, and then walked into the town, where we found there was considerable excitement over my case, which had aroused a good deal of party feeling.

My antagonist Nash, with his friends and witnesses, had pretty well filled up the best hotel, and were indulging in many sherry cobblers, and much boasting and swaggering as to the result of the case, which was to come on on the morrow.

Nash had the impudence to ask me to drink with him, and wanted to shake hands. I told him he was attempting to perpetrate what he knew was a robbery, and that if by some unfair means and hard swearing he succeeded, there would scarcely be room for both of us in Kansas. This took most of the bounce out of him, and he troubled me no more.

I remember well, even now, at this long distance of time, the wondrous beauty of that night in the camp. As I laid on my blanket and watched the " great comet " blaze in the eastern sky, I thought I would not exchange the scene for the finest hotel in the world.

The Court sat on my case for three whole days, from 9 a.m. to 6 p.m., for Nash produced quite an army of witnesses, who swore through thick and thin for him. As the case proceeded, and each of his men swore harder than the previous one that he had been first in the field, I grew more uneasy as to the result. Nash, I believe, made sure of winning, and the thought of what might follow success seemed to weigh on his mind, for many a time I caught his eyes fixed on me with a questioning gaze, as though he were wondering whether I really meant what I had said to him. Be that as it may, he had, as it turned out, no cause for fear, for he lost his case.

The Court decided in my favour, and on payment of $240 and some small Court fees I got my title deeds, and became absolute owner of the claim. That night we had a " high old time " in camp, and next day set out on the return to Monticello in great triumph. Arrived there, we found a crowd of my friends at the ranch, waiting to congratulate me ; for the news of my success had outrun us. We got up an impromptu dance that night, and celebrated the occasion right royally.

As I intended to make the ranch my home, for some time at least, I added to the house and sunk a well. Before doing so I called in a " water wizard," who was highly thought of in those parts, and he contracted to select the proper site for the well for the modest fee of $5, on the principle of " no cure no pay." He stepped about the place with the usual hazel wand in his hand, and presently drove a peg into the ground, close by the house, assuring me I should find water there at no great depth. As a matter of fact I did find an abundant supply of excellent water, at about twenty feet in depth, and cheerfully paid over my $5. I suppose the man was an impostor ; but I understand that many people, even in this enlightened country, believe in this water-magic.

I fear the picture I have drawn of life in Kansas forty-five years ago may be thought over-coloured by those who know nothing of the then state of society in the Far West ; but I can assure them that if I had told of all the desperate deeds within my knowlege, but in which I was in no way an actor, it would be lurid indeed. One more scene of brutal and ruthless murder, of which I was a helpless witness, I must give, since it is characteristic of the times, and of a place where human life was held " at a pin's fee," and also because I took great pains, though without avail, to bring the chief culprit to justice.

It was in the month following my triumph at Lecompton that a young fellow named Walker, whom I had known in Leavenworth, rode down to Monticello on business, and then came on to my place to see if he could buy a yoke of cattle from me. We had dinner, and then smoked and chatted ; for the young fellow was friendly and pleasant, and I was glad to see him. Then we started out to cross the short strip of prairie between my house and Monticello, where the cattle were at work.

Walker was mounted on his horse, and I was on foot, a little ahead of him. Both of us were unarmed ; he because he was a quiet, inoffensive fellow, and seldom carried firearms, and I because I had a very painful whitlow on my right hand, which was in a sling. Things were then pretty quiet and peaceful in Monticello, and I had no idea that Walker had an enemy there, or anywhere else. So we walked on without the remotest suspicion of what awaited us so near at hand.

We had reached the outskirts of the town, when from behind Riche's store the man Miliner and another named McDougal suddenly appeared with double-barrelled shotguns in their hands.

Miliner it was who shot poor Molesby in front of his hotel ; McDougal had been for some time on friendly terms with me.

They halted Walker, and some words passed between

them, the purport of which I did not catch; then without more ado they both fired their shot-guns into the unfortunate man. He fell from his horse, dead, as I thought; but no, he was still alive, and, sorely wounded as he was, scrambled to his feet and ran as fast as he could for a small corn-patch close by the hotel. The ruffian Miliner fired at him again, as he ran for shelter, but didn't stop him. I, all helpless and unarmed as I was, could only throw up my arms. The murderers said, "We have nothing against you, but we mean to finish the d——d scoundrel with you."

They then set off to hunt their victim out of his shelter, whilst several of the inhabitants of the town looked on, without daring to interfere, so terrorised were they by these two ruffians. Just at this moment two of my hay-wagons, with four hands, arrived on the scene, on their way to my ranch. I ran down to them directly, shouting to them, as I ran, to shoot Miliner and McDougal down. Not one of them had a gun, or a six-shooter; but the murderers evidently thought they had, for they bolted forthwith, and then the brave townsfolk turned out and joined in the pursuit!

With one of my hands I climbed the fence into the corn-patch, whilst poor Walker, who thought it was his murderers coming to finish their work, pleaded most piteously for mercy.

We bore him as tenderly as we could into the hotel, and did all we could for him, which was little enough, for he was grievously wounded in the back and side, and died in great agony about ten o'clock that night, assuring me, with his latest breath, that he had no idea why they had shot him.

The moment Walker was safely deposited in the hotel, I wrote a note to my friends in Leavenworth, urging them to at once bring a strong and well-armed party, to hunt down the murderers. By 3 a.m. the next morning a band of seventeen of the "Boys" were at my ranch, having ridden post haste to my summons. All that day and part of the next we hunted the country for the villains, but without success; for, as we heard afterwards, they had fled into Missouri. Had they been caught, "Judge Lynch" would have given them but short shrift.

Now for the sequel to my story, which is even more shameful than the opening chapter, since these cold-blooded murderers were allowed to escape the just penalty of their crime, and that by an act of the Territorial Legislature!

Three weeks after the murder McDougal was arrested at his own ranch, and committed to stand his trial for murder at the next District Court. But, having friends and money, he was immediately brought up before the District Judge, under a writ of *habeas corpus*, and admitted to bail in $4,000.

About six weeks before the sitting of the Court, Pat Cosgrove, Sheriff of Johnson County, having got wind that the chief villain of the tragedy, Miliner, was in hiding at Atchinson, a small town in Missouri, about thirty miles from Kansas City, asked me to bring one of my "Boys," and go with him to effect his arrest, if possible; and I readily consented, for I was most anxious to catch the scoundrel.

To ensure secrecy we said no word to any soul in the place as to our errand, for we had very reliable information, and felt sure of catching our man, unless, by chance, he got wind of our being after him. Crossing into Missouri, we easily obtained a warrant for Miliner's arrest, from the proper authority, and then rode quietly the first ten miles of our journey. After resting our horses, we started, well after dusk, to ride the remaining twenty miles to Atchinson, meaning to surprise the murderer a little after midnight.

The man was a desperado of the worst kind, and wonderfully quick with his shooting-irons. If we roused him some of us were bound to get shot, so you may be sure we went to work very cautiously. It was pitch dark when we reached the town, and not a soul was stirring in the one street it contained ; nor was any light visible ; the whole place seemed wrapped in sleep.

We had such clear directions to go by that, after groping about a bit, we found the house we wanted. Tying our horses to a fence near by, we took off our boots and crept in at the back door, which, luckily for us, was unfastened.

I cautiously lit a candle, and we stood for a moment or two at the foot of the stairs, listening for any sound. But nothing was to be heard ; the silence was absolute. We were pretty sure our man was in the house, but in which room we didn't know, and must risk that. Silently and carefully we stole up the stairs, and in the dead stillness of the house it seemed as though the slight creaking of the boards, and the sound of our breathing, restrain it as we would, must arouse the inmates.

At last we stood on the landing ; on each side of this was a door—which should we choose ? There was nothing to guide our choice, and at haphazard I slowly lifted the latch of that on the right. Peering in, with the shaded candle in one hand and my revolver in the other, I could make out two beds, both occupied. Looking from one to the other, at last I made out Miliner fast asleep in the one nearest the door.

He moved, sat up, and, taking in the situation at a glance, made a grab for his six-shooter under the pillow. But he was just too late, for before he could handle it we were upon him, and Cosgrove had him safely handcuffed in another moment. Now we roused up the people of the house, and told our story. They were not a little astonished to find their place so quietly invaded by three armed men, of whom they had never heard a sound, and they appeared not very well pleased at our visit. However, when they saw the warrant, and knew why we had arrested Miliner, they were appeased, and treated us very well. Next day, starting at daybreak, we marched our prisoner across the prairie, securely fastened to Cosgrove's stirrup, to Kansas City, and the following morning landed him safely in the gaol at Olathy, where he was at once heavily ironed.

The curses he heaped on our heads during the journey were voluminous and powerful, but having got him safe enough, after what we thought was a smart capture, we let him swear at large, without interruption. He seemed to realise that he couldn't escape hanging this time ; but what rankled most in his mind was that if he *must* hang, he couldn't kill me first !

He was committed for trial, on the charge of murder, and, being unable to obtain bail, lay in prison for nearly six weeks before the District Court sat. During that time I was often at Olathy, on County Board business, and there heard from the gaoler and others of the threats our prisoner constantly uttered against me, and how he vowed to shoot me, if only he got free. This made me particularly anxious he should be hanged, and I had a justifiable confidence that that would be his fate.

The District Court was held at Olathy, the county seat, early in July, and on the first day of its opening I rode over with four or five of my " Boys." The Grand Jury found true bills against Miliner and McDougal, and they were brought into Court in irons. Their counsel objected to this, and asked for the removal of the fetters, which the Judge granted, though the Sheriff strongly protested, averring that the men were such notorious desperadoes he would not be responsible for them if they were cast loose.

The little town was crowded with people from far and near, and in the Court itself one could hardly stir, so densely was it thronged with excited spectators. The murder was a particularly atrocious one, even for Kansas, and the interest it created was intense. Walker's two brothers, decent, quiet young fellows, had come all the way from Ohio to see justice done upon the murderers, and if they had only followed my advice they would have seen it.

I was the principal witness for the prosecution, and the first called. All day I stood in the box, examined and cross-examined by counsel, for and against, who, after their kind, managed to spin out even so simple a case as this was to an unconscionable length. However, all things, even criminal trials, come to an end, and by 2 p.m. the next day all the witnesses had been examined, the Judge had summed up, very much against the prisoners, and the jury had retired to consider their verdict. The audience in the crowded, stifling Court still kept their places, discussing the pros and cons of the case ; and the almost unanimous opinion seemed to be in favour of a verdict of murder in the first degree.

At this moment an " Express Rider," his horse all in a lather, galloped up to the door, dismounted, and pushed his way through the crowd, calling loudly for the Sheriff.

Cosgrove came forward, and the messenger handed him an official-looking document.

The babble of talk was hushed in a moment, and every one wondered, and waited, to know what this strange thing might mean. We were not long in doubt, for presently Cosgrove announced that it was an amnesty, granted by an act of the Legislature, and duly signed by the Governor, for all criminal offences committed up to date, whether under trial or not ! Was ever such an act passed by any other legislative body in this world ?

Of course, the reason of it was that many of the honourable legislators, and most of their friends, had serious misgivings as to what might happen to themselves, for deeds done during the " war," and so passed the amnesty.

The trial was over, and the seeming tragedy turned into

a farce ; for now the prisoners were brought in, and, by order of the Judge, released in open Court. But there was a very strong feeling against them both, and especially against Miliner. The crowd of angry men who watched them slink away could have been roused to fury in a moment if the Walker brothers had but said the word, and asked for the justice denied them by the Law. " Judge Lynch " would have done his work promptly, and the world would have been well rid of two remorseless villains.

But it was not to be ; the Ohio men were too gentle, or timid, or too law-abiding, for such an action.

So Miliner and his partner in crime departed unharmed, and for some time thereafter I, metaphorically speaking, slept with one eye open, expecting an attack.

CHAPTER VI

As I said in the previous chapter, mine enemy's escape from hanging caused me no little disquietude ; because, to keep a whole skin, one had to walk very warily, and it did not add to the enjoyment of life to feel that he might be lurking privily behind every corner one turned, or every clump of bush one passed.

The very evening of his unexpected release he came up to me in the town, very civilly, and asked me when I was starting for home, as he would like to ride with me, and talk over our differences. It was nearly dusk, and I said I was leaving at once, that he was welcome to come too, if he liked, but he must keep his hands out of his pockets, for, if he touched his six-shooter, I would let daylight through him.

He laughed, saying I needn't be uneasy, as he only wanted to be friendly, and would certainly ride with me. Very good, I answered, come along then ; I start in ten minutes.

I felt sure he meant to shoot me if he could get the chance, so I told two of my " Boys " to ride behind us, with their six-shooters ready for action. My " friend the enemy " appeared punctually to time, but when he saw I wasn't riding alone he suddenly changed his mind, said he found he had business to detain him in town that night, but would certainly come and see me before long. " You will always find me ready whenever you come," I said ; and so we parted, to my relief, for though I wasn't much troubled with nerves in those days, a dark night's ride alongside a murderer, anxious to add you to the number of his victims, is not altogether enjoyable.

At the end of that month of July I went in charge of one of " Billy " Russell's trains to Fort Kearney, without seeing any more of Miliner, and when I returned home, after some three months' absence, found he had left Monticello for some unknown destination, having made the place too hot to hold him any longer.

I was offered the charge of a train of seventy wagons to Fort Laramie, but I chose that for Fort Kearney, though it was only one of forty-five wagons. The latter journey, though long enough, was only half the length of that to Laramie, and I was anxious not to be away too long from home. I loaded up on the Levee at Leavenworth City, and at the Fort, and started on my long journey to the south of the Platte River, in the Territory of Nebraska, with forty-five teamsters and six extra hands. I had two horses for my own riding, and ten supernumerary ones ; but there was no assistant wagonmaster allowed for so small a train, and I had to look after it all myself.

We travelled for weeks towards the " Big Blue " River, across an open, rolling prairie country ; treeless as a rule, except when we struck a stream lightly fringed with timber. There had been a good deal of rain, so water and grass were good ; a great thing for the cattle, as they got plenty of feed, but it caused many a wagon to stick in the mudholes, out of which they had to be pulled in the way I have described.

We were passing through a rather dangerous Indian country, for the Sioux and Cheyennes were out on the warpath against each other, an occupation which rather whetted their appetite for the plunder of freight trains, if they could catch them unawares. Indeed, only recently a strong band of the Sioux had surprised one in that very country, and killed every man in it after

torturing them by fire, as could be seen from the
" sign " plainly enough.

Not to be caught napping, I always scouted ahead of
my train with three spare hands, keeping best part of
a mile in front of it, with the men widely spread. At
night, or rather before sundown, I formed my wagons
into a corral, and if the cattle were grazing outside at
night, had scouts out round them We frequently saw
bands of Indians at a distance, but they never attacked
us ; probably because they found we were on the alert.

One night on the " Big Blue " we had a bad scare. It
was just after sundown, and we had corralled the wagons,
and all hands were busy cooking at the fires outside the
circle. A little way off, in the gathering gloom, we could
see the scouts and cattle-herders rushing the animals
along for the corral, as fast as they could drive them with
frantic yelling and much cracking of whips. At first I
thought the Redskins were upon us, but as the mob drew
near we could hear the cry of " Buffalo, buffalo ! " and
realised the situation.

The fires were made up, and every man stood ready
with his loaded rifle and six-shooter.

The cattle came lumbering into camp at the top of
their speed, and close at their heels followed the vastest
herd of buffalo I had ever seen. On they came in countless thousands, and the sound of their trampling was
like the distant, dull roar of the surf on the sea beach.
If we couldn't turn them aside, they must surely over-
whelm us by sheer weight and pressure of numbers.
The whole multitude was on the move to pastures new,
and, as was the custom of their kind, travelled at a
steady " lope," or canter ; the hindermost following
blindly the lead of those in front.

However, just as the sea of clashing horns and gleaming
eyes seemed as though it must roll over us, wagons,
cattle and all, our fires, the shouts of the men, and the
volley of rifle fire we discharged turned the front rank,

or rather split it in two. So the great herd passed to right and left of our corral, which stood like a solitary rock in the midst of a wide and raging flood, and did no harm.

For several hours the buffalo streamed past us, so close that we could see the shine of their great bright eyes and the dim outline of their shaggy forms. When daylight came we found we had killed a couple of dozen or so, which was quite as many as we wanted.

There must have been tens of thousands of buffalo in that one herd, and now there isn't a single one on all those wide plains !

After a week's rest at Fort Kearney, which both men and cattle stood in need of, I started back, nearly empty, and, making good time, arrived at Leavenworth City about the end of October, without any incident by the way worth recording.

" Billy " Russell, a man of few words, appeared satisfied with my management of the train, and asked me to winter two hundred of his cattle on my ranch, at $10 a head ; ten per cent. loss to be allowed, but anything above that to be paid for by myself. To this I agreed. He also engaged me to look after some of his cattle farms in the surrounding country, at a salary of $50 a month.

I accepted this employment, though the pay was small, for I was anxious to keep in with Russell, who, as I have said, was a power out West. Though " still of his tongue," he was bluff and outspoken enough at times. To his intimates he was " the Colonel," but not to outsiders. If these gave him the title, common enough in the States, he resented it. " D—— you, sir," he would say, " I'm no colonel, I'm plain Billy Russell, and don't you call me out of my name."

When I knew him he was at the height of his prosperity, but, soon after I left Kansas, came to utter grief. His business was enormous, and very difficult to keep proper control of. Somehow or other he had got to windward of the Treasury at Washington, to the tune of some $6,000,000 ; it was said through the connivance of some of the officials. A committee of Congress was appointed to unravel the affair, and they had to call in " Billy " himself to help them ; of course under the usual indemnity from prosecution, if he made a clean breast of it. This saved him, for there was little doubt that he had dipped his hands pretty freely into the national till.

Early in November I got together four or five hands and set out to fetch my two hundred cattle from one of Russell's "farms " beyond the Kansas River. Winter had set in early ; the cold was intense, and riding was bitter work. I remember halting the first night at a Shawnee settlement near the river, where the Indians put me up as best they could. In the one room their cabin contained sat an old squaw, cowering over the fire ; she looked exactly like a dried-up mummy, except that she breathed and lived. Her great great grandson, the owner of the cabin, said she was one hundred and ten years old, and was the daughter of the great Shawnee chief and prophet Tecumseh. This chieftain was shamefully treated by the U.S. Government, and his tribe treacherously slaughtered and broken up at Ticonderogah, just after the War of Independence.

I worked very hard for Russell all that winter looking after his cattle, which necessitated being in the saddle day after day, and all day often. Indeed all the years I was in Kansas I may say I spent most of my time on horseback.

The wintering of the cattle at the ranch didn't turn out a very profitable speculation after all, for though I had plenty of fodder and corn for them, the weather was very severe, exceptionally so indeed. Then many of the working steers had been " alkalied " on the plains, and many of them died, despite my utmost care. So, as

9

May 10, the time for handing them over, drew near, I was in rather a fix, for I had lost considerably more than the ten per cent. allowed. What in the world should I do ? Now I knew there were a number of Russell's vast herds of cattle that had strayed away from his various " farms," and were roaming wild on the plains. I therefore got together two or three trusty " Boys," and went out to see if I couldn't hunt up some of these on the sheltered and well-grassed river-bottoms I knew of, where they would be likely to winter.

After a rare hunt, I was lucky enough to find nearly as many of these wild steers as I wanted. It was no easy job to drive them to the ranch, but we managed it somehow, and when the handing-over came I was very few short of my number. Russell received them himself, at one of his corrals, and was pleased to express his satisfaction at the condition of the cattle. I said nothing about his wild steers I had caught, and he paid me on the spot.

That winter of 1858-9, the last one I spent in Kansas, was comparatively uneventful. The country was gradually settling down, though not in the way my friends or myself desired ; for the Free State party had got the upper hand, and ruled the Territory, making things somewhat hot for us of the defeated faction.

Though the state of affairs was not altogether so pleasant as it might be, we managed to enjoy ourselves pretty well in the intervals of hard work, and amongst other things had many a good dance. We thought nothing of going ten, fifteen, or even twenty miles to one of these ; and the ride over the hard-frozen prairie in the dry, keen air with a party of girls, who were just as much at home on horseback as the young fellows who escorted them, was almost as good fun as the dance itself.

Margaret Hendricks, she who saved my life when Everard and Cline were so anxious to hang me at Falk's

ranch in the " war " time, often made one of the party
on these occasions. She was the finest and most daring
horsewoman I ever saw ; even in that country, where
all the girls *had* to ride, no one could approach her. She
could break the wildest horse in a surprisingly short time,
and make him do just what she liked. One very handsome Indian pony she had that would come to her call,
and follow her like a dog. She would call him up on
the prairie, make him kneel down, jump on his back,
without saddle or bridle, and go cantering off. Then,
whilst still in motion, she would stand up on his quarters,
quite at her ease ; I never saw anything in a circus to
equal it.

I may say she was as good at taming men as she was
horses, and laughingly averred she managed both by
the power of her eyes ! Probably it was so, for I know
they were large, and dark, and lustrous ; very beautiful
in repose, but flashing ominously in anger. Indeed it
would have been a bold man who dared to take a liberty
of any kind with Miss Margaret ; he certainly wouldn't
have done it a second time.

The state of society, and the perfectly free and easy
terms on which the young folks of both sexes mixed out
West, would no doubt have scandalised " Mrs. Grundy " ;
but in reality I never saw, or heard of, any impropriety.
Moreover the girls were quite capable of protecting
themselves, if necessary, for most of them were handy
with a six-shooter, and many of them good rifle-shots.

Margaret was a beautiful dancer, amongst her other
accomplishments, and, being very pretty and lively, was
in great request as a partner. Though her father was a
Free Stater, he and I were on friendly terms, and he
never objected to my taking his daughter out to dances,
and bringing her home at any hour of the day or
night.

So she and I became close friends, despite the opposition
of her brother, a young fellow of about my own age, but

a bitter Free Stater, who couldn't forgive the part I had taken on the other side. He even went so far as to threaten he would shoot me (though not to my face) if I did not drop the friendship. The girl was very wroth at his daring to dictate to her in this fashion, and I expect must have given him rather a bad time over it.

I remember particularly bringing her home one morning early, from a dance a few miles out of Leavenworth City. The family were all at breakfast, and the father greeted me cordially enough, but the brother sat glum and silent, ignoring his sister's presence, and taking not the slightest notice of myself. Margaret sat silent for a minute or two, after greeting the old man ; then her eyes began to blaze, and at last she burst out, and gave that young fellow such a dressing down as he wouldn't forget to his dying day. If he hadn't slunk away I believe she would have horse-whipped him ! No doubt he was the coward she told him he was, or he would have shot me ; but he never went beyond threats, of which I took no notice.

Margaret, with all her outdoor accomplishments, was equally great in the house ; was a first-rate cook, could spin, and make her own clothes, as indeed all the Western girls did in those days, and was a good musician. Her uncle was a well-known Bishop of the Episcopal Church out West, whose name I have forgotten, and in his family she had been educated, till she was seventeen.

I have dwelt on my friend Margaret at some length because, though she far outshone all her compeers in beauty and accomplishments, she was a true Western girl, of a type which I suppose must, by this time, be wellnigh extinct.

It is forty-four years since I said good-bye to her at her father's ranch, and, if she still lives, she must be an old woman now, though it is difficult to realise that one so full of youth, high spirits and courage should ever grow old. I don't like to think of her in that aspect, but as she was in those far-off days she will always abide in my memory, as long as I shall live.

My sojourn in Kansas was drawing to a close, and I had to choose between giving up my pleasant home and ranch or standing a criminal prosecution, with the probability of a long term of imprisonment to follow. I chose the former, and this is how it came about.

It will perhaps be remembered that I had, unfortunately, to shoot the man Cline in self-defence when Merril Smith and I went to arrest him ; that he was severely wounded, but recovered so far as to be able to be removed to New York, where his friends lived. As time went on, and I heard nothing of him, I fondly hoped that Kansas would see him no more, and at last forgot all about him. I was destined, however, to have a startling reminder of his existence, for the next thing I heard of him was that he was back in Leavenworth City, and, the Free Staters being in the ascendant, had got himself elected Sheriff !

This was in the winter, or rather, very early spring, of 1859. I put a bold face on it, and, directly I heard the news, rode into Leavenworth to see how the land lay.

My friends there reported Cline as breathing the direst vengeance against me, and vowing he would " shoot me on sight."

I met him in the street that day, and we passed each other without a word ; but he didn't attempt to shoot, though I saw he had his hand on his six-shooter in his pocket, just as I had.

I took good care to let it be known in the town that I was quite prepared for Mr. Cline, and always went armed ; and that as to shooting, two could play at that game, as he well knew. But all this bluff notwithstanding, I returned home in a very uneasy frame of mind. I wasn't so much alarmed at his threats of violence, for, desperado as he was, he had had a severe lesson, and I reckoned that would make him very careful ; but what

I did dread was his setting the law in motion against me. His party was in power ; the judges were Free Staters, and my chance of a fair trial was small indeed.

My farm was in good order, and my crops flourishing ; in fact my house and ranch were amongst the best in the neighbourhood, and I was very loth to leave them and all the good friends I had made in that country, which, rough as it was, suited me well in those days.

But I wasn't prepared to risk the probability of a long term of imprisonment, and possibly heavy civil damages as well, even for all this, and made my preparations accordingly.

I got together all the cash that was owing to me, as far as I could ; had prepared, by a lawyer in Kansas City, a deed of sale of all my property to Shoemaker, and a mortgage from him to me, as well as promissory notes for the value, and then awaited events. None of these documents were signed, but were all ready for an emergency.

I don't know why, but Cline made no move till about the middle of July ; perhaps he thought he would keep me in suspense, which he certainly did. About that time, however, I got a message one morning early from my friend Pat Cosgrove, the Sheriff of Johnson County, that he held a warrant for my arrest, and that, if I wished to avoid it, I had best be off at once. By the middle of the day I was ready.

One of my hands brought round two of my best saddle horses for Shoemaker and myself. I buckled on my six-shooter, threw my saddle-bags, with a change of clothes in them, across the saddle, and, with one last lingering look at my pretty ranch, set off at full gallop for Kansas City, *en route* for my far-distant home in old England, which I hadn't seen for seven long years.

In Kansas City Shoemaker and I speedily arranged our business matters ; and I say at once that no one could have acted more faithfully, or more honourably, than did this rough Western Borderer to me in all these transactions.

Everything having been prepared beforehand, I was in time to catch the evening boat to St. Louis. Shoemaker came down to the Levee to see me off, and there we had quite an affecting parting.

Steam was up as I stepped on board ; the boat cast off, and away we went on the first stage of my long journey home, whilst my faithful Shoemaker stood and waved a last farewell.

I had once again escaped safely from a very threatening danger, and for the moment was happy and content.

CHAPTER VII

KANSAS TO CANADA, AND THENCE TO TEXAS

THE journey home, and out again to New York, my sojourn in Philadelphia, and my trip to Canada, I propose to condense as much as possible, only referring to incidents here and there which may be of some interest.

The great Dominion had not been created in my time, and the country I saw round Ottawa was not tempting to settlers.

On the trip down to St. Louis there was an exciting episode which I must tell, since it shows how easily a free coloured human being could be kidnapped by an unscrupulous villain in the days of slavery.

A Northern man had come on board with a light-coloured mulatto woman and her two children. These he entered on the books as his slaves, and of course they were put on the boiler deck, whilst the supposed owner enjoyed himself in the saloon. The woman, who was rather good-looking and had some education, told her tale to one of the passengers. The white man, she said, had made her acquaintance in Kansas City, and persuaded her he would provide her with a good home, and care for her and her children in one of the Free States, I forget which, where he lived. " And now," she said, " I feel sure he is taking me to New Orleans to sell me for a slave, and I am as free as he is. My little ones will be torn from me, but rather than that I will drown myself, and them, in the river."

Her piteous tale impressed her hearers, who repeated it to the captain. He heard what she had to say, and so straightforwardly did she tell her story, that he called a meeting of the passengers to determine what should be done. The supposed owner was haled before this impromptu Court, and both sides were heard. It was evident that the feeling was in favour of the woman, who adhered to her original statement without variation, whilst he contradicted himself, and was manifestly lying. Finally his papers, when examined, were proved to be forgeries, and he confessed his guilt.

It was a bad case of nigger-stealing, the most heinous of all crimes in the South, and the verdict was death ; the sentence to be carried out at the first landing-place. To this however the captain, who acted as president, would not agree, and it was resolved to leave the culprit, just as he stood, on a sandbank in the middle of the river. This was presently done, and I have no idea what became of the scoundrel.

A handsome subscription was got up for his victim, enough to give her a start in St. Louis, where we left her. She had had a very narrow escape, and the poor creature's gratitude to her rescuers I shall never forget.

In St. Louis I interviewed the great firm of Western land-agents, Messrs. Pollock & Co. The senior partner was well known to me, and to him I frankly told my story, placing my affairs unreservedly in his hands. Then I took ticket to New York, crossed the Mississippi, and set out on my seventy hours' journey.

Even in those days America was far ahead of us in the comfort and convenience of railway travelling, with its corridor carriages, dining and smoking cars, etc. But the road itself, and the bridges, were not by any means perfect. For instance, I remember on that journey the conductor requesting all passengers to alight, somewhere near Indianopolis, as a trestle-bridge in front of us was very shaky. We got out and walked ahead of the train, whilst the frail wooden structure trembled and shook with the ponderous weight behind us.

Crossing the Alleghanies the scenery was very grand, and the brilliant moonlight of a glorious summer night touched the mountain-tops and flooded all their slopes with silver ; whilst in the deep valleys, along whose precipitous sides we crept, gleamed far below us the red flares of the blast-furnaces. The glamour of the scene held me entranced, and all that night I sat out on the corridor platform, dreaming dreams of the future before me, till daylight broke the spell.

At New York I put up at the American and European Hotel, and for the first time in seven years revelled in comfort and luxury. Well-cooked dinners, attentive servants, comfortably furnished rooms, and a feather bed to sleep on ! Why, the place seemed a palace after the cabins of Virginia and the ranches of the West.

I had to wait four days for a steamer, during which I did New York and the Hudson River. The city I thought more like an English one than any I had seen in America.

A twelve days' passage to Southampton, in the first-class saloon of a German " Lloyd's " steamer, was a revelation of the comfort, not to say luxury of ocean travel, for hitherto I had been most accustomed to the unsavoury fo'c'sles of ill-found sailing ships.

It was a perfect summer morning as I journeyed up to London through what seemed to me a smiling land of gardens and orchards and pleasant homesteads. Nothing like the fruitful richness of an English country-side in full summer is to be seen elsewhere, that I know of, in all the world. It is almost worth the banishment of years, only to look upon it once again.

So, in full enjoyment of the scene, and with happy thoughts of the meeting now so near, I journeyed home-ward, and in the still, peaceful summer twilight, walked through the quiet churchyard, past the grey old church, into the vicarage home, to receive a greeting so warm that it dwells in my memory still, and will remain as long as I live.

Boys had grown into young men, and children into strapping lads, but except for that, and for the one vacant chair, my favourite brother's, who had passed away, swiftly summoned to that other world in the heyday of youth and manly beauty, and now resting in the quiet churchyard, to the grief of all who knew him, nothing seemed changed. Nothing in the home at least, though some kind friends, who had bade me good-bye so tenderly, were not there to greet my return.

Two months I spent at home visiting friends and relations, and renewing old acquaintances. Then the restless, roving spirit grew strong upon me once more, and I must fare forth again to seek my fortunes in the West. So early October of the year 1859 saw me crossing the Atlantic, bound for New York. Thence I took train for Kansas, in the hope of settling up my affairs and realising my property.

At St. Louis I learned from my friend Pollock that my enemy Cline had obtained judgment against me in the Civil Court, for heavy damages, and had refused to compromise in any way.

Apart from this, there was the criminal warrant out against me, and it was quite impossible to return to live in Kansas, where, under the existing Free State *régime*, I couldn't hope for a fair trial if I surrendered. So, reluctantly, I instructed Mr. Pollock to sell my ranch and claim, now growing daily more and more valuable, as best he could.

But I must have one more look at my Monticello home, at whatever risk. By boat and train then I travelled to Independence, where I found my faithful overseer and friend, Shoemaker, waiting for me with one of my best horses. Soon we were on the road to Monticello, Shoemaker telling me all the news by the way. How good it was to have a gallop once more over the open rolling prairies !

Only a few of my most trusty friends knew of my

coming, and they were at the old place with warm and kindly greetings, though these only made the inevitable parting more sad. They all pressed me to stay on, and they and my other many friends would stand by me to the last, they vowed. But it was no good, I knew, for I had no chance of success against my enemy ; even if they shot him, as they were eager to do, it would only get them into trouble and not help me. So, after one day's stay, I said good-bye to them all, and having paid off Shoemaker and the other hands, sadly enough rode off to Independence once more, on my return to St. Louis.

Having settled my affairs with my friend Pollock, I made up my mind to give up roving, and settle down somewhere in the more civilised parts of the West as a civil engineer. First I tried to enter at West Point, which in those days admitted civilians, but failing there, went through a course at the Polytechnic College in Philadelphia. For one term I managed to keep up with the class I joined, but the strain was too great and nearly broke me down ; so at the end of it I took out a certificate as a qualified surveyor, and gave up the idea of graduating as an engineer.

In the boarding-house at Philadelphia I made friends with a man some few years older than myself, who called himself Thompson and who said he had been in business in the North of England. For a reason I did not know till long afterwards, he had thrown up his business and, with a moderate amount of capital, had come out to the States fully determined to settle down on a farm either there or in Canada. His disqualifications for the life of a settler in a new country were many and palpable ; he knew nothing of farming, couldn't ride, couldn't shoot, and was wholly unused to roughing it, but had plenty of pluck to go through with anything he undertook.

My own inclination pointed to Texas and the wild life of cattle-ranching on the borders of the Indian country ; but Thompson clung to the Canadian idea, and, as he was much more fitted for the *métier* of a farmer in a settled country than for Indian-fighting, we finally agreed to prospect the district round Ottawa, and settle there if it suited us.

For three months we travelled about, by road and river, and saw the country thoroughly, being hospitably entertained by the settlers whenever we put up at their houses, though more often we camped out on the banks of some river or lake, despite the awful mosquitoes which bothered me somewhat, but nearly devoured poor Thompson alive.

We had splendid fishing that summer, and shot a few deer for the pot, but nothing befell us worth giving in detail.

Everywhere there was lumber in abundance, and it seemed to be a thriving business for those with sufficient capital ; but farming in such a country appeared to be hopeless, and meant hard toil without prospect of anything but a bare subsistence. We were full thirty years too soon for the Red River district and the great wheat-growing plains of Western Canada, which now offer such fine opportunities to men of energy, and I soon made up my mind it was no country for me.

To Texas I must go, and "the Colonel," as I had by this time christened Thompson, would fain go with me, though I pointed out, as forcibly as I could, the roughing and the risk he would probably encounter in a wild land like that.

The die was cast, and on the 13th February we took train for New York, *en route* to the sunny south. At New York, where we had to wait a few days because the Colonel's luaggage had gone astray, I remember seeing the ss. *Great Eastern*, then newly arrived from her first voyage from England. From New York we took passage by steamer to Savannah in Georgia, *en route* to New Orleans, and curiously enough met on board a cousin of poor Madison Molesby who was killed by my side at Monticello.

Travelling in the States in the far-away days of which I write was very different from what it is now, but at last, by stage coach and finally by steamer, we did reach New Orleans. That very evil-smelling " Queen of the South " was, as is usual at that season, in the grip of " Yellow Jack," and we were glad to embark on the boat for Galveston and Indianola the morning after our arrival.

Running down the broad Mississippi, how lovely the scene was, with waving cane-fields on either bank, and then miles of orange groves coming close down to the Levee. Years after this, all these latter were destroyed by one fell swoop of King Frost. He laid his icy hand on their green beauty, and blasted them into dead, bare trunks in one night.

Amongst the passengers was ex-Governor Houston, late Governor of the State of Texas. I soon made his acquaintance, and found him a fine specimen of the Southern gentleman, without affectation or " side " of any sort. He had been all through the war of Texan independence, and had seen much Indian fighting on the frontier. The old gentleman was said to be the wealthiest man in the State, owning much land and some fine cotton plantations, and about three hundred negroes.

He had been to South Carolina to buy slaves, and had seventy of them on board with him. All were well clad and well fed, and in all my experience I never saw a jollier lot of darkies. But then, the Governor was the best of masters. It was quite a pleasure to see how the old gentleman and his son treated them. Coming on deck in the morning, they would gather round him, and he would have a kindly word for all, men, women and childen, and it was evident that already master and slaves were on most friendly terms. If all masters had been like Governor Houston, little would have been heard of the miseries of slavery ; but of course the trouble was that they were only chattels after all, and when they passed into other hands their lot might be as wretched as it was then happy.

Whenever I met any one from Texas, either on the cars or on the steamboats, I tried to glean all the information I could about the country, which was entirely new to me, except that of course I had picked up what knowledge I could from the books available. From Governor Houston and from others, but especially from the former, who most kindly answered all my many questions, I gathered much valuable information.

The gist of it was that on some parts of the coast cotton-growing was a very paying industry, but required more capital than we could command. That in Galveston, Indianola, and other coast towns there were fair openings for business, but the climate was unhealthy and Yellow Jack a not infrequent visitor. That for cattle-ranching the best region was in Western Texas, about the Nueces and Pecos Rivers, where the pasture was excellent, and practically unlimited in extent. That, owing to the drought, stock and land too would be cheap.

Of course there were drawbacks, amongst them distance from markets, and Comanché Indians ; in fact it was not quite a country for a timid man, or one nervous about his scalp. But what would you ? You can't have everything you want in this troublesome and perverse world, and I was much tempted to try my luck in the West country, risks notwithstanding.

Galveston seemed a busy place, though not much to look at, for most of the houses were frame, and many unpainted.

The heat was more intense than ever, if possible, and most of the folks were walking about under umbrellas ! I delivered a letter of introduction to a Mr. Mills, a wealthy cotton-broker, who in his turn kindly gave me introductions to Indianola and San Antonio. He fully confirmed what I had heard of Western Texas.

By 5 p.m. we left Galveston for Indianola, by steamer,

and landed at the latter place at five the following morning. Here we were then, after all our travels, landed on the threshold of our El Dorado. All that wide land was before us to choose from. Where should we go, and what should we do?

The Colonel clung rather to the idea of a town, and business of some kind ; my inclinations drew me to the open country, and the free ranching life. At any rate we would have a good look before deciding.

BOOK III

TEXAS, 1860—1862

CHAPTER I

It was on August 5, 1860, that we reached Indianola, a straggling town of about four thousand inhabitants, built in one long, thin line facing the sea, and of rather attractive appearance.

It was with high hopes for the future that I stepped ashore on that land of promise, little thinking of the awful storm of war gathering so fast around us, and which was to involve me and my fortunes in its ruins. Should I have turned back had I known it ? I suppose not ; for I confess that, once I have put my hand to the plough, I don't like turning back. Any way, I was in happy ignorance of what awaited me, and I don't think that any one in the South, except perhaps some few of the leaders, expected war between the two sections. The majority of the Southern States no doubt meant to maintain their " great Institution," and to stand firm for the principle of State rights ; but they thought the North would give way, as it had before.

Nearly forty years have passed since that great fight was fought out to the bitter end ; a fight such as, in many respects, the world had never seen before, with its furious rage, and slaughter and desolation. And now it is almost forgotten save by those who took part in it and witnessed the agony of the struggle.

I volunteered as soon as the State declared for Secession, and saw a good bit of fighting here and there, under the " Lone Star " flag. But as regards the war, which has so often been depicted in all its heroic details by abler pens than mine, I do not intend to dwell upon it ; only to tell what I saw with my own eyes, in my own little corner of the great field of combat.

One reason why I did not see more of the great struggle was that during part of the time it was in progress I was much engaged in Indian fighting on the frontier. Directly the U.S. posts were abandoned, or captured by our forces, the Comanchés, one of the most war-like tribes in the States, and always more or less troublesome, broke loose, and began harrying the out-lying ranches ; murdering men, women, and children, and sweeping off horses and cattle wholesale. To stop this as far as possible and to follow up these murderous bands, was the duty I was so often engaged on ; a thank-less task enough, in which little honour, or glory, was to be gained, but which involved incessant hard work and sleepless vigilance. For the Comanchés, on the war-path, were all mounted on wiry, active ponies. Stark naked as the day they were born, and carrying nothing but their bows and arrows and tomahawks, and riding bare-backed, they travelled light and fast, and were hard to catch. At times they managed to retreat to the hilly country in the north, where the rocky character of the ground made it almost impossible to track them, and we had to give up the chase. At others we succeeded in overtaking them, and their plunder, when they generally showed good fight.

Of these expeditions I shall have a good deal to tell in their proper places, but now I must get on with my story.

The first thing we saw in Indianola was a County election, a free-and-easy affair, the polling-place being in the bar of the chief hotel. The voting was by ballot, but there was not much secrecy in it, as drinks were going liberally, and the voters talked loudly of their favourite candidates. There we were introduced to many of the residents by a Mr. Harrison, a turtle preserver and packer, to whom I had brought an introduction. Everybody was friendly, and hospitably inclined, especially in the matter of drinks ; so that the difficulty was not to get enough, but to avoid getting too much, without giving offence. The intense heat and drought probably led the hospitable Indianolans to wish to moisten their visitors ; any way, they wouldn't let you " go long between your drinks."

That same evening we went out to Harrison's turtle establishment, and were shown the process of curing and the salt-water reservoirs, in which he kept some dozens of the largest turtle I ever saw. On the way out, the heavens suddenly grew black with clouds. There was a sound of rain. The long drought had broken up ; and, just as we reached the house, down it came plump, as though out of a vast bucket. The change it wrought was marvellous ; it was like coming out of a hot oven into a cool, delicious air, and we sat for some hours in a room projecting over the shallow waters of the bay, drinking in the freshness. I am bound to confess there were other drinks however, and it was late before our kindly host would let us return to the town.

This was the first rain since early in April, we were told. Four months of drought in a burning heat like that ! No wonder the people and the land, were thirsty !

We hung about in Indianola till August 20, undecided what to turn our hands to ; at one time thinking of buying a steamboat, to trade along the coast, and then of starting a store. But these prospects came to nothing, so, weary of inaction, I insisted on leaving by stage for Victoria, about twenty-four miles distant, the following day, to see what the country was like in that direction. It had rained almost incessantly during our stay, till our hotel, and the slightly raised ground on which it stood, became an island, accessible only by wading. The roads therefore were in a frightful state, and the four good mules in the stage could only get us along a mile an hour.

It was Court day in Victoria, and crowds of people, bad roads and weather notwithstanding, came in. If we were to prospect the country, we must have horses, and here was the chance to buy ; for there were plenty for sale, though most, owing to the drought, were in bad condition. At last we found two pretty good-looking half-breeds, one four, and the other five years old. The former had only been backed a few times, but the latter was "gentled," and would suit the Colonel. I found my animal not only difficult to mount, but not easy to sit when you were up, for he was one of the worst buck-jumpers I ever rode. His late owner wanted to bet he would throw me before I could ride him a mile, but when I offered to take him up for all the loose cash he had, he backed out.

Next we bought a Texan outfit—saddles, saddle-bags, bridles, etc.—and started the following day for Goliad County, thirty miles distant. For two miles the road lay along the Colets River, through mud almost deep enough to bog you ; then we crossed to the opposite bank and came out on a prairie, high and dry, on which the grass was just starting. In the crossing the Colonel nearly came to bad grief, for the river was in slight flood, and in the middle his horse got into a quicksand and went under. But the water fortunately was only breast high, and the Colonel got clear of his fallen horse with an agility that surprised me, so that nothing worse than a bad ducking befell him.

Arrived at Goliad Court House we determined to prospect the country about the upper reaches of the Nueces River, an affluent of the Rio Grandé.

But perhaps I had better explain what we were looking for. It was a good ranch with plenty of grass and water, and not too many cattle on it. No one in Western Texas cultivated the land ; the climate was far too dry for that, and during all the years I lived in the State I never tried to make even a garden. It would have been labour in

vain. The whole country, therefore, was open and
unenclosed, save for the few acres round each ranch
used for cattle-pens, or corrals, which the rancher had
bought ; so cattle and horses roamed over it at their
own sweet wills, and he who *owned* fifty acres had just as
good a chance as he who owned many leagues, if he
hadn't too many neighbours.

Though the country was good for cattle we found it
too heavily stocked for our purpose, and so struck across
to another stream—the Agua Dulce—*viâ* Banquetta.

Hitherto we had put up at the ranches we came to,
but now made up our minds to camp out and be independent ; far the best way to see a new country. So
at Banquetta I bought a good Spanish horse, to carry
our pack, for $30, and then at the store got the camp
" fixings " and provisions necessary. The Colonel left
it all to me, in simple faith, though he soon regretted
his confidence when he discovered how lightly equipped
I meant to travel. The fixings were two pint tin cups,
to serve as coffee-pots, buckets and cups ; two blankets,
and two overcoats. The provisions were 1 lb. of coffee,
some sugar, hard bread, or biscuit, and a lump of
bacon. All these were put in a sack and, with our
saddle-bags, blankets and coats, fastened pack-fashion
on the led horse.

For miles and miles we rode over a flat country with
plenty of grass, though little timber, steering by compass,
and seeing no one but a Mexican or two, but always
plenty of deer. By sundown we came to a creek, with
water and grass. There we stripped our tired horses,
and picketed them. Very soon I had a brew of coffee
ready, and slices of bacon roasting on sharp sticks over
the fire. A camp supper good enough for anybody ;
at least so I thought, and heartily enjoyed it. Not so
the Colonel, who, not used to camp fare, grumbled
ruefully at the scantiness of the provender.

Then I spread my blanket under me and, with my

Mexican saddle for a pillow and the starlit heavens for
a canopy, soon fell asleep in the balmy air of the summer
night, and stirred not till peep of day. My unfortunate
friend was awake too, and declared he had scarcely
slept a wink the whole night : the ground was so hard,
and the mosquitoes so troublesome !

The second day out we got into a waterless country,
and one that had been pillaged and overrun by Cortinas
and his thieving, murdering Mexican guerillas. For
a day and a night, in the burning heat, we rode without
a drop of water, and it was only when we and our unfortunate horses were clean done up, and could scarcely
move, that we came out of a dense grove of chaparral
right on a Mexican ranch with a good well of water. I
can remember that drink of cool spring water now,
as one of the best I ever had.

For two or three days more we traversed that district,
taking great care not to go so long between our drinks
again ; and then, having satisfied ourselves that it wouldn't
do for us, turned south to Corpus Christi on the Gulf,
at the mouth of the Nueces River. This was partly to
interview an important business man to whom I had an
introduction, and partly to replenish stores, etc., before
taking a further plunge into the wild prairie country of
the west of the State.

Corpus, or rather the upper part of it, is a typical old
Spanish town, with some fine churches and other buildings,
but as sleepy and dirty as are all Spanish towns I have seen.
The bulk of the people were Mexicans, or " Greasers,"
as they were always called in Texas ; but there was a
good sprinkling of Americans in the lower, or business
part. I remember things were rather lively in the
American part, for some men had been shot in an election
row ; a Vigilance Committee had been formed who were
administering Lynch law with much vigour, and perhaps
not quite so much discrimination as could be wished.
Therefore it behoved one to walk warily, and not express

one's opinions too freely, lest contempt of Court should be committed, which is a serious matter within Judge Lynch's jurisdiction.

By the afternoon of September 4, the day after our arrival, we had finished our business, and started with a well-laden pack-horse, on what would probably be a month's ride, to thoroughly explore the country fifty or a hundred miles up the Nueces River, which by all accounts was the ranching district we wanted. Before leaving the town I bought a double-barrelled shot-gun, with which to take toll of the deer; for I felt that the Colonel would no longer endure, without revolt, an unvaried diet of biscuit and bacon. Moreover he had so hungrily eyed the bunches we passed on the previous trip, that it was only fair he should taste venison as soon as possible. I knew he would be disillusioned when he did taste it, for it is the driest of meats; but he must have his chance of forming his opinion of it.

Riding leisurely along that hot afternoon we were overtaken by a man well mounted, and armed, with whom I soon struck up an acquaintance. He was a very pleasant, cheery fellow, and as our roads lay together till we reached a ranch some miles ahead, we became quite friendly, and parted, I think, with mutual regret. He told me his name was Davis, and that he was a lawyer in Corpus Christi.

What strange coincidences and unexpected meetings there are in this world! Here was a man casually met on the wide prairie, chatted with for an hour or two, then parted from; neither of us expecting to see the other again. But Fate willed it otherwise, and we were to meet again twice in this mortal life. At that second meeting, the story of which is rather strange, and will be told in its proper place, my friend probably owed his life to our casual meeting on the prairie near Corpus Christi.

Well, for the best part of a month we rode over the country between the Rio Grandé and the Nueces, and finding nothing to suit us, struck north to Castroville, a small town on the Medina River, twenty-five miles west of San Antonio. Occasionally we put up at a ranch, to get information or to replenish our stock of provisions, but generally camped out. Thompson's lust for flesh was fairly satisfied since, with the gun, we could get as many mule-eared rabbits as we wanted, and every now and then a deer ; but the lying out on the hard ground and the ever-present mosquitoes were a sore trial to him. So was our pack pony too. His manners, when first we made his acquaintance, were not perfect, and did not improve with time. Possibly, with the marvellous instinct of his race, he had found out that the Colonel, whose office it was to personally conduct him at the end of a long lariat, was no horseman and, in his secret soul, somewhat afraid of his charge. Any way, the little demon took advantage of his conductor with fiendish ingenuity. Sometimes he would hang back and refuse to budge ; at others, taking the poor Colonel unawares, run round and round him, winding him up in the toils of the lariat till he was quite helpless, and then drag him out of his saddle. I never saw anything more comical than my poor friend in this plight ; but his language was unfit for publication, and I verily believe he entertained the same vengeful thoughts against the pony as Balaam of old against his quadruped. But the old fellow was good-nature itself, and his wrath was soon appeased.

From Castroville, finding nothing to suit us, we made for the Bandera Creek country, forty miles north, riding through the pass of that name, where shortly before there had been a desperate fight between the Indians and a detachment of U.S. troops and some settlers. The former were badly " whipped," but the latter lost a good many killed, as could be seen from the number

of little wooden crosses dotted about round the scene
of conflict.

This was quite different from any country we had
previously seen ; high rolling prairie, almost hilly, with
much dwarf-oak timber and sedge grass, through
which the Bandera River ran, a beautiful clear stream
shaded by great cedars. A lovely country to look upon,
but not good for ranching, it seemed to me.

Having seen enough of that section, lovely and pic-
turesque as it was, we saddled up and departed, viâ the
Cibollo and Salado Creeks, for San Antonio. That night
we camped near a water-hole, on a rolling prairie with
little grass, not far from the Salado. We hobbled the
Colonel's enemy the pony but let the horses loose, and
in the morning they had vanished. I saddled the pony
and started to hunt them up, leaving Thompson in
charge of the camp.

The ground was dry and hard, and the trail difficult
to follow ; but I tracked it to the Salado Creek, on either
side of which was a good deal of timber and thick brush,
in which I completely lost it. Slowly making my way
through the dense undergrowth for the crossing for
San Antonio, I put up hundreds of turkey-buzzards
quite close to me. Looking round for the dead steer
I supposed they were feasting on, I was suddenly aware
of two men hanging from a live-oak tree just in front
of me. Torn and mangled, almost out of the semblance
of poor humanity, by the loathsome birds of prey, they
were the most gruesome, horrible sight I ever saw, and
with one glance I made off as fast as my pony could
scramble.

In San Antonio I learned the poor wretches were
horse-thieves, who had been caught and hanged by the
Vigilance Committee about a week before.

I shall have more to say later on about this same
committee, and its deeds of ruthless murder ; indeed
I could fill pages with the tales of its crimes, only they

would then be too full of bloodshed. Without that, I shall have to draw a very lurid picture of the state of things in Texas as I saw it ; when lawless men were a law unto themselves, and did such deeds that one shudders to remember them.

Having lost all trace of the horses, I made for San Antonio, and found it the largest and busiest place I had yet seen in Texas. At the livery stable, the boss found me a little dried-up Mexican vacquéro who, he said, for $10 would find my horses, if they had not been stolen, and were still on earth. I struck the bargain with the old fellow, " no cure no pay," and sure enough he brought in my lost property the next evening !

I had left Thompson all by himself in camp for two days and a night, and he hadn't had a very lively time, being convinced that I was lost. For his own part he knew he was lost too, for he had no idea of finding his way across a pathless prairie, and was consequently delighted to see me turn up with the missing steeds. The old fellow had not been short of food, for he had shot, and eaten, several mule-eared rabbits.

We now struck across the prairie to the Medio Creek, situated about fifteen miles from San Antonio, and on the El Paso road to Mexico. There was a ranch there which, from what we had heard, seemed desirable. After a good look round we concluded to buy, if the price was right, though for different reasons : my friend because it was an admirable site for a store, being close to the crossing of the Medio, where most of the trains passing to and from Mexico camped ; I because I thought it a fair cattle ranch, with plenty of water and enough grass. There were a thousand acres of it, belonging to a widow in Castroville, who, we were told, was anxious to sell.

We soon came to terms with the widow, and, finding her title good, paid her $1 an acre for her property. Next, having engaged two German carpenters to put up the buildings we wanted, I rode off to the Atacosa country, about sixty miles from San Antonio, and bought 250 cows and 5 bulls as a beginning.

We both, I think, were well pleased with our new possessions ; certainly the Colonel was delighted to find rest for the sole of his foot, for he was heartily weary of prospecting and all its hardships, and I was glad to have made a fresh start at last.

Throughout December 1860, and January and February 1861, we lived in our camp, superintending the building operations and looking after our cattle, but early in March the Secession movement in Texas, which had long been gathering in force, culminated in an attack on the U.S. troops in San Antonio, and I threw in my lot with the South as a Volunteer.

I do not propose to dilate further upon the causes of the dreadful Civil War, now on the point of breaking out, which have been argued out so fully on both sides ; nor to attempt to apportion the blame for the internecine strife which slew so many hecatombs of men, and devastated some of the fairest regions of the earth. All I will say is that we of the South believed in our very souls that our cause was a just one. We made a brave fight, as I think all the world allows, for what we thought our rights, and, losing, paid the penalty for our mistake, if mistake it were, to the uttermost farthing.

The excitement throughout the South had been growing day by day during the summer and autumn of 1860, and when in November of that year Abraham Lincoln was elected President, it blazed out into Secession, South Carolina taking the plunge into civil war by firing on, and capturing, Fort Sumter.

In Texas the Secession movement was somewhat complicated and confused by the action of Governor Houston. He it was who had brought the State into the Union, for when first freed from Mexican rule it had set up as an independent Republic. When therefore it became clear that the South meant to cut herself loose from the North, Houston conceived the idea of keeping Texas out of the confederacy, making her once more independent, and conquering Mexico ; which seems to show that he had more daring than foresight. However, when he refused to recognise the act of the State Convention, ratifying the ordinance of Secession, that body declared his office vacant, and so an end of him and his schemes.

But I must go back to the beginnings of things, at least as far as I was concerned.

Though I was of course aware that the feeling between North and South was getting more and more embittered, I was too busy that season prospecting to give much heed to politics, and, if I thought of them at all, believed the heat would cool down again, as it had so often done before. I had seen things pretty warm in Kansas, but nothing had come of it all ; so I went about my business, thinking it was a wrangle amongst the politicians which would settle itself in due course. This merely shows how little outsiders know of what is passing around them, and how difficult it is to judge of the awful forces lying hidden in the deeply stirred political passions of a nation. For here was I, and many thousands like me, on the very verge of one of the greatest cataclysms of modern times and wholly ignorant of its imminence !

It was about the end of October that I got the first inkling of what was going on. The Presidential election campaign was then in full swing, and Thompson and I rode into San Antonio to attend a great political meeting, held in the Alamo Plaza. There was a vast crowd assembled, in which parties were fairly evenly divided, for there was a considerable German population in the town and neighbourhood, which was Northern, or Unionist, to a man, while all the " Boys " were of course strongly Southern. There were all the inflammable materials gathered together, only wanting a spark to set them ablaze.

At one end of the Plaza was a long platform for the speakers, and behind it the Menger Hotel, from which floated the Stars and Stripes, so soon to be displaced by the " Lone Star " flag. A well-known and very popular Episcopal Methodist Bishop, whose name I have forgotten, made a most eloquent speech calling upon all who were men to stand up for their sacred rights, and to defend their cherished institutions from the intolerable arrogance of the Northeners. He set the hearts of the Southern men on fire by his strong appeals to their local patriotism, and the excitement rose to fever heat. Revolver shots were fired in the air, whilst through the square rang frantic yells of " Down with the Yankees ; to h—ll with the Abolitionists."

In the midst of this up rose a Mr. Anderson, a man of wealth and education, who had been U.S. Consul at Constantinople. He was a fearless man, for he must have known that to make a " spread eagle " speech to such a crowd was almost more than his life was worth. Nevertheless he pluckily essayed to do it ; but as soon as the " Boys " realised his drift, six-shooters in hand, and with one wild yell, they stormed the platform and swept it clear of friends and foes. Then the shooting grew unpleasantly promiscuous, and Thompson and I cleared out as best we might, and luckily, unscathed. There was more shooting than killing, I believe, for the Unionists showed but little fight ; but the Colonel was horror-stricken at the wild scene, and vowed never to go to an election meeting again as long as he lived—at least, not in America.

An association called the Knights of the Golden Circle had by this time its ramifications all over the South, and was particularly strong in Eastern Texas. Ostensibly formed to protect Southern rights, its real object was to bring about Secession, and all its weight was thrown into that movement.

It had " lodges " everywhere, with secret signs, and

passwords, and all its members were under semi-military discipline. The night of the great meeting I have described, I joined the San Antonio lodge of the K.G.C., and in so doing committed myself as a strong partisan of the Southern cause.

But Thompson wisely held aloof, as indeed he did up to the time of his death, two years after, telling every one that he was an Englishman, and had nothing to do with their quarrels. For the credit of the people, wild and lawless as they were, I must say no one ever molested or reproached him on this account ; but on the contrary, being a good-natured, pleasant fellow, he was well liked and popular wherever he went. Had I but taken the same calm, common-sense view, what a difference it would have made to my future !

CHAPTER II

AN INDIAN FORAY

AT the outbreak of the Civil War, San Antonio was the headquarters of the U.S. troops in Texas, where many forts and posts were held to keep the Indians in check and to guard the Mexican frontier. At the time of my arrival in the country, Colonel Robert E. Lee, as he then was, held the command of the Texas military district, and I had the pleasure and honour of an introduction to him on one of my first visits to San Antonio. It was after the Episcopal Church service, held in the Masonic Hall, that an acquaintance of mine made me known to him. We chatted for a few minutes, and I never saw him again, though I served under him in a subordinate capacity when he so gloriously commanded the Confederate forces.

Let me briefly describe him, as he appeared to me that Sunday morning, Tall, and somewhat spare in figure, with a soldierly bearing that revealed his profession at a glance, he looked, what indeed he was, every inch a gentleman. Courteous, and dignified in manner, but without the slightest assumption, he was beloved by all who came within the charm of his personal influence. At this time he was about fifty-three years of age, but his dark hair was untinged with grey, and his blue eyes were bright and undimmed beneath his black eyebrows. It is said that the bitter struggle between his duty to his country, in whose service he had already spent thirty years of his life, and his duty to his State (he was of the bluest blood in Virginia) aged him rapidly. The awful responsibility

161   11

of the high command he held throughout the war, and the misfortunes of the cause for which he so nobly fought, were enough to bow down any man.

But if they changed his face and bent his form, they left his soul untouched and still attuned to the lofty ideal of duty he followed as his guide through all his life. I think there is no other man who has appeared on the world's stage worthy to be compared with him, save our own General Gordon. To both, self was nothing and duty everything ; and both were " without fear, and without reproach."

Colonel Lee left Texas early in 1861, called to Washington by the President, who offered him the supreme command of the Federal army. But he could not fight against his State, or the cause he deemed to be just, and resigned his commission in a most touching letter addressed to General Scott, his old comrade in arms and commander, dated April 20, 1861. This is given *in extenso* in the *Life and Campaigns of General Lee*, written by his nephew, E. Lee Childe, p. 32.

Colonel Lee was succeeded at San Antonio by General Twig, a very different man. His command comprised a regiment of the U.S. infantry, two batteries of artillery, and a company of cavalry, posted in a strong fort just west of, but adjoining, the town. In the fort were great quantities of military stores and munitions of war, and these our newly established Government was particularly anxious to capture. So in the early days of March, 1861, the " Committee of Safety " made an urgent call for volunteers, which was promptly responded to by all the K.G.C. lodges in Eastern Texas, and to a certain extent by those in the west of the State.

Colonel Ben McCullogh had been commissioned as Commander-in-Chief of the State forces, and soon moved to within a few miles of San Antonio with two thousand men, mostly mounted. There he camped, and was speedily reinforced by five hundred more volunteers, of

whom I was one ; for though our ranch and corrals were
still unfinished, I felt I must obey the call to arms.
It was a formidable force mustered in that camp, for
though it couldn't boast much discipline, all the men
were well mounted, and most of them expert rifle and
revolver shots. With just a little training, what a brigade
of irregular cavalry it would have made! We were not
encumbered by our supply train, for each man was his own
commissariat department, and carried his own rations in
his " malletas."
The night I joined, orders were issued that we were to
parade at eleven o'clock dismounted, and march the three
miles into San Antonio to attack the fort. The position,
as I have said, was a strong one, and could have easily
been held by General Twig had he had any fight in him,
for we had no artillery. We of the rank and file fully
expected a sharp tussle, not only with the U.S. troops but
with the Germans, who made up quite half the population
of the town. Our leaders, I suspect, knew better.
Marching in columns of companies, and in dead silence
in the darkness of the night, we went right into the town
without encountering even a picket-guard. This was
singular enough, and didn't look much as if Twig meant
fighting. Our commander, however, played the game as
though it were in earnest, and occupied every commanding position as he advanced. My company, eighty strong,
was ordered to take post on the flat roofs of those Mexican
houses, the fire from which would command the whole
of the Alamo Plaza. We got up easily enough without
any opposition, and there we stood with loaded rifles for
four mortal hours, and still no shot was fired, though
every moment we expected the ball would open. At
7 a.m. the mystery was explained, for the Stars and
Stripes were hauled down from the fort and the " Lone
Star " flag floated in their place amidst the wild cheers
and hurrahs of all our " Boys."
General Twig had surrendered, without a blow for the

honour of his flag, eleven hundred troops, three batteries
of artillery, and about $3,000,000 worth of stores and
equipment of all sorts. What became of him I know
not, but rather fancy he would hardly care to report
himself at the Northern Headquarters.

After a bit of a spree in the town, to celebrate our
bloodless, but glorious, victory, we were marched back
to camp and there dismissed, each one to his own abode.
Before midnight I was back at our camp on the Medio,
to Thompson's great surprise, for he had prophesied all
sorts of evil concerning our enterprise, and in his heart
never expected to see me alive again.

Though Texas had not as yet joined the infant Confederacy, she had waged war against the United States,
and must be prepared for eventualities. Therefore the
Committee of Safety, shortly after the capture of San
Antonio, called for mounted riflemen, to volunteer for
three months' service.

About the middle of March I joined a company mustered
in by T. Paul, under a Commission from the Committee.
We were forty in number, all good men and well armed,
and reported at Castroville.

Paul had, in bygone times, held a commission in the
Texas Navy, a fleet which I suppose no one in this country
ever heard of before, but he was an old frontiersman and
a fighting man, which was the main thing for us. He
was the only commissioned officer in the company, and
appointed me at once orderly sergeant. Directly we
were mustered we went into camp on the Medina River,
in an old Mormon settlement, where there were several
solid stone houses and a mill. The Mormons had established themselves on the Medina at the time that the
main body of their curious co-religionists were settled in
Nauvoo ; but when the general movement was made
against that body in the States, these folks, like the rest
of them, had to trek to Salt Lake.

Whatever else they are, the Mormons are first-class

organisers in a new country, and know how to make themselves comfortable. Nothing could be better than the spot they had chosen here, and they had made the most of it ; and we could not but be grateful to them for the excellent shelter the old fellows had provided for us against the keen, cold norther blowing.

That night Paul told us his orders were to march at daybreak to Val Verde, forty miles distant, to attack that post, which was held by a detachment of U.S. cavalry. How many of the enemy he would find he didn't know, but thought there were not many more than our number. It seemed rather a large order, but the " Boys " were in high spirits and eager for a fight. Before daybreak our small bugler had roused the camp, and by sun-up we had drunk our coffee and were off on our long ride.

Our route lay, for the most part, by bridle-paths alongside the Medina River, which ran swift and clear between high cedar-clad ridges. We took all proper precautions, and had scouts well ahead, whilst every man rode with his loaded rifle across the horns of his saddle and his six-shooter in his belt ready for use. But perforce we had to ride in single file, and a dozen plucky men, properly posted in some of the narrow defiles, could easily have wiped us out. However, we were not molested, and camped that night about two miles from the post.

We were so confident of capturing the position, where we knew there were plenty of stores, that we had travelled with but small provision of rations, carried on two or three pack-mules ; so my office of issuer of provender to forty hungry men was not a very enviable one, for my comrades had but scant respect for any officer, and none for the orderly sergeant !

That night we lay on our arms, and our pickets and those of the enemy were almost in touch. It passed without any attack on either side, and at daybreak we fell in and marched to within a mile of the fort. There

Paul left his command in charge of the next senior sergeant, an old fighting frontiersman, whilst he and I rode on to the post, I bearing a white flag. A sergeant's guard received us and escorted us inside the fort, outside which I saw strong picket-defences had been thrown up, and I made sure we were in for a fight. Lieutenant Hill, the officer in command, received us very stiffly, and said he meant to hold his post to the last. He had really received orders to retire, as we afterwards learned, but put a bold face on it to gain better terms.

Paul assured him that though he might hold his post against us for a time, reinforcements were coming up and eventually he must surrender ; that General Twig, commanding the district, had already done so, and that therefore fighting would only mean useless waste of life. Our crafty friend was deaf to all reason for some time ; but when Paul offered to let the officers and men march out with their horses, arms, and personal property, which was what he had been fighting for, he at once agreed, and terms were forthwith settled. Hill was to march out next day and report himself, and his command, at San Antonio.

So at two o'clock that day he marched out and we took possession of the post, the stores, ammunition, twelve mules, eighty camels, and two Egyptian drivers, for all of which I had to give a receipt. The camels had been purchased in Egypt by the U.S. Government for transport across the prairies in the dry season, and answered very well. They were very little trouble to us as far as the females were concerned (do they call them " mares ? "—I don't know), but some of the males were the mischief, especially an old gentleman they christened " the major." He was evidently possessed by " Shaitan," and bit and fought like a demon ; but we chained him by the foot to a strong picket-post, and peace reigned in the camel-corral.

For three weeks we remained in these pleasant quarters,

with plenty of good fishing in the Verde Creek, and deer-hunting and turkey-shooting in the brush along its banks. But camp life, however pleasant, soon grows monotonous, so it was a relief to our easy-going but rather wearisome existence when one day an express rider came in, in hot haste, to summon us once more to the warpath ; this time against a marauding band of Comanché Indians. It was night when he arrived, and though his message was urgent enough, nothing could be done till next morning. The Indians had been at their usual work of killing the white men and driving off their horses, on four ranches in the Guadaloupé district. Paul therefore ordered me to detail twenty-five of the best mounted men, including myself, and to be ready to start, with six days' rations in our malletas, by daybreak. How the " Boys " shouted when I gave out the orders ! All of course wanted to go, but that was impossible.

With the first gleam of light we were on the way to the Guadaloupé River, where the Comanchés had begun their fiendish work of massacre and plunder. After about four hours' hard riding we reached a rough mountain farm, which had been the first attacked. Paul and I entered the lonely little cabin, and on the floor of the living-room lay the corpses of two men, one elderly, and the other in the prime of life. Both were scalped, and pierced by many lance and arrow wounds. Two women knelt by the side of the poor remains in bitter grief, the elder one mourning for her husband and her son, the younger for her husband.

The poor old mother told us that the night before the last one, her husband and son, hearing a noise in the horse-corral, turned out to see what it was, and that was the last they had seen of them alive. The terrified women heard the noise of galloping horses and the yells of Indians, and dare not stir. Why the Comanchés did not kill them too is strange, for they almost always made a clean sweep of men, women, and children in these raids.

Anyway, however it was, they were spared, and, when daylight came, ventured out. They found the corral down, the horses gone, and the father and son lying on their faces, dead and scalped. The poor creatures had, with difficulty, carried their dead indoors, and there, in that lonely spot, far from all human help, had watched by them, in anguish and in terror, for a day and a night. There were of course no coffins, and we could not stay to make any, for we must be on the trail of the fiends who had done this work as soon as possible. But we offered to halt long enough to dig a grave, and they consenting, with many tears, we laid the poor fellows to rest under the shade of a live-oak hard by the little cabin. Then with out expert " trailer " leading, we rode off on the broad trail of the spoilers, with wrath and vengeance in our hearts. It was a pitiful sight to see those desolate and forlorn women left alone by the graves of their dead ; but relief we knew was following after us from Val Verde, and we had our stern duty to do.

There were three more ranches swept by the Indians, who in these had killed all the white folks, but they were some miles off the main trail, and we could not turn aside to them ; for we must press on in the hope of catching our prey in the open country. In the hilly, rocky district at the head of the river, no trailer, however expert, could follow Indians ; there they would be safe.

Indian-hunting, in my experience, is not what one would call pleasant sport ; there are so many things you must not do. For instance, you musn't stop to kill any game, however much you may want meat, for your shot may alarm an Indian scout ; you mustn't make a fire in the daytime, lest the smoke should give warning to the watchful foes ; and then you must press on as fast as you can ride on the trail, to have any chance of catching them. For these Comanchés, as I think I have already said, are horse-Indians, and ride active, wiry ponies bare-backed. All the provisions they carry is a little jerked·beef ; their arms are bows and arrows and lances, and, being wholly unencumbered with clothing, they get over the ground, whether mounted or dismounted, at a surprising rate. To catch them without any plunder would be most difficult ; but when they have made a big haul, as in this case, then is your chance to come up with them—only you mustn't lose any time. I may add that the Comanché doesn't want to fight, and won't if he can avoid it, unless the party following him is a very weak one : he wants to get away with his plunder ; but if driven into a corner, will fight like a wild cat.

The trail led up the Guadaloupé, a great part of the way over a boulder-strewn, rocky trail, where it was most difficult to follow, for the " sign " was almost imperceptible. Sometimes through dense cedar-brakes, clothing the spurs of the hills running down to the river, but always through most lovely scenery, if one had only had time to rest and enjoy it. For four days we rode steadily on, never halting except at night, or for the briefest midday rest, and the " Boys " all the while keen and eager for scalps. The fourth day the " sign " grew plainer, for small bands kept coming into the trail, and we judged there was a pretty strong bunch of Indians somewhere, not very far, ahead of us.

That night we camped on a bit of open, rolling prairie close to the river, and there was great excitement, for we believed we were close up to the band. Moreover we had now reached the very edge of the brush-covered, rocky hills, the fastnesses of the Indians, and if we couldn't catch them before they got into them, our labours and toils were in vain.

Our trailer and two scouts went cautiously ahead, when night fell, to reconnoitre. They seemed gone for hours ; in reality it was less than one. Then they came cautiously back and reported they had located the Indians in a thick cedar-brake on the top of a steep ridge, and that, from the smoke of their fires, there must be a strong party of them.

Paul ordered the " Boys " to fall in at 2 a.m., so that
we might attack an hour or so before daybreak.

It was pitch dark as silently, and in single file, we
followed our guide through the cedar-brakes over a very
rough and hilly country. For nearly an hour we crept
on, and then the whispered word was given, and passed
down the line, to halt. We were within five hundred
yards of the camp. Now twenty of the men were dismounted ; the horses were linked and two men left in
charge, and whilst Paul led the frontal attack with
eighteen of the " Boys," I was sent with four mounted
men to the right flank to cut off any of the Indians
who tried to bolt across the ravine on that side.

The young moon just then broke through the heavy
clouds, and by the faint light we could see Paul and his
men creeping up the ridge in line. Then we pushed a
little farther round the flank of the hill, and waited events
rifle in hand, and with straining eyes peering through
the dimness of the night.

Now, as we waited, a single shot was fired, then another ;
then a volley rang out on the top of the ridge and, like
greased lightning, the Indians, on foot, went tearing
through the brush for their lives. Some half-dozen or so
of them bolted across our ravine a bit ahead of us, and
two of them we grassed ; but one got up and ran on. They
seemed to go at a tremendous pace, and in that dim light
we were lucky to hit any of them.

Meanwhile Paul, through the hot-headedness of one
of the " Boys," just missed surprising the camp. He
and his men had crept nearly to the top of the steep
ridge, when he who did the mischief thought he saw
an Indian standing on the edge, peering down, and let
drive with his Sharp's carbine, and hit a gnarled cedar
stump ! The next file followed suit, and in a moment
the Indians were on foot, and bolting in all directions.
By this time our " Boys " had reached the plateau, and
poured in a volley after the runaways ; but they were

scattered, the brush was thick, and aiming in the darkness was impossible, so all they actually bagged was three Indians. No doubt others were wounded but were carried off by their comrades, who make it a point of honour not to lose scalps if they can help it. It was no doubt the suddenness of our night-attack that so scared the Comanchés and made them bolt like that, for as a rule they are no cowards. In the darkness, and in such a country, it was of course hopeless to follow them farther.

In their camp we found all their lances, bows and quivers, and shields, five scalps, various articles such as blankets, saddlery and rifles, the plunder of the ranches, and fifteen ponies.

Of the latter they had a great many more with them, from the size of the trail, but the rest had bolted, or been stampeded by the Indians at the first alarm. By day-break we had made packs of the plunder, and, driving the ponies before us, started on the back trail to Val Verde.

CHAPTER III

THE VIGILANCE COMMITTEE'S WORK

OUR horses were a bit done up by the long stern chase after the Comanchés, and it took us about three days to return to the fort. The next day an auction of the Indian spoils was held, and I bought four of the ponies at $3 ahead ; cheap enough, for they were wiry, useful little beasts.

For ten days we remained quietly at the fort, and then it was " boot and saddle " again for me.

Paul had received orders to send out a scouting party to watch the movements of a body of U.S. troops, supposed to be some hundreds strong, marching from the Mexican frontier, possibly to attack San Antonio. They had been collected from the border forts and posts ; were veteran troops, had two fieldpieces of artillery with them, and it was necessary to keep a watchful eye on them, for though they might be only retiring from untenable positions, they *might* mean mischief. Twenty of our best men then were picked out for this duty, and I was sent in command of them.

So next morning, with four pack-mules to carry our supplies, we started with orders to strike the El Paso road west of Eagle Pass, a hundred miles distant, then get into touch with the U.S. troops and follow them, unobserved if possible, till further orders. Our road lay across the open prairie, or rather our route did, for there was no road ; but my guide knew the country so well, and was so good a frontiersman, that he took us to our point almost in a bee line.

Arrived at the road, I turned up it to the west, sending two scouts to keep about a mile ahead of the rest of the party. For two days we rode leisurely along, and then the scouts reported they had sighted the troops we were in search of. At once I moved my party off the road about half a mile on to the prairie, and took cover in a " mott," or clump, of live-oak to watch the proceedings. It was quite a pretty sight too, for there were, as I estimated, 700 infantry, 2 guns, 8 wagons drawn by six mules each, and a number of officers' servants and led horses, etc., bringing up the rear of the column.

The column marched about fifteen miles a day, and we followed them on their flank, unseen I believe, for they took no notice of us, for fully 250 miles. In reply to a message sent into headquarters by an express rider, I received orders to continue the scout, but to advise Colonel Van Doon, in command at San Antonio, the day before the column would reach the San Lucas springs, within a few miles of the town. This I did, and then rode ahead of the U.S. column and camped near the springs to await orders.

That night I was ordered to move to the Medio close to my ranch, to meet Colonel Van Doon early next morning. Before doing so I had another good look at the troops I had been shadowing so long, and was much impressed by their appearance, for they were as fine and soldierly looking a body of men as ever I saw. If they meant fighting, I was sure they could whip any force Van Doon could bring against them, though they had but a poor chance of getting out of the State, which by that time was up in arms.

I arrived at the ranch, with my command, in good time, and had only just served out a glass of whiskey apiece to the " Boys," when a great cloud of dust on the San Antonio road heralded the approach of the Colonel and his motley crew. He had about two thousand infantry volunteers of all sorts and sizes, armed with all kinds of weapons, and about five hundred mounted men of more presentable appearance. An "aide" now galloped up, and ordered me to move on up the El Paso road as an advance guard, about a quarter of a mile ahead of the main body.

When we came in sight of the U.S. troops I was halted, and ordered to report myself to the Colonel. He, I found, had formed up his infantry in three ranks across the road, with his mounted men on each flank, and it looked as though he expected a fight. I reported all I had been able to learn about the enemy, his ammunition, supplies, etc., and that he was drawn up in line on the crest of a slight rise, with his artillery in position in the centre. I said it looked as though he meant to fight; and if he did—well, he would be a tough nut to crack. The old Colonel, who no doubt was more in the secrets of the enemy than I was, only smiled, thanked me for the way I had carried out my orders, and dismissed me.

We stood in this formation for quite an hour—a very anxious time, I fancy, for the San Antonio volunteers, who certainly were not spoiling for a fight, for at least a hundred and fifty of them had fallen out on the march. Most of them were at that moment being doctored by my friend Thompson at his store with whiskey and such like medicines, to their comfort and his no small profit. At the end of this time a Federal officer, with a sergeant's guard, bearing a white flag, appeared, and in five minutes the news ran down the ranks that the U.S. troops had surrendered.

It may be thought that the U.S. troops in Texas made but a poor show of resistance at the outbreak of the war; but a glance at the map will show that they had no chance of getting away to join their friends of the North. The distance was too great, and they were too completely hemmed in by Southern States, to have any alternative but surrender.

The U.S. troops then were to camp that night on the

Léon Creek, hard by, and next day march into San Antonio and be parolled. Our volunteers were marched back to headquarters, but passed our ranch on the Medio, where they cleared Thompson out of every eatable and drinkable he had, but filled his pockets with coin. Besides this, my astute friend did a good stroke of business with some of the Federal officers in their camp on the Léon. He bethought him that probably they would have some property they would rather sell than hand over to the authorities in San Antonio ; and he was right, for he found them quite ready for a deal, if it could be done quietly. The bargains were soon struck, and by one o'clock in the morning Thompson was back at the ranch with three good ponies, twenty U.S. blankets, and six Colt six-shooters, for all of which he paid a mere song. I'm afraid it was a very questionable proceeding, on both sides, but the Colonel was highly elated with the success of his brilliant idea ; the six-shooters especially being almost invaluable.

Meanwhile our three months' service was up, and we were ordered back to Val Verde to be paid off and mustered out. There, in about a week's time, our company was relieved by one of the lately raised Texan Frontier Troops, and we received our " certificate of service." Then each man went his way to his own place. I afterwards cashed my certificate in San Antonio for $60.

At the ranch I found Thompson had got everything quite shipshape, even to ceilings of " domestic," *i.e.* calico, neatly whitewashed, in the rooms. His store looked quite businesslike, and was well stocked with goods. Two good cattle-corrals were built, and a well dug, about ten yards from the door, in which, at thirty feet depth, there was plenty of good water. The spot had been chosen by a " water wizard," with his hazel twig. Though there *can't* be anything in the twig, it's curious how often these folks strike water first time ; witness my " wizard " at Monticello, in Kansas.

Thompson had also added to our establishment a Mexican vaquéro named Caesario, and his "muger," or wife; the latter to act as cook, for though my friend was an expert in that line himself, he preferred some one else to do the work for him. Everything was in good order and the place already looked quite flourishing; but in the midst of his preoccupations the Colonel had quite forgotten to look after the cattle, and every one of them had made tracks for their old range on the Medina, whence they had come. So the day after my return I started with two Mexicans and six horses on a "cow-hunt."

The first night we camped in the forks of the San Antonio and Medina Rivers, hard by the ancient Catholic Mission of San José. Long as it had been deserted, its walls, of great thickness, stood firm and strong, and round it were numerous outbuildings, and houses for the péons the good Fathers had employed to tend their cattle and cultivate their irrigated lands.

It was when the Mexicans threw off the hated yoke of Spain, early last century, that they despoiled the Church of most of her lands. No doubt she had got hold of vast tracks of country in Texas, as elsewhere; but these "Missiones," scattered over the wildest districts, were centres of civilisation and of industry it was a thousand pities to destroy.

At the time I write of there was scarcely a settlement in all that Medina district; only here and there a small Mexican ranch. These Mexicans were good vaquéros, but much given to cattle-stealing, and when caught *flagrante delicto*, which wasn't often, or even strongly suspected, they were made to "look up" the nearest tree; which being interpreted means hanged, and that of course without trial.

Next morning, starting my boy Antonio to hunt up the horses, and Caesario to prepare our simple breakfast, I strolled down to the river, as the sun rose in all his splendour, to enjoy a bathe in the exquisite coolness and freshness of the dawning. On the opposite bank was a Mexican "pueblo," and I found all the inhabitants thereof of like mind with myself. Men, women, young girls, and children—all were disporting themselves in the beautiful pool, diving, swimming, splashing each other in the bright sunshine ; and not a soul of them wore more than nature's garb ! As they were in no way disconcerted by my arrival, but greeted me with cheerful "Buenos dias, Señor," I was soon amongst them, thoroughly enjoying the fun. I never saw a merrier bathing party, or a more innocent one.

The country I was hunting in was a most difficult one, and after four days' hard work I only managed to collect about fifty head of my cattle. These I drove back to the ranch, and had them herded by day and penned at night. Two more drives I made, and got most of the stragglers back, but it was hard work ! Meanwhile Thompson had bought 150 more from a German who was clearing out for Mexico, and these were added to the herd, which now began to be a respectable size.

One night, whilst I fortunately was at home after one of these drives, a young fellow I had met before, named Dan Ragsdale, put up with us on his way to San Antonio. He owned a ranch on the River Frio, about sixty miles from San Antonio, in a splendid range for cattle, but right in the Indian country ; and what was best from a ranching point of view, had no neighbours within miles of him.

He had 2,000 head of cattle, four darkies, and any number of horses. The war-fever was strong on him, and he was on his way to San Antonio to sell out "lock, stock and barrel," and take a commission as captain in the Confederate service, which had been promised him.

Though I had never seen his ranch, I had often heard of it as the best in all the country round, and when he talked so eagerly of selling I pricked up my ears. Over our pipes after supper he offered to sell to us on most favourable terms : $1,000 down, $5 a head for the cattle we could brand, not counting calves, and three years' time to pay for them by instalments. It was most tempting, and I confess I was as eager to buy as he was to sell ; but we had this Medio ranch and store on our hands, and we must get rid of the one before we could go in for the other.

Finally it was arranged that Ragsdale's offer should remain open for us for a fortnight, by which time he would return for our decision.

I set out then on my third " cow-hunt," with no expectation of being able to take up the Frio ranch. But how often it is that the unexpected happens ! I had been out nearly a week, and was returning home with a good bunch of cattle, when on the Medio Creek I stumbled on an ambulance and a wagon ; the owner whereof, a man named Randall, and his wife, had just pitched camp there. They had started from Arkansas with all their belongings, intending to trek right across the mountains to California ; a sufficiently difficult undertaking at any time, but which the disturbed state of the country made almost impossible.

It sounds almost like a coincidence in a novel, but he asked me if I knew of any place that would suit him, as he had made up his mind to settle in Texas. " Come along," I said, " right away, for I've got the very place for you within two or three miles of where we are."

As soon as he and his wife saw our decent comfortable house, the store, and all the surroundings, they were very pleased, and in a short time we agreed on the terms of purchase. He was to pay $1,500 for the ranch, store, etc., and $6 a head for all cattle delivered. He paid $1,000 deposit, and with his wife and family and four darkies took possession of the house, all but one room, whilst I set off again to round up the remaining cattle. This I did, after another week's hard riding, and then Ragsdale turned up again. We paid him his $1,000 down, and I think he was quite as pleased to sell as we to buy ; for he had got his commission, and was keen to be off to the wars.

I often saw him when he was encamped with his regiment, the 1st Texan Cavalry, at Three-Mile Creek near San Antonio, for the Colonel, commonly called "Daddy" Green, and many of the officers were well known to me. "Daddy" Green was a very fine specimen of the Southern planter, and in former days had seen much service against the Mexicans and Indians. Never was commander, I believe, more beloved than he by "his boys." He led them most gallantly in many a tough fight, and with him it was never "go," but "come."

Near the close of the war he, with his brigade of Texan Cavalry, "whipped" "Commissary" Banks, otherwise General Banks of the Federal Army, in a most gallant fight on the Red River. The dear old boy led his brigade against the Federal infantry strongly posted, with guns on either flank. It was against all the rules of war I suppose, but nothing could stop his boys, with "Daddy" in front of them, and they took the position and the guns, though with heavy loss ; the heaviest and most grievous of all being that of the dear old General, who was literally cut in two by a round shot in the moment of victory. His boys just rode over those Federals, and it was said that there was no such deed done in all the war.

As to poor Ragsdale, he served for some two years, attained the rank of major, and then was killed in Louisiana, pluckily leading his squadron in a gallant charge.

But all this is a digression, though I must repeat the offence to give an instance of the villainous doings of the Vigilance Committee.

The evening I returned from my first " cow-hunt," I was sitting on the " gallery," resting and enjoying the lovely evening, when a two-horse ambulance, with five men in it, drove up. A man named John Atkins I had met before, and two others got down, shook hands, and asked for drinks of whiskey. As the other two remained in the ambulance, I saw there was something up, and asked Atkins what it was. He said they had had a rare hunt after a d——d horse-thief; had found him at last at Fort Clark, where he had enlisted for a year's service, putting his (Atkins's) horse in as his mount. They had recovered the horse, which was tied behind the ambulance, and they were taking the thief into San Antonio.

But his manner as he said this aroused my suspicions; besides, I knew him as a prominent member of the dreaded Vigilance Committee, so I said, " I hope you are not going to hang the poor wretch before you get there." " You've hit it, my boy, first shot," he answered with a laugh; " you get your horse, and come along to see the finish. You bet we sha'n't take him much farther now."

Now one of the two still in the ambulance left it, and came to the house; but the prisoner sat quietly on, and apparently unconcerned. No suspicion of the near-impending fate that awaited him seemed to have dawned upon him. The human ghouls who had brought him along more than 250 miles had played cards with him at each camp, and now were going to murder him in cold blood! It made my blood boil, and Mr. John Atkins never guessed how near he was to getting a bullet through his heart. But if I could have killed all four of these bloodthirsty wretches, and rescued their prisoner, I should have had to flee the country, or their fellow-murderers of the committee would surely have hanged me.

I mastered my wrath then, as best I could, and used every argument I could think of to induce Atkins at

least to let his captive have his chance of trial in the
town. In vain; neither argument nor entreaty could
move him. I had said as much as I dared, and more
than was good for my own security, and could do no
more. So, sad and sick at heart, I walked over to the
ambulance to speak to the poor young fellow; he was
not more than twenty-five, and a well-dressed, good-
looking fellow. Directly I spoke, he said, " Why, I met
you in Kansas, when you were a lieutenant in Miller's
company, and I was in Dunn's." I couldn't recollect
him, even when he told me his name was Jack Young.
He declared he was innocent of the charge, for he had
bought the horse from a Mexican, on the Medina, and
was confident of being able to produce him at his trial.
His trial, poor fellow! How little he knew! I *couldn't*
tell him of the terrible fate awaiting him, and it was
best not. It could only prolong his agony.

But I would try once more what persuasion would
effect with his captors. I might have spared my breath,
for they were as hard as the nether millstone. The
sun was setting, and the murderers were anxious to start,
that they might finish their evil deed before darkness
overtook them.

The victim asked for whiskey, which I had forgotten to
offer him, so I brought him a tumbler. He shook me
by the hand, hoping to meet me again soon; and I knew
I should never see him alive any more. So they drove
off, the prisoner cheery and unconcerned, his escort
laughing and chatting with him, as though they were all
the best of friends. In less than half an hour the brutes
would hang him! I watched them, in the crimson
glow of the setting sun, until they disappeared round
a " mott " on the prairie, and then, with a feeling of
utter helplessness, turned back to the house.

That night I scarcely slept, and at daybreak was on
horseback, following the trail of the ambulance; drawn,
as it were, by some irresistible attraction; feeling sure

at one moment of what I should find, and the next hoping the murderers *might* have relented. Thus hoping, fearing, I rode on for about three miles, and then saw what I really expected : Jack Young hanging from a China-tree hard by the trail !

In hot haste I rode on into San Antonio and reported to the City Marshal what I had seen. The deed was recognised as the handiwork of the all-powerful Vigilance Committee, and no one dared to interfere with its dread decrees. Only some Mexicans were sent out by the city authorities to cut down the victim and bury him on the spot where he died. And so an end, as far as this world's justice is concerned. I have, alas ! seen many die by Lynch Law, but never so cold-blooded a deed as this one.

CHAPTER IV

A RANCHER'S PARADISE

HAVING agreed terms with Ragsdale for his ranch, and paid our deposit, all we had to do now was to ride into San Antonio, see his lawyers, and put matters in proper legal train. This we did in a very few hours, and became duly " seized " (I think that is the legal phrase) of the coveted Frio ranch.

I must say they do these things better in the States than we do here. Why, it is easier, and less costly, to transfer the ownership of a great estate, that may be worth millions, over there, than one tumbledown old cottage here !

That fixed up, I engaged an old frontier Mexican, Juan Garcia by name, to go out to the Frio with me, and ride round the home range. Juan was well known to me as a first-rate vaquéro, and though he had never been actually on the new ranch, knew its whereabouts, and the lay of the surrounding country. I have no idea how old he was, nor do I think had he himself ; any way, he looked like a dried-up mummy, a little bleached by long exposure to the sun. On foot he looked old, and decrepit almost ; but put him on a horse, however wild and unbroken, and he seemed transformed. He could ride all day, and every day, and after the longest " cow-hunt " seemed as fresh as paint. He was a good shot with rifle or six-shooter, and furthermore—a great consideration in view of where we were going—wasn't afraid of Indians.

His costume, like that of all his kind, consisted of

buckskin pants, nearly as ancient as himself, gaiters much adorned, Mexican fashion, with tassels and laces, and long mocassins, to which were affixed a huge pair of silver spurs, the pride of his heart. The upper part of him was clad in a short jacket, or jumper, of canvas, which displayed much brown skin between itself and the buckskins, and on his head he had a huge sombrero, under which the old fellow looked like a vast mushroom on a short stalk.

Juan and I then started on our somewhat perilous journey, armed with rifles and six-shooters, and carrying for provisions, in our malletas, coffee, dried beef, and hard bread. Our shortest route lay across the prairie to a ford on the Medina River, but we neither of us knew the exact position of the ranch, so had to pass through Castroville and take a very dim trail to the San Francisco Creek, about twelve miles.

The crossing of the San Francisco had an evil repute ; for about a month before the Lepan Indians had surprised a small party of cow-hunters there, killing one and wounding another, the latter a man named Lemmons, who afterwards did a lot of cattle-driving for me. However, we got over the creek all right, and there before us lay the open, boundless prairie with never a sign of a trail on it.

Juan said our direction, he thought, was about west, so for that point we steered by the sun, riding over fine rolling prairie, dotted here and there with great live-oaks, and in the bottoms, dense white chaparral. Not a living being, nor any sign of settlement, did we see all that day ; only now and then a few stray cattle, and plenty of deer and peccary, which we dared not shoot for fear of betraying our presence to the watchful Indians.

That night we camped on the Seco Creek, by Juan's reckoning, about fifteen miles from the Frio, and after dark made a small fire to boil our coffee and heat up our dried beef. This done, we put it out, lest the smoke should be seen, lariatted our horses to prevent their straying, smoked one pipe, and then laid down on our blankets, with our saddles for pillows and our arms by our sides, frontier fashion. The moon was high, and the night full of light. Very beautiful to look on in its vastness and its stillness, and I lay for a short time contemplating the wondrous scene, and thinking of the past, and of the uncertain future before me ; also I confess wondering if there were any Indians about, and how a scalping-knife would feel. But not for long ; for soon the soft cries of the whip-poor-wills, the distant howls of the coyotés, and the grumbling of the bull-frogs in the creek sent me into a dreamless sleep, till Juan roused me as the first glimmer of light showed on the eastern horizon. That worthy declared he had slept with one eye open, but I rather doubt it. Indians or no Indians we were bound to make a fire, for a pint of good coffee is almost worth risking your life for. We drank this, perhaps enjoying it the more for the risk we ran, ate a bit of dried beef, slightly broiled on the embers, and set off due west again, still seeing no trail, though we had expected to strike one of Ragsdale's before this. I found afterwards that the reason was that he never used the same trail twice, either in riding or sending a wagon, into San Antonio. A wise precaution in an Indian country like that.

However, we soon began to strike big cattle-trails, all leading in one direction, which we were sure must be the Frio, and followed them at a smart " lope." Presently all doubts were at an end when we struck a number of cattle, all with the I.X.L. brand, which I had bought from Ragsdale. I was delighted with what I had seen so far, and recognised that I had struck the finest cattle-range I had ever laid eyes on. Miles and miles of clean mesquite grass extended on all sides, and all the cattle fattening on this pasture were in splendid condition.

The cattle and deer trails soon led us to dense chaparral of " cat-claw " mesquite and prickly pear, with wide cattle-roads through it. Here and there this would open out into hollows, or cañadas, perhaps a hundred yards wide, with lagoons in them, round which grew beautiful grass, clear of brush, but dotted about with live-oaks, palmetto, and mesquite-trees. This chaparral, I found afterwards, extended back from the river about four miles, and along its length for about thirty miles : a very home and paradise for game of all sorts.

As we rode along that morning, troops of turkeys would rush across the trail ; deer would jump up, almost under our horses' feet, and bunches of " javalines," or peccary, bolt from their wallows on the margins of the water-holes into the brush with angry grunts and fierce snapping of their tusks. Signs, too, were not wanting of mustangs coming down to drink, and as old Juan, whose regular calling was mustanging, rode behind me, I could hear him muttering to himself, with much satisfaction, " Que buena, que chula " ; which, freely translated, means " what a beautiful place ! "

Coming to the river itself, we found the banks of loamy clay about seventy feet high, with many cattle and bridle tracks leading down to its boulder-strewn bed, and on the opposite side, hard by the bank, were the ranch buildings plainly to be seen. Where we had struck the Frio it was easily fordable, but above and below that point it spread out into lakes of clear, blue, cool water, full of fish and abounding in alligators and " alligator gar." Indeed the river, for nearly the whole of its course, is a succession of these lakes or " water-holes," as they are called in Western parlance.

My lot, I saw, " had fallen on a goodly heritage " when I bought this Frio ranch. But there were two drawbacks to my enjoyment of its advantages : the first, over which I had no control, the Indians ; the second, my own per- verse desire to mix myself up in the great War of the Secession,—the last being more fatal to my prospects of success than the first. If I had only stuck to my own business of cattle-raising, for, say, ten years, I have no doubt I should have been the fortunate owner of the finest range and the biggest stock of beeves in all Texas. However, it was not to be ; and regrets are useless, or worse.

Climbing up the western bank of the river, whose margin was lined with mulberry-trees and live-oaks, entwined with " mustang " grape-vines to their very summits, we found ourselves outside the high mesquite picket-fence surrounding the ranch. Our approach was greeted in so vociferous and threatening a manner by about a dozen hounds and " Arkansas curs," that I thought it wisest not to dismount before some one came out to quell the riot. Long and loudly I shouted, and after some minutes an ancient darky cautiously peeped out of the door and, having carefully reconnoitred us, came forth. The poor old fellow was overjoyed when I explained who I was, for he and his old woman had been left in charge by Ragsdale with only the dogs to protect them from the Indians, and so terrified were they that they had slept in the chaparral every night.

Aunt Martha, his wife, fixed us up some corn-bread and venison, with a good brew of coffee, and whilst this was preparing I took a look round my new homestead. The house was of hewn logs, with two rooms, one above and one below ; the former reached by a broad stair-ladder outside. At the back a log kitchen with dirt floor, and alongside it six " acaldes," or Mexican picket-houses, for the hands. Behind them again, good log " smoke-houses " and fowl-houses ; the whole surrounded by a strong picket-fence enclosing about half an acre of ground dotted about with beautiful trees. The house had a rough gallery round it, a pleasant shady place to sit out on ; but it was wholly innocent of glass, the windows being only closed by shutters.

Outside the fence were the cattle, calf and horse,

corrals, all well fenced with high, strong picket-posts,
and the former was capable of holding 2,000 cattle.
With the ranch went the freehold of a square league of
land, or 1,920 acres ; whilst all the splendid grazing
ground for miles round was practically, for the time
being at least, as much my own as if I had bought
and paid for it.

To the west of the ranch, which stood on a knoll, there
was an extensive view over the gently undulating prairie,
covered with the richest of grass, and sprinkled with
fine timber which gave it a park-like appearance. Could
heart of cattle-rancher desire anything better, anything
more perfect for his business ? The *amari aliquid*
was the Indians, and there was no doubt one would have
to keep a wary eye on them to retain one's scalp intact.

The Comanchés knew the range well, and the Lepans
considered it their special property. Only the previous
spring the former had swept this very district, killing
fifty men, women and children, and getting safely away
with a big drove of horses. But " what can't be cured
must be endured," and these Indians were certainly
incurable, and, as Artemus Ward said, " pison wherever
met." It was only the steady march of civilisation that
could rid the country of them, and that has done its
work long years ago now.

After breakfast, and having rested and fed our horses,
we started out to ride down the west side of the Frio,
about twenty-five miles to the junction with the Nueces
River. I had seen a good deal of "frontier" in Missouri
and in Kansas, having ridden over nearly the whole of
the latter, but a wilder country than this I had never
beheld. Not a human being, nor sign of one, did we see,
but plenty of bunches of I.X.L. cattle, in wonderful
condition and as wild as bucks. Deer, and peccary too,
were in abundance, and towards sundown, as we neared
the forks of the Nueces, a great drove of mustangs,
perhaps one hundred and fifty strong, passed ahead of

us at a gallop, making for their watering-place on the river. Old Juan was frantic with excitement, and I could hardly restrain him from galloping after them, by telling him he should come, by and by, and rope as many as he liked.

That night we camped on a water-hole of the Frio, under a grove of splendid " peccan " trees. Seated under one of these, watching Juan getting ready our supper, a piece of good luck befell us ; for along the deer-trail, a few steps from me, came a troop of turkeys, strutting leisurely to water. At the head of his harem marched a stately gobbler, unconscious of aught but his own dignity and grandeur. Though it was a risky thing to shoot in a place like that, the old fellow was too tempting to resist, and I knocked him over with a shot from my six-shooter.

Juan had him plucked in double-quick time, gave him a coat of clay, scooped out a hole, and baked him therein on the wood ashes. No *chef* or professor of the culinary art can, with all his appliances, produce a dish to beat this. Be it deer-meat or turkey, or any other meat, no way of cooking it equals this ; but perhaps a beef's *head* treated in this fashion is the supremest dish of all. It makes one hungry, even now, to think of it.

Next day we rode back up the east side of the Frio, seeing many cattle, and plenty of unbranded calves, which showed that Ragsdale, since the war-fever had attacked him, had let his stock go ; all the better for us perhaps. At the ranch we stopped for an hour, stripped the horses, and fed them, whilst we breakfasted. Then off again, and rode ten miles or so *up* the west side of the river, seeing more cattle, and a pack of " lobos "—large wolves, not to be confounded with the small prairie variety, or coyotés. Here we saw very fresh Indian sign, which showed that a considerable band had struck the river at this point and turned up it, travelling north.

Having no desire to run into these gentry, and being

moreover more than satisfied with what I had seen of the range, which indeed was unsurpassed and unsurpassable, we crossed the Frio and struck across the prairie for the Seco Creek, *en route* for the Medio. The Indians being so near, we made no fire in our camp that night, and went coffeeless to sleep, but saw nothing more of the Comanchés, or their sign.

Next morning we were in the saddle before sun-up, and reached Castroville in safety that afternoon. The little town was in great excitement, for the Indians were on the warpath again, and had killed a German settler in the Atacosa country, about twenty miles south of the Medio, and the other side of the Medina River.

My old friend Paul, with whom I had served before, was getting up a command to follow them, and nothing would do but I must go with him. Tired as I was, I couldn't say no, under the circumstances ; for men were scarce on the frontier, and his command, so far, consisted of only fifteen young Germans, none of whom knew anything of Indian fighting. So I agreed to join the scout at noon the following day, at a small ranch south of the Medina, and bring one or two more with me if possible.

In the meantime I was bound to return home to get a fresh horse ; for the one I was riding was about done up, and it was all I could do to get him to the ranch, quite late that night. Thompson was really glad to see me turn up, for he had begun to think the Comanchés had got me, and of course was delighted with my report of the Frio ranch.

He had heard that the Indians were out across the Medina, but no particulars of their doings ; however when I told him I was going to join Paul's scout next day, he at once said he would go too. " I have nothing to do with fighting the Yankees," he said, " but this Indian business is different, and if I'm going to live on this frontier, I must do my part like the rest of you." The good old fellow seemed delighted to go, and as " his soul was in arms and eager for the fray," I was very pleased to have him with me, especially as there was no one else I could enlist.

He saw to everything for me ; got the horses, arms, and provisions ready for the morrow, whilst I threw myself on the bed, just as I was, and slept like a rock till the Mexicans called me before daybreak. Then, after a swim in the cool water of the creek, and a hasty breakfast, we set off for our twenty-mile ride across the prairie ; the Colonel in the highest spirits at the prospect of this his first brush with the Comanchés, and I as fresh as paint again. We reached the rendezvous a good hour before the rest of the command, and, for my part, I was glad to get to the end of the journey ; for there were too many Indians about in the neighbourhood, and we two might have been jumped on by a big bunch of the brutes at any moment.

At the ranch we learned that the Comanchés had killed two more settlers, one of whom had been scalped, after being tortured to death with lance-thrusts. The " sign " showed plainly enough the diabolical ingenuity of the wretches, for it was as easy to read as a book.

They had roped him, and driven him round in a circle, prodding him the while with lances, till he had died, literally covered with wounds. They had also, which was very unusual, attacked a big ranch, but had been beaten off by the owners, who were well armed. Moreover they had got together a big drove of horses, and had killed a great many cattle, and were much bolder and more careless than usual, knowing just as well as we did that the frontier was no longer protected by U.S. troops, and that our best young " braves " had gone to the war. Indeed at that time we suffered terribly from Indian raids, owing to these causes, and no outlying ranch was safe from attack, so that very many were abandoned by their owners.

When the command appeared, and I had had a look

round, I can't say I was much impressed by the appearance of the men. They were well mounted and armed, but I couldn't feel very sanguine as to the result if we did come up with the enemy ; for except Paul, Demp. Forrest and myself, none were real frontiersmen, or used to this kind of work. However they all seemed very keen, and so after a short halt we set off, nineteen in number, on a trail the most inexperienced could follow, it was so wide and plain. At dusk we struck the Comanché camp of the previous night, and all next day followed it as fast as we dared go. We were evidently overhauling the Indians, who were hampered and delayed by the big bunch of horses they were driving, and I felt sure we should catch them, and have a fight. The trail was now heading for the Presidio crossing of the Rio Grandé, and the only fear was lest they might get over into Mexican territory before we came up with them, for there they would be safe from pursuit.

The third day we pressed on as fast as our tired horses could go, with Demp. Forrest the trailer and two scouts well ahead ; the rest riding two and two, with Paul and myself leading the van. The excitement was intense, for now the Rio Grandé was not so very far ahead. Would the devilish murderers escape us after our hard ride ? Even the rawest German trader was keen for blood now, and my friend was quite wild ! I could scarce realise that it was the same placid, good-natured old Thompson ; but I suppose it was the tale of the poor young German's awful death that had roused the fight latent in him.

About midday Demp. came riding back, at full gallop, to report that he had located the band, camped in a brushy cañada, about three miles from the crossing, and that all seemed busy cooking and eating. Round their camp he had seen a big lot of the stolen horses, perhaps two or three hundred in number. There was plenty of brush for covert, near the cañada, and, as the Comanchés seemed careless and off their guard, he thought we might possibly surprise them if we hurried up.

Rifles, six-shooters, and cartridge-belts were carefully examined, and off we set at a lope, Paul leading, and I bringing up the rear of the column to prevent straggling. I confess I felt rather anxious as to how our raw recruits would behave. An Indian yell, before the brutes charge, is not a pleasant sound to hear for the first time, and I wasn't sure how my young friends' nerves would stand it. If any of them gave way, we should have the Comanchés charge into us to a certainty ; and they outnumbered us by more than three to one. Most of them, I was glad to see, seemed still keen enough, though one or two, I fancied, had cooled down a bit in their ardour, and these I resolved to keep close by me when the pinch came.

Now, as we pressed on over the rolling prairie and between the thick standing clumps of nopal, our scouts came back and reported there was no hope of a surprise, for the Indians had left their camp and, having mounted, had taken up a position on a " lomo," or ridge, hard by, where they evidently meant to fight. No men fight harder than these Comanchés when driven into a corner, but here their retreat over the river was secure ; so it was doubtful whether they would make a big fight to save their plunder, or bolt to save their own skins.

Paul formed his little troop in line to the front, and, advancing to about eighty yards from the ridge, dismounted his men ; the horses' reins were thrown over the men's left arms, and orders given to reserve fire till Paul gave the signal. Then every man to mount in double-quick time and have at the Indians, six-shooters in hand.

Hardly were we ready when the Comanchés came on, in V formation, at a good hand canter down the hill, between sixty and seventy in number and yelling like demons. They had let drive their arrows, and a young

13

fellow named Petersen got two of them, one in his shoulder
and the other in his thigh. It was a nervous moment,
though Petersen was the only man hit ; but the fellows
stood steady, even those I had thought doubtful, gripping
their rifles and waiting for the word.

"Fire, boys!" shouted Paul, and at about fifty or
sixty yards' distance we poured in our volley. Six
Indians dropped, and others we could see were wounded,
perhaps a dozen of them, but they stuck to their ponies.
It was too hot for them to stand, and the formation
broke at once, and wheeled about in full retreat up the
slope. It seemed only a moment before we were mounted,
but even as we started in pursuit the active Indian ponies
had topped the ridge and disappeared. Helter-skelter
they went for the crossing, only half a mile away, and
before we could catch up with them were over in Mexican
territory, where they knew our boys wouldn't follow
them.

We had done pretty well, considering the composition
of the command ; but of course could have cut up pretty
well the whole of the band if we had had enough men to
divide, and secure the crossing. We gathered about two
hundred horses, after a good deal of trouble ; so the
Comanchés didn't get away with many.

Well pleased with the success we had met with, we
camped on the field of battle, and feasted right royally
on a fat yearling the enemy had left behind.

Poor Petersen was badly hurt ; but the arrow-heads
were cut out and the wounds dressed as well as might be,
and we got him back to Castroville, where he eventually
recovered.

All, as I have said, were well pleased ; but none more
so than old Thompson, who vowed he had grassed one
buck and, if he knew it, would never miss another Indian
hunt.

CHAPTER V

WHEN we returned to Castroville, after the Indian fight on the Rio Grandé, the German inhabitants (we always called them " Dutch," though I don't know why) gave us quite an ovation, and feasted the whole party with their best.

A list was made of all the brands on the captured horses, and a notice stuck up that the owners could reclaim them on payment of a small fee. Those not claimed within a fortnight were, with the Indian trophies, sold at public auction.

Randall, who had bought our ranch, was not ready to pay the balance due, so we did not hand over possession. I filled up the time of waiting by hunting cattle, and, after another three weeks' hard riding, collected another twenty-five of our brand, which made up our number in the corrals to five hundred.

Being a member of the K.G.C., and having voted for Jeff Davis for President and served three months under the Committee of Safety, I was pretty well known in San Antonio as " sound on the goose," which meant a good Southern man, and at this time was a good deal in the town and in the camps of instruction. In the latter I met General Wasp in command, General Sibley, Colonel Green, and many others, with whom I became very friendly. At this time the war-fever ran very high in Texas, and throughout the South. The battle of Bull Run had been fought and won, and every one was sanguine of victory. It was with all of us only a question of how

long it would take us to whip the Yankees, and what we
should do with them when that was accomplished ; we
were indeed proceeding to dispose of the lion's skin before
we had slain him ! For myself, I was just as sanguine
and as excited as the rest, and never dreamed the South
could be beaten. It was the common opinion that the
war would not last more than six months, or at the
outside a year ; and that, if England and France would
acknowlege our independence, it would be over directly.
It is easy enough to laugh at our shortsightedness and
vanity now, and the proud Southerners paid a heavy
enough penalty for it too ; how heavy, in the downfall
of their pride and the ruin that overtook them, no one
can realise who was not an eye-witness of the *débâcle*
in 1865.

Now, in this summer of 1861, I was almost carried off
my feet by the prevailing excitement ; and when General
Wasp offered me a captain's commission in the Partizan
Rangers, these being raised for service in Tennessee, it
was hard to resist the temptation. But I had this Frio
ranch on my hands and Thompson to look after and
consider, so I had to decline with many thanks, though
I told the General, if the war lasted, I should serve, if
only in the ranks. I may say I was as good as my
word, for I did serve eventually, and under General
Wasp too, who, though an old West Point man, was not
a brilliant commander.

About the time I am writing of, I happened to be in
San Antonio staying with some friends, and was a witness
of a deed perpetrated by the Vigilance Committee that
almost surpasses in cool villainy any of its doings.

It was a lovely evening, and many people were strolling about the Plaza, whilst under the shade of the trees
surrounding it, numbers of Mexicans were seated at tables
playing their great gambling game of " Monte." A
young Ranger from the camp of instruction, with perhaps
too much aguadiente in him, appeared and began jumping

over the tables, some of which he capsized. Five or six of the city marshals ran up, and after a big fight arrested him and carried him off to jail. A simple drunken row, common enough in those days, of which one took no notice ; but it was to have a tragic enough ending for the unfortunate young Ranger.

Next morning, at about ten o'clock, I walked over to the Court House with my host, Mr. Sweets, the Mayor of San Antonio, and we were both much surprised to see a crowd of several hundreds in the Plaza fronting the court and jail.

I sat by Sweets' side whilst he disposed of several trifling cases, amongst others that of the Ranger, who was charged with creating a disturbance. His case was dismissed with a caution, and the next one called on. But the young fellow, a smart-looking, soldierly man, though acquitted, seemed in no hurry to regain his freedom, but, on the contrary, begged the Mayor to keep him in custody. He gave no reason for his strange request, though no doubt he had a strong suspicion of what awaited him outside. The Mayor said he had no power to detain him, and he must go.

I remembered the crowd we had seen, and stepped to the door to see what was going on. There was nothing much in its demeanour to attract attention, but it had gathered thickly round the door, as though patiently waiting for something, or somebody, and at the back I saw two well-known members of the dread committee. Hastening back to Sweets I told him I didn't like the look of the crowd, and thought there was mischief afoot. I don't know whether he heard me, for just then the Ranger was asking, more earnestly than before, to be detained in custody. Anyway, his answer to the request was short and sharp.

" Nonsense, my lad, you have been acquitted ; I have no power to keep you, and you must go." The Ranger said never another word, but, with a shrug of his shoulders, turned on his heel and marched out to his doom.

The moment he stepped outside, the human wolves, waiting for their prey, set on him, dragged him across the Plaza, put a rope round his neck, and strung him up to a tree in less time than it takes to relate. I saw it all, but of course was absolutely powerless to help. I however went off, as fast as my horse could carry me, to the camp to tell the tale to the victim's comrades, in the hope that they would avenge his murder. Quickly they ran to get their arms, but the General fell in two regiments of infantry and marched them into the town to keep order, or I verily believe the villainous committee would have had to mourn the loss of some of its leading members that day. They were well known to every one in the town and neighbourhood, but the excitement died down, nothing was done to them, and their evil power remained unshaken.

The young fellow's drunken escapade had of course nothing to do with his hanging ; it only gave his enemies the opportunity of catching him away from his comrades. It seems that two years before, the Vigilance Committee had hanged a brother of his on some pretext or other, and the Ranger, who had only recently arrived in San Antonio, had openly threatened that he would shoot Asa Minshul and Solomon Chiswell, the leaders who had murdered the brother. These rascals therefore, to save their own skins, had organised the hanging I had witnessed.

It made one's blood boil to think that these cowardly villains could terrorise a whole State like this, and murder with impunity any one against whom they had a spite. They took no part in the war, and never one of them fired a shot for their country and its cause, about which they talked so loudly, but stayed at home, and ruled those who did the fighting by their terrible secret power.

The ramifications of this secret society, which in its

constitution was something like the Italian Mafia, of evil notoriety, were very wide, but though the leaders were perfectly well known, the rank and file, who obeyed their behests without question or hesitation, were difficult to identify. Some of course were known and shunned, as much as those ouside the organisation dared to; but the terrible part of the thing was that one never knew whether the man you met on pleasure, or on business, or in whose house you stayed on terms of friendship, might not be a member, and denounce you. A terrible state of society, truly; but no private organisation could hope to cope with it, and in those disturbed times public law and order were in abeyance.

The head of the committee, and the man who pulled the strings, was Asa Minshul, a well-to-do merchant and store-keeper in San Antonio. When I first met him he was about fifty years of age; short, stout, and florid, he looked what he was, a prosperous tradesman. Moreover he was a shining light amongst the Wesleyans, in whose church he often preached and prayed with much unction. I have often been in his house, which was about the best in the town, and in which his two daughters, who were well educated and musical, gave very pleasant parties.

Now, as soon as I found what terrible power this man wielded, and how necessary it was for one's good health to be friendly with him, I confess with some shame that I cultivated his acquaintance. The old ruffian was no doubt fond of his two girls, and with them I struck up quite a friendship—not entirely disinterested perhaps, though they were pleasant enough; also, at times, I attended his ministrations in the Wesleyan church, and listened to the confounded old hypocrite's long-winded discourses, with what patience I might. All this was somewhat ignoble no doubt, and not a thing to boast of; but there was always that rope that the old fellow was said to carry in the tall white hat he invariably wore, and one would do a good deal to keep it from off

one's neck. Talking of that rope, there was a good
story current in San Antonio, though I can't vouch for
its truth, as I was not present at the scene ; at any rate,
if not true, it was " well invented."

The old rascal was preaching one hot Sunday afternoon
in the Wesleyan church to a crowded congregation, and
by his side on the pulpit-platform he placed his hat. As
he vehemently denounced sinners, and urged to righteous-
ness his listening flock, the perspiration trickled down
his forehead so fast that he paused, and stooped down
for his handkerchief, lying in his hat. But, in his excitement, he quite forgot what else his hat contained, and
hurriedly seizing the handkerchief, drew out with it a
coil of rope !

Randall being still behind in his payment, the Medio
ranch couldn't be handed over, and I couldn't take up
my abode on the Frio. So, as it was necessary to have
some one in charge, I hired a Mexican and his wife to
look after the place. Then I got old Juan to find
three other vaquéros, besides himself, to help me drive
and brand on the range. So this trip we were quite a
party ; the man and his wife travelling in my wagon,
and the other four Mexicans and myself mounted.

Never I think were human beings more delighted to
see me than the two poor old darkies at the ranch, for
they had made up their minds that they had been
abandoned as a prey to the Indians.

We hunted, for about a week, up and down the Frio,
and in the forks of the Nueces, and branded two hundred
calves, some of them nearly yearlings. Game as before
was very abundant, and we lived on turkeys and deer-
meat. Every now and then we scared up a bunch of
mustangs, but, as they always galloped like mad for
the thick chaparral, the Mexicans only managed to
rope one ; a beauty that I can only describe as a dwarf
horse. Him I gave to old Juan, to his huge delight.

When we had finished our work and were about to

leave, the Mexican in charge wanted to come away too, before he lost his scalp, and it was with great difficulty I induced him to stay, and only on the promise to relieve him very shortly.

The Indians of course could have raided the ranch at any time that they pleased, but there were few horses there at that time, and that is why they left it alone. Cattle were of no account in their eyes, but horses they were always keen to steal. We had already bought fifty Spanish mares, at $5 a head, and fifteen " cow " horses at $25 apiece, but these were all on the Medio still, for if they had been left on the Frio unprotected, the Indians would have driven them off directly.

It was now about the end of October, 1861, and General Sibley was organising his Texan Brigade of 3,000 mounted men, or three regiments in all, for his expedition to New Mexico. There it was supposed the Northern forces were weak, and that he would easily overrun the country ; with the result that probably the Far Western States, including Arizona, and even California, might join the Confederacy. It was a foolhardy scheme to send the flower of our Texan youth on a march like this of 800 miles, into a country where they had no base of operations and could get no reinforcements, and no help, unless they met with complete success. But our leaders were crazy, I think, in those days, and believed they had the game in their own hands ; so no enterprise was too rash for them to undertake. I saw that gallant force march away, with drums beating and flags flying, and every man, from the General downwards, confident of victory.

Alas ! A few months after, I saw the first detachment of the remnant come straggling back on foot, broken, disorganised, and in an altogether deplorable condition.

The tale of disaster is soon told. The march in the fall rains was a most arduous one, but the men and horses were of the best, and struggled through it bravely.

General Canby, of the U.S. Army, was in command against Sibley. This officer was, long years after this, prominently engaged in the war with the Sioux Indians, led by their chief Sitting Bill, when that tribe made its last stand for its hunting grounds and its freedom. Sibley was at first successful in several engagements, notably at a place called Val Verde. But his losses were heavy ; California and the rest of the Far West stood firm for the Union, and no reinforcements could reach him. The South, even if the difficulty of distance could have been overcome, could not spare a man. Canby, on the other hand, drew all the troops and supplies he wanted from California, and gradually wore down his opponent.

The remnant of the Texan Brigade, reduced to less than half its original strength, commenced its retreat, harassed throughout the greater part of that weary 800 miles by the victorious enemy. The retreat became a rout, and the brigade ceased to exist as an organised force. It was a heavy blow to Texas, and to the Confederate cause, which could ill afford to lose such men as these.

In the following month of November, Randall still being behindhand with his payments, and we unwilling to hand over without a settlement in full, I went out to the Frio again, to see how my Mexican was getting on. This time I went quite alone, and, taking my best horse, Brownie by name, did the journey in one day. Not a pleasant trip for a lonely man to take. I started just before daybreak, and halting only once at midday, to rest my horse for a brief hour, reached the ranch at sundown. You may be sure I kept a sharp look-out for Indian sign, but saw none, and was unmolested, both going and returning.

I found the vaquéro all right in health, but in a blue funk at being left so long alone in that dangerous spot. By this time the hounds and curs, that had been so threatening at my first visit, had got to know me, and gave me a friendly greeting; and right amongst them, on good terms with all, was a pet deer that Ragsdale had tamed and given me. It would follow me about the place like a dog, and usually slept in the house, though free to wander about wherever it wished. I have always been fond of pet animals—horses, dogs, cats, monkeys, peccaries; even a badger is a friendly beast, as I know from experience, if kindly treated, and all are interesting—some of them very lovable. But of all the hosts of pets I have owned in my long life this deer was one of the most friendly and fearless. Of course, like so many of its kind, it came to a tragic end, and at the hands of my friend Thompson, of all people!

At his first visit to the ranch he saw the poor little fellow browsing quietly in the chaparral near the house, and shot it, for a wild one! It was his ignorance of the ways of the wild creatures that led him to do it; but when he brought it home in triumph, I was so vexed and grieved, and abused him so roundly, that we had a desperate quarrel, and didn't speak for a fortnight, though practically alone at the ranch. At the end of this time I could bear it no longer, and said, "I can stand this no more; either we must make friends, or part—one or the other. I am sorry if I said too much. What do you say?" He grasped my hand, and shook it warmly; and so an end of the foolish quarrel, the only one we ever had.

That night I slept at the ranch on a "cowskin," *i.e.* a skin rough-tanned and stretched on a frame, which makes an excellent couch. For the next two days we hunted the chaparral for hogs, of which Ragsdale said he had about 300, and I came to the conclusion he was about right in his calculations; but most of them were so wild, and could travel so fast, they would have given good sport to a "pig-sticker."

When I got back to the Medio, I found Colonel Sydney

Johnson, with a small detachment, staying at our ranch. He had resigned his commission in the U.S. Army, of which he was a most distinguished officer, and was on his way to Richmond to take up an important command under the Confederacy. He had, as a captain, done good service in the Mexican War, and, next to Colonel Robert Lee, had the highest repute of any officer in the U.S. Army. He was a strikingly handsome man, of splendid physique and most winning manners; in fact he was a Southern gentleman of the best type. Soon after his visit to us he was promoted to the rank of general, and given the command of the trans-Mississippi district. There he did good service, but early in the following year, at the battle of Shiloh, when leading one of his regiments in a charge, he was twice wounded; the second time mortally, and died on the field. The South lost in him one of its best soldiers and bravest men.

Poor fellow! I well remember how we sat and smoked and chatted on the "gallery" at the ranch, after our frugal dinner; and how cheering it was to listen to his sanguine views as to the assured success of the Southern cause. Next morning we drank success to the South; shook hands warmly, and parted, with the mutual hope we might meet again when the troubles were over. The brave man's own troubles were soon over, for within a few months of our parting he was dead on the field of honour, and was spared the bitter grief so many of his comrades endured at the ruin of their country and their cause.

Now at the end of November Randall paid up the balance due, and we handed over the store, ranch, cattle and everything to him, and prepared to move out to the Frio. We already possessed a good wagon, but bought an "ambulance" for extra transport, as there were many impedimenta to cart out to our new diggings. In San Antonio I managed with some difficulty to hire three Mexican vaquéros as permanent cattle-hands, and two of these were blessed with "mugers" and several offspring. The establishment was completed by the hiring of a nigger woman as cook.

Thompson looked after the armament of the garrison, and bought three double-barrelled shotguns, three rifles, and plenty of ammunition, including a good supply of slugs; most useful in case our friends the Comanchés looked us up, which they were pretty sure to do sooner or later. For stores we laid in a good stock of coffee, sugar, flour and bacon; and so, with the wagons well loaded with the Mexican women and children and our and their "plunder," we set out for the Frio two days before Christmas 1861.

It was almost like a patriarchal procession of old, for ahead of the wagons went Thompson, the three vaquéros, and myself on horseback, driving before us the fifty mares and fifteen "cow-horses" for cattle hunting. Our progress with the heavily laden wagons was slow, and it was not till late in the afternoon of Christmas Eve that we reached the ranch. Thompson was delighted with what he saw of the range, though he vowed it smelt of Indians.

By the time we had got the wagons through the chaparral and over the difficult crossing it was nearly dusk, but we soon had our furniture, such as it was, in the house, and settled the Mexicans in their huts or acaldes. Then, in honour of the occasion and for a sort of house-warming feast, I shot a fine fat yearling, which provided a sumptuous dinner for all hands. How those Mexicans did eat! You wouldn't believe that human beings could put away so much solid meat at a sitting, but it wasn't often the poor beggars got beef like that unless they stole it; and in that case there was always the afterthought of the rope to follow if they were found out.

CHAPTER VI

GENERAL HOOD

RAGSDALE, as I said before, had "let his stock go," and there was an immense amount of work to be done in driving and branding calves and yearlings.

On Christmas day no Mexican can be got to work for love or money, so the "fiesta," as they call it, was kept as best we might in that out-of-the-way place; not without memories of other Christmas days, so different from these, and distant friends, and holly-decked churches in far-off England.

My friend Thompson was very reticent about his past, and never spoke of it, at least not till the great parting was nigh at hand, when he told me why he had left his home and friends and come out to the Far West. For him as well as for myself that day was haunted by remembrances, and, though we tried to be cheerful and jolly, I think the gaiety was rather forced, and silence often fell upon us. But work must be done, and it is the best antidote to carking care and haunting regrets. So next day I sallied forth with three Mexicans to drive cattle, and came back with a good bunch. It was that same evening that Thompson shot my pet deer, as previously related.

Early in the following January (1862) we invited three friends from San Antonio to come out and have a week's hunting with us, and had some very good sport, which we all thoroughly enjoyed.

Deer, peccary and turkeys were very abundant, espe-

206

cially the peccary, which were a sure find in the chaparral along the Frio banks ; the only difficulty was to
get them out of the dense covert of thorny bush. This
was four or five miles wide on either side of the river,
and extended for about forty miles along its banks.

All five of us would sally forth, after early coffee,
well mounted and carrying shotguns and six-shooters.
Amongst our miscellaneous collection of dogs were five
well broken to " javalines " or peccary ; a very important
matter, for if your hounds are not used to the ways of
these little pigs, they are apt to get terribly cut up by
their razor-like short tusks. They are generally found,
in the daytime, in the chaparral near the water, in
bunches of four or five, and, when put up by the hounds,
go off at a clinking pace for a short distance, the pack
in full cry after them. Presently, being fat and short
of wind, they set up against a tree or rock, ready to
charge the first comer, be it man, or horse, or dog. They
are absolutely fearless when cornered like this, and
nothing will stop them but death ; so the dogs that
hunt them soon learn by sad experience not to get too
close. I have had dogs that would kill them, but they
were new to the game, and always got badly cut up.

The hounds then being thrown into covert, we rode
along outside, or followed the narrow cattle-paths as
best we might, riding to the music of the pack as fast as
the awful cat-claw thorns would let us. Presently the
sound showed the run was over, and the peccary " set
up," and it was a race who should get up first to shoot
the pig or pigs. Our friends from San Antonio, being
new to the sport, and eager for blood, got terribly torn
by the thorns at first, but soon learned caution. In
this way we often killed half a dozen peccary of a
morning. We never ate the meat, though why I hardly
know, except that no one in Texas did, unless it was the
Mexicans when short of flesh. I have been told since
that peccary hams are considered quite a delicacy in

Central America, but never having tasted them, can't say. The Mexicans generally took the hides off, and they made capital mats and floor-coverings.

To get deer was a more difficult matter in that thick covert, though there were any number of them on the Frio in those days. The usual way was for the guns to take post on the deer-trails leading down to the river, and then to turn every available dog into the chaparral, on the chance that the deer might break for the water and give a shot ; but it was very uncertain work, and one might wait all day without seeing a deer. Another way was to beat the comparatively open brushy glades under the live-oak trees, round the great water-holes or miniature lakes, and in that fashion good sport was often to be had.

For the wild turkeys we used to go down to the river after supper, a little before sundown, and take post near the roosts with guns loaded with buckshot. The Frio in dry weather formed a series of small lakes from one hundred to four hundred yards in length, with subterranean connection between each, and the water was beautifully clear and blue. Round all there were fringes of splendid live-oaks, and there the turkeys came nightly to roost, their favourite spots being clearly to be seen from the " sign " under the trees.

Hiding oneself near the selected roost one could sit and smoke at ease, with the certainty that some old patriarch of a gobbler would presently come along with his harem of perhaps ten or a dozen hens. As the sun dipped below the horizon, and the brief twilight began to fade into darkness, the gobblers commenced to summon their families to bed, and the chaparral soon resounded with their cries. Then, solemnly marching down the path to its own particular roost, would come the procession, in single file, with stately steps. With much flapping of wings, for it is difficult to raise so heavy a body off the ground, the leader flies up into the tree, and his family quickly follow him, one by one. Not till all are settled must you shoot, or the first shot will scare the whole lot away. When all have flown up you can shoot three or four, or more perhaps, without the others moving; only you must be careful not to show yourself. In those days the turkeys didn't seem to know what the report of a gun meant, though they understood well enough that a man was an enemy; now I daresay they are wiser—*i.e.* if there are any left to profit by the experience of their forbears.

Another way to get them wholesale, was to walk down the river, following the cattle or deer trails of a moonlit night, and shoot them off the various roosts you came to. Doing this, I have often shot twenty or more of a night, but that was only when I was sending a wagon into San Antonio and wanted a load for my various friends there, not forgetting that holy man Mr. Asa Minshul, with whom, as I have explained, I was particularly anxious to keep on friendly terms.

By the by, on one of these walking shoots Thompson nearly killed me. He was walking close behind me and, by some carelessness, let off his gun. One of the buck-shots cut my pants and grazed my leg; it was a narrow escape, one of the narrowest of the many I have had. "Now, old fellow," I said, "it's my turn, so you walk ahead, and let me have the next shot."

As the result of the shoot, our friends carried away with them, in my wagon, two deer and forty turkeys, and were mightily pleased with their sport.

On the prairie there were many coyotés, or prairie wolves, and "lobos," as the Mexicans called them; the big grey variety of the same species. At that time neither of them afforded us any sport, for our hounds were not fast enough to run them with any chance of a kill. Later on we got a small pack, specially for the purpose, and had some rare good fun with them.

The coyoté is the most artful, sneaking, thieving

brute in creation, and makes himself a great nuisance on the ranches. How wonderfully Mark Twain has described him, in his celebrated monograph! The beast is all Mark says, and a little more; for though he lives chiefly on carrion and any unconsidered trifle he can steal, he is not above helping himself to a sick calf, if he can catch it away from the cow, and chickens he is death on! And what a pace the gaunt, mangy-looking " varmint " can travel! Since my Texan days I have seen many a good fox bustled along by a fast pack of hounds, but a coyoté, I believe, would have the legs of the fastest and outlast the staunchest.

The " lobos " were thundering great brutes and did us a lot of damage, especially in calving time, when they killed many calves. They couldn't do much with the cattle, or bunches of mares and horses, for these, when attacked, formed square to receive the enemy; the former with their heads, and the latter with their heels, outwards. But they snapped many a yearling and young thing, if they could catch them away from a herd. We rid ourselves, as much as we could, of these pests with poison, sticking a good dose of strychnine into any dead beast found on the range, or into offal laid for the purpose. But I am bound to confess that we were more successful in killing the lobos in this way than the coyotés; for the latter were so artful, and so keen of scent, it was very hard to catch them.

For the first two months of the following year, Thompson, the Mexicans, and I were on horseback every day, and all day, gathering cows and calves in the home range and making ourselves thoroughly acquainted with it, so that we might know where to find the cattle when wanted; for these have their different feeding grounds, scattered far and wide over the range.

There were plenty of rumours of Indians on the move, which caused us some uneasiness, and much trouble, for we had to corral the horses every night. Early in

February a big band of them passed within a couple of miles of the ranch, as we saw from their trail. They killed half a dozen or so of our cattle, but didn't molest us further, possibly because they thought we were too strong and well armed. Passing us by for that, or some other good reason, they went on to the head of the Hondo River, about twenty-five miles from us, and there killed, scalped, and mutilated a settler named Reeders and his two sons. These poor fellows had, in a measure, courted their fate by doing a deed which, though it was highly applauded all along the frontier, where Indians were " pison," was a very brutal and barbarous one, worthy only of the Comanchés themselves.

Six months before they met their fate, the Reeders, who were old and experienced frontiersmen, having seen Indian sign about their ranch, penned their horses one night, and lay up, armed with their rifles and six-shooters, in the corral. Sure enough, an hour or two before dawn a big bunch of Indians rode up, threw down the corral bars, and began to drive out the horses. The Reeders let drive into the thick of the Comanchés, but in the darkness couldn't aim, and only killed two of them. The rest bolted, leaving their dead behind them, which shows they were properly scared by the unexpected attack.

So far so good ; but the Reeders, not content with having killed two of the thieves, proceeded next day to flay them. Then they stretched, dried, and rough-tanned the skins for saddle-tree covers, razor-strops, belts, etc. This was soon " orated round " on the frontier, and won the perpetrators much kudos amongst the ranchers. But the wiser, cooler ones shook their heads ; the Comanchés, they knew, would be revenged for this insult to their dead, and the Reeders had better look out, or they would get them to a certainty.

They were right, for in less than six months the Indians followed them from the ranch, when they went cow-hunting, and caught them unawares, no one knows how. When they didn't come back, search was made the following day by their nearest neighbour, and the poor mutilated bodies found not far away. The poor widow, robbed in one day of her husband and her sons, all she had in the world, was broken-hearted, and died not long afterwards in San Antonio.

On this same raid the Comanchés attacked a ranch near Dhannis, in the same country, not far from Fort Inge, formerly held in some force by the U.S. troops, to keep down the Indians and protect the frontier. The men, as the Indians probably knew, were away cow-hunting, so they killed, and scalped, the mother and her two little girls, three and five years old. At that ranch alone they got over one hundred horses, and crossed the Rio Grandé unmolested. There were no troops to follow them, and the settlements were so sparsely scattered in that region, it was hopeless to organise a scout for pursuit ; indeed, before the news reached us, they must have been close to the Mexican border.

Talking of Forte Inge reminds me that I forgot to mention that I met there, when Thompson and I were prospecting the previous year, a U.S. officer who, at the time I am now writing of, had made himself one of the most brilliant reputations in the Confederate service. I refer to General Hood, a man of indomitable courage, whose fiery spirit and power of leadership prompted his men to such deeds of valour as all the world wondered at. His story, I suppose, is all but forgotten now, for things move so rapidly in these times, and there are so many fresh excitements, that the great and heroic struggle of the Confederacy itself is almost like a half-remembered dream, even to those who took part in it. His name, however, should never die, but live for all time on the scroll of deeds of honour.

I will, as briefly as may be, recount how he, and his Texan Brigade, covered themselves with renown at

Gaines' Mill, in the great fight with McClellan, on the Chickahominy ; but first as to our meeting in the wilds of the Mexican frontier.

He was then about thirty years of age, a simple lieutenant of U.S. cavalry, in command of the post.

Thompson and I pitched camp one evening close to Fort Inge—*i.e.* we had off-saddled our horses and were cooking our supper, when Hood strolled over, probably to see who we were, and what we were doing.   I remember now what a splendid man he was to look upon, every inch a soldier, and withal most courteous and genial.   I suppose he satisfied himself we were decent men, though I am free to confess our appearance, and get up generally, must have been but a poor recommendation, for we had been looking round for more than a month, without change of raiment.

Be that as it may, after a few minutes' talk he pressed us to come into the fort to sup with him.   " We rough it out here, as you know," he said, " but at any rate, I can do you better than that dried beef you're trying to eat ; so come along, and we'll have a game of cards after supper."   We accepted the cordial invitation willingly enough, and after a supper which was sumptuous to us, fresh from a diet of dried beef, biscuit and coffee, played euchre with him and his officers till midnight.   Then, after a very friendly parting, and refusing an invitation to sleep in the fort, since we must look after our horses, we went back to our blankets and saddle-pillows. Departing at sunrise, we saw no more of our kindly host.

The next time I met Hood was soon after the war, when he had turned his sword, not into a ploughshare, but an office ruler, for he was keeping store in New Orleans.   He was the same genial, pleasant fellow, without side or swagger, and no one would suppose, from talking to him, he had ever done anything out of the common.   I remember his left coat-sleeve was empty, the result of one of the many wounds he received in the gallant charge at Gaines' Mill.

On the morning of June 26, 1862, General Lee commenced his daring attack on the strong position held by the Federals, under General McClellan, on the Chickahominy, near Richmond, the Confederate capital. The Federal general had 120,000 men in line, and General McDowell was hastening to join him with 40,000 more. So there was no time to be lost, for General Lee had only 70,000 under his command.

In that series of combats lasting from June 26 to July 1, and known as " The seven days under Richmond," and in which Lee first revealed himself as a great captain, two incidents stand out with prominence. The first, General James Stuart's daring ride through the Federal lines, with twelve hundred men, when sent to reconnoitre the enemy's position. It was indeed a brilliant feat of arms this young officer (he was only thirty) performed. For three days, from the Thursday morning till the Saturday night, he and his gallant men rode over the enemy's position, and found out his strength and his weakness, with the loss of only one soul, the brave Captain Latarie, shot dead the first day. With this single loss, he contrived to capture many prisoners, horses and mules, and to destroy millions of dollars' worth of stores and provisions.

The second notable incident was Hood's charge with his Texans, on the evening of June 27. By the morning of that day Lee had driven back the Federals from position after position, and McClellan had made up his mind to withdraw his forces to the James River. To enable him to execute this movement it was essential that his right position, where General Fitz John Porter, one of his ablest divisional leaders, commanded, should be held at all hazards. It comprised a range of precipitous wooded heights, at the foot of which ran a boggy creek, beyond which was open ground cumbered by fallen trees.

In the brushwood on the slope lay hidden thousands of sharpshooters, half-way up extended a stong force of infantry, ensconced behind a parapet of trunks of trees, and behind this a second parapet of the same nature, also strongly held. Beyond the top of this well-guarded height, the ground dipped down into a narrow ravine, and on the summit of the further slope was a third line of infantry, and a strong force of artillery.

General A. P. Hill's division had been repulsed from the right of this formidable position, and, to save him from destruction, Lee ordered General Longstreet to make a feigned attack on the left. But to be of any service to Hill, the latter saw he must convert his attack into a real one, which he most gallantly did. With terrible loss he carried all the defences, up to the top of the first height; but his men recoiled from the concentrated infantry and artillery fire poured on them from across the ravine, and they could make no progress.

It was at this juncture that Hood and his Texan Brigade were called upon for the desperate duty of capturing this stronghold. Of the four regiments composing it, three had been almost wholly cut up by the Federal fire, and one remained in reserve, five hundred strong. It was the 4th Texas Infantry, and at that moment was lying on the ground below the crest of the slope, for shelter from the withering fire.

Hood spoke a few words to them as they lay, telling them what they had to do, and that he knew they were the boys to do it. Then he ordered them to fix bayonets. Up they rose at his command, and over the top of the rise and into the ravine they went, that gallant five hundred, with a cheer that was heard above the din of battle. The colonel fell immediately; but Hood was leading his boys, and they would follow to the death.

Through the extended ranks of these heroes passed the broken lines of the Third Brigade, recoiling from the awful fire from that fatal palisade; but, nothing daunted, they still held on to what seemed certain destruction. The hail of bullets thinned their ranks—Hood himself was wounded twice, one shot breaking his left arm—but on they went without pause, over the dead and dying.

Now the remnant of that wonderful five hundred—I don't know how many there were, but not much more than half—were close to the rampart. Their comrades watched with bated breath ; was it possible they could storm it ? To such men, and to such a leader, all things were possible ; but the Federals didn't wait to see, for, terrified at the fierce attack, they rose up and ran. Helter-skelter after them clambered Hood and his men. The work was won, and the Confederate flag floated over it, amidst the frantic cheers of the onlookers.

I don't think our own British annals contain a more gallant deed than this, and it warms my heart now to remember that I have met the man who did it.

CHAPTER VII

THE HORSE-STEALERS

ALL that spring of 1862 work on the range was almost incessant, for there was a very good " crop " of calves. We were generally in the saddle soon after daybreak, and by midday would drive home from ten to twenty cows, with their calves at foot. Then, after a short dinner-hour, out again on fresh horses, returning before sun-down with yet another bunch. This hunting up of cows and calves sounds, I daresay, easy enough work, but on a big cattle-ranch like ours, where the cattle ranged over miles of country, it was no child's play. For the cows, half wild as they were, with the instinct of their race hid their calves in the chaparral, where it was hard to find them. But they had to be found, for success in ranching depends on the careful and thorough manner in which this calf-hunting is done. If you don't look sharply after them, the half of your " crop " will be lost, killed by " lobos " or coyotés, or eaten up alive by maggots.

The last were, I think, the most destructive of all our enemies, for the blow-flies were more numerous and active than any one in this country would credit. Once the brutes had found, or established, a raw spot, be it ever so small, on a calf, or even on a cow or steer, it was all up with them if not promptly seen to and dressed with sheep-dip.

So we worked hard, but with great success, for that spring and early summer we branded more than a thousand calves and young things.

The range was unequalled by any I have ever seen,

and the prospect of success seemed assured ; the Indians were the only drawback to this rancher's paradise, and even these one soon ceased to worry about, though of course proper precautions, such as corralling the horses at night, were always taken. There was certainly a fortune in the ranch, with anything like good luck ; for if the stock was well looked after we should be the owners, in a few years' time, of at least ten thousand cattle, and these some of the finest in all the States ! And yet I was foolish enough to throw away this splendid chance because I must needs meddle in the quarrel between the North and South, and go a-soldiering with the latter !

About once a month, at this period, I rode into San Antonio, seventy miles of rather risky riding, to get the news of the war ; for on the Frio we heard nothing, and rarely saw a white man, so far were we from the beaten track. The ups and downs of the great struggle the Confederacy carried on so bravely, against such fearful odds, were most exciting ; and more and more, resist it as I might, I felt drawn to take my part in it. And yet for a brief period longer I managed to keep away from it ; and mainly because of the necessity of protecting our property from the marauding Indians.

On one of these trips I hired three more Mexican vaquéros to help in the cattle-driving, making, with those we already had, eight in all ; and not too many for all the work to be done.

We managed the calves as follows : When driven home we penned them in one or other of the corrals set apart for them, and then drove the cows out ; no easy matter sometimes. Night and morning the cows returned to suckle the youngsters, and then were turned out again. It was quite a sight to see hundreds of these anxious mothers waiting round the corrals to be let in. And the row they made with their lowing was astonishing ! But at night the din was even greater ; for to the lowing of the cows was added the bellowing of the bulls and

A CATTLE CORRAL

the squealing of the stallions. Round the corrals were placed big logs of wood, in which holes were bored with a 2-inch auger to hold salt for the stock to lick. To these came the bulls with their cows, and the stallions with their " mañadas " of mares, but always at night ; and the noise of their battles, the howling of the great " lobos" and the barking of the coyotés, that followed the stock for a chance victim, answered vociferously by all our dogs, made night hideous indeed ! But a long day in the saddle was an excellent soporific and, after a bit, one could generally contrive to sleep through it all.

Whilst cattle-driving we often came across big bunches of mustangs, but seldom went after them, for unless you have a very strong party and the best of horses, it is very difficult to run them down. Though the hardest, toughest little brutes in the world, they are very troublesome to "gentle," and never are what one would call comfortable mounts ; in fact they are more bother than they are worth.

But on one of our drives on the Leona River, one of the Mexicans sighted afar off a big bunch that had some stray horses running wild with it. So, with two of my best mounted men, I started to run the mustangs in the hope of cutting out the horses. For five good miles we galloped as hard as we could go, and then one of the " strays," which turned out to be a Spanish mare in foal, tailed off. Leaving one vaquéro behind to rope her, I went on after the bunch with the other, and eventually cut out both the other horses and roped them too. I was short of " cow-horses," so this was a stroke of luck ; and I returned to the ranch, after a week's camping out, in high feather, with my three horses and 150 head of cattle. These " strays " had Mexican brands on them, so they had come from over the river, or I should have had to hand them over to their owners.

On another occasion that same spring, low down on the Frio, my Mexicans and I came on a large bunch of mustangs, with many foals in it. Having no cattle under herd at the time, I determined to run it, and cut out some of the youngsters. The mustangs were quite a mile ahead of us, and the moment they sighted us went off at a tremendous pace. I knew the foals couldn't stand that long, so pressed on after the bunch as hard as I could. One by one the little fellows dropped out till, after we had run the mañada for about eight or nine miles, we had left a good many foals behind us. Then, as it was getting dusk, we took the back trail, and picked up six of the youngsters without much trouble; for their friends and maternal relatives having long since disappeared, they seemed only too glad to follow our horses.

Next day I got them home to the ranch and shut them in a calf-pen, where they very soon learned to drink cows' milk out of buckets, and throve mightily thereon. In a short time they were the cheekiest, most mischievous, and most amusing party on the ranch. Five of them lived to make very good cow-horses; for they could carry a Mexican cow-hunting all day, and every day, though only little rats of things to look at, not more than about twelve hands high.

About this time a young fellow named Jack Vinton came out to us from San Antonio, where he was loafing about and doing no good. His father, Colonel Vinton, was a West Point man, and had been in command of the U.S. troops in Texas prior to General Twig of surrender fame. The youngster was rather a lively youth; he was only nineteen, and had, I fancy, given his father some trouble. The Colonel, with whom I was very friendly, therefore asked me to give an eye to him, when he himself left San Antonio for the North, on the eve of the outbreak of the war. In that, being a Northern man, he served on the Federal side with some distinction, rising, if I remember right, to be Adjutant-General to the Forces. So Master Jack came out to us, and made himself useful on the ranch, which was the very place for him ; for he was as hard as nails, a first-rate cowboy, and not afraid of Indians, or anything else.

Just then we were kept pretty well on the *qui vive* by these gentry, plenty of their sign being seen about the range, and Jack was a very desirable addition to our little party. We had by this time a strong party of " Greasers," but these Mexicans are no good for Indian fighting. If they are cornered and can't get away, they will fight ; but if there is a chance to run, they take it like a shot.

As a rule, the Comanchés never *showed* themselves near the ranches in early spring ; but as the season advanced, and the leaves thickened, they began to get to work. Lying hidden in the dense chaparral, in parties of twos and threes, they gradually collected together what horses they could pick up on the ranges. During that time one might pass close to them and, though quite alone, not be attacked. But when they had got together a good lot of horses, they were ready for serious business, and started in to kill and scalp all they could come across ; the worst time being usually before the full of the moon.

I could fill many pages with accounts of their murderous doings, for in those days they had the whole frontier of three or four hundred miles at their mercy But it would only weary the reader with the dull monotony of bloodshed : here and there solitary cow-hunters killed, scalped, and mutilated, or defenceless women and children massacred in some lonely ranch. Indeed, for the time being, the wretches had things pretty much their own way ; but by and by it was our turn, and I shall be able to tell how we now and then took it out of our friends the Comanchés and the Lepans.

At this time too we were a good deal bothered by the frontier Mexicans from the State of Nuevo Leon, who crossed the Rio Grandé into Texas to steal horses. As most of these gentry had been vaquéros on the cattle-ranches, they knew the country thoroughly, and where to lay their hands on what they wanted, so that it was most difficult to catch them, and in most cases they got clear off with their plunder. When caught, they of course " looked up " the nearest convenient tree.

Here is a story of their doings, and of the summary justice meted out to a small party of these thieves we by good luck managed to catch.

It was in the month of May that one of our Mexicans told me a party of his compatriots had come in to steal my horses, and those on a big ranch on the Hondo, some thirty miles away, belonging to Pete Burleson. I promptly sent a note to Burleson, to let him know what was up, and to ask him to keep a look-out for any sign of the thieving Mexicans, so that we might know where they were making for, if they had been about his place. That same night my Mexican brought a note from Pete, saying he had found " sign " of a bunch of horses being fresh driven for the Rio Grandé, and that the trail pointed for the San Felipé crossing ; that he, with three or four more, would meet me next day on the Carisa Creek, near the " old Presidio crossing," where he would camp.

By daybreak next morning Jack Vinton, two of my best Mexicans, and I started and, picking up two fellows, named Bennett and English, on the Leona, made Burleson's camp on the Carisa before sundown. Our two parties made up eleven, all told. As soon as it was light enough next morning, we saddled up and, with Jack Bennett, a capital trailer, leading, soon hit the trail, which, sure enough as Pete had surmised, led towards the San Felipé crossing. There was no time to be lost, if we were not to have our trouble for nothing, and we " loped " on it as fast as we could go. Bennett declared the trail was so fresh the thieves *couldn't* be far ahead of us ; but on we went, mile after mile, and still they were in front of us.

We had ridden a good thirty miles, and twilight was

deepening into dusk when, topping a ridge on the prairie, we came right on our quarry, camped in a " mott " near a water-hole about four miles only from the river. One of the thieves was mounted, and was herding the stolen horses ; the rest had off-saddled and, believing themselves quite secure from pursuit, were cooking supper. The mounted man bolted the moment he caught sight of us, and got clear off, though two of our boys hunted him right up to the river's bank. The others—there were four of them—were surrounded in the " mott " before they knew what was up, and they at once surrendered, rather than be shot there and then.

Pinioning them securely, we set a guard over them, and then gathered the stolen horses, twenty in number, six of which bore my own brand. As it was now nearly dark, my Mexicans were set to herd the horses, whilst we cooked supper and fixed camp. The fate of the prisoners was reserved till next morning, when it would be decided, as usual, by the vote of the majority of the party. This voting, I may say, was a mere formality, for in such a flagrant case as this, hanging was inevitable.

After breakfast the next morning we stepped aside a few paces from the camp, and Pete Burleson, as the senior present, put the question to each individual. " What shall we do with the prisoners ? " Now, no doubt, these thieves deserved hanging, if horse-thieves were ever to be hanged ; for all of them had recently been employed on the ranches they had robbed, except mine ; but there was always something horribly cold-blooded and cruel to my mind in this hanging, and I am glad to think that I never did vote for that punishment, in all my Western experiences. In this case I voted for flogging the prisoners, and turning them loose on the prairie, and my Mexicans voted with me. But of course we were in a minority of three, and the majority of eight went for hanging.

When told the decision, the miserable wretches took it

quite calmly, all but one, Carildo by name, and he had
served one of our party, Jack Bowles, as vaquéro. He had
evidently no hope of mercy, and did not beg for life,
only that his old master would shoot him, and so save
him from hanging. So he was shot, and the other
three were hanged on live-oak trees hard by the camp ;
and then we set off home with the recovered horses,
most of us in high spirits at our successful catch. It
was necessary to teach these " Greasers " that the
ways of horse-thieves are hard, but I confess the live-
oaks, and their horrible dangling burdens, haunted me,
so that I felt sorry I had been at the catching of them ;
which was perhaps foolish, not to say weak.

At the end of this month of May 1862, two of my
neighbour ranchers, Louis Oje and Mont Woodward,
who had big cattle-ranches on the frontier, about twenty-
five to thirty miles away from us, made up a party,
with myself, to hunt stray cattle in the forks of the
Nueces. We took eight vaquéros and plenty of spare
horses, and, making our headquarters in a dilapidated
mustanger's hut, with corrals near by, handy for penning
the cattle, spent a week there, doing some good driving.
At night we sat round the camp fire smoking and yarning,
but most of our talk was of the war, and of the terrible
hardships of the Confederate troops, especially under
Stonewall Jackson.

We were all experienced frontiersmen, owning big
ranches on the borders of the Indian country, and were
inured to hard knocks and a rough life. It might be
thought we had enough to do to hold our own against
the Comanchés and Lepans, who would give us as much
fighting as we could want, and who would probably
harry our stock if we went off to the war. These con-
siderations, in our earlier talks, made us reluctantly
agree that we *could* not leave, at any rate not till things
were more settled on the frontier ; though how they
could ever be so, whilst the war lasted, was difficult to

see. But still, night after night we went back to the same subject, for our heads were full of it, and we could talk of nothing else.

At that time McClellan was invading Virginia, by way of the peninsula, and threatening Richmond, the capital of the State and of the Confederacy. The Federal commander was said to have more than 150,000 men under him in the vicinity of our capital ; whilst McDowell Fremont, Franklin, and other division leaders of the North were hastening to reinforce him with 60,000 or 70,000 more. To oppose this terrible array of armies, thoroughly equipped and armed, with all the resources of the Northern States behind them, Generals Sidney Johnston, Lee, and Jackson had no more than 70,000 ill-clad, half-starved men. A ragged crew to look upon, these ; but for all that the best fighting men of the South, and, under such leaders as Lee and Stonewall Jackson, all but invincible. The tale of their doings set our hearts on fire, for we were all ardent Southerners, and it was a tale to inflame the coldest blood. Yet we *couldn't* go and do our share, and take our part for the cause we believed in, and which so sorely needed every man who could carry a rifle. We had made up our minds, and so an end of it. This lasted for a day or two, and talk languished over the camp fire, till we fell moody and silent. The last night had come, our trip was over, and the next day we should drive our captured cattle home to our ranches, brand calves, fight Indians, hunt horse-stealing Mexicans, and leave our friends and foes to battle it out in Virginia. It seemed a tame conclusion to arrive at. But what would you ? We couldn't help it.

The last pipe was smoked for the night, and the blankets were spread. We were going to turn in, when Mont Woodward, who hadn't spoken a word for an hour, rose, stretched himself on his long legs, and opened his mouth to some purpose. " Blame me, boys, I can't stand to think of it any more. The cattle may go to

15

h——, or the cussed Injuns may eat 'em for all I care.
I'm goin' to 'list right off. Soon's these beef are at the
ranch, I make tracks for San Antonio right away."

Mont had solved the problem for us. Louis and I
jumped to our feet together. "We'll go too, Mont,"
we said in one breath. And that is how I became a
Confederate soldier.

When I told Thompson my resolve, he tried hard to
dissuade me from it ; but seeing my mind was made up,
said he would do his best in my absence, if go I must.
He was getting to be quite the vaquéro himself, and,
having young Vinton, with a good lot of Mexicans, to
help him, I felt fairly easy in my mind at leaving him.

As to the Indians, I knew the old fellow wouldn't run
any unnecessary risks, and wouldn't go far from the
ranch by himself.

So in the last days of May I set off for San Antonio,
where I was to meet Ojé and Woodward, for we had
made up our minds to enlist in the same corps and serve
together.   Sure enough they rode in together, the same
evening of my arrival. We learned that a man named
Duff, of the firm of Duff & McCarthy, contractors and
merchants, was raising a company of Partisan Rangers for
the service, and that, we thought, was just the corps for us.

The partners were both well known to me, for they were
my agents and " merchants," through whom I transacted
all my business. So next morning we three walked over
to their office and I, being a valued client, was promptly
ushered into the sanctum. When I told my errand, and
that I had brought two more recruits of just the sort to
suit him, Duff said he would be very glad to have us,
for he wanted men badly, if we had made up our minds ;
though, if he were in our position, with our property
and cattle on that dangerous frontier, it would take
a good deal to induce him to enlist. The end of it was
we were sworn in there and then, and became Partisan
Rangers in Duff's company.

BOOK IV

IN THE CONFEDERATE SERVICE

CHAPTER I

VERY pleased was I that, at last, I was enlisted to fight
under the banner of the Confederacy, and my one desire
was to go to the front, where, in Virginia, Lee and Stonewall Jackson and the rest of our gallant leaders, were
fighting their heroic battles against such desperate odds.

I make no boast of this. Why should I ? I enlisted
of my own free will, and against my own interests,
which should have led me to stay at home to protect my
property ; and my object was to strike a blow for the
noble cause I had at heart. As to that cause, I did
not then doubt that it was a sacred one, and that the
Southern States were justified in resisting to the death
the oppression of the North. But as to the representa-
tives of that noble cause in Texas—the local nobodies
who ruled the roast, and exploited us for their own base
and selfish ends—I was very speedily disillusioned.

In times of convulsion and strife, great leaders, of
the purest patriotism, are thrown up to guide and direct
affairs at the centre of the movement, if there is any
vitality in it, any great principle for which a nation is
struggling. But in the outlying districts, the extre-
mities of the body politic, the pulse of patriotism seems
to beat but feebly. There the scum of the population
rises to the surface, and there corruption and self-
seeking are rife.

This generalisation may appear a sweeping one ; but
I think it is borne out by history, to take only what
happened in the Franco-German War, our War of

Secession, and the late Boer War. At any rate it was absolutely true as regards Texas, and the outlaying States of the Confederacy. For there loud-tongued local nobodies talked themselves into power and position, and used them to rob their suffering country, and to defraud the soldiers fighting her battles. And of all these harpies, none were worse than my friend, and immediate commanding officer, Captain Dunn—that is, be it understood, in his own small way. His opportunities for peculation were never very great, but such as they were he, I am bound to say, made the most of them.

Instead of going to the front, I was kept hanging about in Texas month after month, sent here and there to arrest supposed Unionists, or to hunt down imaginary express riders carrying mails which only existed in the fuddled brains of our leaders—fools' errands, on which I and my comrades rode many and many a weary mile, knowing only too well the real nature of them. And all this time I was in the toils of this villain Dunn, and couldn't escape by any honourable road, for I had enlisted for three years, or for the war. I could have got away by malingering, as many men did, and making it worth our Captain's while to connive at it, but this I could not do. So I served on under him, and found him to be not only the scheming rascal so many were, but as cowardly, cold-blooded a murderer as I had ever met even in the roaring days of the Kansas " War."

I don't purpose to tell in detail the story of my service in the State with the Partizan Rangers ; that would be wearisome and monotonous. But a few incidents must be given, to bear out what I have said ; and one in particular, at the remembrance of which I shudder still, shall be described at some length, shameful as it is.

Now to my story.

Directly we three were sworn in we were sent to join our camp about two miles out of San Antonio, where our

THE AUTHOR IN RANGER UNIFORM
Photographed at San Antonio, 1863

p. 230

horses were valued by the Commandant, and paid for in Confederate notes. For already, even at this period of the war, there was no cash in the country ; everything was paid in notes, at an ever-increasing discount. Even these notes, after a time, became scarce, and then every one—merchants, storekeepers, down to the very barbers—issued promissory notes of their own, wherewith to pay their debts. Perhaps not quite a " new way to pay old debts," but a very bad one, for it led, naturally enough, to any amount of fraud and swindling, not to mention forgery.

For ten days we were kept hard at work drilling, but unfortunately under instructors who knew but little more of the mysteries of the science than we did ourselves ; so I fear we were not very proficient at the end of that brief period. For all that we were a useful body of irregular cavalry, for the most part hardbitten frontiersmen who would give a good account of themselves in any fighting for which they were adapted. All the more shame to waste their services, fooling about in Texas, as the authorities did. At the end of this time I was sent off with two others, at a moment's notice, in pursuit of a man supposed to be carrying despatches from some of the disaffected Texans, into Mexico. Some one dreamed this phantom express had passed through Castroville on his way to the frontier, and we were to catch him somewhere before he got to the Rio Grandé.

That day we rode fifty miles, neither at Castroville, nor at any of the neighbouring ranches, getting any tidings of the fugitive. All next day we pursued our imaginary quest, with the same result : no one knew, no one had heard of such a man as we were after. So the third day we returned to Castroville and, on the evening of the fourth, to San Antonio, where we learned that our company had that morning marched for Friedricksburg, a town some eighty miles to the north, there to proclaim martial law in that county.

Two hours we rested, and then set off to overtake the
company : rode on till 1 a.m., then off-saddled and lay
down on our blankets for a couple of hours' sleep. Starting again at 3 a.m. we came up with the company just
as it was breaking camp for the second day's march.
That night we camped within eighteen miles of Friedricksburg ; and I confess I was fairly done up, for I had
been in the saddle for best part of five days and nights.

Friedricksburg was a town of about 800 inhabitants,
almost all of them Germans, and Unionists to a man.
The object of our expedition was to compel these people
to take the oath of allegiance to the Confederate Government, which most of them did, though some cleared out
and took to the mountains rather than perjure themselves.

After three days' halt in this town forty of us, of whom
I was one, were detailed to march to camp Verdé, forty
miles distant, to overawe, or convert into Southerners,
more Germans of Northern proclivities.

From this camp two Rangers and myself were sent
out to arrest about a dozen supposed disloyalists, in
various parts of Medina County. Two days we were on
this hateful duty, during which we arrested about ten
unfortunate wretches and took them into San Antonio,
where the rest of our party had already arrived.

Three days we rested there, and then set off to rejoin
the company, which presently we found had marched
away from Friedricksburg and was meandering about
the State, doing goodness knows what—certainly no
earthly good. We found it at a place called Blanco,
whence we all marched back to San Antonio and went
into camp again, after three weeks' absence on this war-
like expedition, during which all we had done was to
bully a few inoffensive Germans.

Next, on June 26, five of us were started off to
catch seven armed niggers, supposed to be driving stolen
horses into Mexico, and who had last been seen about

twenty-five miles from camp. I knew the thing was a humbug, but orders had to be obeyed. Three days we followed that will-o'-the-wisp, and then discovered the seven niggers had dwindled to two, and they were driving their master's horses !

In the early days of July a man came into camp and reported he had seen tracks of some shod mules near the Frio River, leading in the direction of the Rio Grandé, and that he had been told by some old donkey, on a ranch near by, that he often saw tracks he couldn't account for. Our sapient commandant at once jumped to the conclusion that secret communication, and of course treasonable, was going on with Mexico. I told him the Presidio road, to which the tracks pointed, was the last one a spy would use ; but he wouldn't listen, and five of us, including myself, were dispatched at a moment's notice on another fool's errand. Eight days' hard riding we had on this little trip, in pouring rain most of the time, during which we covered some two hundred miles—of course, all for naught ! The night we returned to camp, pretty well done up, and our horses dead beaten, we were warned to be in readiness for a review of all the troops in camp by General Herbert, in command of the district, who was to inspect us next day.

At 4 p.m. then we were all formed up in the Alamo Plaza in San Antonio, the force comprising four infantry companies and two of Partizan Rangers. The infantry were rather a mixed-looking lot, dressed in all sorts and varieties of uniforms, or none at all. The Rangers, though in much the same plight as to uniforms, were really a fine, soldierly lot of men, for the most part mounted on good horses. There were some queer specimens of humanity on parade that day, but the queerest of all was our own Commander, who on foot resembled a bullfrog, and on horseback Sancho Panza.

We formed up in double line, cavalry in front, and in the middle of the Plaza a wheezy civilian brass band discoursed such music as it could. Then presently appeared our gallant General, surrounded by a heterogeneous staff, as ignorant and pretentious as himself, and followed by a small boy on a diminutive cow-pony, who acted as his orderly. The chief duty of the staff, aided by the small boy, seemed to be to keep back a crowd of about three hundred people, who lined the square and wanted to fraternise with their friends in the ranks whilst the performance was going on! This was soon over, for when the General had ridden down the ranks, looking as wise as he knew how, we marched past him once, with some difficulty, and then were dismissed. The whole thing was a farce, and I was thoroughly disgusted with the humbug of it; for the so-called General knew no more about soldiering than his boy orderly, and indeed was a storekeeper who probably had never seen a shot fired in anger in his life, but had been promoted by some back-door influence.

At this time the remnants of Sibley's Texan Brigade began to straggle back from New Mexico in woful plight. It was in the end of October in the previous year that it had marched out, three thousand strong, the flower of Texan youth, with high hopes of victory; and now it was a broken, disorganised rabble, ragged and half starved. The horses had nearly all died, and such of the men as returned had tramped hundreds of miles with scarce a whole boot amongst them. The whole business had been shamefully mismanaged by General Sibley, who was absolutely incompetent, and yet was entrusted with a command like this!

Perhaps the most astonishing thing in the whole affair was that Sibley was not brought to a court-martial, but, on the contrary, was promoted, and held in high honour by the rascals who ruled us in Texas.

Small wonder that the Confederate cause fared so ill in the Southern and Western States, with such people at its head !

On July 19 the two companies of Partizan Rangers, our own under Dunn and the other under Captain Freer, marched out once more for Friedricksburg, in the vicinity of which it was reported that 1,500 " Bushwhackers," mostly Germans, had taken to the mountains, and were plundering and burning the ranches of the Southern loyalists. Furthermore, they were said to be well armed, and intended fighting their way northwards to join the Federal forces. Those who, like myself, knew the country and the people, didn't believe one-tenth part of this yarn, but our leaders swallowed it whole, or professed to, and made great preparations to put down this formidable insurrection.

Amongst other steps to this end, our redoubtable Captain Dunn was appointed Provost-Marshal, with full powers to deal with the rebels. These, the sequel will show, he exercised to their fullest extent, committing atrocities that even his superiors in San Antonio would not have sanctioned.

We marched by easy stages to Friedricksburg, and there found most of the inhabitants remaining quietly in their homes, though a certain number of misguided men had taken to the mountains, *en route* to join one of the Federal armies. Their numbers were variously estimated, but, as far as I could make out, they did not exceed a couple of hundred.

The morning after our arrival we marched out fifteen miles to the west of the town and pitched camp on a stream called the Pedernalio, with the intention of remaining there about six weeks. Here Captain Dunn issued his proclamation announcing his appointment as Provost-Marshal, and giving the inhabitants three days to come in and take the oath of allegiance to the Confederacy ; threatening to treat all those who failed to do so as traitors, who would be dealt with summarily at the discretion of the officer commanding.

Meanwhile we remained in camp enjoying the rest and the beautiful scenery. The spot we had chosen was an ideal one : a gentle slope, dotted with majestic live-oak trees, and at the foot a clear running stream of coolest water, abounding in fish. Under a great rock, half-way up the slope, gushed forth a spring of delicious water, which went singing on its downward course to the river. From the summit of the rising ground the eye could range, in that clear atmosphere, over miles and miles of rolling prairie, green with lush grass after the rains, and dotted with clumps of timber, like some vast park in the old country ; a veritable paradise of Nature's own making, " where only man was vile "—and pretty vile too some of us were ! Mightily we enjoyed ourselves for a time, for the weather was beautiful, and fish and game of all sorts abundant.

Presently, however, sinister rumours as to Dunn's intentions began to spread, and it was said, amongst other things, that he had given certain of his followers to understand that he wanted no prisoners brought into camp. The majority of the men, especially those who were Southern born, were utterly opposed to such deeds ; and many of us, myself amongst the number, openly declared we would do all in our power to put a stop to them. But amongst the command there were many " whitewashed " Yankees, and even, I am ashamed to say, some Scotsmen, who were ready tools for Dunn's infamies, and believed in converting Union men to the true faith by means of the halter.

I soon noticed that neither I, nor any of those who thought with me, were sent out on scout. It was very suspicious, as presently many parties were detailed to scour the country who rarely, if ever, brought in any prisoners, and were very reticent about their doings. Amongst these, two parties of twenty-five each were sent out with wagons to bring in from the scattered ranches the wives and children of those who had taken to the mountains, and, I fear, to harry their homes. In four days they returned with the wagons full of prisoners— four or five men, and eight women with their little ones. The latter were sent on to Friedricksburg, and the former confined in the guard tent.

It was a pitiable sight to see all these poor folks stripped of their property, such as it was, earned by hard toil and exposure on a dangerous frontier ; and I could not but contrast their treatment with that of well-known Abolitionists in San Antonio, who, because they were wealthy, and made friends of the mammon of unrighteousness, were not only unmolested but specially favoured in all sorts of ways. Many of these were German Jews, who did nothing for the South, but monopolised trade, and got all the contracts for supplies given them by the military authorities, with whom they shared the plunder of the unfortunate soldiers.

These prisoners, I afterwards learned, had been informed against by a Dutch tavern-keeper in Friedricksburg who was often out in camp drinking with Dunn, and who had private spites against most of them, which he took good care to pay off.

I forgot to mention that very few of the outlying settlers came in to take the oath before the expiration of the three days ; probably because they were more occupied with procuring a living, and protecting their families from Indian raids, than with politics. Possibly, too, many of them never heard of Dunn and his proclamation until they were arrested.

The day after the return of the wagons, one hundred of us, of whom twenty belonged to my company, were warned to prepare seven days' rations and to go on a scout into the mountains to find and attack the Bushwhackers' camp. One of the prisoners, an old soldier, and a friend of Dunn's, had been released, and he was to act as our guide and betray his friends, if possible, into our hands.

We all set off in high spirits, for we had soon tired of inaction, and here was a chance of a fight against men who really were in arms against our country, and were well armed too. This, at any rate, was better work than harrying harmless, defenceless people, whose only desire was to be let alone to earn their bread in peace.

The first day's ride took us over a rather rough prairie country, in which we passed several small homesteads, ruined and deserted. At sundown we reached what had been a well-cultivated little farm, situated in a pretty, well-watered valley. The owner, a Northern man named Henderson, had gone to the mountains, but his wife, also from the North, had been brought into camp with her numerous children. I had felt very sorry for her then, for she bore her misfortunes with a quiet dignity that was very touching ; but when I saw her desolated home, and how, in that out-of-the-way place, they had made so prosperous a little settlement, all now wasted and destroyed, it was most grievous.

They had fenced and cultivated about twenty acres of good land on the side of the valley, cleverly irrigated by the stream running through it. Now the crops were trampled and destroyed, and not a living thing was to be seen on the place ; even the bee-hives in front of the comfortable log house were overturned and empty. The poor little furniture in the living-room, and the loom in the kitchen, had been smashed ; and all this had been done by some of our marauding parties by our Captain's orders. It made one utterly ashamed to be serving with such men ; but there was no help for it now !

The following day we struck the Guadaloupé River, and, travelling up its course, soon passed beyond the region of settlements. The stream itself was most beautiful, running clear and strong over a rocky bottom and between high cliffs crowned with giant cypress-trees. Here and there it would open out into cool, shady pools, just deep enough for a delightful swim. By one such as this we made our noonday halt, and soon were cooling our fevered skins in such a bath as made full amends for the burning heat of the morning's ride. Then on again, still following the river, over ground rising more and more, and growing more difficult for the wagon to follow us over.

The next day we left the main stream of the Guadaloupé and struck across to its southern branch. There, about midday, we found a deserted camp of the men we were after. It was admirably situated in the midst of cedar-brakes, and had been left perhaps four or five days before, after being occupied for quite a month.

These Germans apparently meant business, for they had cut rude human figures on the trunks of some of the big trees, and had used them for targets for their rifle practice. From their "sign" I reckoned there were about 160 of them, and the event proved I was not far wrong.

The trail led about west, towards the Rio Grandé, and it was evident from this direction, and from the start they had, that our scout would be a long one. So we concluded to halt where we were till next day, to rest our horses, and fix up bread and coffee enough for three days; for the wagon could follow us no farther over the rough country we had reached. Soon we were busy enough, baking bread and "parching" coffee; and that finished, all of us, except the guard, and two energetic souls who went out hunting, were soon stretched out on the soft grass, under the canopied shade of the great trees, enjoying an unwonted siesta. Towards evening the hunters returned with a small bear they had killed, so they said; but it was so miserably poor as to be uneatable, and they were very riled at being told they must have found it dead of starvation!

Our party was divided into messes of five each, and our scanty provisions of bread, bacon, sugar and coffee were carried in turn by each of the members in a sack swung across the cantle of the saddle. The first turn at this was taken by one Billy Mac, of which more anon.

The morning's ride led us over a tremendously rough and hilly country, and we could only follow the trail in Indian file, till we struck the head of the Medina River. Here the country became rough, rolling prairie studded with timber, and we pushed on along the wide trail at a smart pace, till we called a short halt at midday. Then it was discovered that a dire misfortune had overtaken our mess, for the miserable Billy had dropped the whole outfit! The villain had found out the loss in time to have gone back for the bag but was afraid to do so, and so held his tongue. We five unfortunates were in a pretty plight now, for all we had amongst us was a couple of loaves of bread and a lump of bacon, and our comrades had only barely enough for themselves. The language addressed to the culprit will not bear repetition. Though naturally forcible, it only relieved our feelings, but did nothing for our hunger.

Now as we rode along that afternoon, another trail came into the one we were following, showing the Bushwhackers had been reinforced by another party.

It was, for the most part, desperate country to ride over, for we were well in the mountains, and frequently had to dismount and lead our horses down rocky slides. Towards evening the trail led us to a large water-hole on the head of the Frio River ; perhaps the only one to be found for many miles of its course, which showed the enemy had good guides. Here we watered our thirsty horses and filled our canteens and, after a brief rest, pushed on again. We were nearing the Rio Grandé, and if we were to catch the Germans we must keep on without pause. The full moon rose gloriously, and by her light we rode, and clambered, and slid till midnight, when we camped for a brief rest on a rough and narrow plateau, where there was a little grass for the horses but no water. From the elevation on which we stood we could see that the whole country to the south-west was on fire. It was a magnificent sight, probably caused by the Indians firing the dry cedar-brakes, which burnt like pitch-pine.

That night again all the talk, till sleep claimed us, was of the prospects of a fight. Would the Germans stand or run ? My own idea was that they would get over into Mexico if they could, but if caught would fight desperately. They had, no doubt, heard of the character and the doings of our commander, and would sell their lives dearly rather than fall into his hands. Moreover, most of them were old frontiersmen and good marksmen. But what they actually did must be told in the next chapter.

16

CHAPTER II

THE FIGHT—AND AFTER

BEFORE sun-up next morning we were in the saddle again, and about ten o'clock struck the eastern branch of the Nueces River, where, there being good water and grass, we halted for breakfast and to graze our horses. Thanks to Mr. Billy, my breakfast consisted of a few mouthfuls of bread, and nothing but water to wash it down! But there was a good feed for our horses, who wanted it badly. What tough, good animals these Texan horses are, mostly of the old Spanish stock! They had had a rare rough journey over that terrible country, but, so far, none had knocked up. My own, which was one of the best little animals I ever rode, was a bit tucked up, but as game as ever.

We were traversing the eastern watershed of the mountains bordering the Rio Grandé and the Mexican frontier, in which all the streams of Western Texas, such as the Pecos, Medina, Nueces, and Frio, take their rise. Most of these, high up near their sources, run dry except in the heavy rains, or at best give only a scanty supply of water in pools, and at long intervals. But fortunately the Nueces was an exception, for we found it running strongly, though only a few, inches deep, between cliffs a hundred feet high, and over a bed of solid rock of about the same number of feet in width. On this the trail was easy enough to follow, for the Germans' horses were all shod, and had left white marks on the rocks.

The rocks above our heads were rich with untold

wealth of honey, and the river full of fish, but we could not pause to take toll of either.

The fugitives were not far ahead of us now, for at two o'clock, close to another of the branches of the Nueces, we came on their camp in which they had slept the previous night. The fires were still smouldering, and great chunks of half-cooked beef were lying about. It was pretty plain they did not know they were being followed, or surely they would have waylaid us in one or other of the narrow defiles in the river. There, from under cover of the cypress growth on the edge of the cliffs, they could have shot us down at their ease, and not one of us could possibly have escaped to tell the tale.

They were evidently lulled into false security, for they were not hurrying their flight, nor had they any rear guard out to cover their retreat. That being so, near as they were to the frontier, we made sure of catching them before they could cross, and probably that very night. We pushed on, the country getting worse and worse, and we generally on foot, as it was impossible to ride, till the light failed us, and then halted for the night. There was some talk of marching again when the moon rose, but both men and horses were too done for that, and we had to rest till morning. There was no water for any of us, and for our unfortunate mess no food, except a lump of raw bacon.

Famishing and parched with thirst, we struggled to the top of the dividing ridge of the watershed next morning, and then led our horses down the most precipitous descent ever attempted by mounted men. Wonderful to say, the horses all got down without serious mishap; but before we had negotiated the worst of it, we were spread out in a straggling line nearly three miles in length. Again, if the Bushwhackers had only known it, what a chance they had to cut us up!

At midday we struck a water-hole on some stream, which held a little muddy, evil-smelling liquid, but a perfect godsend to both men and horses. Then we five miserables boiled our lump of bacon, and drank the soup ; the only food we had tasted since the previous morning.

Round this water-hole the " sign " of the fugitives was quite fresh, and we followed on the trail with all due precaution, keeping scouts out ahead, lest we should stumble on them unawares. We had only ridden on about two miles from this spot when our scouts came hastening back to report that our long stern chase was at an end. They had found the camp of the Bushwhackers about three miles away, on a small prairie surrounded by cedar-brakes, on the other side of the western branch of the Nueces. The prairie, on our side of the stream, ran up in steep rocky cliffs, and from the top of these the scouts had overlooked the camp.

The enemy were supposed to be about 150 in number, and they had two hundred horses grazing on the prairie round their camp. From the fact that they had no scouts out, and their general carelessness, it was evident they hadn't the slightest suspicion they were being followed.

There were three officers with us, a man named Cole McCree, a lieutenant in Davis's company of Partizan Rangers, being in command of the whole party, with Lieutenant Harbour of the same company, a rough but good sort of fellow and a "number one" Indian fighter, under him. A Lieutenant Luck was in command of our detachment of twenty, and in view of the crime so soon to be committed, in which he took a leading part, it may be well to give his antecedents.

A Yankee by birth, and an entirely uneducated and ignorant man, he was a horse-dealer and livery-stable keeper in San Antonio, with a reputation for sharpness in trading which, to say the least of it, would compare favourably with that of most of his kidney. In fact, he was an unscrupulous rascal who would cheat his own father—if he could. Till some time after Secession he was a strong Union man, but when the Confederacy seemed likely to come out on top, he became the hottest of hot Secessionists. By Dunn's influence he was elected junior lieutenant in our company ; but not by my vote, for I never thought him fit for even 4th Corporal.

We then, being halted on the return of the scouts, these three went forward to reconnoitre the position before forming the plan of attack. In about an hour they came back, and orders were issued for a night attack, to be delivered just after midnight. Then we moved about a quarter of a mile up a ravine running at right angles to the river, where we were securely hidden, and there off-saddled, and spread our blankets to await the coming fight with what patience we might.

I may say we were all pretty confident of whipping the Germans, and the general idea seemed to be that they would show but little fight. I thought, as I said before, that we had a pretty tough job before us, unless we could effect a complete surprise of the camp, and that, with undisciplined troops and incompetent leaders, was not very likely. However we were to put the question to the test of experience very soon, and in the meantime there was nothing to be done but to rest and be thankful for that blessing.

About eleven o'clock my comrade and I were roused out of a sound nap to find the whole party falling in. Arms were carefully inspected, hats were discarded, and a white handkerchief tied round our heads ; then leaving our horses under a small guard, for the attack was to be made on foot, we marched off in single file, by the light of an overclouded moon, over breakneck rocks and down the steepest slides. Silence had of course been strictly enjoined, and for their own sakes was kept by all, so that, as we slowly crept up and down those dreadful rocks, not a whisper was heard, not a sound was audible save the tramp of feet or the noise of a falling stone. Into the bed of the stream we slid, one by one, down the steepest declivity of all. It was only knee-deep, running strong and clear, with great boulders scattered everywhere. Though no word was spoken, one could see the intense excitement of the men as they paused for a hurried drink of water, and clutched their rifles and crept stealthily on again.

Our detachment led up the stony slope that would land us on the little prairie where was the camp ; and our orders were to wheel to the right on the top, creep through the cedar-brakes, and line up on the far side of the camp. The rest of the party, marching straight to the front, would form line on the near side of the camp. The enemy's pickets were to be captured without noise and, the camp not being disturbed, the whole force was to wait till daybreak came, and at the sound of a signal shot from McCree's pistol, charge right in.

It was beautiful in theory, but how the man could have expected us to carry it out successfully in practice, I don't know ! Of course there was a frightful muddle, as we shall see ; all orders and pre-arrangements were forgotten, and confusion reigned supreme directly the first shot was fired. We managed our part of the business very well, and crept through the brakes, to within about 300 yards of the camp, without in any way alarming the enemy or seeing any outpost. Then we halted in dead silence. Hardly had we done so when a rifle shot, coming from the far side, rang out in the stillness of the night. Some idiot, over-excited, had loosed off at a sentry, and instantly the camp was in a buzz, like a swarm of bees. Men ran hither and thither in great confusion, and if what had happened had been foreseen, and orders given to charge at once, no doubt we could have carried the camp with little loss. But no one knew what to do, and we on our side lay low, waiting for developments. Presently the Germans, having recovered from their surprise and got their arms, fired a volley at our comrades on the far side, but without much execution in the darkness of the night. This was replied to by our people, and the firing became general on their side.

So far we hadn't fired a shot, and our presence was unsuspected ; but now two of their picket-guards came running in a few yards in front of our position, driving some horses before them. One shot was fired without effect; three more followed, and a heavy thud told that one at any rate was killed. One of our party ran out and brought in the dead man's arms, a Colt's six-shooter and a Jäger rifle.

From where we lay to the cedar-brake round the mott, or clump of timber, was about fifty yards of open ground, and we were now ordered to double across this independently, and then find what cover we could. In the darkness, made more intense by the shadows of the great trees, all got across safely and, taking cover at varying distances from the camp, opened fire on its defenders. Some of the men blazed away in great excitement, and didn't do much execution, but suffered some loss through foolishly exposing themselves ; one of our party getting a bullet through his arm and one through each thigh.

The defenders still showed a bold front, and dared us to come on. They even threatened to charge out on McCree's party, some of whom were inclined to bolt, but were promptly rallied by Harbour.

On our side the bullets were whistling pretty thickly over the heads of six or seven of us who were fighting together, and from our then position it was difficult to return the fire with much effect. Very cautiously then, now crawling, now dodging behind trees, I worked my way up to the edge of the mott in which the camp stood, followed by my comrades. There for a brief space we kept up a galling fire on the defenders, but when four of our party had dropped, one with a bullet through his head, and the others severely wounded, we, the three survivors, had to retire the way we came.

The defenders by this time had lost very heavily, and began to make off in small parties through the thick brush.

From our side a few of us pursued one of these, but soon lost them, and when we got back the camp had been taken, with a loss on our side of twelve killed and eight wounded.

The defenders suffered very severely in comparison with ourselves, fighting as they did in close formation in the centre of their camp, while we were more or less behind cover. In the narrow space inside the mott lay sixty dead and twenty wounded. One poor creature, with yet a little life in him, but unable to move, lay across the camp fire. Pulling him back, I put out the fire, but death mercifully put an end to his sufferings in a few minutes. The scene was a ghastly one, and for a time there was plenty to do separating the wounded from the dead and dressing the hurts of the former as best we could, for we had no surgeon with us.

Seeing there were plenty of willing helpers for our own poor fellows, some of the more humane of us did what we could to ease the sufferings of the wounded Germans. They had fought a good fight, and bore themselves so pluckily I felt sorry I had taken my part against them. We bound up their wounds, and gave them water, and laid them as comfortably as we could in the shade. Poor creatures, how grateful they were!

By this time some of the boys had cooked breakfast, for there was an abundance of provisions in the camp, and I fell to with them, with an appetite, having tasted nothing, except the bacon soup, for two days. Hunger appeased, I went down to the creek hard by to see if any poor wounded creature had crawled there and needed assistance. I did not find any, but happened on a cool spring bursting out below a great tree-shaded rock, and sat me down to rest a few moments.

It was Sunday morning, and my thoughts turned to a far-away country church, where presently a simple service would be held, and those so dear to me would be worshipping. What a contrast to the scene of bloodshed and evil passions I had just left!

But not for long could I indulge in daydreams, for there was plenty of work to be done. The wounded had to be attended to again, and then the numerous horses belonging to the Germans had to be gathered. There were about 200 of these grazing about in all directions, some of them badly wounded by stray shots during the fight.

By four o'clock we had got them all together, and put the worst of the injured ones out of their misery.

Then I hurried over to where we had left the German wounded to see how they were getting on, and was surprised to find them gone. Asking what had become of them, I was told they had been moved to better shade a short distance away. With this answer I was quite satisfied, and never dreamed the brutes with whom I served would be guilty of foul play, especially after the gallant fight the enemy had made.

Just then one of our own wounded called for water, and I brought him some from the cool spring. As I was giving it to him, the sound of firing was heard a little way off. I thought at first they were burying some of the dead with the honours of war ; but it didn't sound like that either. Then, possibly it might be an attack on the camp ; so I seized my rifle, and ran in the direction of the firing. Presently I met a man coming from it who, when he saw me running, said, " You needn't be in a hurry, it's all done ; they've shot the poor devils, and finished them off."

" It can't possibly be they have murdered the prisoners in cold blood ! " I said, not believing that even Luck would be guilty of such an atrocious crime. " Oh, yes ; they're all dead, sure enough—and a good job too ! " Feeling sick at heart, though I hardly even then credited his report, I ran on, and found it only too true.

It seems they were asked if they wouldn't like to be moved a little way off into better shade. The poor creatures willingly agreed, thanking their murderers for their kindness. They were carried away, but it was to the shade and shadow of death, for a party of cowardly wretches went over and shot them in cold blood.

This was Mr. Luck's work—the remorseless, treacherous villain ! And I vowed to be even with him for it, if ever I got the chance. Meanwhile I denounced the bloody deed in as strong language as I could use, telling the perpetrator, to his face, what he was, and what every decent, honourable man would think of him as long as he lived. He handled his six-shooter, and looked as though he would like to use it on me ; but the coward was afraid to shoot at a live man, as I told him. Fortunately some of my own comrades backed me up, or I have no doubt it would have gone hard with me ; as it was, the scoundrel played me a scurvy trick, and gave me the most awful day's work I ever did in my life.

I brooded all the rest of that shameful day on the best course to pursue : there was no hope of bringing the murderers to justice, for I felt sure Dunn would uphold them, and that General Wasp would support him. My only chance then was to get out of the company, or to attain such a position in it as would enable me to stop such deeds.

In justice to Cole McCree, who was a brave and kindly man, I should mention that he was severely wounded in the fight, and had no knowledge of the crime committed by Luck and his friends. The latter's chief motive, I believe, was to prove his zeal and devotion to the Southern cause, and by these base murders make himself popular with the authorities in San Antonio. What their character was, I have already described, and Luck's idea of how to please them confirms all I have said about them.

Immediately after the fight a couple of the boys were sent off, post haste, to Fort Clark, supposed to be some thirty miles distant, to fetch the surgeon stationed there. Till midnight I was off duty, but after that had to help tend the wounded, some of whom were in great pain ; and we had no appliances with which to treat them, nothing much to give them except cold water. I always remember, to the credit of poor humanity, how patiently they bore their terrible sufferings.

It was quite necessary, for the sake of the wounded, and for sanitary reasons, that we should move out of camp as soon as possible. Our own dead were buried in one long trench, but those of the enemy were carried to where the murdered prisoners lay, and there left for a prey to the buzzards and coyotés.

So the day after the fight we were all busy, making litters for the wounded, packing arms, ammunition, etc., captured in the camp, ready for transport, it being arranged we should set out for Fort Clark at daybreak next morning. My comrade Ojé and I suggested using horse-litters, which we knew all about. But Luck wouldn't listen to this; nothing would suit him but hand-litters. He had no doubt laid his plans to pay out myself and the comrades who had stood by me in the row, though we had no suspicion of the abominable trick he was going to play us, more especially as he loudly declared he would take his turn at the bearer work with the rest of us.

That night the doctor arrived, and was promptly at work; but several of the cases were very serious, and would not, he said, live to see the fort.

Betimes next morning, the litters, of long cedar poles with blankets laced to them, were ready with their sad loads, and the horses packed with the plunder. Four bearers were allotted to each litter, or thirty-two in all; sixteen of whom, being all that were fit for duty, were taken from our detachment. The mounted men marched ahead with the guide, carrying our rifles, water-kegs, blankets, and everything except water-canteens that we took for the immediate use of the sick. The first stage was to be about five miles; there the mounted party were to halt till we came up, and we were to be relieved by fresh bearers. Louis Ojé and I, with two other men, carried our comrade and friend Mont Woodward, who was desperately wounded.

Wagons and ambulances had been sent out from the fort to meet us, or rather would be so sent, as the nature of the country wouldn't let them go much more than five or six miles in our direction.

Hardly had we started when one of the horses, loaded with rifles not very securely packed, got scared, or didn't like his load, and away he went, kicking and plunging and followed by three others. Down the steep hillside and through the thick brush they went, shedding rifles at every stride; and may be going still for aught I know, for we never saw them again, nor the forty rifles they carried between them.

Soon the mounted men disappeared down the trail ahead of us, and we plodded on, consoling ourselves with the thought that, though the load was heavy and galled our shoulders badly, we should get a rest and plenty of water at the end of five miles. The sun was terribly hot, but we kept on, with occasional short rests to give the sufferers water to quench their burning thirst. For ourselves, as I have said, there was none.

For nearly three hours we tramped, and climbed, and slid over that awful country, before it dawned on us we were deserted by that scoundrel Luck and the rest of the party. When it did so dawn at last, many of the men threw themselves on the ground, and declared they could not, and would not, go any farther. We certainly were in a dreadful plight, but what was ours compared with that of the unfortunate men in the litters? It was plain we were sold, and would have to carry our burdens, through that dreadful heat, perhaps fifteen, perhaps twenty miles, without a drop of water. But for the sake of our suffering comrades we must go through with it— if we could. The doctor, who was with us and behaved like a man, taking his turn at the litters, backed by some of us, at last got the men going again.

Ojé and the three others of us picked up our litter and started, and the rest soon followed, the doctor bringing up the rear, to see that none lingered behind. To add to our troubles, and they were bad enough, we were in a dangerous Indian country, and had no arms with us, not even a six-shooter!

Our own poor comrade Woodward was past utterance, for he was at the point of death, but the groans of some of the other poor creatures were piteous to hear.

To cut a long story short, we staggered on till near sundown, when we came out on a high rolling prairie on which we saw traces of wheel-marks—joyful signs indeed that we really were on the road to the fort, for till then we had not been sure we were right. On the prairie were plenty of nopals, or prickly pears, with ripe fruit on them ; and how good the juice was to our cracked lips and parched throats! Just after sunset, painfully stumbling along with our weary burdens, we saw two wagons and two ambulances coming over the prairie. Was ever sight more delightful to longing eyes ? In one of the former was a plentiful supply of water, and I don't think any I ever tasted seemed so good as that.

Soon we had the wounded stowed in the ambulances, and ourselves, as best we could, in the wagons. We were five miles from the fort, and had come, they told us, a good thirty from the scene of the fight. It was the most awful journey I ever made. My shoulders were cut to the bone by the litter-poles, my feet were bleeding from the sharp rocks, and I was utterly broken down, as indeed were all of us, including the doctor, though he, good fellow that he was, still had pluck and strength enough to attend to his charges directly we reached the fort.

By-the-bye, Luck's excuse for leaving us in the lurch was that, when he left the bearer party, he had gone in search of water, and lost his way. It was too thin, and no one believed it.

CHAPTER III

A RIDE FOR LIFE

It was nearly ten o'clock at night when we reached Fort Clark, and found supper ready for us in our camp under some beautiful mulberry-trees hard by the creek. But I was too sick and done up to do more than drink a little coffee, and scarce could crawl about or eat for two days. Next morning I did manage to get up to the hospital to see how the wounded were. It was an airy, commodious building, and the good doctor was doing all he could for his poor patients ; but most of them were in a very bad way, and eventually five, out of the eight we had carried so far, died in hospital. The only wonder is that any of them survived the terrible hardships of that journey.

My own poor comrade, Woodward, was still unconscious, and evidently slowly passing away. He died that night, happily without further pain. He was the only son of his mother, and she was a widow. How should I break the awful news to her ? This I had to do, when I got back to San Antonio, and I dreaded the ordeal more than I can tell. But it had to be done.

Fort Clark had been built about six years before by the U.S. Government, and was capable of accommodating four companies of troops. It was situated at the head of the Los Moros, a small stream which runs into the Rio Grandé some thirty miles to the south.

The country round was rolling and open for the most part, but here and there was a good deal of brush, in

which deer, bear, and turkeys abounded and, as the river
was full of trout, it was a sportsman's paradise. Settlers
there were scarce any in those days, and they only cattle-
raisers ; but as the valley of the Los Moros was very
rich, and easily irrigable, I daresay it is all under cultivation now.
For a week we rested in the fort, and then, the day
before the command started to return to San Antonio,
Loo Ojé and myself got leave to ride across to the Frio,
to visit our ranches, before rejoining at headquarters. As
Indians were in the country, we rode very cautiously, and
camped at night east of the Nueces River, away from
water and without making a fire. Next morning, pretty
early, we reached Uvaldé, a small village, where we got
our horses watered and fed, and our own wants supplied.
There we learned that close to where we had to cross the
Frio, a bunch of Indians had camped, and killed a cow,
and that farther up, on a small creek, they had killed and
mutilated two settlers who lived at the head of the Frio.
It was supposed, though no one knew for certain, that the
Indians had surprised these unfortunates in their camp
before daybreak, and killed them as they slept. All this
made us even more cautious, and didn't seem to add
much to the pleasure of our ride across the prairies.
However, we jogged on, keeping a bright look-out for
Indian "sign." At about four o'clock in the evening we
were close to the crossing of the Frio, when we were aware
of a number of buzzards hovering over the opposite bank
of the river ; but as we knew the Indians had recently
killed a cow there, thought they were after that, or rather,
what remained of it. So we rode down the steep bank
of the river to water our horses, and then dismounted,
to climb the opposite one. I was leading, and as I neared
the top of the bank, saw a line stretched, with beef drying
on it, and horses picketed on the edge of the brush. Instantly I turned about, as did Ojé, and we reached the
bed of the river, apparently unseen.

There we looked to our arms, and, after a whispered consultation, agreed to ride some three or four hundred yards up stream, climb the bank, and reconnoitre the Indan camp on horseback. This may seem foolhardy, but our horses were fast and fresh, and there wasn't much fear of the red devils catching us, if it came to riding. We climbed the bank all right, then mounted, and turning back to our left, rode very cautiously through the brush, which there was rather thin, and not very wide. Presently we saw, about a hundred yards ahead of us, two Indians, apparently busy cooking at the camp fire. They seemed not to see us, or at any rate took no notice of our presence ; but as we didn't know how many there might be about, we thought it wisest not to alarm them, and so turned sharp to our right, to get out of the brush, on to the open prairie.

Just as we emerged on to the grass, seven Comanchés burst out of the chaparral, about three hundred yards from us, yelling like demons, and brandishing their spears, as they galloped down on us on their bare-backed ponies. We " stood not on the order of our going," you may be sure, but stuck spurs into our horses, and went off as fast as they could lay legs to ground.

The Indians had burst out on us at full gallop, and before our horses could get well into their stride the devils were not much more than a hundred yards behind us. Too near to be pleasant ; for now they began to loose off their arrows at us, but, what with the pace we were all going, and the distance, didn't touch us.

By this time I knew we had the legs of them, and that, barring accidents to our horses, we could ride clean away from them. So we got our revolvers out, and easing down a bit, let them overhaul us, till they were perhaps not more than eighty or ninety yards behind. Then we turned in our saddles, still at a gallop, and let drive at them. One of us, I don't know which, made a lucky shot, and hit one of the ponies, for down it came a regular cropper, and lay quite still. It was a sad pity it wasn't the Comanché himself that was hit, but there was some consolation in the thought that the gentleman would have a longish walk back to camp.

The remaining six held on after us as hard as ever, so now, instead of keeping on down the Frio, for my ranch, we "turned to sunset," in which direction the prairie was more level, and let our horses go. For an hour longer the yelling demons followed us, like a yelping pack of hounds, but gradually tailed off more and more, till they saw it was no good, and gave up the chase. When we were quite sure we had shaken them off, we slowed our horses down to a jog trot, and reached the ranch just as darkness fell, very thankful for having saved our scalps by so near a shave.

I found Thompson pretty fit, and all well at the ranch, except that the previous night the Indians, no doubt the same party who had given us such a gallop, had killed one of our horses right close to it. All the others had been penned, and a good watch kept as soon as Thompson heard Indians were about; but this one refused to be driven in, and so met his fate. The Comanchés had also killed a poor young fellow who owned the nearest ranch to us on the eastern side, and run off several horses from his place. There was just an off-chance we might catch these marauders, if we were smart. Therefore I immediately sent out a Mexican to get up fresh horses, and got a young fellow staying at the ranch to ride down to a party of cow-hunters, working about fifteen miles below us on the Frio, and ask their help.

That evening he returned with five good men and true, keen to have a go at the Comanchés. With Thompson, young Vinton and myself, we were a party of eight, and, after some supper and an hour or two's rest, set off on our quest. Riding steadily best part of the night, we reached the Frio crossing, where we had seen the Indian camp, soon after daybreak. Cautiously reconnoitring

17

the position, we found it, as I feared, deserted ; and worst of all, the wily Comanchés had so scattered that it was hopeless to follow the trail. So there was nothing for it but to return ingloriously to the ranch, which we did the same afternoon.

On the back trail we found the dead body of the pony we had killed during the chase, or rather what remained of it, for the Indians had carried off the hind-quarters to eat, and the buzzards and coyotés had been busy with the rest. The head and neck were still nearly intact, and I found on examination that the bullet had struck it just behind the ear, which fully accounted for the sudden drop.

After two days' stay at the ranch I set out to return to the command at San Antonio, where I arrived at the end of the week, and found my company encamped on the river-bank near the town. Over our pipes and coffee that night I heard from some of my comrades, with whom I was very friendly, of Dunn's infamous doings at and in the neighbourhood of Friedricksburg, both before we started after the Germans and whilst we were away.

I mentioned in a previous chapter that I had not been on guard, nor had I been sent out on any of the scouting parties that harried the country round ; those for these duties had been chosen from Dunn's creatures, and had acted on the hints he gave them that he wanted no prisoners. He was too cautious to give positive orders to that effect. The unfortunate prisoners, whose only offence was that they secretly sympathised with the North, were placed under the charge of the guard, and in the morning were reported to have escaped. They had been quietly taken away and hanged at some little distance from the camp.

One man had been brought in by a patrol one morning, accused of being a Northern sympathiser. Nothing could be proved against him, and that same night he was released, and given a pass by Dunn. He went away happy enough no doubt, poor fellow, at his escape from such clutches. Next morning his body was found hanging in the woods near by, with the throat cut from ear to ear. Many of these murdered victims were fathers of families, and some of them greyheaded old men. These people were not taken with arms in their hands, there was no force of the enemy in the country, and we had no similar acts to avenge. Further than this, martial law was in force, and summary justice could have been executed on any real offenders by legal methods.

So there was no shadow of an excuse, no possible palliation, for these diabolical midnight assassinations. What motives could have actuated the perpetrators of these murders it is hard to conceive. Probably there were two. The first, the mad lust for blood, and the enjoyment of killing for killing's sake aroused in men of the baser sort, whom the lawless condition of society had brought to the top, and whose evil passions were unrestrained by any power outside themselves; the second, the desire of Dunn and his creatures to prove themselves ultra-Southern in principle, and so make friends with the State authorities, in order to enrich themselves by further pickings and stealings from the public purse. Be that as it may, there was little doubt that more than twenty unfortunate men had been done to death in this shameful manner in and around Friedricksburg by Dunn's connivance, if not by his positive orders.

There was a very strong feeling in the company against him and the other officers, which I did all in my power to stir up, and eventually a requisition was signed by a good many of the better sort, calling upon them all to resign. He, however, braved it out, cajoling some and threatening others, till there were but few names left and we had to drop the matter. My position, and that of the few who had stuck out, was not a pleasant one; for I was a marked man, and there was the prospect staring me in the face of a rope on a live-oak, and myself dangling at the end of it. The man was quite capable of murdering me, or any one else that stood in his way, and I don't mind confessing that I felt very uneasy, and was very careful with whom I consorted at night just then. My only chance was to get out of the villain's command, and with that object half a dozen of my friends and myself requested permission from General Wasp to quit the company and join one of the regiments of the Texan Brigade which, under Hood, was doing such splendid service with General Lee in Virginia. This, through Dunn's influence, was refused, though every available man was urgently required in Virginia to fill up the gaps in the gallant brigade, and for the moment I was at my wits' end. I could have got away easily enough by malingering, and making it worth Dunn's while to connive at it ; but there are some things a man *can't* do, and that was one of them.

It would be tedious to tell of all the efforts I made that autumn of 1862 to get out of my enemy's clutches— what hundreds of miles I rode, trying to recruit men for a battalion being raised for Confederate service by a Major Coopwood, in which I was promised a captain's commission if I could bring in forty men. Failing in that attempt, because most of the men I approached preferred State service to fighting with Lee in Virginia, where real hard knocks were going, I tried my hand at recruiting for Dunn himself, who was empowered to increase his command to a battalion to serve in Texas only. In this enterprise I was working with a man named Adams, a cattle-rancher, and a great friend of mine.

We were solemnly promised by Dunn, in his most plausible manner, that if we could recruit forty men, one of us, whichever we liked, should have a captain's commission, and the other a first lieutenant's. He had arranged with the General that the officers were not to be elected by the men, as was customary in Partizan

Ranger corps, but to be appointed by himself. So he said. We both had great doubts as to the reliability of these promises, but at last were talked over by the specious rascal; which says a good deal for our simplicity, and something for his cleverness.

We scoured the country in all directions, and when we had secured nearly thirty men, brought them into camp and had them sworn in.

By this time there was a good deal of grumbling amongst the men, many of them declaring they wouldn't serve if deprived of their privilege of electing their officers.

We therefore saw Dunn about it, and he again assured us there certainly would not be any election, and we could absolutely rely on getting our commissions as soon as we had made up our number. Notwithstanding this we both had an uneasy feeling we were going to be done, but having already taken so much trouble, resolved to go through with it. So we set to work again to make up our number, and, after about three weeks' hard riding, returned to camp with ten more recruits. No election had taken place; and after hanging about in camp for some days, during which Dunn repeated his assurances as to our commissions, we both asked leave to go to our respective ranches, which was granted.

I was away for a week, and on my return learned that the day after I had left, an election of officers had been held, and both Adams and myself had been left out in the cold, whilst creatures of Dunn's had got the commissions promised to us!

When I tackled him about it he was quite ready with a plausible excuse, saying that despite all his efforts the men had insisted on their right to elect their officers, and that it was my own fault for going away that I was not chosen. If I had not been an enlisted soldier and under his command, I think it would have gone hard with Mr. Dunn at that interview; but as it was, I could only grin and bear it as best I might. How the brute must have chuckled at having so badly fooled me ! We hung about in San Antonio or in the neighbourhood week after week, and for all the service we were to the Confederate cause, might just as well have been disbanded.

Horse-racing and gambling were the chief occupations of the officers and men, though the latter was strictly forbidden by the regulations ; yet it went on in camp from morning to night, and all night, leading, as may be supposed, to the utter demoralisation of all concerned. Quarrels and bloodshed were common enough among the gamblers, and were taken little notice of, as they were everyday occurrences. One such row I remember witnessing on the main plaza in San Antonio. I was strolling across it on my way to visit a friend, and was startled by a bullet whizzing past my head. I turned and saw a man running for his life towards me, and another staggering after him, with uncertain steps, but shooting at the fugitive as fast as he could loose off.

I was pretty well in the direct line of fire, so dodged behind a tree to await events. Peeping round the trunk I saw the pursuer steady himself for a moment and take deliberate aim. This time the bullet found its billet, for the runaway, who had just reached the corner of a street, fell headlong, shot through the heart. He was a captain in a corps that had been christened " the Brigands," and had recently returned from New Mexico with the remnants of Sibley's Brigade. A gambler and a thorough desperado, he had been playing cards with the other man, who was also a Confederate officer, and on some paltry quarrel had struck him with his knife, but failed to kill him. Having no six-shooter on him, he then took to his heels, with the result described. The survivor recovered from his wound in due time, and no notice of the homicide was taken by the authorities. Such fracas were common enough in those days, and human life was cheap ; why should they trouble them-

selves about such trifles ? In fact, of real discipline
there was practically none, and with such a man as Dunn
in command, could be none.

I remember about this time one of his favourites, who
had assisted in his midnight murders, got on a spree,
and returning to camp very drunk, cursed Dunn and all
his officers in unmeasured language, declaring they
were thieves and murderers, and everything that was
bad, and that they dare not punish him because he
knew too much of their doings. " A pretty Major we've
got," he shouted ; " why, he did six months with a ball
and chain on his leg, and ought to have them on now ! "
Next morning the drunken rascal was given sixty days'
furlough, to recruit his health ! He was quite right,
they dared not punish him.

The day after this, quite a number of the same set
raised a general row and free fight, and it was quite
evident that such an insubordinate crew would, if we
went into action, be a greater danger to their officers
than to the enemy.

It was about the end of October that I saw Pyron's
regiment of Texan Rangers march through San Antonio,
en route for New Mexico, where both they and he distinguished themselves greatly. Pyron, though originally
a barkeeper, was a natural born soldier, and withal a
very quiet, unassuming man. His men, as fine a body
of irregular cavalry as you could wish to see, well mounted
on their own horses, had elected him colonel, on his
merits as a fighting man, and he deserved their confidence.
How I wished I could have served with him ; for every
day I grew more and more disgusted with my present
position, and with the incompetent, scheming rascals
who commanded us.

One evening about this time, on my return to camp,
I found everybody in a frantic state of excitement. A
report had come in that Cortinas, the notorious Mexican
guerilla, had crossed the Rio Grandé with two thousand

men to raid in Texas, and we were under orders to meet him. I didn't believe one word of it, and thought it only one of the many " shaves " always being started in camp to enliven the deadly monotony of existence. However, it was true enough we were under orders to march next morning into the town, and thence to the Rio Grandé as soon as transport could be provided.

As I expected, there proved to be little, if any, foundation for the report, and I made up my mind to go recruiting again, if I could obtain leave from Dunn, for General R. Baylor's Brigade, then being raised for Confederate service.

After some demur he gave me the leave I wanted, stipulating that I should recruit. for him, as well as for General Baylor, to which I had reluctantly to agree as the only means of temporary escape from him and his hateful command.

CHAPTER IV

THE FOUR MEXICAN DESERTERS

WHEN the command marched away for the Rio Grandé I remained a day or two in San Antonio making my preparations, and there met a friend who held a commission to raise a company for General Baylor. I agreed to work for him on the understanding that I was to be first lieutenant if we could raise the men required.

All along the Mexican frontier, from the Colorado to the Rio Grandé, there had been stationed a frontier regiment, enlisted for State service. It had been stationed in detached posts, at wide intervals, along this extended line for about a year, and was now going to be reduced from ten companies of 120 men each, to the same number of eighty each. Here was a chance to get a good number of recruits, if only I could persuade them to come with me and see some real soldiering. The first post I visited was high up on the Frio, some sixty miles above my ranch, and commanded by a Captain Dix, with whom I was acquainted.

It was now November and, for Texas, bitterly cold. I had perforce to ride long distances between halts, and as I couldn't carry more than one blanket, for fear of overloading my good horse, suffered much at night. Moreover, it was known that bands of Indians were out depredating and killing in the country through which my route lay, and I dare not make a fire ; it would have been more than my life was worth.

However, I saw nothing of the Indians themselves, though plenty of their " sign," which didn't add to the pleasure of the ride, and arrived safely at Dix's post. There I was welcomed kindly enough, but alas! found three recruiting officers had been there before me, and that the few men they had failed to enlist were not the sort who wanted fighting ; indeed I believe they had joined the frontier regiment in the hope of keeping out of it. After a few days' stay I left for Fort Clark, where was another frontier post, and made it in two days' ride. The fort was held by two companies of Confederate cavalry under command of Captain Carolan, an old friend, who put me up during my stay.

The camp of the frontier detachment was about four miles below the fort, on the Los Moros Creek. There the following day I tried my hardest to get men for our company, but not one would enlist for Baylor's Brigade, though several were willing to join Dunn's command, notwithstanding that I told them quite frankly all about it. Finally, after three days' stay, and finding I couldn't do anything else, I enlisted some twenty men for Dunn, though I felt almost ashamed of myself for doing it.

From this camp I rode to another on the Rio Grandé, about thirty miles distant, travelling down the valley of the Los Moros ; a wonderful stock country, and abounding in game. This detachment was commanded by a Captain Rabb, who had been absent from it some weeks, leaving his orderly Sergeant in charge. What sort of a disciplinarian the Captain himself was, I don't know, but the Sergeant had no sort of control over the men. They lived comfortably enough in huts made of grass, and hunting, fishing, horse-racing, and gambling filled most of their time. No guards even were mounted, and no duty of any sort done ; it was only playing at soldiers.

Not long after my visit the Comanchés looked them up one night, stampeded their horses, and drove off the lot before they knew what had happened. At this camp I couldn't even enlist men for Dunn ; they all said they were too comfortable where they were, and didn't want any change ! One thing I mustn't forget, as it shows what sort of men these were. High up on a pole, on the top of their commissary store-hut, grinned a human skull. I was told it had belonged to an unfortunate German, who with others of his countrymen had been killed by these valiant warriors, when attempting to cross the Rio Grandé some months before. They were quite indignant when I suggested it would be more seemly to bury the poor remnant of humanity, evidently regarding it as a trophy to be proud of.

Being certain by this time that there was no hope of getting men for my friend's company in Baylor's Brigade, I wrote to him to that effect. I was sorry for myself that it was so, and especially for his disappointment ; for he had fought bravely in the ranks of Hood's Texan Brigade, and been badly wounded at the great battle of Sharpsburg.

From the camp on the Rio Grandé I returned, the way I came, to the post near Fort Clark. There, on this visit, some of the boys suggested I should try to raise a company for myself, which several of them said they would join. I didn't feel hopeful of success, and told them so, but that if I saw a chance of making up the number I would return to them. From Fort Clark I rode to another camp at the head of the Nueces River, but met with no success there ; and so, sick of recruiting for the time being, returned to San Antonio. Dunn, who was there on sick leave, professed to be much pleased with the twenty men I had got for him, and gave me leave to continue on recruiting service as long as I wished.

My company, I found, was still near the Rio Grandé, though the Cortinas raid had, as I expected, turned out to be a hoax. So hateful to me was the thought of rejoining the company and loafing about in camp, that, after a few days' rest in San Antonio, I made up my mind that even unsuccessful recruiting was better than that, and so started out west again.

During my absence General Herbert had been succeeded in his command by General Magruder. The former was an indolent, imbecile puppy, who knew nothing of soldiering, and was by no means a fighting man. The latter came to us with a great reputation for daring, which he had gained in Lee's Virginian campaign—notably in the desperate fighting at Gain's Mill.

Herbert, the incompetent, had abandoned Galveston to the Yankees without striking a blow, to the great disgust of all Texans, and especially of the inhabitants of the town, who had worked untiringly at the earthworks they threw up, and spent all their substance in arming them. Galveston was one of our few ports of entry for goods, which were scarce enough in Texas by this time, and our new General set to work to retake it. He collected a force of Texan Rangers, about one thousand in number, all good fighting men, and put a couple of hundred of them on board two little coasting steamers.

The U.S. cruiser *Harriet Lane*, with a crew of about 250 all told, lay off the port, about a mile distant, owing to the shallow water. One pitch dark night Magruder, and his two little steamers, drifted quietly down on the unsuspecting Yankee, boarded her smartly and, after a sharp tussle, captured her, with small loss to the attacking party. The Northerners ashore heard the firing, but could render no assistance to their comrades ; indeed they didn't know what had happened till daylight broke and they saw the Confederate flag flying on their cruiser. That day, as soon as the stores, ammunition, etc., had been removed, the *Harriet Lane* was burnt where she lay, to avoid recapture, for the Confederates, alas ! had no port into which to take her.

After this disaster the Yankees made but a feeble resistance, when Magruder and his Rangers assaulted the town and captured the garrison. This signal victory shed a gleam of hope over all the State, and infused joy and gladness into all the Rangers' camps, where the men had been until now depressed and disheartened by the ineptness and mismanagement of their commanders.

When I speak of "camps," I should perhaps explain that in the Ranger corps, which were the most irregular of irregulars, there was no such thing to be seen as a military camp in the ordinary sense : no ordered array of tents in lines, with ambulances and wagons drawn up in parks, nor horses on picket lines at regular intervals. The camp consisted only of the men and the horses, scattered about as suited each one's fancy or convenience, generally under the shade of the splendid live-oaks so common in the country. A blanket formed the man's bed, and his saddle served him for a pillow.

On my way up country this time I stopped at my ranch to have a look round, and spent a couple of days with Thompson. The good old fellow gave me a most kindly, friendly welcome, and cooked me a regal supper of venison steaks with his own hands. I was pretty hungry after my sixty-mile ride, and did ample justice to my friend's cooking. Then when coffee had been brewed, and the pipe of peace lighted, one realised it was worth even the sixty-mile ride to be at "home" again. It wasn't much of a place to be sure, but it was the only "home" I had on that side the Atlantic, or was likely to have for some time to come, and the magic of the word seems to endear the humblest shanty to one's heart.

The next day was Sunday, and we spent it quietly strolling about the place : a restful, peaceful day such as I had not enjoyed for months past. In the evening Thompson, at my request, read several chapters from the Bible, and read them very well. I daresay, if some of my rough Ranger comrades could have looked in on us, they would have been astonished ; though why I hardly know, since even from a literary point of view there is no grander book than that, and in the roughest, wildest periods of my rough life I have always delighted in its pages.

On the Monday we took a good look round the range, and found the stock doing well, and the crop of calves larger than I expected.

Thompson, I should have mentioned, had sold out his share in the ranch, and stock, to me nearly a year before, intending to return home and settle down there once more. But still he stayed on month after month, and looked after the place for me, and did it very well too. He evidently had some trouble on his mind, which he didn't like to confide to me, though every now and then he seemed to be on the point of doing so. Poor old fellow, the time was drawing near when he would give me his confidence ; but that, alas ! was just before we said " good-bye " for ever.

After this brief rest I started again on a fifty-mile ride to the nearest Ranger camp. There I stayed but one day, as no good was to be done, and then rode over to a ranch owned by a Doctor Jones, a friend of mine about sixty miles above me on the Frio. Poor fellow, I found him in the lowest of spirits, for the Indians had run off all his horses the week before ! It was now Christmas Eve, and there was to be a great dance at Fort Inge, twenty-five miles away, to which I was invited, and rode over to combine business with pleasure, if possible. Close to the fort I overtook the surgeon of the post, a Doctor Dodd, a very good fellow indeed, but more of a fighting man than a doctor, I should say ; for though he was a surgeon in the Confederate service, he had no diploma, and owed his title to the fact of his having invented a cure for maggots in cattle !

The hospitable Doctor gave me a pressing invitation to stay at his comfortable quarters, which I accepted, and there introduced me to his wife and daughter. The dance was a great success ; for everybody who came had travelled long distances to be present, and came to dance and enjoy themselves, not to look on.

Two violins formed the band ; and indefatigable they were, for they played till nearly daylight, except during an interval for supper, which was a solid sit-down affair, with an abundance of eatables and drinkables. I need hardly say there were no dress-suits and no kid gloves, and indeed I don't suppose any of us possessed such things. The girls of course were in their best, with perhaps an added ribbon or two, and the men in their riding costume, but it was all very hearty and pleasant and informal.

On the afternoon of Christmas Day I left my hospitable friends and rode over to Uvaldé, where I expected to find some recruits. In this I failed, but met a man who wanted to buy beeves for the army, but could find none, chiefly I suspect because the owners didn't like Confederate paper-money. I told him I would sell him as many as he wanted, and would gather them in two days. So off we started for the ranch, but got benighted twelve miles from it ; and as it was pitch dark, and there was no road, had to camp on the prairie.

Sunday we rested, as I always did when possible ; but on Monday morning Thompson and I started driving, with the Mexicans, and by midday on Tuesday had three hundred splendid fat beeves penned. My cattle, running over such a great range, were almost wild, and it was exciting work driving them, as well as uncommon hard riding.

My man picked one hundred and fifty, and agreed to my price, $75 (paper) a head ; but it must be remembered that $1 specie was worth about $6 paper. Having got the cattle together for him, I found the confounded fellow had left his money at Uvaldé, and I had to ride back there with him to get it. There I met Captains

Rabb and Dix, who told me their companies were in camp at Black-Water Hole on the Frio, and were about to be disbanded with the object of making one company out of the two, for frontier service. They gave me a cordial invitation to go over with them, and stay till the reorganisation was completed, when probably I might pick up some recruits. Dix was a particularly good fellow, and I gladly accepted. Arrived at the camp, I found it was on the identical spot where, four months before, as previously related, the Indians had surprised, killed, and mutilated two unfortunate settlers. This had happened only a day or two before the seven Comanchés gave my comrade and myself such a chivy across the prairie, and no doubt it was the handiwork of the same gentry.

Dix had quite a budget of newspapers in camp, which I read most eagerly ; for I had had no news of the outside world for weeks, and under such conditions a newspaper is such a treat as stay-at-home folks, who get their paper regularly every morning, can hardly realise. From them it was that I learned the news of Magruder's gallant feat of arms at Galveston.

I stayed on with my friends a few days, and then, having picked up three or four recruits, returned to the ranch. There I found that one of my best Mexicans, a young fellow named Antonio, had been foully murdered by a party of cow-hunters within a few miles of the place. The story is so characteristic of the utter lawlessness of the frontier, and of the callous brutality of the frontiersmen, that I think I must give it, as shortly as possible.

It is the custom in a cattle country like Western Texas, where stock runs almost wild over vast areas, to hold periodically what are called "long hunts." These last sometimes for several weeks, and great herds of cattle are collected, from which the respective owners cut out their own property, and drive them home. Each ranch sends as many hands as can be spared, to help in the drive.

Antonio was the smartest, best hand we had, and a favourite with everybody, from his willingness and cheeriness. Thompson then sent him, and another Mexican, to help on this occasion.

It seems that early in the hunt a small stock-owner, of more than doubtful reputation, named Maccay, lost his six-shooter, and pitched upon Antonio as the thief. The unfortunate boy had often been left in charge of the ranch when he might have gone off with as much as a thousand dollars, besides arms and other things; moreover he had a six-shooter of his own, and being, as I believe, innocent, indignantly denied the charge. As he would not confess, the brutes put a rope round his neck, after disarming him, threw the end over a branch, and hoisted him off the ground several times, until, what with the torture and the fear of death, he confessed, not that he had stolen the pistol himself, but had seen a strange Mexican take it, and hide it where he could find it if they would unloose him, and promise not to kill him.

This they did, but of course the poor lad couldn't find it, for the very good reason that it hadn't been stolen. Then he offered to give them his own pistol, which was quite as good as the lost one, and to pay them any money they asked, as soon as he got back to my ranch.

But all to no purpose. They kept him tied for a couple of days, and then Maccay and two more said they would take him back to the ranch, and left the rest of the party, ostensibly for that purpose. They took him to within about six miles of the ranch, and then, having some sort of an excuse for a murder, couldn't resist the temptation, and turned aside into the almost impenetrable chaparral, and there hanged him. Two days after the hanging, the pistol Antonio was supposed to have stolen was found where it had been accidentally dropped!

18

I was furious when this outrage came to my ears, but it was impossible for me to punish the offenders single-handed ; and my comrades of the company, who would have helped me, were far away on the Rio Grandé. It was worse than useless to seek redress from the authorities, for law and justice did not exist, or at any rate could not be moved to action, as I knew full well. This being so, and I being determined that, if possible, these brutal murderers should not go unpunished, I was constrained to try to put old Asa Minshul and his Vigilance Committee on their track. Accordingly I rode into San Antonio, saw the old rascal at his house, and told him my story. He at once admitted that some hanging ought to be done, and he would see to it, if the murderers came into town. To send any of his myrmidons out to the Frio was too much of an undertaking, to punish the murderers of a mere Mexican boy. If they had hanged an American, it would have been different, and he would have done the job with pleasure—which I quite believed.

Before we parted he advised me, most strongly, to get leave from Dunn to take out half a dozen of my comrades and do the hanging myself, adding, with a horrible leering wink : " It's a job after his own heart ; he's sure to give you leave." And so we parted ; he cheerily promising me that my friends shouldn't want for a rope, if they came within his reach.

On that ride down to San Antonio, whilst I was crossing a brushy prairie about twelve miles from the ranch, I suddenly came on a party of four mounted men, whom at the first glance I took to be Indians, but soon saw were Mexicans. They saw me at the same moment, and made a run for it. Seeing there must be something wrong, I set off after them and, my horse being fast and fresh, whilst theirs were ridden out, soon overhauled them. Six-shooter in hand, I halted them, and saw, to my relief, that the rifle each man carried was strapped fast to the saddle. Dismounting them, I made them hand me the rifles one by one, and then demanded who they were, and what they were doing.

After a deal of prevarication they at last confessed they were deserters from the Confederate service, running for Mexico. Down on their knees they went, and begged and prayed, as only Mexicans can, that I would let them go. They would gladly leave their horses and arms, and everything they had, with me, if only I wouldn't take them into San Antonio : " Por el amor de Dios, y todos los santos, señor," they pleaded. My *duty* undoubtedly was to take them in and hand them over to the authorities for trial by court-martial ; but then it was a hundred to one that the bloodthirsty mob would seize them before I could do so, and hang them in the plaza.

I pondered these things in my mind for a minute or two, whilst the poor devils still knelt and prayed, and then I resolved to let them go. Never were miserable mortals more relieved and thankful than they when I told them they could go. They called down the blessings of all the saints they knew of on my head, and then, handing over to them the few provisions they had in their malletas, I gave them the order to march. When they had gone a short distance I dismounted, fastened the rifles again on the saddles, and set off, driving my cavalcade before me, on the road to San Antonio.

My arrival there with my plunder caused some little stir, and many were the questions asked by the boys as to how I had made the capture. When I told them the facts, which I did, except that I said the prisoners had escaped in the night, most of them shook their heads incredulously, being firmly convinced that I had killed them, as they themselves would certainly have done. It was a terrible state of affairs which then existed in Western Texas ; for it had come to this, that it was the rule to take a man's life, if only any kind of pretext could be found for so doing. I never heard or read of anything like it, except perhaps in the French Revolution.

When I reported myself to the Government officials to hand over the horses and arms, I was told they knew nothing about them and, if I couldn't find the owners, I had best keep them myself ; for, as far as they could see, I had the best claim to them. So after a time, when no claimant had appeared, I sold the rifles and sent the horses down to the ranch.

CHAPTER V

THE COTTON-STEALERS

ABOUT the middle of January and a day or two after my return to San Antonio, two companies of our regiment were ordered to march to Brownsville, on the lower Rio Grandé, opposite to Matamoras, there to join a force under General Wasp holding that post against a threatened attack by the Yankees.

I found on rejoining that some change had taken place for the better in the command, but I was still very dissatisfied with it and anxious to leave it. Of this however there was no immediate chance, so I had to do the weary march of about three hundred miles to Brownsville with my company. The worst of it was that, with a commander like General Wasp, and the staff of incompetent rascals serving under him, there was but scant prospect of seeing any real fighting, or striking a blow in our country's cause. Their real object in moving on Brownsville was the better to carry on their speculations in cotton, and to rob the Confederate Government, whose one available asset it was, by sending it across the Rio Grandé into Mexico for cash, which they put into their own pockets, as I will explain further on.

The weather was awful, and the rain incessant, so the march was not a picnic ; but most evils have their compensation, and in this case we didn't go short of water, and generally had good grass for the horses.

How wonderfully keen is the Hebrew's scent of a profit !

In these troublous times no small number of them

appeared in Western Texas, though goodness knows
where they sprang from. Probably, as the buzzards
wind carrion, so they scented the corruption which was
so rife in the State, and saw their profit in it. On this
march we had to cross a sandy waste of some miles in
extent where, even in this wet season, there was no water,
save in a muddy hole, far away from human habitation.
Hard by this we found a Dutch son of Israel had literally
pitched his tent, with the humane intention of supplying
the hunger and thirst of passing troops with hard crackers
and cheese, to be washed down with " rifle whiskey,"
the latter far more deadly in execution than most of the
weapons after which it was named. Abraham however
was not entirely disinterested in the matter, for the scale
of prices he proposed to charge for his viands was, to say
the least of it, exorbitant. Moreover he was apparently
infected by the poison of Abolitionism, for he stoutly
refused to accept payment in good Confederate paper ;
nothing but hard dollars would do for him. At this
the boys were highly incensed, for I don't think that any
of them had so much as a single specimen of that commodity about him.

The majority pronounced him a malignant traitor, and
were for hanging him on the spot. That they would have
done so I have not the slightest doubt, had there been
a tree convenient for the purpose. But there wasn't
one within several miles ; so Abraham's person was
spared, but his goods were taken, payment being made
in paper money. He was amply avenged, I believe, by
the intolerable thirst produced by his salt cheese and
poisonous whiskey.

About six miles from Brownsville we pitched camp, there
to await the arrival of the rest of the command. Close
by was a long, narrow lagoon, connecting with the Rio
Grandé, and on it, and in its reedy, swampy margins, the
biggest show of waterfowl I ever beheld. Ducks of all
sorts, teal, widgeon, snipe, plover, coots, and an immense

variety of wading birds, were everywhere to be seen ; but none of us possessed what my comrades called a " scatter-gun," so we couldn't take much toll of them.

It was now the end of January, and spring was coming on apace ; the season down near the Gulf being quite a month in advance of the western part of the State. There the trees were barely budding, whilst here many flowering shrubs, especially the Wisaches, were blooming freely, filling the air with a delightful perfume.

Next morning some of us rode into the town, and found it quite " a place," doing a large business with Matamoras, the Mexican town on the opposite bank of the river ; indeed, since the outbreak of war it was only *viâ* the Rio Grandé that any goods could get into the State. The majority of the inhabitants were Mexicans, but there was a good sprinkling of Americans, and the town boasted a commodious market-house, three churches, and a well-built fort on the high bank of the river. Several small steamboats, plying to and fro across the stream, added to the bustle of the scene, and indeed it seemed quite a metropolis to eyes so long accustomed to the wild solitudes of the frontier.

That night there was to be a great " fandango " held in a plaza on the outskirts of the town, and I must needs go and see it, with some acquaintances I had made.

Round the square stood rows of orange and china trees, under which were stalls, or booths, for the sale of sweetmeats, light refreshments, and liquor—especially the latter. Gambling was going on everywhere : under the trees, at tables set out for the purpose, and in booths. Monté of course was the great game, and money seemed changing hands freely, there apparently being no dearth of hard cash amongst these gentry. In an open space in the centre of the plaza some two hundred couples were dancing to the music of a feeble string band. Waltzes were the favourite dance ; and as all Mexicans, both men and women, are fine performers, it was quite a pretty sight.

Matamoras, to which I crossed in the steam ferry next day, was a thriving town too, but purely Mexican, the cathedral and the best houses being built of " adobe " (sunburnt clay) and painted in various colours. The streets and plazas were wide and well laid out, with orange and china trees bordering them, but dirty and evil-smelling to a degree. Here, as elsewhere in Mexico, the chief occupation of the natives seemed to be gambling. One wonders where and how they get the money they stake ; they certainly don't appear to work for it.

Many of the houses in the main plaza, and the cathedral itself, were bespattered with bullet-marks and other signs of the severe fighting which took place the previous year at the election of the Governor of the State of Nueva Leon, when several hundreds of the combatants were killed. Such scenes were common enough at Mexican elections in those days, but now that wonderful man President Porfirio Diaz has changed all that, and order and good government prevail where chaos reigned.

In Matamoras I met several Northerners I had known in Texas, who had cleared out for political reasons. From them I got a sight of some of the New York newspapers and read their version of events, which I need hardly say, was very different from that of the Southern press. Vicksburg was still holding out, but the long siege was telling on the garrison, which could hope for no help from General Lee, who had his hands full in Virginia. Evidently the expectation in the North was that when the place fell, and the whole length of the Mississippi was open to their gunboats, the South would be brought to her knees. I confess it seemed to me the supposition was correct, for when Vicksburg was taken by the Yankees the Confederacy would be cut in half, and the struggle *must* end.

The fall of Vicksburg, which soon after took place, was a terrible blow to the South, but the end was not yet. Both friends and foes had failed to realise what the indomitable courage and wealth of resources of Lee could do, in face of the overwhelming odds against him, and no one, especially in the North, dreamed he could hold his own, as he did, for more than a year longer.

The newspapers in the South had constantly buoyed us up with assurances that the North was heartily sick of the war, and would shortly make peace, on terms such as we could accept. Eagerly I scanned every Northern paper I could get hold of for any indications of such a feeling. There were none. All declared the war must be prosecuted to the bitter end, at any sacrifice of blood and treasure, till the Secession was ended by unconditional surrender. No hope of peace could be found : only victory or ruin lay before us, and who could doubt which it was awaited us ?

As I had fully expected, there was no sign of any movement on the part of the Yankees against us ; but we remained on, some of us in the fort and barracks, and the rest encamped about half a mile below the town, for many weeks. There was no real soldiering to be done, and I spent my time, when not actually on duty, in hunting and fishing, or visiting friends in Brownsville and Matamoras. One result of our being so long quartered so close to the Mexican border was that we lost a very large number of men by desertion. It was so easy for those who were sick of soldiering to slip across the river, that they couldn't resist the temptation. Patrols were kept on the watch on our side to stop this, but without much effect, though one of them mistook me for a deserter, and nearly shot me in his zeal for the service.

One day I left my valuable horse, one of the best I ever had on the other side, in camp, whilst spending the day in Matamoras, and when I returned at night it had disappeared. I didn't know for certain it had been stolen, though probably it had been, since horse-thieves, and every other sort of thief, abounded in that no-man's-land. In this uncertainty I hunted for it several days, up and down the river, but finding no trace of it had to provide myself with another mount. This was no easy matter, but at last I found a horse in Matamoras which had been the notorious Mexican guerilla Cavajal's charger, and bought him in default of a better.

I hadn't had him many days before he went lame, having apparently strained his shoulder. A swim often does good in such cases, so I stripped and rode my horse into the river.

I had got some few yards out from the bank, heading as though I were going to cross the river, when from a point about a hundred yards up stream a zealous patrol let drive at me with his rifle. The bullet whizzed past my head too near to be pleasant, and I at once turned my horse for the bank, shouting to the fellow not to fire. Whether he heard me or not I can't say, but he paid no attention, and fired two more shots before I could scramble ashore. Fortunately for me my zealous friend was a rank bad shot, or he must have plugged me, especially as he was doing his target practice lying down. I need scarcely say I never swam my horse in the river again as long as we remained in camp.

One day we all went up to Brownsville to see the 3rd Texas Regiment inspected by General Wasp. The men turned out very well, and were a fine body, though of mixed nationalities, for the regiment was made up of American, Irish, Dutch, and Mexican companies. The officers were rather a motley crew, having been, as usual, appointed by political influence rather than for their military qualities. The Colonel commanding, by the name of Locky, was a doctor in some practice in San Antonio. A strong Secessionist, he had been a member of the State Convention, and thus got his appointment. Personally he was a very pleasant fellow, though a thirsty one, but was entirely ignorant of military matters. The second in command, Colonel Bushel, was an old Prussian officer who understood his business, and was the only efficient officer in the corps.

The Major, a man named White, had served some years, so he said, in the U.S. Navy; he was an habitual drunkard, and neither knew nor cared anything about soldiering. The senior Captain, Kaupmann, was a heavy, besotted-looking lager-beer Dutchman, a stone-mason by trade, who had got himself elected, no one knew how, and was rarely quite sober. The others were for the most part barkeepers, or people of that class, and wholly unfitted for command.

I have given these descriptions to show how affairs were managed, or rather mismanaged, in Texas, far away from the control of the Confederate executive; of course at headquarters things must have been very different, or the collapse must have come much sooner than it did.

The coast of the Gulf is subject to very severe storms of wind, which rise at times almost to the force of a hurricane, and make life in camp a perfect misery by filling the air with choking dust. In one of these a Yankee brig, laden with clothing and stores of all sorts for the Northern troops in New Orleans, came ashore on our side of the river. Company B was sent down to guard the wreck, which was breaking up and washing ashore all sorts of goods. At first the boys had a " high old time," and many of them secured plunder enough to have set up " store " on their own account. But presently this was stopped, and the rest of the things sent up to Brownsville, where they were confiscated as the property of the enemy.

At first the order was that everything was to be sold by auction for *cash*; no paper-money to be accepted. This was rather more than the soldiers would stand: they were paid in paper, and it was beyond a joke for the authorities to refuse to accept it. Accordingly the order was rescinded, and then the Hebrew speculators, in collusion with our General, swarmed to the auction to buy up everything worth the having. But the boys wouldn't have this either, and promptly ran them off the premises, as they did a lieutenant of the 3rd Texas who started buying for the expelled Jews. Our excellent commander intervened to stop the expulsions, but the boys were in no mood to be trifled with, and wouldn't listen to him.

The goods not sold that day were sent back to store, and the clothing, of which we all stood in great need, it was given out, would be distributed fairly amongst the different companies. That very night it was reported the store had been broken into, and the bulk of the clothing stolen. The real thieves were Captain Kaupmann and his friends : the supposed burglary was only a blind !

But the most laughable thing was when we were allowed into the store to select one garment apiece from the remnant left by these rascals. After long search I found a decent coat without any name on it, for already almost everything worth having had been appropriated. I was walking away with it, when Captain Kaupmann asked what I was doing with his coat ! I told him I had already counted sixteen garments with his name on, and I thought that was enough even for him ; besides, this one had no name on it. Blandly he smiled, the old Dutch thief, and said : " Gif you vill loke *inside* de slief, you vill zee my names." Sure enough the old villain had pinned it inside, so that it might not be removed. I threw it at him without further parley, and left the store in disgust.

I have previously referred to the robbery and swindling carried on by our General and his crew in relation to the sale of cotton, and perhaps this is the place more fully to describe the method or methods, for they had several, by which they managed it.

The Confederate Government having no money, except the paper currency it created, paid the blockade runners, who brought ammunition, arms, and all kinds of supplies, in cotton or certificates for cotton. In the early stages of the war, cotton was fairly plentiful, and the paper-money at, or about, par. Soon, however, it began to depreciate, and the holders of cotton, who had at first taken it freely, would only accept it at an ever-increasing discount. General Wasp then proclaimed martial law—illegally, I believe—in Western Texas, and under it made the paper-money legal tender at par, not only for cotton, but for all other goods. This measure, supposed to be for the benefit of the Government, was really enforced to enable his agents to buy the cotton for other than hard cash. Every one, at first, had been allowed to take cotton into Mexico, which was the only way traders could obtain goods. Now a system of permits was established, and these were only given on an undertaking on the part of the holder to exchange his cotton for goods, to be brought into Texas.

As a matter of fact, the permits were given to the creatures of Wasp, and the rest of the ring, and to no one else. These gentry bought their cotton for paper, and sold it for specie in Mexico. They bought no goods, or at least only such as suited them, and put the dollars into their pockets, less the heavy percentage they had to hand over to their patron.

Many of these people, who at the outbreak of the war were poor, amassed very considerable fortunes, made in this manner.

The Confederate Government, finding that under this *régime* cotton came in but slowly, whilst it was urgently required to load the vessels waiting for it (at one time there were no fewer than seventy ships lying in the mouth of the Rio Grandé to load with cotton), appointed an agent with extraordinary powers to collect it. He was empowered to impress teams, teamsters, and labourers, and could take all cotton required for State service, at a fixed price, payable in Confederate paper.

Only a man of the highest character and of proved probity was fitted to fill such an office as this. The man selected, no doubt through local influence, a New York Jew of the name of Warter, was of the worst possible antecedents ; for he was a speculator and a gambler, and had been branded by public advertisement as a coward and a liar ! The teams and the teamsters he impressed, to the great loss and inconvenience of their owners, and the large sums of money entrusted to him by the Government, were mainly used for his own speculations, in which of course his friends shared.

This was well known to be going on throughout the State, but so terrorised were the people by the rascals in power that no one dared to take any steps against them, and, as far as I know, they carried on their robberies with impunity up to the very last. To be sure they all cleared out directly the " break up " was known, and before the rule of the North was established in Texas ; which was a wise precaution on their part.

The ordinance issued by General Wasp, under martial law, by which paper-money was made legal tender *at par*, had never been very strictly enforced except for the purchase of cotton, and when it had served its purpose, was withdrawn. Immediately on this the value fell away, day by day, till at last one had to pay fabulous prices in paper for everything : $30 for a very common pair of shoes ; $10 per bushel for corn ; $10 per pound for coffee ; $500 for a very ordinary horse ; $2½ per pound for sugar ; $75 for a beef-steer ; $5 for a water melon, and so on, and so on.

Perhaps I have dwelt at too great length on this disgraceful cotton-selling business, but it made a great impression on my mind at the time, as an instance of how " the wicked prosper." One more story I must however tell relating to it, which for brazen effrontery beats everything in my experience. But it is too long for the end of a chapter, and must be reserved for the next one.

CHAPTER VI

THE RAID INTO MEXICO

I MUST premise that the story I promised to tell at the end of the last chapter was not part of my own personal experience, for I had left Dunn's command and the Rio Grandé before the ridiculous farce was enacted. It was, however, told to me by friends who were eye-witnesses, and I believe there is no doubt of its truth. Moreover, it was the talk of the whole State, provoking mirth in some, and shame in others, each according to his nature.

It was well into the autumn of 1863, and Messrs. Wasp, Dunn and Co. had done good business with their cotton-stealing, but still had several bales left, which they had not been able to get across into Mexico.

Now probably General Wasp's disgraceful conduct was actuated by two motives : funk for his own precious skin, and a desire to cover up his wholesale peculations. Which was the more potent of the two, is hard to say ; probably the last one, though he was undoubtedly a coward without shame.

One morning a terrified Mexican ranchero came galloping into Brownsville with a report that the Yankees had landed in force at Boca del Rio, a small port at the mouth of the river, and were marching, horse, foot and artillery, on the town. At once all was confusion and terror in the place, and many of the officers were for evacuating it forthwith. But even General Wasp couldn't do that ; so he sent out the gallant Captain Dick Turner, with his company of Partizan Rangers, to reconnoitre and report ; Wasp and Dunn remaining in Brownsville " between a shake and a sweat " whether to fight or run. Turner was a windy, gassy fellow who, with his tongue, could whip a whole regiment of the despised Yankees unaided. Certainly he was a poltroon, but he was one of Dunn's basest creatures, and no doubt was deep in the confidence both of that worthy and of the General. Therefore it is not clear whether the report he brought back was the offspring of his fears, or whether it was made at the suggestion of his superiors.

Be that as it may, he returned the second day, in hot haste, with the report that he had sighted a force of Yankee cavalry and artillery, several thousands strong, marching on Brownsville. So overwhelming was their strength that it would be madness to attempt to hold the place ; the only chance to save themselves was to clear out at once, which he should certainly do himself, whatever any one else did. Some of the Rangers with him told me afterwards that all *they* saw was a big herd of cattle being driven over the prairie in the dusk of the evening, and that it was these that Turner mistook, or chose to mistake, for Yankee cavalry !

In the panic and excitement that followed on Turner's report, a regular drunken spree set in, every one, from the General downwards, being more or less drunk. Orders were given to fire the barracks, Government stores, buildings, and cotton. As I have said, there wasn't much of the latter remaining, but what a splendid opportunity the burning of it gave these rascals to cover up their frauds on the Government ! What they had failed to account for had been burnt to save it from the Yankees ! So unfortunate ! But what else could they do ?

Order and discipline were at an end, and the various regiments and detachments began to clear out on their own hook. The burning went on merrily, Wasp and Dunn lending a hand themselves, and all the while the flames from the beautiful barracks lit up a scene of disgraceful orgie.

By this time the Yankees were said to be close at hand, and it was high time for the gallant General to save his precious life. He was probably worth about $100,000, mostly made during the last six months. The cash was safe on the other side of the Rio Grandé, and he couldn't afford to be killed by these murdering Yankees !

It was now that he made what the wags called his celebrated strategic movement to the rear, and in an ambulance drawn by four good horses, attended by a small escort, never called a halt till he reached Kemp's ranch on the San Gertrudes, 125 miles from Brownsville ! He was followed by some of the soldiers and a small crowd of civilians ; but these unfortunates couldn't keep up with his headlong flight, for he had relays of horses, and they had none.

The best of the joke, if joke there can be in such a disgraceful episode as this, was that not a single Yankee had landed at Boca del Rio when all this took place ; and it was not till Wasp and his straggling command had got safely back to San Antonio that a small force did land. Even then it approached Brownsville slowly, and with great caution, believing that the story of its evacuation was a trap to draw them on. Was there ever such a General, ever such an exploit, since war was a trade ?

But I must give one more of his exploits, and then I have done with him, for some time at any rate.

It was about a couple of months before the hurried exit from Brownsville, that a young half-bred Mexican named Vidal had, by Dunn's influence, been given the command of thirty Mexicans, drafted from various companies of Rangers, and sent on scouting duty to the mouth of the Rio Grande. This too was after I had left the command. This man had served in my own company, and I knew him well as a vain, trifling fellow without any experience, who cared for nothing but gambling and drinking. But he was son-in-law of a man named Kennedy, who had amassed a fortune speculating both in the North and in the South, and who was connected with Wasp and Dunn in their cotton transactions. This was of course enough to get him the billet.

About this time Dunn had, whilst yet money was to be picked up at Brownsville, to his great disgust, been ordered off to Eastern Texas with his command. He moved out of the place, and camped about eight miles off, till he could get the order rescinded (which he eventually did), and this left the garrison rather weak. In fact all that remained were General Wasp's personal escort and a company of citizen volunteers, enrolled for home defence. Vidal knew Dunn had been ordered away, and, thinking he was gone, believed Brownsville to be in a defenceless state. So he " went Fanti," and played the mischief on the frontier.

Dunn, before he marched out to his camp, sent two couriers, both of the old company in which Vidal had served, down to his camp, to order him to rejoin the command. To their great surprise, they met him already on his road to Brownsville ; but he explained that he had already received the order by a messenger, and was on his way there. The couriers, who were, as I have said, old comrades of Vidal's, suspected nothing, and of course turned back with the party. They all rode together, apparently on the most friendly terms, till they came within about twelve miles of the post. Then they halted, and Vidal invited his old comrades to have a drink with him ; and, whilst they were taking it, he and some of his men shot both of the poor fellows down.

One of them, named Dashields, a friend of mine, who had joined the service at the same time as myself, was the only son of an old army officer, who at the time of

Secession edited a paper in San Antonio. Him the treacherous villains killed on the spot. The other man, though sorely wounded, got to his horse, and managed to ride into Brownsville before his pursuers. He arrived, speechless, but signed for pencil and paper and wrote his tale before he died.

Dunn, who happened to have come into the town from his camp, refused to believe that his pet could have been guilty of such baseness, but averred the treachery must be the work of guerillas, or a party of marauding Yankee cavalry. However, he sent orders for his command to march back to the post forthwith, and sent out my friend Jack Vinton, with a party of ten men, to reconnoitre and ascertain what Vidal was really doing. Vinton had not gone far before he encountered the rascal with a party which he had increased to about one hundred in number, by picking up " greasers," which can always be done along the Rio Grandé when any plunder is to the fore. Vinton of course couldn't attack with his small party, and Vidal seems to have come to a halt, in some uncertainty as to his future movements, supposing that the escape of the wounded man would have put the garrison on the alert.

Now if Wasp and Dunn had only gone out at once, they probably would have caught, and destroyed, the whole of the murdering gang, and so saved many lives and prevented the destruction of much valuable property. But they, like Vidal himself, were better hands at murdering defenceless people than fighting, so they set to work erecting breastworks of their precious cotton-bales, and getting a gun into position, against the attack of this paltry band of Mexican cut-throats !

Vidal, finding he was not attacked, turned back down the Rio Grandé, and raising the cry of " Muerto à los Americanos ! " plundered all the ranches in the district, and murdered all the Americans he could lay his hands on.

Two days after the murder of the couriers, the gallant

warriors in Brownsville, having partly recovered from their scare, sent out two companies of Rangers in pursuit. These, if they could have come up with Mr. Vidal and his Mexicans, would have made very short work of them. But unfortunately the rascal got wind of what was up, and scattered his band, all of whom got safely across the river into Mexico, where they eventually joined Cortinas, the notorious brigand and guerilla leader.

Now having told these two stories, which seemed to fit into this place, I must hark back to the doings on the Rio Grandé, whilst I was yet a sergeant under the gallant Dunn's command. And one of them at any rate was remarkable enough, I think, to be worth the telling.

It may be remembered that in Chapter II. of the previous Book I mentioned having casually met a man named Davis outside Corpus Christi, shortly after Thompson and I landed in Texas. Davis was a lawyer of some standing and, though a strong Northerner, was popular with a certain section of the people, and had been elected a Probate Judge. When Secession took place he had, like many others, to clear out, and went North, where he was given a commission as Colonel to raise a regiment for Federal service out of the disaffected elements in South-west Texas and the deserters and the renegades who had crossed into Mexico. With this object he established his headquarters on the Mexican side of the Rio Grandé, a little way above Boca del Rio, and near a small frame building dignified by the Mexicans with the name of a Custom House. Close by this a detachment of Mexican troops, some thirty in number, was quartered to guard the passage of the river, across which two small ferryboats plied by day, but were tied up on our side at night, since the ferrymen lived there.

Davis, aided by two Texan renegades named Height and Monson (the latter a desperado of the worst character, who had shot two men near Corpus Christi and then bolted into Mexico) had collected together about three hundred deserters, and was, it was reported, about to take them by sea to New Orleans to join the Yankees there.

This then was the position of affairs when, one Saturday afternoon in April 1863, the bugles sounded the fall-in at our camp near Brownsville, and Major Sampson, when the parade was formed, called for 150 volunteers for a night expedition. We were not told the nature of the service, nor where we were to go, only that probably there would be some fighting; and almost every man in the six companies stepped the six paces to the front. " Boys," said he, " I can't take you all ; wish I could ; but I guess six hundred's too many for the job. So each captain must pick thirty of his best mounted men—that'll be quite enough. And look sharp, and get a day's rations together, for I'm off by sundown."

I was one of those chosen from my company ; saw my horse well fed, got my rations ready, and, with the rest of the party, fell in just before sundown. After an examination of arms and horses, about which latter the Major was very particular, explaining that we had a long, sharp ride to do that night, he gave the word to march.

Once clear of the camp we wheeled to the right and, keeping close to the deep fringe of chaparral that lines the river-bank nearly to its mouth, moved at a sharp trot in the direction of Boca del Rio, distant about forty miles. It was a lovely summer evening and, as the last gleam of daylight died out, we rode along at a smart " lope " over the open prairie by the light of the moon, which however would set and leave us in darkness in some four hours' time. So we pushed along to make the most of the light, every one wondering and guessing what we were after ; for, so far, the secret had been well kept, if indeed it was known to any one except the Major, and none of us knew our destination.

For about two hours we kept going, "loping" and trotting, and then our commander halted, dismounted us, to ease the horses for a few moments, and told us he was going to cross by the ferry, just above Boca del Rio, into Mexican territory, capture the Custom House and its Mexican guard, and then surprise Davis' camp. He was going to take him and his officers, and burst up his precious regiment of deserters and renegades ; and as he had two good and reliable Mexican guides with him, thought it would be easy enough to effect the surprise, if only we could secure the Custom House guard before the alarm was given.

Now these deserters and their boasting talk, which we heard of in Matamoras and in our camps, had riled the boys very much, and they were "blue mouldy" to get at them. So when the Major had unfolded his plan of campaign they were wild with excitement, and raised such a cheer as set the chichalakas and turkey-cocks in the chaparral hard by crowing and gobbling vehemently. For my own part, though I was as dead against the deserters and the rest of the crew as anybody, I thought the proceeding an unwise one ; for the more successful we were in our raid, the greater would be the insult to the Mexican Government, whose territory we were going to violate, and I thought it bad policy to embroil our-selves with people who, so far, had been friendly to our cause.

About 3 a.m. we reached the ferry, and found the two boats tied up all right on our side. Leaving our horses under guard, we quietly crossed in two trips, and formed up in dead silence under the high bank, within a few yards of the Mexican guard house. The moon had long since set, and save for the glimmering light of the stars, darkness reigned.

A whispered word of command was passed down the

ranks, and noiselessly we crept up the bank past the Custom House, standing presently round the guard house, where no light was visible, and all were apparently fast asleep. The surprise was complete, for in less time than it takes to tell, the thirty Mexicans were prisoners, and their arms secured. Never did I see men so scared as they were when they found themselves prisoners in our power.

Evidently they hadn't a very high opinion of us, for they seemed to think they would be murdered, and many fell on their knees and begged for their lives. Great accordingly was their relief when Major Sampson assured them their lives were safe, and that if they kept quiet they would probably be released in an hour or two.

Davis' camp was about two miles away, and the road to it lay through the dense chaparral nearly the whole distance.

Sampson left five men, with loaded rifles and six-shooters, in charge of the Mexicans, and the rest of us set off, marching two abreast along the narrow path in the inky blackness of the night, the two Mexican guides leading the way. From them the Major had learned that Davis, Height, and Monson occupied a good-sized hospital tent, pitched in the centre of the camp. Twenty picked men were therefore told off to secure these three, at all hazards, when the rush was made.

It was not altogether a pleasant stroll along that black path, where you could scarcely see your hand before you ; for if Davis had an inkling of what was afoot he could cut us up to a man. Fortunately for us however, he had not the remotest idea of what was in store for him. So secure did he deem himself on neutral territory, that when at last we emerged from that horrible path into the comparative light of the space around the camp, we found no picket, not even a sentry mounting guard. By the dim starlight we could see quite a number of tents, and on each flank wagons drawn up, whilst outside them were many horses picketed. In the centre of the camp, standing by itself in a small open space, was the hospital tent sure enough ; and now, if the three men we particularly wanted were in it, we had them right enough.

It was now, as I guessed, about 4.30 a.m., and still quite dark. Not a sound was to be heard : the whole camp was fast asleep, unconscious of the fate awaiting it so soon. In dead silence, and on tiptoe, we filed right and left, the twenty picked men in the centre, and then waited for the signal to charge. This was to be a single shot fired by the Major.

The shot sounded, loud and startling in the stillness of the night, and then, with a volley from all the rifles, and one wild yell, we were amongst the tents. In less than five minutes, we twenty told off for the duty had Davis and his friends securely tied. None of them made any resistance except Monson, who fought like a wild cat and wounded two of the men badly with his bowie-knife before he was overpowered. The rest of the renegades, completely surprised, for the attack to them was a veritable " bolt from the blue," showed but little fight, and those who did were speedily shot down. Those who could, bolted right and left into the dense chaparral, where we didn't attempt to follow them. Only two prisoners, besides the three leaders, were taken.

By the time it was all over, the first faint streaks of dawn began to show in the east, and it was time for us to be off, before the whole country turned out. So hastily collecting all the arms we could carry, and exploding the ammunition, we set off at a smart pace for the ferry, bringing the five prisoners along with us. There we released the Mexican guard, and by six o'clock in the morning were safely across on our own side of the river again. Our only casualties were one man killed, and the two wounded by Monson. It was a smart bit of work, and well managed, though I still thought it very foolish to risk the bringing down upon us the wrath of all Mexico just for the fun of breaking up the nest of renegades.

It was a most lovely summer morning that Sunday, and as we halted for breakfast under the shade of the live-oaks, where the horses had been left over night, all were jubilant over the complete success of our little trip, and no one gave any heed to possible troubles to come.

After a couple of hours' rest, which we had well earned, we started on our return to camp. About noon we halted near a clump of live-oaks, and dismounted. Major Sampson moved quietly about amongst the boys, evidently taking their opinions on some matter of importance, though he never came near me. What it was, was soon made clear; for in about ten minutes' time Monson, Height, and the two other prisoners were dangling from the limb of a live-oak hard by.

Monson no doubt richly deserved his fate, for he was a thorough-paced scoundrel, whose only redeeming feature was his pluck. Against the others nothing particular was known except their desertion from the Confederate forces. For this doubtless they deserved death by all the laws of war, but they ought to have been tried first in all due form by court-martial. Sampson's excuse for the murders, for such they were, was that if he handed over the prisoners to the proper authorities in camp, there would probably be such a rumpus kicked up by the Mexicans, over the raid, that they would have to be released and sent across the Rio Grandé again.

Davis was spared, and taken into camp under strong escort. There the desire amongst the boys to hang him was very strong; but General Wasp and Dunn, much as they would have liked to string him up, were afraid of the consequences of such an act. They therefore told off a party of twelve reliable men to guard him, with myself as Sergeant (to which exalted rank I had then attained) in charge: probably because they knew I had always resolutely set my face against private and amateur hangings. The next day, about midnight, when all the camp was quiet, I received an order to take the prisoner over to General Magruder's camp beyond Brownsville, and hand him over to the Provost there : a wise precaution I believe, for if the boys had known he was being removed, they would have lynched him to a certainty. As it was I got him safely away, and was very glad when the Provost in Magruder's camp relieved me of my troublesome charge.

As I had anticipated, the Governor of Nueva Leon, in whose jurisdiction the raid had been made, was furious at the insult put upon his country, and demanded the instant release of Colonel Davis and a full apology for the violation of his territory. With these demands General Magruder at once complied, and both he and General Wasp having denied all knowledge of the raid, the matter dropped.

In after years, when the war was over, I met Davis again in Indianola at the house of my friend and partner Doctor Hughes. He told me that during that night's march to Magruder's camp he fully expected to be strung up on every tree we came to, and that he thought he was mainly indebted to me that such was not his fate.

CHAPTER VII

MY FRIEND GOES HOME

ABOUT this time we were startled in our camp by the firing of salvos of artillery and volleys of musketry over in Matamoras. Flags were hoisted on all the public buildings, and crowds of Mexicans went about cheering and shouting themselves hoarse. In the evening the town was illuminated after a fashion, and a grand "fandango" held in honour of a glorious victory gained over the French under Marshal Bazaine.

The very next day, curiously enough, there were more rejoicings, though not on quite so extensive a scale. This time it was the Yankees celebrating the fall of Vicksburg, and the practical ruin of the Confederate cause. Both these jubilations turned out to be somewhat premature ; for the Mexican "victory" proved in reality to be a severe defeat, and Vicksburg, sorely battered, and in desperate plight, still gallantly held out.

A lieutenant in my company named Luck, to whose misdeeds I have before referred, especially after the fight with the German Unionists from Friedricksburg, had now to resign his commission, as the boys insisted on his retiring.

I was persuaded by my friends amongst the better-class men to put up for the vacancy, and, though I was sick of trying to get a commission, consented. I got a clear majority of votes, but was done again by Dunn's trickery. The man who stood next to me was put up to demand a recount, and then it was worked so that our positions were reversed, and I came out second.

Luck, immediately he resigned his lieutenant's commission, was appointed by Dunn Captain and Quartermaster of the regiment.

A scene which took place just after this election is perhaps worth relating, because one of the actors in it behaved with pluck and generosity : a combination of qualities not often found amongst our rough frontiersmen. A dispute about some trifling matter arose between two members of our company named Adams and Cranham. The first, an old acquaintance of mine, was a Western stock-raiser, a rough, open-hearted fellow, with plenty of pluck, and much liked by everybody ; the other a little backwoods schoolmaster, and would-be lawyer, ill-tempered and spiteful, with a sharp edge to his tongue.

In the course of the dispute Cranham grew very abusive, and Adams, who suffered from rheumatism and walked with a stick, threatened to strike him, if he gave him any more talk. Cranham at once clapped his hand to his six-shooter, and dared him to do so. Adams raised his stick, and the other fired point-blank at his head, and missed, though he was so close that his hair was powder-burned. Cranham then started to run, firing as he went ; and Adams, forgetting all about his lameness, darted after him. In about twenty steps he caught him by the shoulder, and, as the runaway pointed his pistol at him again, grasped it by the muzzle and wrenched it out of his hand by a quick turn of his wrist.

His adversary then took to his heels, crying for mercy as he ran. From ninety-nine men out of every hundred in that camp he would have received none, but Adams was the exception. He was a splendid shot, either with pistol or rifle, and as Cranham ran, screaming with terror, he covered him for a moment ; then dropped his muzzle, and walked up to where we were standing, saying quite coolly, " I couldn't shoot the poor devil like that."

Both men were placed under arrest by the captain of the company ; but there was so strong a feeling amongst the boys on Adams' behalf, that they were both shortly released, on condition that they dropped the quarrel, to which my friend at any rate readily agreed.

About the middle of April 1863 our company, then quartered in Brownsville, was ordered to rejoin the regiment, stationed some twelve miles below the town ; a detachment of twenty men being left behind, which would be relieved in a fortnight. I volunteered to remain with this detachment, and it was fortunate I did so, for my old friend Thompson turned up at Brownsville the very day after the company marched out. He, as I have already said, had sold out his interest in the Frio ranch to me more than a year before, and was now on his way home. He had come to Brownsville partly to say good-bye to me and partly in the hope of getting a passage in a blockade-runner homeward bound from the mouth of the Rio Grandé. Our meeting was most cordial, for save and except for the foolish quarrel at the ranch over the pet deer he shot, which was entirely my fault, we had been warm friends since we first met in Canada, three years before.

He looked pretty well, but complained of his head, and a general lassitude and weariness.

The next day he seemed worse, was feverish and restless, and that afternoon I got my friend Doctor Jones, the head of the medical service on the Rio Grandé, to see him. He said he had a mild attack of yellow fever, but with care and good nursing thought he would be all right again in a few weeks. With some difficulty I got him a comfortable lodging in the town and, with the aid of a Mexican woman, tended and nursed him myself for the next fortnight. Then I was obliged to rejoin the regiment ; but as my friend was already on the road to convalescence, I left him with a fairly easy mind, promising to return as soon as I could. I spent four days in camp, during which we had almost incessant drill, in preparation for inspection at Brownsville by General Magruder. Then we marched into the town for this function, and I found Thompson so much better that, though still weak, he was out of bed and dressed.

Magruder overhauled us thoroughly, for with all his faults he was a *real* soldier, and a fighting man. He was a West Point man, and held the rank of colonel in the U.S. Army at the time of Secession. On that he was made major-general, and given the command of a division under Lee, with whom he did good service and saw much hard fighting in Virginia, when McClellan was foiled in his first attempt on Richmond. But it was said that it was owing to some fatal weakness of his that he failed to bring up his division in time to block McClellan's retreat on the James River, so saving that commander from an overwhelming disaster. Anyway, he was relieved of his command shortly after this occurrence, and sent down to Texas. Whatever his faults, he was the best officer by far that we had seen in Texas since the war began.

He seemed pleased with our turn-out and appearance ; and indeed we were, as far as men and horses went, a fine body of irregular cavalry, and could have given a good account of ourselves, if only we had had a capable leader like himself. As to drill, I'm afraid that was not our strong point ; but that was the fault of Dunn and his crew, and I believe Magruder gave these gentry a bit of his mind on the subject of their ignorance and inefficiency. So it was reported, and I most sincerely hope it was true.

After the inspection we rode back to camp, and there had to remain on duty till the following Friday. Then I got leave till the Sunday night, and rode up to Brownsville to look after Thompson. Unfortunately he had had a slight relapse and had taken to his bed again, but the doctor I called in, in Jones' absence in Corpus Christi, made light of it; said he had been doing too much, but with care and quiet would soon be all right again. So I left him that Sunday afternoon, without any apprehension, and never dreamed that our final parting was so near at hand.

That ride back to camp was a memorable one, for a comrade who rode with me, and myself, were caught in a sudden tornado some miles short of it. An inky blackness spread over the sky with extraordinary rapidity, and almost before we could take shelter in the chaparral, down came the rain in bucketfuls. All that night it poured down upon us, and without blankets, or cover of any sort, we sat shivering and drenched to the skin. Arrived at camp, we found our comrades in not much better plight, for their tents had been blown in all directions, and the whole show was a wreck.

The day we returned an order was read out on "dress-parade," converting us, whether we liked it or not, into the 33rd Regiment of Texas Cavalry, in the regular Confederate service, taking our tents from us, and reducing our transport to four wagons to the regiment. This created a great deal of dissatisfaction amongst the boys; for service in a local Partizan Regiment, for which they had enlisted, was very different from that in a regular corps. To me it brought a hope of escape from the service I hated so much; for in the regulars substitutes were allowed, whilst in the Rangers they were not, and I made up my mind to get one as soon as I could.

Till the Thursday evening we were busy with drills and inspections, and it was not till Friday morning that I could get leave to go back to my sick friend. I found him decidedly worse, though he didn't seem to realise it, but was cheerful, and very glad to see me. "I am always better when I have you with me, old friend," he said. "Don't leave me if you can help it, till I'm all right again."

I had a week's leave, and would be with him all that

time, I told him, and at the end of that, hoped he would be up again. But in my heart of hearts I had no such hope, for it seemed to me the end of all things earthly was close at hand for my poor friend, and the thought was hard to bear. I went off at once to the doctor, and asked his opinion. He had seen Thompson an hour or two before, and said there was no danger, though he certainly was very weak. Might I call in the post surgeon, and would they both see him together? He had no objection, and presently, after consultation, I was assured by both that my fears were groundless, for with good nursing my friend would pull round. That, at any rate, he should have, poor old fellow, as far as I could give him it. All that Friday night I sat up with him, and all Saturday never left him. He was very patient and quiet; but he was growing weaker and weaker, and, notwithstanding the doctors' opinion, I felt sick at heart, for as I watched his thin, drawn features I knew there was no hope.

On Saturday evening, as the daylight was fading, I was sitting by his side, whilst he apparently was dozing. I suppose I looked sad and worried, as indeed I was, for he suddenly opened his eyes, and placing his hand on mine said, " Don't worry yourself about me, my dear fellow; I shall be all right again soon, if you can stay with me and look after me." I declared I wouldn't leave him whatever happened, till he was better. " But you must be back in camp by the end of the week. You mustn't get into trouble for me; I have been trouble enough to others, without that," he said. Then, with a weary sigh, as talking to himself—" I daresay that'll be long enough." He lay quite still after this, and, thinking he was asleep, I was gently moving away when, once more, he laid his hand on mine and said, " Don't move; if you don't mind listening, I should like to tell you who I am, and how I came to leave home, just before we met in Canada."

And this is what he told me, as I sat by his side in the deepening gloom. There was nothing very romantic in it ; only the tragedy of a commonplace life, that so many of us carry about with us for years, hiding it so carefully from our friends behind a smiling, cheerful face, whilst our hearts are heavy within us.

He had been station-master at one of the principal stations of a great railway in the North of England. He had a pleasant home, and a good wife, and lived happily and comfortably in the northern town for about five years. Then one night the Edinburgh express ran into a shunting goods-train just outside the station, and there was a frightful smash : carriages piled on each other, dead, dying, and mutilated passengers, making such a scene as only those who have witnessed such an accident can realise. He was exonerated from all blame for the accident, which, like so many of the kind, had been caused by the carelessness of a signalman. But the shock of the awful scene he had gone through was too much for his nerves, and he sent in his resignation.

The directors of the company gave him a month's leave during which to reconsider the matter ; for he was a valued official, and they wished to retain him. But it was no good. The very sight of the station, and the rush and roar of the trains, so unnerved him that it seemed to his disordered imagination every one was pointing at him as the cause of the disaster.

All this I may say was inexplicable to me, for he always seemed a cool, placid man, the very last one to be troubled with nerves, whilst I knew him. However, in his then state of mind there was nothing for it but to throw up his employment. This done, he left the town, dropped his real name, which had become hateful to him, and took that of Thompson. For a short time he went into farming in an out-of-the-way place in the extreme west of England. But wherever he went he was haunted by the fear lest he should meet some one who knew him, and would whisper, "That's the late station-master of —— who caused that awful accident."

It was becoming a monomania with him ; so at last his wife agreed with him that his only chance was to leave England, and start life afresh in a new country. When he had found a new home, she would come out and join him. In this, as we know, he had failed ; and now, poor fellow, he was going home to his wife, who was eagerly expecting him, he said. Would I write to her by the first opportunity, and tell her how it was he had been so long on the journey ? He gave me her address, and said he had told her all about me, and what friends we had been, and how pleased she would be, poor soul, to get a letter from me.

I promised him to write by the first chance ; but presently he looked questioningly at me and said : " But after all it is perhaps hardly worth while to write, I shall be home almost as soon as your letter." He did go " home," poor fellow, before I could write, for he died in my arms next morning at sunrise.

He was sleeping quietly, after a restless night, and I lay down close by him. Suddenly I heard him gasping and struggling for breath. I held him a few minutes in my arms ; then I laid him back upon the bed, for my poor friend was dead.

At sunset that lovely Sunday evening we laid him to rest in the cemetery hard by the town. An Episcopal clergyman read the solemn Church of England burial service, and then the doctor, and the little party of mourners who had followed with me, left him to sleep for ever, a stranger in a strange land.

My poor friend's death was inexpressibly sad to me, and I mourned him truly as an honourable, open-hearted man, fearless, and truthful in all his dealings. How I regretted having persuaded him to come to Texas ! But then I didn't know his story, or his aims and objects had I known them, things might have been different.

The following day, hearing that Dunn was in town, I went out and asked him for sixty days' leave to attend to my own business, for I felt very reluctant to return to camp just then ; and besides, I had had no tidings from the ranch for some time, and didn't know whether the Indians had cleared out the whole place or not. He said he was very sorry he couldn't grant me this, as all furlough had been stopped by the General's orders, but added, " Now you are in the regulars, why don't you get a substitute ? " Well, it was almost a mockery to ask such a question ; for such things are very rare commodities, and when one by good fortune was found, the authorities were very fastidious about accepting him, unless the applicant were a favourite. However, I said, " Am I to understand, then, you will accept a substitute in my place if I can get one ? "

" Certainly," he answered ; " I will recommend his acceptance by the General, for it rests with him."

How strangely things happen in this world sometimes ! That very evening a young fellow, evidently a sailor and an Englishman, met me in the town, and asked me some question—about a lodging, I think it was. So we got into conversation, and he told me he had come over in a coaster from New Orleans, and been discharged ; that he was sick of the sea, and had some idea of joining the Confederate service : could I put him in the way of it ? " Why," I said, " you've come to the very man who can, and who will put something into your pocket too ! "

Then I told him how I wanted a substitute, and was willing to pay him $150, if that would suit him. He jumped at it, and we struck the bargain at once. I took my man—Osborne was his name, to the hotel—and then went straight off to my friend Dunn again to tell him what I had done.

I wasn't surprised to find that he raised all sorts of difficulties directly. No Englishman would do at any price, and only an American citizen over twenty-five years of age could be accepted. As may be supposed, I was pretty mad at this, and told him he knew as well as I did that what he asked was impossible to get, and if it were possible, would cost three or four thousand dollars. We were alone, so I told him straight he had fooled me often enough already, and I wasn't going to let him do so any more. " I am going now to Colonel Luckett and General Wasp, and if they refuse my substitute, which I don't believe they will, I tell you plainly, Major Dunn, I will serve under you no longer," and with that turned on my heel and left him.

To cut a long story short, Colonel Luckett, who commanded the brigade, sided with me, and thought I was being unfairly treated. He was a good fellow, and had always been friendly with me. " Come right away to the General with me," he said ; " I think I have enough influence with him to fix this up for you, whatever Dunn may say." He was as good as his word, and by Friday evening everything was settled ; my man Osborne was sworn in, I paid him his money, and was a free man once more—free, above all things, from the hateful command of the man Dunn, to serve under whom was a disgrace to a self-respecting man.

And yet, when it came to parting with some of my old comrades, I couldn't help regretting the severance. The majority of them were right good fellows, rough frontiersmen as they were, and many a good turn they had done me ; showing their confidence in me too by voting for me when I ran for lieutenant. Not a man amongst them blamed me for going, though I confess I felt a sort of sneaking feeling in my heart of hearts, as though I were deserting them in what might be the hour of danger. However, I consoled myself with the thought that after all I wasn't going away to lead an easy or luxurious life, but back to the exposed Indian frontier, where the few and scattered inhabitants, it might truly be said, lived in a state of chronic warfare, and had hard enough work to protect their property, let alone their scalps.

So, on May 12, 1863, just a year after joining them, I left the Partizan Rangers, now the 33rd Regiment of Confederate Cavalry, with many a warm hand-shake from old friends, and many a hearty wish for our speedy meeting again.

After spending a few days in Matamoras with acquaintances I had made, I bethought me I had promised to inquire for letters for a friend in Brownsville, and so strolled into the post-office, a wooden shanty with racks round the interior, in which letters are deposited till called for. Whilst the Mexican postmaster was deliberately searching for the name I had given, I glanced round and there, right opposite me, saw a packet addressed to myself in my mother's handwriting! Then I examined a flyblown list of letters uncalled for, which was stuck against the wall, and found there were two more for me. I hadn't heard from home for months, and was delighted with my unexpected find.

The letters had been addressed " Care of the South Western Express Company," which, so far as I could learn, had no existence except in the fertile imagination of an English newspaper man who had advised those having friends in the South to so address their letters. How mine ever got to Matamoras still remains a mystery ; but I got them, which was the great thing, and was happy in their possession, the more so that my finding them in that unlikely place was a pure chance. Having finished my business in Matamoras, I set out with a friend who was going 125 miles of the way to Victoria, on my eight days' ride to San Antonio, which I reached without any misadventure.

CHAPTER VIII

IN COMMAND AT LAST !

I MUST now explain that, from the middle of May 1863, to the beginning of November 1864, I neglected to keep the rough diary I had hitherto written up pretty regularly —partly from want of time, partly because nothing of much interest happened, but chiefly I fear because I was idle. But in the latter month, being a good deal at the ranch, and the rest of the time in winter quarters, with the frontier company I then commanded, I wrote up notes of anything I could remember of importance during the interval. From these, therefore, I resume my story, such as it is.

From San Antonio I rode off to the ranch, after one day's rest. There I arrived late in the evening, to the great surprise of the Mexicans, for I was the last person they expected, or wished, to see. Having no one to look after them, these gentry, after the manner of their kind, had been taking things very easy, and everything had been neglected. Calves had been left unbranded ; horses allowed to stray miles away on the prairie, till the only wonder was that the Indians hadn't cleared out the lot. However, I soon changed all that, and kept the lazy rascals hard at work from morning till night ; they, no doubt, the while, heartily wishing me back on the Rio Grande, or anywhere else.

The night of my return I heard there was a Mexican beef-buyer in the country, about twelve miles above me ; and as I was in dire need of cash for current expenses, I started out next morning with some of my vaquéros to his camp. Finding I could do business with the Mexican, I set to work cattle-hunting for eight days, collecting a good bunch of fat stock, which I sold for $2,500, and so returned to the ranch in much contentment.

One day I rested there, and then, as I was quite out of stores of all kinds, had to ride into San Antonio again, sending my wagon on ahead of me. I found the town in great excitement over the fall of Vicksburg, and General Lee's Pennsylvania campaign. The former event I looked upon as a most serious disaster for our cause, and a blow so staggering that it would probably compel the South to capitulate very shortly. In this of course I was mistaken, for the desperate struggle continued, with increasing bitterness, for two years longer ; the dauntless Lee, with ever more and more diminishing forces facing his foes with a resourcefulness and rapidity of movement that made the whole world wonder and admire.

The heart of the whole Southern people was lifted up to that hero, as the heart of one man, in worship and in admiration ; and how anxiously and eagerly every soul watched and waited for tidings of his great deeds ! But now, in the cold light of afterwards, it is easy to see, though hard to say, that it would have been better for the South had her hero been a smaller man, and less selflessly devoted to her cause : her death-struggle would have been shorter, and the sum of her awful agony reduced.

But still in San Antonio I found every one, especially the non-combatants, and above all the neswspaper editors, very warlike ; they were going to whip the hated Yankees to a certainty ! What, however, troubled these worthies more than the disasters of the war was the rapid fall in value of the Confederate paper-money, which now was at a discount of about 88 per cent. " Where would it stop ? " was the question in every one's mouth ; and it was only those who had some foresight who realised that, if the South lost, it would be abso-

lutely worthless. Fortunately these were a very small
minority, or I don't know what would have happened.

Returning to the ranch after a week in San Antonio,
I had to start out again to look after some stock some
miles up the Frio, so there wasn't much respite from
the saddle for me. Whilst camping there an old acquaintance, of the name of Johns, turned up somewhat
unexpectedly. He had served in the old company
with me, but, suffering much from rheumatism, had been
discharged. He came of a good Virginian family, and
was an old bachelor, very eccentric in his notions and
habits, but, take him altogether, a very good fellow.

I knew he was as poor as a rat, so invited him, when
he got his discharge, to come up to the Frio, and if he
had nothing better to do, he could put up there as long
as he liked, and I should be delighted to have him. So
now he was on his way there, and I was glad enough to
see him, for life on a ranch by oneself is but dull work.

I'm afraid his first night on the Frio was not very
pleasant, for the rain came down in torrents. In those
days I never got up for rain, unless I was fairly washed
out ; so I rolled myself in my Spanish manta, which
is nearly impervious to water, and slept through it
pretty well. Not so poor Johns, who said next morning
he had wandered about disconsolately all night, to try
and keep himself warm.

About sunrise the rain ceased, and I unrolled myself
from the manta to find the Mexican had prepared the
usual breakfast of fried beef, corn bread, and coffee.
After this I was strolling a little way from camp when,
behind a clump of live-oaks, I came on a lively scene.
An American lad, not more than eighteen years old,
had his six-shooter pointed at one of my vaquéros, and
was threatening to shoot him, whilst the latter, with
his knife drawn, and his eyes gleaming with rage, was
telling him in Mexican, not a word of which did the
lad understand, to make a sure shot, or he would kill

him with his knife. I very soon put a stop to the row, the cause of which I have forgotten ; but it was lucky I turned up when I did, for a minute or two later on, one or other of them would have been dead.

The country was too wet to do much riding, so I turned back to the ranch, and Johns with me. He, poor fellow, was, I think, the most awkward man on a horse I ever beheld, and the rheumatism, which had stiffened one of his knees, didn't improve his horsemanship. He hated riding, which was not to be wondered at, though a most unusual thing in Texas, and never would get on a horse if he could help it. Of course in a country like that, of " magnificent distances," he had to ride, but it was always pain and grief to him.

It was now early in the month of July, and the heavy rains had changed the whole face of nature with a suddenness which always struck me with wonder, often as I had seen it. Months of drought and fervent heat burn the prairies brown : even the evergreen live-oak leaves seem scorched and withered, and all the land parched and dry, till one yearns for the sight of something green. Then the heavy clouds gather, down pours the torrent of rain for perhaps forty-eight hours without ceasing, and the whole scene is changed as though by a magician's wand ; the grass springs fresh and green, the flowers bloom ; lagoons of pure water fill the dry hollows, and all things living rejoice in the transformation.

Most of that month Johns and I remained at the ranch, branding calves, looking up the stock, and generally getting matters straight. In our spare time we amused ourselves fishing, and shooting turkeys, deer, peccary, etc. ; but as I have already described sport on the Frio, I do not propose to do so again. Johns was very keen on what he called " gunning," or hunting, and, when I was too busy, or too lazy, to go with him, would often sally forth, mounted on his old Mexican pony, by himself ;

and a queer figure he looked—something like the immortal Don of blessed memory.

One evening he returned from one of these solitary trips, a stranger figure than usual. What he had done with himself I couldn't make out at first, but as he drew near, I saw he had stripped off his pantaloons and in them was carrying, in front of him, a young fawn he had captured. It was tied up as in a sack, but objected most strongly to this mode of conveyance, and struggled so violently that, just as he got into the corral, it burst its bonds asunder, leaving the pants torn and ripped almost beyond repair.

Johns' face was a study as he ruefully turned over and examined his ruined nether garments; but presently he dropped them and set off, with his shirt tails flying in the breeze, in pursuit of his fawn, which, left to itself, was making off out of the corral. The little thing was quite young, so Johns, with the help of one of the Mexicans, soon ran it down; but the chase whilst it lasted was most comical. The pants were apparently beyond repair, but the old fellow was both persevering and ingenious, and stitched them together somehow; indeed he had to, for at the moment they were the only pair he owned.

He was a great hand at tanning alligator-skins, making them quite soft and pliable. As there were plenty of the brutes in the river, he kept all hands on the ranch supplied with excellent leather for mocassins, besides selling quite a quantity of the skins in San Antonio, where they were in great demand.

One day about this time, riding home to the ranch, I saw a number of buzzards hovering over the edge of the chaparral, a sure sign something lay dead, so turned out of my way to see what it was, and was rewarded by finding a fine fat buck, just killed by a panther. It was in such splendid condition that I took the liberty of helping myself to a good bit of the loin, which I tied

behind my saddle and carried home. I'm afraid when
the founder of the feast returned he didn't find much left,
for by the time I had loaded up my share of the spoils,
about fifty buzzards were hard at work on the remainder,
and it wouldn't take them long to pick the bones.

In the beginning of August I rode, with a friend, to
Eagle Pass on the Rio Grandé, 160 miles West of San
Antonio. It is a small town, chiefly inhabited by
Mexicans, and just across the river is the Mexican pueblo
of Piedras Negras. It is a port of entry, through which
a good deal of cotton always passed into Mexico, and this
had been largely increased by the war, and consequent
blockade. Though a miserable one-horse place, the
war had brought it a good deal of trade of one sort and
another, and the object of my trip was to see if I couldn't
sell my friend the Alcaldé of Piedras Negras some of my
beeves for the Mexican market.

He received us most hospitably, putting us up very
comfortably, for his house was the best in the place,
and he was a man of some wealth. What was more
important to me, he said he could take a good lot of
my cattle, and would come over to the ranch, in a week
or two's time, to get them.

In Piedras Negras quite a number of renegades and
deserters from the Confederate service had congregated,
and seemed to have things pretty much their own way
there. I was well enough known to many of these gentry,
some of whom assumed rather a threatening aspect ; so I
took care to be well armed with a couple of six-shooters
whenever I went out in the town. Lucky for me I did, for
one morning I got into a crowd of about twenty of them,
and was told my name was down on a black list of men
who were doomed ; that sooner or later they would
" get " me, and then drive my stock over into Mexico.

I was in a pretty tight place, one against twenty
ruffians, but my only chance was to put a bold face on it.
So I whipped out my six-shooters and faced the lot of

them, saying, " You'll never have a better chance to get me than now, but the first one that handles his weapon is a dead man. Hands up every one of you, or I'll loose off ! " Up went the hands like one, and I saw they were either cowed by my getting first draw, or else by good luck were all unarmed at the moment—the latter, probably. Just then the Alcaldé and two of his friends turned into the plaza and, seeing what was in the wind, joined me at once.

Now, having some backing, though I don't know that my friend the Alcaldé was much of a fighting man, I turned to the crowd, that still stood " hands up " before my levelled six-shooters, saying : " If you want my cattle, and dare to come for them, I promise you a good time before you get them, and I'll meet you half way if I know you're coming. Now you can get." And they went. But when Don Miguel Ramos, the Alcaldé, heard what had taken place, he agreed with me that a longer stay in Piedras Negras would not be healthy ; so before my friends the deserters could organise an attack, which no doubt they would have done under cover of night, we cleared out, and saw no more of them.

On the way back to the Frio we met a Mexican, who said a large band of Indians had been seen in the neighbourhood the day before, and were supposed to be still in the country. We kept on, but rode very cautiously, making no fire, even at night. I was very uneasy, wondering what had happened at the ranch, and whether Johns had heard the news and penned my horses in time. On the last day of the journey my uneasiness was not relieved by coming across fresh sign of a very large band. However I had been most fortunate again, for the Comanchés had passed my ranch some miles to the right ; probably because they had got what they wanted lower down the river. Johns had seen nothing of them, but had heard they were in the country, and had taken the precaution to pen the horses.

I found a party of Mexicans waiting for me at the
ranch with a large bunch of mustang mares, just caught,
which they wanted to sell me. I declined the offer,
for full-grown mustangs can never be tamed in a wild
country like that, and as soon as the clogs are taken off,
make for the prairie and their old haunts again. They
are pretty little creatures, running between twelve and
thirteen hands high, and when caught quite young,
and very carefully gentled, make very good cattle-ponies,
being active as cats, and wonderfully tough. But a
full-grown mustang, fresh off the prairie, is about as
wild a thing as you can imagine ; yet the Mexican
vaquéros, in their high peaked and cantled saddles,
with a blanket rolled in front, to keep their knees down,
generally contrive to stick on.

The animal is blinded, and the fore-leg strapped up.
The Mexican vaults lightly into the saddle, pulls off the
blind, the mustang is let go, and the fun begins. With
arched back, and head between his fore feet, if he can
get it there, the little animal jumps all ways at once,
whilst his rider drives in those awful spurs, and plies
his " quirt," to try to get him into a gallop. Once he
succeeds in that, the fight is won, for he never lets him
stop whilst he has a kick left in him.

But the next time he is mounted, much the same
performance goes on, and a mustang never becomes
what you would call " a mount for a nervous gentleman " ; not even a horse-dealer could conscientiously
so describe him, I think.

At the end of August my friend the Alcaldé from
Piedras Negras turned up for the cattle, and stayed with
me a week whilst we were hunting them for him. During
this hunt a wild steer came very near doing for me.
He charged right at me, and as my horse, usually a very
good one at the game, turned to avoid the rush, he
stumbled. In a moment the steer was on us, and over
and over we went in a confused heap of man and horse.

When I came to myself, on a lounge in the house, I was surrounded by all the Mexicans in the establishment ; the women kicking up no end of a row, and declaring, " Es muerte ! el pobre señor ! " But I wasn't dead, or anything like it—only stiff all over, as if I had been well beaten ; and it was some days before I could get up into the saddle again. It seems that just as the steer bowled us over, one of the Mexicans, riding close behind me, roped him, and so stopped his charging again ; probably so saving my life.

Every evening of his stay the Alcaldé, who had a great gift that way, entertained us with Mexican " cuentos," or tales ; many of them very good, and all well told. It is quite a custom with these people to yarn like this ; and in that out-of-the-way country, where there are no books or newspapers, and where none could read them if there were any, they will gather together in some friend's house and listen nearly all night to a good narrator.

The stories I fancy are traditions handed down from father to son perhaps for centuries, for many of them have their locale in old Spain ; though most of them have their scene in Mexico, and are tales of hunting, cattle-raiding, love and war, and vendettas fought out between neighbouring pueblos.

I traded with the Alcaldé to our mutual satisfaction, and he and his peons drove off a fine lot of fat beeves, whilst I received a good solid sum in hard dollars ; so that, for the first time for many a day, I had cash to the good, and began to lay by money, which I hoped steadily to increase if things kept right. If only peace could be restored, and the frontier be protected from Indian and guerilla raids, I felt confident of ultimate success. But alas ! there was no such good fortune for me. The South was determined to accept no terms short of independence, and the North was equally resolute not to grant it.

The fall was a very seasonable one ; my cattle were

flourishing, and increasing rapidly, and I had high hopes of being able to run over to England in the coming spring, if only for a short visit. But these pleasant dreams were soon dispelled, for in the month of October 1863 the Legislature of the State passed an ordinance rendering all able-bodied men between twenty and fifty years of age liable to serve, either in the Confederate army or with the State troops. In fact it was universal conscription, and I was wondering how soon I should be called out, and what service I should have to join, when I received an order from Governor Murrough to enrol a company for the protection of the adjacent frontier and the upper Rio Grandé. Accompanying it was a commission as Civil Magistrate for the district. Though the company was to be raised primarily for frontier service, it was liable to be ordered anywhere, or against any enemy, at the sole discretion of the Governor.

The service was a popular one amongst the frontiersmen, who had suffered so terribly in life and property from the raids of Mexican guerillas and Indians, so I soon enlisted and enrolled the requisite number of eighty men. Each man brought his own horse and arms, for which he was paid by the State, as soon as mustered in—in paper, of course. As soon as the enrolment was complete, I ordered the men to hold an election for officers, and was very much pleased and flattered when they elected me to command them ; the more so as the election was perfectly free and independent on their part, and was managed by ballot, so that no unfair pressure could be applied by anybody.

I may say at once that I was very proud of my little command ; for all, or nearly all, were good and tried frontiersmen, well mounted and armed, and ready to go anywhere and do anything in the way of fighting. Certainly there wasn't a finer body of men in all the State of Texas, and, if I had to soldier, I was content to do so in their company.

CHAPTER IX

My company was not attached to any regiment, so I had no " ranking officer," as they say out West, and was my own commanding officer, and indeed was, for a long time, the sole authority, civil or military, in a very wide district.

I didn't bother my men with much drill; it was sufficient for me that they could ride, and shoot, and perform the simplest evolutions, which I held were the three essentials for an irregular corps such as ours.

The first service we were sent on, was to go to the assistance of Colonel Benavides, who, with a force of State troops, was holding Lorado, on the middle Rio Grandé, against a threatened attack by Yankees and Mexican guerillas. My orders were to report myself to the Colonel at the earliest possible moment, as he was daily expecting to be attacked by a force much stronger than his own. The distance was just over two hundred miles, and we did it in four and a half days, arriving before the enemy had crossed the river. Though there was no fight, for the mongrel crew of Yankees and guerillas, as soon as our presence was known, cleared out, yet our forced march was not in vain. As they retreated down the Mexican side of the river, we could not of course follow them, though my fellows were very keen to have a go at them.

After a week's rest at Lorado we returned to the Frio district, and had only been back a few days when news reached me that a big band of Indians had been killing, and raiding horses, some miles to the north of us. The next morning we started in pursuit, and the following day hit the trail, a very plain one, made, my trailer said, by at least one hundred Indians, driving nearly double that number of horses. But they had a week's start of us, and ride as we might, we couldn't catch up with them. So after a ten days' ride, which took us right up into the mountains, we had to turn back, being nearly out of provisions, and none being procurable in that wild country, though fortunately there was plenty of water. The weather was very cold, and the men suffered a great deal from that, and from scanty rations. It is no joke sleeping on the ground, with only one small blanket over you, when the frost is keen enough to freeze the pools and water-holes, but my fellows bore it all without a murmur. Of course I fared exactly as they did, and doing everything I could for their comfort, I believe became popular with the whole command.

December, I think, was the coldest month I ever experienced in Texas, for even down on the prairies we had constant frosts, severe enough to freeze the shallow pools and lagoons. It was cruel work camping as we usually did, and sleeping on the bare ground with only the sky for shelter, so I formed a permanent camp for the company a few miles up the Frio. It was situated in a sheltered hollow hard by the river, handy for water, and where the boys, if they took the trouble, could get plenty of fish, and game of all sorts. All hands working with a will, good warm bush huts were soon built, and the men were as comfortable as frontiersmen ever expect to be in their rough lives.

Having fixed up the camp to my satisfaction, and got everything in good order, I handed over the command to my 1st Lieutenant, and gave myself leave to go down to the ranch to spend Christmas. I took a couple of the boys with me who were very keen to see some sport with a scratch pack of hounds I had

21

just got out from San Antonio. They were foxhounds, originally brought down from the Northern States, and though perhaps not what you would call here "fashionably bred," were a useful lot, with plenty of dash and music. There were only five couple of them, but they could bustle the big "lobos" and smaller, though more artful, coyotés, properly. My friend Lieutenant Jack Vinton, of the Rangers, came up just before Christmas, and we four had many a good gallop.

We would start of a morning, just after sunrise, when the air was beautifully cool and fresh, and the dew lay thick on the prairie grass. Dotted here and there were "motts," or clumps, of white chaparral, and big patches of long grass, favourite lyings for both kinds of wolves, so we hadn't got far to draw, and were sure of a find.

The "lobos" were great grey brutes, rather bigger than the European wolves one sees at the Zoo, and go a tremendous pace. But there was so much game about in the country, and they, in addition, made so free with my young stock, that we generally found them pretty full, and not in condition to run away from the hounds. When empty, they certainly had the legs of them, and would make for the dense chaparral along the river, where they were generally lost.

The country, for miles and miles, was open, rolling prairie, with no coverts on it except the motts I have spoken of, scattered here and there at wide intervals. Therefore if the lobo was roused out on the prairie, a few miles from the brush on the river-bottom, we were sure of a good run of perhaps an hour or more, and at a clinking pace ; for scent in the early morning was generally very good, and there were no fences to stop hounds or men, and no coverts big enough for the hunted wolf to dwell in. Of course we were not always in luck's way, no sportsman ever is, but we rarely went out without having at least one good run, ending with a kill more often than not.

By ten or eleven o'clock, when the sun grew too hot to be pleasant, our day's sport was done, and we made for home, to enjoy the usual substantial breakfast of fried beef or deer meat, or wild turkey, with perhaps a dish of delicious fresh-caught fish. The only accompaniment to these viands was the everlasting corn bread ; and the drink was strong coffee. We had no vegetables, for no one, American or Mexican, ever thought of growing any, in Western Texas at least. At certain seasons of the year however the Mexicans used to gather the young flower stalks of the magie plant, and the tender shoots of the nopal, or prickly pear, when they were about as large as a hen's egg. Both of them were very good boiled, especially the latter, which has a flavour of asparagus about it. At first, I confess, one misses vegetables very much ; and bread and meat day after day, for months together, gets somewhat monotonous, but, *pace* the vegetarians, it can't be an unwholesome diet, for many Americans, and vast numbers of Mexicans, lived and thrived on it, and it alone, for years.

It should be borne in mind, however, that the people who lived on this diet led active lives in the open air, otherwise it might not have suited them so well.

Early in January 1864 I received an order to send a detachment of twenty-five of my men to join a Major Hatch, and serve with him in an expedition into the Indian territory, away up in the mountains to the north-west. The detachment was to go under command of my 1st Lieutenant, whilst I remained on the frontier with the rest of the company.

The Comanchés had been more troublesome than usual, and had raided the upper settlements, murdering, burning ranches, and driving off stock wholesale. The authorities therefore determined they should be rigorously followed up, and the war, if possible, carried into the enemy's country, for a change ; more especially as, contrary to custom, the Indians had, on this occasion, carried off some unhappy women and children captives with them.

The season of the year was most unfavourable for such an expedition, which I knew must be most trying for the men; and knowing more of Indian fighting, and of the country, than my Lieutenant, I determined to go myself. Accordingly I reported myself in Major Hatch's camp two days after the receipt of the order. He had fifty men with him, fairly mounted, but very inferior to my boys in every other respect.

The next day I was sent on ahead with my men, to impress cattle for the command, which had to be driven along with us for provisions. Having everything ready I awaited the command at a creek called Piedra Pinta, where, the very morning of its arrival, I learned that the fresh trail of a large band of Indians going down to the lower settlements had been seen just to the east of us. I urged the Major to stay where he was with his command, to guard the passes into the mountains, whilst I sent an express to my company to take the trail, when if they didn't come up with the Indians themselves, they would probably drive them into our hands. But he knew better, or thought he did, and insisted on following the trail himself.

Of course I could only obey, but I sent an express to my second in command, ordering him to get on the trail forthwith and follow it as fast as he could. If he had only obeyed his orders, he most likely would have driven the Comanchés back to us; but he too knew better, and instead of following the trail struck across country to where he *thought* the Indians would make for, intending to waylay them on their return. The savages however, thinking my whole company had gone on the expedition, took their time, killed three men, drove off a good " caballado," and made their exit by another route, to the intense disgust of the boys. So much for making cocksure of knowing the movements of Indians !

We of Major Hatch's command of course missed the Indians too, and they got off scot free. We had also lost valuable time in this wild-goose chase, and the original raiding band we set out after had of course distanced us completely, so that we had no chance of coming up with them before they got back to their fastnesses.

Now, to add to our difficulties, we were called off on another false scent, which Major Hatch followed with alacrity. He had sent a scouting party up to Presidio, on the Rio Grandé, who returned with a yarn that two companies of Federal troops from California were coming down on Fort Lancaster, on the Pecos, and even now must have taken it. I told him I didn't believe a word of it, since the man who would attempt to march an unsupported force like that right across from California, at that season of the year, was only fit for an asylum. But he wouldn't listen to reason. So to Fort Lancaster we went, a week's march there and back, only to find the whole story was a hoax, and no Yankees were within hundreds of miles of the place ! After a brief rest, which we were obliged to give the horses after this useless marching and counter-marching, we returned to Piedra Pinta, there to resume our original scout into the Indian country.

Piedra Pinta, as the Texans called it, though it was properly " Piedra Pintada," or Painted Rock, was a fast-running, shallow creek flowing for some distance between steep cliffs, on many of which were paintings made by the Indians. Some of these were mere signs, left by a raiding band, to give information to their comrades who might pass that way. But others were rude sketches of the white men they had slain, and the scalps and other trophies they had taken in their raids. The colours they invariably used were red, white, and blue, but how they obtained them I don't know.

The weather grew colder and colder as we left the lowlands, till at last, when we were well in the mountains, we all suffered much from it, for from the nature of the service we could carry no extra clothing, and had but one blanket apiece. Moreover we were obliged to be very sparing with our rations to make them last out the trip. The second day's march took us well beyond the farthest settlements, and that night we camped at the San Felipé springs, which are the most remarkable I ever saw. They are the sources of a small stream of the same name which runs into the Rio Grandé, and the two of them rise from the bottom of an immense rock-basin. The water, which is said to be unfathomable in depth, is a beautiful clear blue colour, and full of mountain trout. What the depth really is I don't know, but I heaved in a good big rock, and watched it sink down and down in the crystal pool till it dwindled to a speck and then vanished, apparently without touching bottom. What a splendid site for a cattle ranch this spot was ! for there was the best of water, and all the surrounding land for many miles carried, even at that season, a great crop of grass.

Our next camp was at Devil's River, where were more Indian paintings, only this time in a cave. They were much the same as those at Piedra Pintada, though one quite recent artistic effort had apparently been made for our special benefit, as it depicted quite a large number of warriors with their bows and arrows, many of them carrying what looked like scalps.

We had now reached a fine game country, and in the ravines running back from the river saw many bears ; whilst now and then a herd of antelopes, headed by some veteran leader, would come galloping up to within thirty yards or so, stand stock still for a minute or two, and then, having satisfied their curiosity, scamper off as fast as they came, in ever-widening circles. Scanty as our rations necessarily were, the boys were sorely tempted to shoot some of the antelopes, and I had hard work to stop them. On such business as we were engaged in, it would have been madness to run the risk of alarming Indian scouts, who for all we knew might be lurking near by. So the game went untouched, and the boys grumbled, but obeyed orders.

At this camp some of the boys brought me lumps of ice, many inches thick, as a curiosity. I should have been better pleased if they could have brought some fuel; for all we had were some stalks of dry " bears' grass," and what, in border lingo, are called "buffalo chips." These together were barely sufficient for cooking purposes, and left no surplus for warming our chilled blood.

Near our next camp, by a big water-hole called " Yellow Banks," from the colour of the water, we found fresh Indian sign, and the remains of a recently slaughtered horse. These Comanchés esteem horse-marrow the greatest delicacy in the menu, and, epicures that they are, will often kill an animal for the marrow in its bones, leaving the rest of the carcase for the buzzards and coyotés. These latter follow hard on the Indians' trail to pick up any unconsidered trifles left behind in their camps, and, artful, sneaking, furtive brutes that they are, somewhat closely resemble, in many of their ways, the " humans " they scavenge for.

I think I have already mentioned that all these Indians in Texas are fond of horse flesh, preferring it to beef; but what they like best of all is mule flesh, so the owner of a mule in these parts has to keep a sharp look-out, if he doesn't want to have it run off. In my time the stockmen didn't go in much for mules, as they are no good for cattle-running, but there were plenty of them in Mexico.

Our next march lay over " Deadman's Pass," a steep and narrow defile in the mountains on the trail to El Paso, on the Rio Grandé. At this spot, a couple of years before, a considerable party driving cattle into Mexico had been waylaid by the Comanchés, and killed to a man; hence its ill-omened name. It was the very place for such an ambush, for the steep mountain sides that closed in on the track were strewn with huge boulders, and two hundred resolute men could easily have held it against two thousand.

A few miles beyond the pass we struck the Devil's River again, close to Fort Hudson, which before the war had been a U.S. post capable of accommodating two companies of cavalry. It was now a complete ruin, everything but the adobe walls, which wouldn't burn, having been burnt by the Indians. Wandering round the ruined fort, I came on the little graveyard hard by it, the last resting-place of some dozen brave fellows who had once guarded this solitary, far-away outpost of civilisation, and probably had fallen victims to their crafty foes. Once carefully tended, the graves, and the simple mementos at their heads, were rapidly falling to decay, like their unconscious tenants, and one sadly wondered what were the life-stories lying buried in that neglected spot, and whether those who perchance still mourned their loss knew of their desolate resting-place, where only the mournful wolves and weird owls sang their dirges.

Passing on from this melancholy ruin, we marched up the valley of the river and camped that night at Peccan Spring, a noble basin of clear blue water, though not so fine as the San Felipé. Here again were abundant Indian sign, comparatively fresh, and we began to hope that we might before long come up with the band. Here, too, was more game than ever, antelope and javaline (wild hogs) being very numerous. Buffalo sign were all round the springs too, and now on the hillsides we began to see a few black-tailed deer, a large species with tufted tails, which is only found in the mountains near the upper Rio Grandé. As we rode along we often flushed coveys of quail, of which there are many varieties in Texas, the most beautiful being a rather large one with a glossy blue head and neck and silvery specks on the body-feathers.

As the Indian sign was so very plain, and the band couldn't be very far ahead of us, I was ordered to take sixteen of my boys to scout on the trail and bring back what information I could glean to Major Hatch, who remained in camp with the rest of the command. We took no pack-animals, but just four days' rations in our malletas, and with us went the best trailer and Indian fighter I have ever met in all my frontier service. This was Dan Westfall of the Leona, so called from a terrible adventure that befell him in a little cabin he owned on that creek.

In some ways he much resembled Fenimore Cooper's hero " Deerslayer " in his mode of life, for he had made his living by hunting and trapping on the borders of the Indian country, and was in great request as a guide whenever Indians were to be followed.   No trail was too indistinct, or difficult for him, and he was up to every dodge and manœuvre of the wily Red Man.   With the old-fashioned long Kentucky rifle, which he always carried over his shoulder, whether afoot or on horse-back, he was a dead shot, and being as cool a hand in a tight place as ever I met, was invaluable for such work as we were engaged on.   He was remarkably " still of his tongue," and it was rarely one could get him to talk of his doings ; but now and then, sitting round the camp fire, when the day's work was done, he would open out to one or two friends, and was always worth listening to.   On one such occasion, on this very trip, I got him to tell the story of his escape on the Leona, and a wonderful one it was, which perhaps it may be interesting to tell in another chapter, when we have done with this scout.

I kept the trail with Westfall and another guide, about three hundred yards ahead, the rest following in Indian file.   The country consisted of stony, bare ridges, with only here and there a little brush, and the trail on such hard ground was not easy to follow.   But Westfall kept on, hour after hour, and never seemed for one moment in doubt, even when to eyes like ours, accustomed to Indian sign, no vestige of a trail was visible. His eyes were fixed on the ground as he rode along, never speaking a word, never turning or hesitating ; it was more like a hound following a line with unerring nose, than a human being guided by vision.

That night we camped, as soon as the light failed us, without water, on one of these bare ridges, and I took my turn of guard with the rest. Nor, when it was over, could I sleep ; for I knew the Indians, in unknown numbers, were not far off, and in such an exposed position a surprise would have been fatal. Soon after we started in the morning, I saw, far away to the south-west, two columns of smoke, some miles apart, rising straight up in the still morning air. I touched Westfall on the arm, and pointed. " As I thought," he said, " the darned critters are making for beyond the Pecos. A bad country to follow 'em in : too much brush." Presently the smoke disappeared ; the fires had been put out, and the Indians were on the move again.

All that day we rode on over much the same country, following each other in Indian file, silent and alert. Much the same, only with this addition, that now we were in a region where every sort of scrubby, prickly cactus grew and flourished, and made riding a difficulty. The commonest kind was one the boys called the " bayonet cactus," a sturdy thing growing only about six inches high, but studded with thorns as stiff and as sharp as a penknife. Do what they would the unfortunate horses couldn't help treading on them, and several were badly lamed, notably one of the two I had with me.

No water the previous night and no water all day had given us all a pretty bad thirst, the unfortunate horses suffering even more than their riders. But just before nightfall the trail led us to a rocky basin that held enough water to give us, horses and all, a good drink round, and then to fill our canteens. The Indians had camped here, and killed and eaten a cow, as we thought, about two days before. So it was evident they were taking things leisurely and, so far, had no idea they were being followed. After a couple of hours' rest I therefore started again and marched on well into the night, by the light of a brilliant moon, camping at last not far from the Pecos River.

"Pecos" is a corruption of the Mexican name for the stream, which is Rio Puerco, or Pig River—I presume from the dirty colour of its waters and the muddy character of its banks.

When next day the trail led us to the river the prospect was not inviting, for the current ran strong and deep, and quite 150 yards wide. On our side there was no timber to make rafts; so there was nothing for it but a swim in the ice-cold water, and some of the boys couldn't swim at all. These, and indeed some of the others, were very unwilling to cross under these conditions, so there was nothing to be done but to give them a lead, which I knew they wouldn't refuse to follow.

After some prospecting up and down stream, I at last found a place where the banks shelved on either side and there was only about fifteen yards of swimming to be done. Here we crossed safely, and, what is more, kept our arms and provisions dry. Of course we all, swimmers and non-swimmers, kept hold of our horses; but two of the latter, in their fright, let go, and were nearly drowned, when we fished them out with our "lariats." It was a great relief when all were safely over, and I confess that, though not one of those who hanker after a fight, I would rather have fought Indians, or anything else, under fair conditions, than swim that stream. We were of course as wet as drowned rats, and, to add to our discomfort, a cold drizzling rain set in, so that our plight was miserable enough for the rest of that day. But what befell us across the Pecos must be reserved for another chapter.

CHAPTER X

WESTFALL'S STORY

WHEN we had straightened up a bit after the crossing, we rode on again for about two hours through, as Westfall had foretold, a brushy country with, here and there, a little timber on it. A risky country to follow Indians in with so small a force as mine. Every man therefore kept his loaded rifle unslung and we advanced very slowly, with scouts out wide on either flank, and Westfall and myself following the trail well ahead of the rest. In this order we crossed a wide shallow stream, the name of which was unknown to any of us, with still thicker brush on the far side.

It was now growing dusk, and I therefore halted my party in a mott of thickish timber, where we might have some chance of defending ourselves if attacked. Though, as far as we could see, there was no Indian sign about, I took every precaution to guard against a surprise. The horses were picketed just inside the mott, and four sentries were posted a short distance outside it. The drizzling rain still fell and the moon was hidden behind heavy clouds, so that there was but little light, which was in our favour ; for if we were attacked, the enemy couldn't see us in our shelter.

Now the boys, thoroughly drenched, and miserably cold, begged so hard for a fire to boil some coffee on, that against my better sense I consented, and a small one was lighted in the centre of the mott. The coffee certainly was very grateful, and seemed to me the most delicious brew I ever tasted ; but it nearly cost us our lives. The coffee done, I saw the fire put out, and then the boys lay down to sleep if they could ; but not before I had given them strict orders that no one was to fire a shot, or even to utter a sound without my orders, if by chance we were attacked.

Presently all was still in the camp, and not a sound was to be heard save the stamping of the horses and the heavy breathing of the weary men, who, cold and wet notwithstanding, seemed fast asleep. It was not my turn for guard, which I always took with the rest, but I felt so uneasy, partly on account of that blessed fire, that I couldn't sleep. So I spent the weary hours of that long night creeping as noiselessly as I could round the outskirts of the mott, and occasionally visiting the sentries, to make sure they were on the alert.

It must have been towards morning, though still quite dark, and I was returning from a visit to the sentry on the lower side, when I heard some of the horses give quick, uneasy snorts, and in another moment the sentry on the upper side came running in with an arrow sticking in the fleshy part of his arm. The other three got back unharmed in double quick time, and sooner than it takes to tell, the boys were aroused, and standing to arms.

No word was spoken on our side, and as noiselessly as possible I had the horses brought into the middle of the mott, out of harm's way.

Peering out in the dim light one could see the Comanchés were a strong band, probably 150 in number, some few of whom were armed with rifles. Evidently they didn't know our strength, or our weakness, and their game was to find it out if possible. They came, yelling and screaming, at full gallop up to within twenty or thirty yards of our shelter, and then halting, poured in a volley from their bows and rifles. We all this time stood silently behind the cover of the trees, and suffered no harm from the shooting.

Finding they couldn't draw our fire, and not caring
to charge in on us while our rifles were loaded, they
ceased firing, and set to work cursing and taunting us
as cowards, in very voluble Mexican. One big buck
Indian, who stood not twenty yards from me, was
certainly a master of the art of cursing, and so irritated
me that I was sorely tempted to drop him in his tracks.
All the time he orated and jumped about, flourishing
his tomahawk, I had him covered with my rifle, and
how my fingers itched to pull the trigger ! But better
sense prevailed, and I let him scream on unharmed.

With a power of language I cannot hope to repro-
duce, he anathematised us as cowards, including in
the same category all our relations paternal and maternal ;
then told us how many scalps and horses there were
in their camp, if we dared to go and get them. All
this time I neither spoke nor moved, only watched my
friend, finger on trigger, and rifle at the ready.

Standing a few yards from my post was a young
and excitable Irishman named McCarthy. Up to
now he had held his tongue, and stood quite still, like
the rest of us ; but when the big buck shifted his ground
opposite to McCarthy, and appeared to address his
uncomplimentary remarks to him personally, it was
more than his Celtic blood could stand in silence. He
couldn't speak Spanish, or Mexican, as we always called
the lingo, but he knew that " cobarde " meant coward,
and he wasn't going to be called that for nothing. Out
he jumped from behind his cover, and shouted in the
richest of Cork brogues ; " Coward bedad am I, ye red
divvil ? I'll let ye see ! " and was going to pot my
friend the buck with his rifle. But the moment he
spoke, and almost before he had finished his defiance,
a rifle shot rang out from amongst the band of Indians,
and over went poor Pat. I thought he was killed to a
certainty, for he lay quite still for a few minutes. Presently, however, he scrambled to his feet and, picking

up his rifle, beat a hurried retreat to his tree, with all the talk knocked out of him. He had had a most wonderful escape, for the bullet had struck the broad brass clasp of his pistol-belt in a glancing direction, and, save that all the wind was knocked out of him, he was unhurt.

I think it must have been about two hours that the Comanchés kept up this infernal din, during which time the boys obeyed orders, and neither answered nor returned the fire. Then, quite puzzled by our silence, the Indians drew off to their own camp, to my great relief. All that time I made sure they would charge in on us every minute, and had they done so, but few, if any, would have lived to tell the tale of that night's leaguer.

I don't quite know why they didn't charge, but Indians are very wary and suspicious beings, and it is difficult to fathom their motives. Probably they thought we must be a strong party, having followed them so far up country : then our absolute silence, and the holding of our fire, possibly made them suspect we were waiting for day-light to attack them with greater advantage. Any-way they cleared out, and when I came to reckon up the casualties, found that only three horses and the sentry had been wounded by arrows, and none of them seriously.

We remained in our position for some hours, and it was not till after I had very carefully reconnoitred the surrounding brush, to make sure the enemy had really retired, that I moved my little party out and drew off in the direction of the Pecos again. Very warily and cautiously we retreated, not feeling sure, for the first day or two, that the Comanchés were not following us. I did not take the back trail, but struck higher up the river, in the hope of finding a better crossing, which we eventually did, and returned to camp in six days, where I reported my doings to the Major.

We had pretty nearly finished our provisions before we started back, but managed well enough on coffee once a day, and antelope meat, without bread of any sort. By the by, I think this class of venison is about the meanest stuff you can find in the shape of meat, being lean and dry and tasteless to a degree. It took us six days' steady marching to rejoin the command, for our horses were a good deal done up, and several had been lamed by the bayonet-cactus thorns.

As soon as we had got well away from the Comanché band and there was no longer any fear of their following us, we made ourselves as comfortable as circumstances would permit, and, when wood could be found, indulged ourselves with good camp-fires at night. Round these we smoked and yarned far into the night, if the fire was good enough ; for all of us were frontiersmen, and most of us had had experiences of one kind or another, and more or less interesting. But none of us could compare with Dan Westfall, whose life for nearly thirty years had been one of adventure ; first on the prairies of the great West, amongst the Sioux Indians ; then on the wide stretching plains between the Missouri and the Rockies, even before the most adventurous emigrant had dared to push his way across that awful desert. When tired of killing buffalo for their " robes," he had hunted grizzlies on the foothills of the Rockies, and slain many a wapiti and mountain sheep on the higher slopes. These were his pastimes, or lighter occupations ; his serious business was that of trailer, or guide, to many an out-of-the-way U.S. post or fort on the confines of civilisation. And it was that business that brought him down to Texas, a few years before the war, moved thereto by one of the officers with whom he had served, and who was taking over one of the posts on the Rio Grandé frontier.

On this scout across the Pecos, Westfall and I had camped together, and shared each other's rations. I

had known him for some time, and had always admired
his sterling qualities and indomitable pluck, but in the
closer intimacy of this expedition quite a friendship
had sprung up between us, which lasted till I left the
country. It was the night before we rejoined the command, and Westfall, Jack Vinton and I were enjoying
the warmth of a good big fire in a sheltered hollow,
whilst we smoked and chatted. The talk was chiefly
between Vinton and myself, for the hunter was, as usual,
more inclined to listen than to use his tongue. We were,
I remember, discussing the tactics of the Comanchés,
when they had us penned in that mott, and Vinton said :
" If they hadn't been cowards they would have rushed
us out of that fast enough." Then Westfall spoke.
" Don't you run your head agin that idea, Jack, or it'll
likely bring you to trouble afore long. Injuns is no
cowards, but they're skeery o' traps—skeery as wolves.
That's how them Lepans didn't raise my har, over
on the Leona. They suspicioned it was a trap." " Tell
us the story, Dan," I said, " and I'll brew another pan
of coffee, if you will." And he, probably because he
was in a talkative mood for a wonder, told us the following yarn, which I will retell in my own language :

About six years before, Westfall was living on a small
ranch on the Leona Creek, about thirty miles from the
Frio. With him lived a Frenchman, who was his sole
companion ; both were bachelors, and of course looked
after themselves. Though in Texan parlance the place
was called a " ranch," it was merely a two-roomed
cabin, the walls of which were split poles, and the roof
" clap-boards," or riven timber. It was enclosed by a
fence of stout pickets, forming a small yard round it.
There were no windows, and the floor was of beaten
earth ; just such a poor little place as was common
enough in those days on the outskirts of civilisation.
When not engaged as trailer, or guide, for one of the
frontier posts, Westfall and his friend spent their time

22

in hunting deer and antelope, or the wild cattle which were then pretty plentiful in the thickets of the Leona, varying these occupations by trapping wolves and other " varmint " for their skins.

It was a lovely spot he had chosen for his cabin, as I can testify ; for hard by, the Leona ran between high banks, shaded by splendid walnut and " Peccan " trees, whilst in front stretched the boundless prairie, shining golden in the setting sun-light. Before the cabin stood a giant live-oak, and almost from beneath its roots bubbled up a clear, cool spring of water.

Now the Leona was the centre of the old hunting grounds of the Lepan Indians, and was a district much frequented by them even in those days. But Westfall was too well used to Indians of all sorts, and their ways, to be scared at them ; nevertheless he never stirred out unless armed with his deadly Kentucky rifle and six-shooter, and kept a wary eye open for any sign of their presence, thereby often giving timely notice to out-lying settlers that they were in the country. It was perhaps not an ideal location for a nervous man, but then Westfall wasn't troubled with that complaint ; and as game was abundant, and it was handy for his scouting work with the U.S. troops, the place suited him well enough.

He and his chum had lived in the cabin nearly a year, without molestation, when one morning in the early summer time they returned from fishing in the creek to rest during the heat of the day. The trees were in summer foliage, and the moon was at the full, a time that Indians always choose for their raids ; but no fresh sign had been seen, and neither of them had any suspicion that the Lepans were out on the warpath.

The water-bucket was empty, and the Frenchman stepped out to the spring, just beyond the fence, to fill it. As he turned back to enter the yard, an appalling

Indian yell burst from the thicket behind him, and he
dropped his bucket and ran for his life. But he had
no chance ; the Indians had made sure of their victim,
and he fell, transfixed by three arrows, mortally wounded
at Westfall's feet, who, the moment he heard the yell,
had jumped to the door, rifle in hand, to cover his friend's
retreat. As he did so his favourite dog, a large and
fierce one, dashed out to attack the Indians, but presently
crawled back with an arrow through his body. His
master, who had already dragged the wounded Frenchman inside, opened the door to let the poor dog in,
and received a bullet wound in his thigh and two arrows
in his body. The Lepans, seeing he was hit, made a
dash for the house, but Westfall, who was an unerring
shot with the rifle, dropped two of them in their tracks,
and the rest fell back for the moment, giving him time
to close the door. Fortunately there were three loaded
rifles in the house, and, in addition, his own and the
Frenchman's six-shooter.

His respite was but brief, for the Indians, recovering
from their check, burst into the yard again with furious
yells. But Westfall, wounded as he was, meant to sell
his life dearly ; and if he was to die, many " braves "
would die with him. Firing, through the openings between the picket wall, the two loaded rifles, and then
emptying his revolver into the crowd, he killed one and
badly wounded several more, and once again the savages
gave way, with howls of rage and terror. Then he
reloaded his weapons as quickly as he could, and, for
a few minutes, knelt by the wall—for already he was too
weak to stand—grimly awaiting the next assault. He
had no hope of escape, for outside the fence were a couple
of dozen Lepans, howling for his blood ; and he was alone
with his dead friend, and his dead dog, and gradually
growing weaker and weaker from loss of blood. Faintly
to his ears came the sound of the Indians' shouts and
taunts, and their challenges to the supposed *defenders*

to come out and fight ; then all was silence, for he had
swooned.

How long he lay in that deathly swoon he didn't know,
but when he recovered consciousness the moonlight was
shining in between the crevices of the wall, and all was
still. As he slowly raised himself on one arm, for he
was weak and faint from loss of blood, a bar of light fell
across the upturned face of the dead Frenchman by his
side, and he remembered what had happened. But
why the Indians hadn't scalped him and his friend he
couldn't understand ; they certainly hadn't, for his
hair was still upon his head.

If they were really gone they must have thought, from
the rapid firing, and their heavy losses, that several men
were in the house, and so dared not attack again. Then
too the dead silence that followed the last volley, when
Westfall had fainted, probably made them fear a trap,
of which they are always suspicious. But the first thing
to be done was to draw the arrows, and staunch his still
bleeding wounds ; then he would crawl out, and see how
the land lay.

He took a drink of whiskey, which fortunately was
handy, and then, with desperate pain, pulled out the
arrows, and bound up his wounds with strips of his
shirt. Next, after a brief rest, he opened the door,
and, trailing his rifle after him, crawled out into the
yard. There lay, close to the door, a dead Lepan,
with his arms by his side as he fell. He no doubt was
the last one killed ; the other two had been removed.
Dragging himself outside the yard, he saw his other two
hounds lying lanced and dead ; and all around tracks
of blood were visible in the moonlight, left by the
wounded savages.

He lay long with his ear to the ground. Sound there
was none save the nameless voices of the night, and the
distant howling of the coyotés. The Lepans seemed to
have gone.

Exhausted, and almost hopeless, he got back to the cabin and laid himself down on his bed till daylight came. He was parched with thirst, and there was no water in the house ; but drink he must, so dragged himself to the spring, and drank long and deeply, and was refreshed. All that day he lay on the bed, thinking what he should do. It was clear he couldn't remain long in the house with those two ghastly companions, and he hadn't strength to remove them.

The nearest place where he could get help was Fort Inge, and that was nearly thirty miles away. It was hopeless to drag his wounded limb that weary road ; better to die where he was, or crawl into the brush and hide himself there, like some stricken animal. That was his first thought ; then the indomitable spirit of the man revived, and he resolved to try that awful journey. He knew he couldn't possibly do it unaided, but there was the bare chance a scouting party might find him ; and it was at any rate better to die on the road than in that awful place.

Having made up his mind, he ate a little of the cooked food which luckily was in the house, and lay quiet till nightfall. It would be cooler travelling by moonlight, and the Indians, if still in the neighbourhood, would be less likely to see him. As soon as it was dark then, he took his six-shooter, a little dried venison, a large flask with whiskey, which he filled up with water at the spring, and set off to crawl to the fort. Did ever such a traveller before attempt such a journey ?

For two days and nights he dragged himself along on hands and knees, tortured with pain and parched with thirst, such thirst as only the badly wounded know. Then, even his iron nature could no more, and he lay down, as he thought, to die, under the shade of a live-oak, by the side of the trail, ten miles from his ranch. There, when all hope had vanished, he was found by a scouting party from the fort, who had heard that the

Lepans were out, and was on the road to the Leona to pick up the trail.

A rough litter was soon fixed up, and he was tenderly carried into the fort, where he arrived more dead than alive. But the post surgeon was a skilful man, and Westfall had a marvellous constitution, so he recovered, and in about three months' time was busy with his hunting and his Indian trailing, just as if nothing had happened.

This was the story he told, and I believe every word of it was true ; for I had heard long before at Fort Inge of how he was found on the trail, and carried thither in that awful plight.

When he had finished, he handed me his beloved rifle. " Count them notches under the stock cap," he said ; there's one for every Lepan I've wiped out with her since that day, an' I guess I'm nearly level with the varmints now." There were fourteen tallies on the stock, and room for more !

The Westfall ranch was deserted, and wholly gone to ruin and decay, when last I saw it, but just before what had been the door was a grassy mound, beneath which sleeps the hapless Frenchman ; and at its head a rude cross placed there by Westfall in memory of his dead friend.

CHAPTER XI

THE DESERTERS SURRENDER

WHEN we returned to the command, we found it had been strengthened by the arrival of a Mexican Company under the command of a Captain Pattinia, who knew the Rio Grandé country pretty well. The Major was so uplifted by this accession of strength that he was greatly minded to march off to Fort Lancaster again, to attack another imaginary force of " Feds " said to be in that neighbourhood. This time, however, we managed to dissuade him from such a wild-goose chase, and got him to set about our legitimate business of Indian-hunting ; not that I, for one, had much hope of catching them with such an unwieldy command as ours, operating in such a country as they had retired to.

We marched for Beaver Lake, at the head of Devil's River, and camped there at 2 p.m. on the second day, halting thus early since that was the last water we should touch for fifty miles. We had not been camped more than an hour when the picket-guard came riding in to report that a small party of Indians had been seen driving a band of horses. They were coming in the direction of the lake, and would pass the head of the ravine in which our camp was placed, and which completely hid us from their view. In a moment every one, from the Major down, was in a frantic state of excitement ; men were running hither and thither, saddling their horses and setting out to attack the Indians, without any order or method.

Seeing that this confusion could only end in letting

343

the Indians escape, I got the Major to let me halt and dismount all but twenty picked men, and to take up a position with them at the entrance to the ravine, where was plenty of cover for an ambush. Having placed my men, who were mounted, and with rifles unslung, so that the Indians couldn't well escape us, I climbed up a small rise and peered through the brush to watch for the approach of the enemy. Presently the party, ten in number, driving a lot of horses before them, turned the shoulder of a hill and entered the valley I was watching. They were quite half a mile away, but I saw at a glance they were not Indians, but white men, from the way they sat their horses. When I saw this I formed my men across the ravine, and as the strangers came into sight round another corner, rode out and ordered them to halt.

In a moment they wheeled about, and bolted as hard as they could gallop up the valley, and we after them, helter skelter. The horse I was riding was fast and the men soon began to string out behind me, till there were only five at all near. As soon as I was within hailing distance I ordered them to halt, or I would fire, and they at once dashed into a thick mott, with open timber round it. There they dismounted, and looked as if they meant to make a fight of it. Things looked ugly. But I was anxious to avoid useless bloodshed, so I waved my handkerchief as a flag of truce, and rode up to within some fifty steps of their position and called on them to surrender, promising their lives should be safe if they did so. No answer came, but all their rifles were covering me ; and the position wasn't pleasant, for one or more of them might have gone off by accident.

Meanwhile my boys were coming up in twos and threes, and presently the leader of the party stepped to the front, still with his rifle at the ready, and asked who it was that called on him to surrender, and whose command it was. I told him my name, but said nothing about Hatch (whose reputation for good faith was

not of the best), feeling sure that I had sufficient influence,
backed by my own boys, to enforce due observance of
my promise.

The Major was coming up now, with fifty of his men;
so, if the men were to be spared from immediate hanging,
there was no time to be lost. " Two minutes more, and
if you don't surrender I attack; but if you throw down
your arms, your lives shall be spared." I pulled out my
watch. My twenty boys behind me were fingering their
rifles, all eager to charge. Slowly those minutes passed;
the leader, who seemed a determined fellow, hesitated
till they were nearly gone. He glanced at the Major's
troop coming along at a gallop, and back at his own little
band. Evidently he was a real fighting man, and didn't
like the thought of surrendering. But just as time ex-
pired, his better sense prevailed. He lowered his rifle:
" I surrender to you, and accept your conditions."

The moment he spoke, I ordered my Sergeant to take
their arms; then turned my horse, and galloped back
to meet the Major. " They are either bushwhackers
or deserters," I said; " but I have accepted their surrender, and pledged my word their lives shall be spared."

Now Major Hatch had much the same taste for
hanging defenceless people as the old villain Dunn, of
evil memory, so he received my report with an ill grace:
" You had no right, I guess, to give any such promise.
If they're deserters, a quick ' look up a tree ' is what
they deserve; but I reckon you must have your way,
else you'll git your dander up." Having secured this
unwilling consent I rode back to the mott, where by
this time the men were disarmed, and placed them under
guard of my own boys. Then we collected their horses,
about thirty in number, and marched back to camp.

I at once spoke to my boys about the prisoners, telling
them I expected our present commander would be trying
the same game with them that Dunn had so often played
with other poor wretches before, but that I relied on

them to prevent foul play, and to see that my pledged word was respected. "We'll see you through, Cap, you bet," they all said; and I felt more easy in my mind. The prisoners, it turned out, were deserters, and I had no sympathy with them; all I wanted was that they should be handed over to proper authority to stand their trial, and that I was determined should be done.

I found, or rather had good ground for suspecting, that the old trick was about to be played with them. A weak guard of Hatch's own men was to be mounted over them; then some of his ruffians, in the dead of night, would take the prisoners, without resistance from the guard, and hang them up a little way from camp, on the plea that they were trying to escape. I had known this done too often by Dunn, when I had no power to prevent it. Now I had some power I was going to put a stop to it.

I went straight to the Major, and told him plainly that I insisted on having these men properly tied, so that they couldn't escape, and on having a strong guard mounted to protect them. He tried to laugh it off; said, " If I was so mighty fond of these rascals, how could I be so cruel as to want to tie them ? " Then, knowing my man for the coward that he was, I made up my mind there was only one way to secure my object, and save my honour, and that was to commit right down mutiny.

" Don't think, Major Hatch, you can fool me in this business. I know what's in your mind, and in the mind of your confederate, the scoundrel Luck. Plain speaking is best for us both. If those prisoners are hanged, with your connivance, whilst with your command, your life shall pay the penalty. Now see to it that I haven't to shoot you." He went deadly pale, and I turned on my heel, knowing the prisoners wouldn't be hanged whilst I was alive.

Luck was the man who, as a lieutenant in the Partizan Rangers, had been very prominent in the massacre of the German prisoners after the Nueces fight, described in a previous chapter. He was now a private in Hatch's command, and was hand-in-glove with him in this hanging-plot, as I well knew. I therefore, to make assurance doubly sure, took an early opportunity of telling him that it would not be good for his health to take any part in such doings, and, I think, convinced him on that point.

The unfortunate prisoners were quite aware of their parlous position in Major Hatch's hands, and seemed to look to me for protection; so as soon as I had done with the Major and Mr. Luck, I stepped across to the guard and told their leader that he, and the rest of them, could sleep in peace, for I guaranteed no harm would happen to them. He seemed reassured, but said: "If I'd known that skunk Hatch was in command, I'd never have give in, but fought it out, as you saw I'd a mind to. Stranger, you didn't do just fair not to tell me, but I'll trust you now, for I've no one else I can trust."

The following morning we resumed our march, striking for the Pecos above Fort Lancaster, in order to beat up the Indian camps from above, rather than follow the trail I had found, which would have been a roundabout road. Moreover, the Major still dreamed there were "Feds" in that locality, and was anxious to pass near it on that account.

Very early in the morning I rode on ahead of the main body, with twenty men, to clear out a spring fifty miles away, that Westfall knew of, and which, as it was the only water available for nearly a hundred miles, the Indians would be sure to fill up. We reached the spring at sundown after a thirsty ride, and found it filled up sure enough. All hands set to work to clear it, and when we had about finished the command came up. It was now nearly 10 p.m., and it took us the rest of the night, and well on to midday on the morrow, to water the horses and stock, and even then many of them went short. Taking what water we could in our canteens, we made another dry march that afternoon, with another dry camp at night.

By the middle of the next day, riding over an open, rough country abounding in game, we reached a pretty little running stream a few miles above Fort Lancaster. Here we called a halt by its pleasant banks, and revelled in an abundance of cool delicious water, and a plentiful supply of wood for the camp-fires. From this spot I was sent on with a small party to reconnoitre Fort Lancaster for the Major's imaginary "Feds," the main body of the command following after me. Of course I found no sign of the enemy, nor indeed of any other living creature ; and as to the fort itself, the Indians had burned everything about it that was consumable, leaving nothing but the walls standing, bare and gaunt.

At the confluence of the two rivers, and close to the ruined fort, we halted two days to recruit our jaded stock, and here the boys killed a great number of antelopes, and caught no end of fish, so that the camp-kettles were well filled for a time at any rate. By this time we had several men on the sick-list, and many horses were so done up that they were unridable, and I strongly advised that all such, together with the prisoners, should be sent back under escort, since they hampered our movements. But my commanding officer thought differently ; though how he imagined sick men, lame horses, and prisoners could help to catch Indians, is more than I know.

From Fort Lancaster I went on scout again ahead of the command, with sixteen Mexicans, detailed for the duty, and seven Americans who volunteered, Westfall again going with me as guide and trailer.

I can't say I was anxious to take the " greasers " on such duty, for they are not to be depended on in a tight place. However, it was the Major's order they should go, and I had no option in the matter. We crossed the

Pecos by a ford and made for some Indian camps, located some miles beyond by our scouts, but found them deserted. The Comanchés build no permanent villages, but being nomadic in their habits make temporary camps where grass is good and game abounds, and then after a while move on to " fresh fields and pastures new."

The evening of the second day, after a dry and thirsty ride, we descended a steep mountain-side, down which we could with difficulty lead our horses, and in the valley found a stream of clear running water, with clumps of timber on its banks. On the mountain-top was another of these curious Indian look-outs : a shallow, wide cave, adorned with their hieroglyphic paintings and signs of all sorts.

That night we camped in a mott convenient for defence, and, though it was bitterly cold, made no fire till an hour before dawn ; and then only sufficient to cook our dried beef and boil our coffee. Oh ! that morning brew of coffee ! No dwellers of the city can realise half of what it means to the poor wretch who has laid out on one thin blanket in the freezing air of the mountains through the weary night, till his teeth chatter and his very blood seems congealed.

The day was as hot as the night had been cold, so, after working up the valley for some miles, in the hope of striking a leading trail, I pitched camp at midday. Having placed picket-guards on a mountain-top, perhaps half a mile away, which commanded the country for a considerable distance round, I lay down to take a nap.

But my slumbers were soon disturbed by one of the boys on picket coming in to report that he had seen an Indian scout come riding down the valley, till he reached a point where he could see our staked horses, when he had turned round and galloped back for his life. I gave the order to saddle up at once, and sent Westfall and a couple of the boys on to inspect the sign and make sure the picket was not mistaken. Soon he came riding back to say there was no mistake, for the sign of an Indian horseman was plainly to be seen.

There was every probability that this scout would bring down on us a large party of his friends, and the " greasers " began to get very nervous, as I knew they would at a pinch. I had that morning sent back two of my boys to camp to report my movements, and so had only five left. The Mexican Sergeant, who seemed thoroughly scared at the prospect of a fight, begged to be allowed to return to the command with his party, to hurry it up to our assistance, and when I refused, seemed inclined to go without leave. This had to be put a stop to at once ; so I told him, and his men, that if any one of them dared to leave I would have him shot on the spot. This quieted them for a bit, but I could see they were in such a funk that, if the Indians did come down on us, they would only be in the way. So after talking it over with Westfall and the other boys, who were all anxious to stay, I concluded after all to let the " greasers " go. It was by our reckoning about thirty-five miles, as the crow flies, to the camp, and I knew they would reach it by midnight, and bring the command to us by the middle of next day.

Never did men get under weigh so quickly as these did, when they got the order to go ! They were off down the valley like a flash ; all but one, and he was a half-breed Indian, who hesitated, and then came back, saying he was ashamed to leave us. But I had given my orders, so I told him all he had to do was to obey, and he must go now with the rest.

The " greasers " having departed, and the evening drawing in, Westfall and I made up our minds to look out for some defensible spot, where we might have a chance to hold our own, if attacked, as we fully expected to be, in the night. So we rode up the valley till we came to a very narrow ravine, on our left hand, shut in by lofty precipitous cliffs on either side ; indeed it was more like a cañon than a ravine, being only some thirty yards wide, and not far from its mouth grew some dwarf live-oaks. We tied our horses behind these, and felt we had got a position we could defend, for some hours at any rate, against a hundred Comanchés.

Two of us stood guard, whilst the other three slept; but I confess I was too uneasy to sleep myself when my turn came ; for if the Indians did find us, I knew they would never leave us without taking our scalps. So it was a blessed relief when day broke at last, and we found ourselves unmolested. Promptly we saddled up and followed the valley, looking for the trail of the Indians to whom the scout belonged, which I made sure we must hit before long. In about an hour's time we struck it, coming in down a ravine that crossed our valley, and heading for the Rio Grandé country. It was plain to be seen that the party was a big one, driving a lot of loose horses. Westfall opined there were not less than two hundred of them, and that probably they were the same lot that had attacked us before. Probably they had not attacked us now because they knew Alexander's command was on their track, and they wanted to push on with their plunder. Anyway we had a lucky escape.

Near where we struck the trail, high up on the mountain-side, one of the boys on outlook duty found by accident an Indian cave, used as a kind of storehouse. In it were several spare lances, cooking-pots, pairs of leggings (the only article of clothing the mounted Comanchés wear) and many " cased " hides, *i.e.* hides scraped till quite transparent.

After following the trail till we were sure of the direction to which it was going, we turned back to the valley creek, to catch fish for dinner and await the command. Soon we had a nice lot of mountain trout broiling on the embers ; a feast indeed for hungry men whose dinners for the past two days had been of the scantiest.

Just as we had finished, up rode the advance party of the command, much surprised to find us with our scalps on. The Mexicans had told them such a tale of our perilous position that they had struck camp directly they heard it, and had ridden all night to our rescue, though with little hope of finding us alive.

We camped in the valley that night to rest the horses, and next morning followed the trail over a tremendously rough, hilly country ; my duty being to bring up the rear with the pack animals, beeves, and prisoners. No water all day, after leaving the creek, and none at night, and—perhaps worst of all—no tobacco left ! It was not a very cheerful state of things, for I was too thirsty to eat anything, and was just lying down to seek forgetfulness in sleep, when I was startled to hear shots and shouts in the direction of the guard. Running there, I found that the ten prisoners had made a bolt for freedom, and that only two had been caught. Though the whole camp turned out to scour the country, the other eight escaped in the darkness of the night, and were no more seen.

Poor creatures, without horses, arms, or provisions, their chances of reaching any of the settlements were remote indeed, and probably they would die of hunger and thirst. Sorry as I was for their evil plight, I couldn't help feeling relieved by their escape, and wishing the other two had gone also ; for I was always uneasy lest some of the bloodthirsty villains in the command should take them and hang them out of hand.

But soon prisoners, Indians, and all other minor troubles were forgotten in the dreadful sufferings we now had to endure for want of water, as will be set down in the next chapter.

GIANT CACTI ON THE RIO GRANDÉ BORDER

p. 352

CHAPTER XII

WATER! OR WE DIE!

THE next three days' march of this ill-starred expedition are very memorable to me, for during them not a drop of water could we find, and we all came near dying of thirst. It has often been my fate to endure the pangs of hunger, but I venture to say they are not to be compared to those of thirst. Hunger can be appeased in various ways, but for thirst there is only one remedy, and if that cannot be found, it grows hour by hour more maddening and unendurable.

In that arid mountain region we were frozen by night and parched by the sun's rays shining down on us from a pitiless, cloudless sky by day. The rocks glowed with the fervent heat; the very ground seemed baked under our feet, and for miles and miles we tramped, when our horses gave out, over a desolate, treeless country where only cacti in endless variety, each one more prickly than its neighbour, flourished exceedingly. I have no doubt the Comanchés chose this route for the express purpose of stopping us by thirst, and the artful rascals nearly succeeded in killing us whilst they themselves contrived to subsist on the little water they found in small rock-basins known to them, which they took care to empty before our arrival.

If we human beings suffered tortures from thirst, our unfortunate horses and cattle were in even worse plight, for there was hardly a bite of grass for them, and all were lamed by the cruel thorns. As for the miser-

able beeves, their feet were so worn by the rocky ground
that the trail could easily be followed by the blood they
left behind them, and it was only with the greatest difficulty they could be urged forward. Indeed many of them
died by the way, and were left as a prey to the buzzards
and coyotés that attended us in the well-grounded assurance that a feast would soon be forthcoming.

The first day after the escape of the prisoners we
found, about midday, a little off the trail, a scanty supply
of water in a rock-basin enough to give us men a short
drink all round, but leaving no surplus for the animals,
and at night we camped without water.

All next day we followed the trail, which, as far as
we could make out, ran parallel to the Rio Grandé, at
a distance of probably forty miles, over the same barren,
desolate country. Already some of the horses and
beeves had to be killed, being unable to travel farther,
but the pack-mules still held out fairly well.

Westfall and the other guides advised that we should
strike at once for the Rio Grandé, as, in their opinion,
we shouldn't find water otherwise for three or four days.
But the Major was in one of his obstinate fits, and insisted
we should follow the trail as long as possible, and when
it was no longer possible, then make for the Rio Grandé.
Knowing nothing about Indians and their artful dodges,
he thought they must be making for some creek or stream
unknown to the guides. There was nothing for it therefore but to obey.

Next day again no water, for man or beast ; and our
tongues clave to the roofs of our mouths, for it was now
fifty-four hours since we last drank. The men were
growing mutinous, and declared they would no longer
follow the trail.

That night the Major wanted to hang the two remaining
prisoners, for the men wouldn't trouble to guard them,
and he feared they would escape. " A good thing too,"
I answered, " if they do, poor devils, but you shan't hang

them whilst I'm alive." And with that he had to be content.

When the third cloudless sun rose on our misery, the men could no more be controlled, for we, and they, knew that if we didn't find water soon we should die, and we struck for the Rio Grandé. Far away (oh, how far it seemed!) in the dim distance rose a chain of lofty mountains which our guides said were on the other side of the river. For them we steered our course, and tramped on mile after mile, leading our horses for the most part ; and still the mountains wore that tint of blue that only far distance gives. Should we ever reach the precious life-giving water that flowed at the foot of their slopes ? We were a hopelessly disorganised rabble now, and those who still had horses that could be ridden pressed on as fast as they could go, the Major amongst them.

I was in charge of the rear of this rabble, and did all I could to bring along the pack animals, and the beeves that still could travel, for without them we should starve even if we lived to reach the river. But when darkness fell it was impossible to keep them together, for men and horses and cattle were mad for water.

About midnight, I think it was, I came up to a camp fire, round which some of those who had pressed on ahead were lying utterly done up. No man greeted his fellow, no word was spoken ; we just threw ourselves on the ground and lay there in silence and despair. To sleep was impossible ; the pangs of thirst prevented that. It was two days since I had eaten anything, but hunger didn't trouble me—water, water was my only thought.

A little before daybreak next morning we staggered to our feet and set out once more on our weary quest of the river. The beeves, horses, and pack animals that could travel had disappeared. They had gone straight to the river, and Westfall and I, and a few more, kept together and followed their trail as best we could. In silence, and something like despair, we tramped on, for, if we didn't find water in the next few hours, death stared us in the face.

Now the stars began to pale, and with the first glimmer of dawn we saw the dim outline of the mountains we had striven so long to reach. Then with the full light of day we could see the ravines that scored their sides, and the forest growth on their slopes, and hope revived, for the river couldn't be so very far off now. " How far, Westfall ? " I whispered. " Fifteen miles, I reckon," he answered in the same tone, and we pressed on without another word.

How long it took us I don't know, but the sun was high in the heavens, I remember, when we reached the river—only to find we couldn't get at the water, for it ran between precipices more than a hundred feet high, which were quite unclimbable. As far as the eye could reach it was the same, up and down stream. It was heartbreaking to see the beautiful clear-running water, so near and yet so far away !

The cattle-trail we had followed turned up-stream, and we took that direction too, hoping that the instinct of the animals had guided them aright. For quite two miles we followed where they had gone, and then struck an old, well-worn Indian trail evidently leading to a crossing, and in another mile were at the water. No drink I ever tasted in all my life was like that one !

Fortunately the stream was shallow, running over a hard gravelly bed ; for if it had been deep and muddy many of the stock would have been drowned. All our missing animals had got to the water ahead of us and many of them were standing knee-deep in the river, whilst others were already cropping the grass on its banks. When all had slaked their thirst, we crossed the river and climbed by the Indian trail to a plateau where was some grass for the stock, but not an atom of shade to shelter under. Then, thirst being appeased, hunger became insistent, and we cooked and ate the first food we had tasted for many a long hour.

The primary wants of man and beast being satisfied, and all being filled with meat and drink, each after his own kind, everything began to wear a brighter aspect. We, who yesterday were a broken, hopeless rabble of despairing men, took a fairly rosy view of things in general, and if we had only had some tobacco, would have been quite cheerful, I believe !

After a sleep under the shade of my blanket, I took my rifle, and strolled down the stream with a couple of the boys who were going fishing. Not a quarter of a mile from camp they halted to try a deep pool, and I sat on the rocks to watch them. Behind me was a steep escarpment of loose stones, boulder strewn, on the Mexican side. The stones began to rattle down, and I turned to see a magnificent black-tailed buck making off along the slope. He was broadside on, and the place was so steep that even he couldn't go very fast. But there was no time to admire his proportions, for already he was about fifty yards off ; so I got on to him as soon as I could. The bullet hit him just behind the shoulder, and with one tremendous bound he fell dead, and rolled down to within a few yards of where I sat. He was a noble-looking fellow, with a fine head, and, what was more important from our then point of view, in rare good order. Whilst one of the boys went back for a pack-mule the other one and I skinned the buck, and that night we feasted right royally, for there was venison and fish enough for the whole of my own command.

We rested in this camp a couple of days, and had ample leisure to admire the wild and desolate scenery around us. The river, about a hundred yards in width, and very deep, except at its rare fords, ran clear and bright over its rocky bed, through a channel that seemed as though hewn out of the solid grey rock to a depth of one hundred feet and more. The country all around rose in mountain after mountain, like the waves of some vast sea, only broken at intervals by lofty conical peaks, and in the far distance by the still loftier summits of the Sierra Madre, which themselves seemed to melt at last into the clear blue of that wondrous sky.

No grateful shade-trees were here, or luxuriant grasses, but rocks that pulsated with heat under the pitiless glare of the cloudless sun. But wherever there was a scrap of earth that could give a foothold there was a cactus growing ; some many feet high, like stiff green poles, others only a few inches from the ground : a world of thorns and heat and drought.

Desolate and forbidding as this region was, we all enjoyed our brief rest immensely. Whilst some of the boys went fishing or hunting, others were busy slaughtering and drying beef, and making the hides into mocassins ; only the inveterate gamblers and loafers indulged their ruling passion, and lay round under the shade of a blanket playing " monté " with greasy packs of cards.

During the halt the Major sent a scouting party up the river, but they returned, after a twenty-mile ride, saying they could find no watering-place in all that distance, nor any sign of Indians. Our guides and the old Mexican Captain said we were about two days' march from San Carlos, near which was a favourite camping-ground of the Muscalaros Indians ; and, as the horses had now picked up a bit, the Major concluded to try to catch some of that tribe. It was quite hopeless to hunt Comanchés in our then condition ; indeed they were more likely to hunt us, if they were aware of our plight and were in any force. So rather than do nothing at all, after all our toils and sufferings, we would have a try for the others, especially as their location was not very far out of our direct road back to the settlements.

Sending a scouting party ahead, we set off once more, keeping always in reach of the river. But ill-luck still attended us, for the scouts found the Muscalaros' camp had been moved long since, and a small band they came across cleared out at once ; and they were in no condition to pursue them.

The few cattle we had left were unable to travel farther, so we halted long enough to kill, and cut up for drying, all that were fit to eat. By this time nearly the whole command was on foot, the horses having given out ; provisions were getting scarce, and it was absolutely necessary to return whence we came. To dream of hunting Indians of any sort was sheer folly ; the only question was how best and quickest to get back. I didn't like the route the Major proposed to follow, nor had I much faith in his guides, so I asked leave to take my own road with my command, and to report to him from my own head-quarter camp on the Leona. To this he agreed, so we parted the following morning, I taking with me the two remaining prisoners, who, not too well guarded, escaped near the Rio Grandé, and, I hope, got safely over into Mexico.

Neither Westfall nor myself, nor any of the boys, had ever been in that section of country before, and we had no compass to guide us. Moreover, to add to our difficulties, the weather set in misty, so that we couldn't see the sun for several days. On parting from the main body we boldly left the river and struck across the country in a line which Westfall was sure would bring us out all right, though we might perhaps suffer somewhat from want of water. We were leaving broken-down animals every day, and almost all of us were on foot : our meal and flour had quite given out, though we had still a little dried beef left, and in this condition it was essential to take the shortest road. It certainly was a risky thing to do, but I had unbounded confidence in my guide, which in the end was quite justified, for he eventually did bring us out all right, and we beat the Major and the rest of the command by three days. I don't propose to tell what befell us day by day on this march, for it would only be wearisome repetition of hardships endured, more or less cheerfully, by us all. Once only had I any real trouble with the boys, and that was on the third day we had passed without seeing the sun. They grew very uneasy, and thought we must be lost in that awful sea of rocky hills ; for, said they, it was impossible for any man to find his way without even the sun to guide him. I could see Westfall was getting bothered by their grumbling, and that it had to be stopped at once. So I fell them in, and told them he and I had chosen the line we were taking ; that we knew it was the right one, and they had to follow it, whether they liked it or not. All the same I confess I was very uneasy, and it was an immense relief when next morning the sun shone out, and we saw we were not far out of our right course.

We were fortunate in finding a good water-hole the second day ; then we had a couple of dry marches ; and so it went on, but we were never reduced to the dire straits we had been in before we reached the Rio Grandé. One day we were lucky enough to run across a good bunch of javalines, or peccary, near a water-hole on a dried-up creek, and killed four of them ; a welcome addition to our scanty larder.

The morning after this we saw a column of smoke rising from a hollow a mile or two ahead. As this could only come from an Indian camp, we looked to our arms, and advanced in readiness for an attack, sending scouts before. It was an Indian camp sure enough, and the fresh sign showed a party of about twenty, with a big bunch of horses, had just left it. It was hopeless to follow them, for we could never come up with them, unless they had kindly waited for us, so I reluctantly kept on my way down country.

Now Westfall spotted two mocassin-tracks on an old trail, leading in our right direction ; so we followed them, and in a few miles they brought us out on the lower Rio Grandé. Thank goodness we had at last got out of the treeless waste we had wandered in so long, for all along the river there was fine timber, and we marched on under its delightful shade in much comfort. The hackberries, growing on low bushy trees along the river-bottom in great abundance, were just ripe, and we devoured them wholesale. The fruit, rather larger than currants and very sweet to the taste, is a great favourite with the wild turkeys, which grow exceeding fat on this dainty diet.

Hard by where we first struck the river was another of the curious Indian painted caves, and in it we found sign of our escaped prisoners. So after all the poor wretches hadn't perished in the stony wilderness, and would probably now get safely down to some of the Mexican pueblos on the river.

Turning a projecting angle of rock, a little below the cave, Westfall and I came suddenly on a couple of Indians, cooking at a small fire. They saw us before we did them, and vanished like snakes into the thick brush close by, in which it was hopeless to pursue them. They left behind them a fine " blue-cat " fish, nicely broiled on the embers, and the smell thereof was so appetising that we were fain to taste their cookery ; and, finding it most excellent, left nothing but the bones for the rightful owners.

We followed the river down to the mouth of the Pecos, and now reached a section well known to our guide, and indeed to many of the boys, so that all anxiety as to our route was quite at an end. Following a plain Indian trail leading down to the Mexican settlements, we crossed the Rio Grandé, there very deep and swift, about twenty-six miles from the San Felipé springs, and camped by them at night.

Our dried beef being finished, the boys were ravenous ; so next morning, before daybreak, I sent on a party to hunt up a beef at Sycamore Creek, our next halting-place, and have it cut up and ready for our arrival. When we got to camp, we found a cow had been not only killed and cut up, but was nearly cooked ready for us. I don't think the boys waited for it to be overdone, for they set to like so many wolves, and presently cleared up every scrap of meat. To watch them devour that cow was something like the far-famed sight of feeding the lions at the Zoo.

From this camping-place we marched thirty-five miles to Elm Creek, all on foot; for now, my good horse that had carried me with occasional rests all the journey, gave out and had to be led. That day's march took us through Fort Clark, where we got a small supply of meal and coffee and, more welcome than either, a little tobacco. Thence two long marches brought us back to our camp on the Leona, which we had left ten weeks before on this wild-goose chase ; and I think we were lucky not to have left our bones in that terrible thirst-land.

CHAPTER XIII

THE CALIFORNIAN RAIDERS

WHEN I got back to camp, after the pleasure trip with Major Hatch's command, I found my stores of ammunition, clothing, medicines, etc., had run so low that I was obliged to go into San Antonio for fresh supplies. There I found every one much excited about the threatened invasion of the State by the Federal General Banks, commonly known amongst us of the Confederate Service as " Commissary Banks," from his supposed disinclination to move without an abundance of creature comforts, more especially for his own use. He had collected a considerable force on the Red River between Arkansas and Texas, and boasted he would sweep the State of rebels.

The gallant Magruder and his Texan boys, than whom there were no better fighters in the South, when properly led, met him just within our boundary and, with a far inferior force, inflicted on him a signal defeat. It was a gallant fight, and splendidly won, but I was not present at it, though my boys and I volunteered to a man to go with Magruder, whom we all recognised as a leader of men ; but it wasn't to be, for the authorities had other uses for us.

An expedition was being organised to attack a body of three or four hundred Californians who had established themselves at Fort Lancaster, in the south-western part of the State, where they were assuming a threatening attitude, and attracting to themselves many deserters from our service. Indeed, desertion was at that time rife in Texas, and had increased to such an alarming extent that, especially in the west of the State, the men were going off in bands of from a dozen up to two hundred at a time. Many of these joined the Federal forces, whilst the most part scattered over the Mexican frontier and lived by indiscriminate plunder.

The command of the Fort Lancaster expedition was given to Major Hunter, an old Texan frontiersman, and an able commander, who since the outbreak of the war had, with his company, been stationed on the north-western frontier.

It was whilst we were waiting in San Antonio to know if we might join Magruder that the Adjutant-General of the State ordered me to report, with all my command, to Major Hunter, and to be ready to start for Fort Lancaster in a few days. It was a great disappointment at the time, but Hunter was, as I afterwards found, a first-rate man, who thoroughly understood his business, and I had no cause to regret serving under him.

At this time a Colonel Franks, a well-known and rather notorious character in Texas, was organising a force to recapture Brownsville, on the Rio Grandé, which, after General Wasp's shameful skedaddle, had been occupied by the Yankees. Franks and I were well known to each other, and for that very reason, I was somewhat surprised to find that he had begged the authorities to send my command with him. Though I had no very high opinion of the man, I was willing to join him, for we all thought the Federals would make a fight of it at Brownsville; in which however we were mistaken.

It was flattering to our vanity to be in such request, but, as it turned out, it was just as well the Adjutant-General stuck to his original order, for Franks' force did nothing, nor was capable of doing anything, being composed mainly of deserters and loafers of all sorts.

These gentry flocked to the gallant Colonel's standard under the well-founded belief that there would be but little discipline, and no danger. In fact they expected a " good time," with plenty of gambling and a sufficiency of plunder. In the result the Colonel and his loafers lay round in camp, doing nothing, for several months until the Yankees evacuated Brownsville, when they boldly marched in and occupied it.

Franks was, as I have said, a well-known character in Texas, and a type of a class of men common enough in the State in those days. He enjoyed the reputation of a " fighting man," and was I think the most inveterate gambler and the hardest swearer I ever met, even out West ; indeed his power of " language," especially when the luck went against him, was almost grotesque in its resourcefulness. With a Colonel's commission in his pocket, and supposed to be earnestly engaged in raising a regiment for State service, he was generally to be found in one of the most notorious gambling dens in San Antonio " dealing " monté with all the riff-raff of the place, whilst youngsters of his own regiment stood round " bucking " at him, i.e. backing his luck.

Notwithstanding all this, I am bound to say that " Old Rip," as he delighted to be called, was fairly popular with most of the people, being hail-fellow-well-met with everybody, free with his money, and equally free with his six-shooter. As to his military experience, he had for a short time, years before, commanded a ranging company on the frontier, and had also commanded the volunteers who fought the Mexican bandit and guerilla leader Cortinas, when he raided into Texas in 1859.

Early in April 1864, at the very time I received the order to report to Major Hunter, a law was passed changing the conditions of service of my frontier company, and making the men liable to serve wherever they might be required, either in or out of the State.

That being so, I asked, and obtained, permission to resign my commission and hold a fresh election, which I thought was only fair to the boys, though if I had not been re-elected I should have had to serve in the ranks.

The boys were much disgusted at the arbitrary changes in their service conditions, but were somewhat cheered when they knew they were to go to Fort Lancaster with Hunter, who was well known to most of them, though they would have preferred going with Magruder. The day after my return I held the election for officers under the new conditions. They were perfectly free to choose whomsoever they liked, and somewhat to my surprise, and much to my gratification, they re-elected me almost unanimously.

My boys had by this time quite got over the effects of the last abortive expedition, and, having provided themselves with fresh horses, were fit to go anywhere and do anything in the way of fighting they might be asked to. Two days were spent in preparing rations, looking thoroughly to saddlery and equipment, and then we rode out, seventy-five strong, to meet Major Hunter at Dhanis, on the Eagle Pass road, distant about thirty miles from camp. I reported myself that evening in his camp, where he had already a command of about five hundred Rangers, all picked frontiersmen, well armed and mounted. He only waited our arrival to start ; so next morning at daybreak we broke camp, and set off on our three-hundred-mile ride to the fort.

Hunter, as we rode along, told me his information was that the Californians, who were supposed to number about five hundred, were encamped in the difficult brushy country between the fort and the Rio Grandé. There they had established themselves in a strong position, and for some time had been busy plundering the ranches and small settlements on either side of the river with fine impartiality. Having been left unmolested for some time, they probably had grown care-less, and kept but an indifferent watch, especially at night. His plan then was to push on steadily till within a day's march of their position and, having carefully reconnoitred it, make a night attack.

We covered about thirty miles a day and arrived quite fresh and fit on the evening of the ninth day at our last camping-place, on a clear running creek, about twenty-five miles from the enemy's stronghold. It was a bright night, and the full moon riding high in the cloudless sky made it almost as light as day. Leaving me in command of the camp as next senior officer to himself, Hunter set off with three of his best scouts, after a couple of hours' rest, to examine the position. If he did not return by noon next day, I was to conclude he had been taken or killed, and was to assume the command and attack the enemy in the way I thought best.

That night passed slowly enough, at least with me, for I had a sort of foreboding that Hunter, who didn't know what fear meant, would do something rash and get himself into trouble. The morning wore on till towards noon, and I was just giving orders for the command to fall in to march to Hunter's rescue, feeling sure the Californians had got him, when he and his scouts came riding down the slope across the creek. He laughed long and loudly at my anxiety about him. " Give us a drink, my boy, and something to eat, for I'm starving, and then I'll tell you all about it."

The tale was soon told. Following the beaten trail past the fort, which seemed deserted and in ruins, he had arrived within a quarter of a mile of the Californians' camp, about two hours before daybreak, without en-countering any pickets. There he left the horses in charge of one of the men and, with the other two, crept cautiously forward. The moon by this time was falling low in the west, but still gave all the light he wanted.

A plain enough trail led to the foot of a wooded bluff on which the camp was placed, and there he nearly blundered on a picket of three men; but luckily they were fast asleep, stretched comfortably on their blankets.

Passing away to the right, he and his scouts crawled through the brush that covered the steep slope, till they reached a cleared space, studded thickly with tents. Not a soul stirred, and not a guard was to be seen. Half a dozen or so horses were picketed near the tents. The rest must be under guard somewhere else; but where? Retreating down the slope as they came, they found the far side of the bluff almost precipitous, and strewn with loose stones.

It was too risky to pass these, so they retraced their steps and, giving the sleeping picket a wide berth, passed round to the left of the position. There, coming to the edge of a wide open space, they saw quite a crowd of horses picketed under guard, for they could hear the men laughing and talking and see some of them, under a big live-oak, dealing monté by the light of a flaring torch. Having found this side of the bluff, like the right, a steep brushy slope, Hunter had seen enough, and made the best of his way back to our camp. He was in high glee, for now he was sure of success.

" The trumps are all in our own hands, and the game's as good as finished, if only we work it cleverly, and some darned blunderer doesn't scare them. Now for a good sleep, my boy; have the command ready to march an hour after sundown, and see to all the rifles and six-shooters in the meantime."

By the hour appointed supper was over, the men, all eager for the fray, were mounted, and we set off in the highest of spirits. I well remember now what a glorious night it was, as we rode over the prairie by the light of the brilliant moon, with the cool night breeze to fan us after the burning heat of the day. But I don't think many gave much heed to the beauties of nature, for before us was the prospect of some real fighting under a leader we were all glad to follow.

The plan of attack was thoroughly explained, and all the men carefully detailed for the various parts they had to play, before we started, so that there should be no confusion, so fatal and so difficult to avoid, with any troops, in a night attack. The command was to halt half a mile from the camp, and all the horses, except 150, to be left with a reserve of 125 men ; for Hunter, daring as he was, was cautious withal, and would avoid risks if possible. He himself would lead a hundred picked men up the right slope, to surprise the camp, whilst 250 dismounted and 100 mounted men were to take up position on the left, to intercept the fugitives and secure their horses.

We took our time on the march, jogging along quite easily, for we had seven hours to do the distance in and prepare for the attack. It was just after three o'clock when we reached our halting-place, and the moon was all but down. In a very few minutes the horses were linked, and the reserve fallen in, under command of the second senior captain, with strict orders not to move except by order from the Major or myself. Even then no word was uttered above a whisper, and the boys, excited as they were, were wonderfully quiet as yet ; would they keep so till the curtain rang up ?

The Major and his hundred passed away to the right, to avoid the picket, and presently disappeared in the darkness and dead silence. Immediately he had done so, I led off my 350 to the left, guided by the scouts who had been over the ground the night before. We marched in column, four abreast to keep touch and avoid straggling in the dark.

Arrived as near the edge of the clearing as we dared venture, I gradually formed my party into line as well as I could ; the dismounted men on the right, and the mounted on the left. Then we waited. Not a sound

24

came from the sleeping camp away on our right; only to our front we could hear the faint stamping of horses' feet, perhaps a couple of hundred yards away, and the voices of their guards. How slowly the time passed; would Hunter never begin?

Now, in the stillness of the night, one of the horses in the clearing ahead of us neighed, long and loudly, probably because he had winded us, and directly one of our own answered him. Some one shouted from the guard: "There's a horse loose, whose in thunder is it?" Men came running towards us as we stood in silent ranks. If one of my boys fired at them, as they well might in their excitement, all our well-laid plans were spoiled.

I dared not move, but held my breath and clenched my teeth. What could Hunter be doing all this time? The horse-seekers were pushing through the brush, coming straight to us; in another moment we must be discovered.

No, thank goodness! our luck still stuck to us; for now, away on the hilltop, I heard a single revolver-shot, and following on it instantly, a volley from the hundred rifles; then yells, and screams of terror, and desultory firing. For a brief space this went on, and then down the brushy slope, on our right front, came the Californians, helter-skelter, a mob of fleeing, panic-stricken men, whose one thought was to get to their horses and escape.

Meanwhile, the moment I knew Hunter was at work, I ordered an advance of the dismounted men at the double, directing the horsemen, the moment they were clear of the brush, to pass away to the left and get round the picketed horses, to prevent a stampede. Coming out on the clearing I found, as far as I could see in the dim light, an open space between the horses and the foot of the slope, which the fugitives must cross. Here we halted.

As soon as; judging from the sound, they had gathered pretty thickly there, I ordered my boys to fire a volley. What was the effect it was impossible to see, but the cries of terror that resounded from the brush, and from the clearing, showed that the double surprise had entirely routed the enemy, who were scattering in all directions. Without waiting to reload, I led the boys at the double across the clearing, but only the dead and wounded remained; the rest had, under cover of the darkness, disappeared into the brush.

Now the order to "cease fire" was given, for fear we might shoot our own people, and Hunter, leaving a detachment to hold the camp, joined us with the rest of his men. The surprise was complete, and we congratulated ourselves and our men on the smart way it had been carried out. Of my party not a man had been touched, the enemy having been too demoralised, when they came into our hands, to fire a single shot.

Hunter's party had not been so fortunate, for a squad of them, leading the charge through the camp, had received a hot fire at close range from some of the enemy who made a brief stand, and four men were killed and ten wounded, four of them very seriously. Of the Californians we found in all some thirty-five dead and twenty severely wounded, those able to move having got away into the brush. When daylight came we rounded up the captured horses, and found we had got some 250. Very few had been taken away by the fugitives; the rest had broken loose, and were lost in the brush.

A strong scouting party was sent out to follow the enemy, but soon returned reporting that they had crossed the river into Mexico, whither we did not pursue them. There, we heard afterwards, they met with a hot reception from the ranchers and people of the settlements they had plundered with impunity before we broke them up, so that many were killed, and the rest scattered to the four winds of heaven.

We feasted royally on the ample provisions left behind by the enemy, and then, after a brief rest, having burned the tents and what plunder we couldn't carry away, set off for Fort Clark, with the wounded borne on improvised litters. We had no surgeon with us nor any ambulances, and so were obliged to seek both at the post. There we camped for some days, whilst the post surgeon attended to the wounded of both sides. Four of our own poor fellows died of their wounds, but the rest being soon fit to travel, we borrowed four ambulances and brought them back with us to our camp.

Hunter, having pressing business to attend to, left us the day after we reached Fort Clark, and set off with a small escort for headquarters, leaving me in command. After leaving the fort we kept together for a few days, and then the companies dispersed to their respective camps under their own commanders.

The captured horses and other plunder were sent into San Antonio, and sold for the benefit of the command in general. So ended a successful expedition, well organised, and well led by its able commander, to whom all the credit of the result was due.

CHAPTER XIV

THE JUMPING " BUCKS "

As soon as we got back from the Fort Lancaster expedition in the month of April 1864, the usual exchange of detachments took place ; those who had been on leave returned to duty, and those who had been on service went home to attend to their own affairs. I therefore took a spell of leave at the ranch, handing over the command to the senior Lieutenant, English by name. There things I found were not in a very flourishing condition. The Indians had swept off several of my horses, and many of my cattle had been stolen by so-called Government agents, Mexican raiders, and other thieves.

But the worst news I got was the disastrous end of a cattle speculation I had gone into with a man named Bacon, a cattle-buyer in San Antonio. At that time there was hardly any market for beeves in the States, whereas in Mexico they fetched a fair price, and in hard dollars, not paper-money. Accordingly, I arranged with the aforesaid Bacon to take a drove of about four hundred cattle across the Rio Grandé, of which he was to provide one half and I the other.

Unfortunately, it was just when I was ready to start on this trip that I was ordered to join Hunter's expedition, and of course I couldn't go. But the cattle were already at the ranch and all the arrangements were made, so some one must take them. Bacon wouldn't go himself—he was a dealer pure and simple, not a rancher—but he recommended a half-bred German

named Blackaller as a trustworthy, competent man
for the business. So this rascal went off with our cattle,
whilst I went Californian-hunting to Fort Lancaster.

Now it seems all went well till the drove was nearing
Eagle Pass, when Blackaller learned that a stringent
law had been passed by our Legislature, prohibiting
the export of cattle, and enacting heavy penalties for
those even attempting to evade it. At first, so the
vaquéros reported, he thought of trying to run the
cattle across lower down the river, but finding that the
passes were all strongly held by frontier guards, he
finally drove them on to the prairie between the Carisa
Creek and the Rio Grandé, and there turned them adrift
to fend for themselves. I need scarcely say the fellow
never came near me again, which was perhaps as well
for his health.

For many months I was too much occupied with
Indian-hunting and other things to look up these cattle,
and it was not till the spring of the following year 1865
that I could find time to recover them. They were all
properly branded, and I may say that I managed to
recover the most of them, but in doing so had one of
the narrowest escapes of losing my scalp that ever befell
me, which shall be told in its proper place hereafter.

That spring and summer the Comanchés and Lepans
were more troublesome than ever, and gave us little
rest or peace. I don't propose to tell of all the hunts
we had after them, as there was so much sameness in
them ; but one or two may be worth mentioning as illus-
trating their methods of fighting.

Early in the month of May, whilst I was still at the
ranch, the Comanchés came into the country and killed
and scalped three men, not far from my neighbourhood.
I sent down to my camp at once for a dozen of my boys,
and the day after their arrival took a scout round to see
if we could hit a likely trail to follow. The second day
we came on one which I guessed was made by about

fifteen or twenty mounted Indians. It was quite fresh and easy to follow, and after riding hard on it for a couple of hours we came in sight of the scoundrels. There were fifteen ponies right enough, but the Indians were riding double, so there were thirty of them all told, nearly half of them armed with rifles.

Directly they saw us they formed up in their usual V shape, expecting us to charge. But I had no mind to do that, for though we probably could have whipped them, it would have been with a heavy loss on our side. The country was for the most part level and open, but broken here and there by hollows. Away to the right, about two miles distant, was a low hill with a mott of good timber on it, and no covert near it except a few scattered live-oaks. Here was the very position for us, and without dwelling a moment, for it we rode at a gallop.

The Comanchés, who were rather nearer the mott than we were, tried all they knew to cut us off; the dismounted men running by the side of the mounted, and all yelling like demons. However, we were just too quick for them, and got into the mott a hundred yards ahead.

The Comanchés then halted, and seemed rather uncertain what to be at. Meantime we had dismounted, and got our horses behind as good cover as we could. I posted my men under cover at the edge of the mott, ordering one half to give the Indians a volley when they came on, and the other to reserve their fire in case they tried to charge home. Presently the Comanchés hardened their hearts and made a charge, screaming and yelling with all their might, and dancing about at such a rate that it was uncommonly hard to hit them. We held our fire till they were within about sixty yards; then the six rifles spoke, and two of the dancing devils dropped. The rest fell back into a hollow, and for some minutes were quite quiet; then out they charged again, only to retire as before, but this time they carried away three wounded with them.

This performance, varied by occasional potting at us, from behind the live-oaks, went on for more than an hour, without doing us any damage except slightly wounding a horse. Some of them had white men's scalps in their hands, and these they flourished about, taunting us with being afraid to come out and get them.

The chief, a big buck Indian, as naked as the day he was born (as indeed they all were, save for their buck-skin leggings and a plentiful daubing of paint), tried his hardest to make his followers charge the mott. After a long harangue, he suddenly made a rush for a live-oak about fifty yards from the mott, and planted his lance in the ground by the side of it. Some half-dozen of his men followed him; the rest hung back, despite his vehement exhortations.

The old fellow was plucky enough, for though we made it pretty hot for him, he held his ground, and annoyed us greatly by jumping out every now and then and taking a snapshot at any one unwary enough to show even the tip of his nose.

The thing got to be a nuisance and had to be put a stop to, for quick as he was in his movements, just flashing out from his tree and back again like lightning, he was making very good shooting. I therefore called up Jake Hillson, a splendid rifle-shot, and told him to wipe out that buck for me. " I've had half a dozen pulls at the crittur already," he said, " but he's so tarnation smart in his jump, I can't git him nohow."

" Lay your rifle on the spot he jumps to, and when he comes into your sight, pull, and it's odds on your nailing him."

Once more our friend jumped out and back, untouched ; but the next jump was his last, for Hillson's rifle rang out, and the Indian sprang into the air and fell dead in his tracks, shot through the heart. The fall of their chief dashed the courage of the rest, and they retreated into the hollow, taking the body with them ; but not before one of the boys knocked over another, who had turned round to flourish the scalp he carried at us. After waiting half an hour, and finding they didn't renew the attack, we sallied forth to find the Indians had gone, riding off double again as hard as they could go. We found the bodies of the chief, and two other Indians, thrown into a water-hole in the hollow, but the wounded they carried off with them.

We had given these gentry a pretty good lesson, at slight cost to ourselves ; for all our casualties were the wounded horse, and one of the boys slightly hit by one of the shots of the vanishing chief just before Hillson bowled him over. I did not feel inclined to follow them any farther, for it was risky work to tackle them in the open, well-armed as they were, with so small a party, and so returned to camp next day.

At the end of May 1864 an organised band of renegades from Texas collected in Mexico, hoisted the Union flag, crossed the Rio Grandé, and took the small town of Eagle Pass, where they looted the cotton stored for export to Mexico. Expresses were sent out at once to summon all the frontier regiments within reach, to turn these rascals out. It was boot and saddle all up and down the district, and in double quick time my command was *en route* for the Rio Grandé. We were, however, turned back after a few days' march, as our services were not required, the renegades having dispersed at the first alarm of the approach of reliefs.

A garrison of two companies of Rangers was left in the town, who drove off and killed a good many of the ruffians when they returned a second time. Some of them retired to Mexico, but a strong band moved up the river to the San Felipé Springs, plundering as they went. There they were encountered by a frontier force under a Captain Minshul, son of old Asa, of Vigilance Committee fame, who surprised and captured a number of them. These, to the number of about thirty, he promptly hanged, thereby proving himself a true chip of the old block.

The next bout with Indians I may mention was late that same summer; and curiously enough there was then a repetition of much the same jumping performance as in the previous one, only this time we had the Redskins penned in a mott instead of being penned ourselves.

I was in camp with the command on the Leona, when a runner came galloping in with a most urgent message from the brothers Rheeders, begging me to come to their help against the Comanchés, who in some force were raiding the country, and sweeping it of horses. They had already killed and mutilated the men, women and children on two ranches, and there was no time to be lost if the other settlements were to be saved. The brothers, of whom there were two, were holding their ranch, with eight more good men, and thought they could keep the Indians off till we arrived.

I got that message an hour before daybreak, the runner having ridden all night without drawing rein. He was well mounted, and made a dash from the ranch, with the Indians at his tail for some miles; but his horse was too good for them, and he shook them off, carrying with him, however, one of their arrows, stuck fast in the cantle of his saddle. Within an hour I was on the road to the Hondo, with twenty-five of my best-mounted men, and with sixty good miles to ride before nightfall. Steadily we pushed along, and just at dusk made the ranch, where you may guess my friends the Rheeders were right glad to see us.

The Comanchés had cleared out at our approach, so there was nothing to be done that night but to rest in preparation for the next day's work. The folks at the ranch saw to our horses and got us a good supper; then, whilst they mounted guard against a surprise, we of the command stretched ourselves on our blankets, where best we could, and soon slept the sleep of the weary.

The first streak of daylight next morning saw us all on the trail, which was easy enough to follow, for the Indians were driving a big bunch of horses they had stolen, and we knew they would make a fight of it rather than allow them to be recaptured. Our horses were fresh as paint again after their rest and feed, and we pushed on at a sharp lope, confident we should overtake the thieving villains and whip them; which we did, for we were thirty-five in number, all well armed, and used to the game. The brothers reckoned that the Indian band was at least sixty strong, but only a few of them appeared to have rifles; I think their estimate was near the mark.

In about two hours we found the Comanchés in a thick mott crowning a low hill near the Hondo, with a brushy ridge running back from it to the dense chaparral that lined the banks of the creek; an awkward position to attack, and one from which the Indians could easily retire, if they found it untenable. I saw at once we couldn't hope to get many of them; but could we recover the stolen horses? They had got a bunch of about a hundred securely hidden in the mott, and they had to be captured somehow or other.

I halted my little party about three hundred yards from the Indian camp, in a hollow, and then crept forward to reconnoitre the position. From the top of the low ridge on which I lay, I could see that between me and the mott there were some scattered live-oaks, and here and there some brushy cover, through which the boys could creep pretty close to the base of the hill. Behind me the hollow trended round, till it ran up to the wooded ridge at the back of the mott. I rejoined my boys in a few minutes, dismounted them, and left the linked horses in charge of two men.

I had no doubt that the Indians thought we were a much stronger party than we were, else they would have fought us in the open, as is their usual custom. To keep up the delusion, and effect a surprise, which scares Indians badly, as indeed it does most people, I sent my senior Lieutenant, Dan Williams, with eight picked men to creep round by the hollow and get unobserved on to the ridge in the rear of the mott. There he was to lie quiet till I gave the signal for my boys to charge, which would be one shrill blast on my whistle. Hearing that, he was to fire a volley into the Indians, and kick up all the row the boys could raise. Away he went with his little party, and I moved my men up to the edge of the ridge and ordered them to lie down with intervals between them of about ten yards.

Very few of the Comanchés could be seen, for most of them were hidden behind the trees, and didn't show ; but one big buck, whom I judged to be the chief, from the bunch of eagle feathers in his hair, stood out watching our movements, having no doubt caught a glimpse of us as we topped the ridge. To attract their attention, and let Dan get round unseen, I now ordered the boys to commence individual firing as fast as they could, but before they did so I took a pot-shot myself at the gentleman in feathers, but missed him, which was a bad mull, for he wasn't more than a hundred and fifty yards off. The bullet must have whizzed pretty close to him, for he gave such a jump I thought he was hit ; but he was only scared.

The enemy promptly replied with a volley of arrows, all of which fell short, and a few rifle shots, which did no damage.

We kept this up till such time as I thought Dan and his men had reached their position ; then I ordered an advance to the foot of the slope, all of us creeping and crawling through the long grass and brush, which fairly hid us. This brought us within about eighty

to a hundred yards of the mott, at which range
Indians are more deadly with their bows and arrows
than they are, as a rule, with rifles.

The buck with the feathers was an extra good shot
with his bow, and one could see him peering round the
tree for a chance at any one who showed himself. The
grass in which we lay was so long that to get a shot
it was necessary at least to show one's head above it.
The moment one of the boys did this, out popped my
friend, and let drive an arrow, generally unpleasantly
near his mark. Once he hit it, for as one of the boys
next to me raised his head and shoulders to take a
snap at another Indian, the chief, quick as lightning,
sent an arrow through the fleshy part of his left arm,
and then began to whoop and dance in triumph.

The time to charge had nearly come, for I felt sure
that Dan must already be at his post; and I had too
many wounded, and couldn't afford to lose any more.
But if I could polish off that chief before I gave the
order, it would have a demoralising effect upon the
enemy, and perhaps save some lives. Hillson, my
prize shot, wasn't with the party, so I must even try
what I could do myself.

By this time the big Indian, having been missed
several times, had grown careless and over-confident,
and, instead of popping back the moment he had shot,
paused an instant to see the result. I had carefully
marked where he jumped to; and now I knelt up to
tempt him out, and laid my Sharp's rifle on the spot.
I hadn't more than a few seconds to wait, finger on
trigger and eye on sight; but whilst I did so a couple
of arrows came hurtling past me, unpleasantly near.
Out came the chief, to see if he couldn't do better than
his men, and the instant he came into my sight, I squeezed
the trigger. I had got him sure enough this time, for,
to my great relief, he fell forward on his face, and lay
like a log.

Seeing this, I blew my whistle long and loudly, then gave the order to charge, and away we went at the double. Hardly were the words out of my mouth when, from the ambuscade, rang out Dan Williams' volley.

The Indians in the mott, who till then showed a bold enough front, and evidently meant fighting, were now cowed and terrified by this sudden attack on their rear, and ran for their lives ; so that when we reached their camp none but the dead and wounded were to be seen. Through the brush they went, as only themselves, or scared peccary, with hounds at their heels, could go, and it was quite useless to follow them. The ruse had succeeded perfectly and Dan had managed his surprise so cleverly, and got so close to the camp, that when he opened fire he bowled over seven of the unsuspecting enemy.

Poor Dan ! he was a right good fellow, and a first-class Indian fighter. If he had any fault it was that he was too plucky, and held Indians too cheaply. Unfortunately this cost him his life not long after this, as I shall have to tell in its proper place.

Our victory had been cheaply won, for our casualties were only three men wounded by arrows, only one of whom was dangerously hurt. On the other hand we had killed ten Indians, recovered all the stolen horses, eighty-seven in number, and captured many of their ponies, as well as much spoil in the shape of spears, bows and arrows, blankets, etc.

It was not advisable to linger in the mott, lest the Comanchés should rally and attempt to retake the horses ; so as soon as we had collected all the animals, and packed the spoil, we set off on our return to the Hondo, well pleased with our morning's work.

CHAPTER XV

WHILST we were away on the Indian hunt last described, two inoffensive Mexicans were basely murdered on the Leona Creek, not far from the headquarters of my command. A man named French, a well-to-do cattle-rancher, was the perpetrator of the deed, which would hardly be worth mentioning—murders were such common occurrences in those days—if it were not for the signal vengeance his two sons wreaked upon all those concerned in the punishment inflicted on their father. These young fellows, Jim and Dick French, were both in my company ; plucky, dare-devil boys, and first-rate frontiersmen, though the eldest was only twenty-one, and the youngest twenty.

The whole story, including the lynching of the murderer, is so characteristic of the Texas of those days that perhaps it is worth telling.

According to the evidence of his own vaquéros, two Mexicans came from across the Rio Grande to buy beeves from French, and brought with them solid silver dollars to pay for them ; scarce commodities in Texas in those days, when all the money we ever saw was Confederate paper. It was these same dollars that cost the poor fellows their lives. After the usual bargaining and hag-gling, the price of the beeves was agreed, and French set out with the two unsuspecting Mexicans to hunt them up.

The dollars being too heavy to carry cattle-hunting, were left behind at the ranch. When the devil put it into French's head that he might have the dollars, and keep the cattle too, I know not ; but it got there pretty early in the expedition, for the murders were committed on the morning of the second day out. The little party were camped on the edge of the dense chaparral that lines the sides of the creek, and, after the customary cup of coffee, one of the Mexicans went out to hunt up the horses for the day's work, and with him went the only vaquéro French had brought with him. It doesn't appear whether this latter had any suspicion of foul play, but at any rate, instead of hunting up the horses he hid himself in the brush hard by, and saw all that happened.

No sooner had Mexican No. 1 got out of earshot, than French suddenly clapped his six-shooter to the head of No. 2, who fell without a groan. The body was dragged into the chaparral, and the murderer returned to wait for the other victim. Presently he came back with the horses, and he too was shot from behind. The body having been disposed of as before, French sat down and had his breakfast as though nothing had happened.

The trembling witness, lying hid in the brush, was afraid to come out, lest he too should be shot ; so after waiting for him some time, his master set out for the ranch, driving with him the cattle they had collected. But before doing so he took the saddles, bridles, and blankets of the Mexicans, and hid them too in the chaparral, turning their horses loose to find their way home.

When he got back he told his people that the Mexicans and he had quarrelled about the quality of the cattle, and they had gone off to buy beeves elsewhere, and would come for their money when they had got what they wanted.

He no doubt thought he had managed the business very cleverly, and had no fear that his crimes would ever be brought home to him. The non-appearance of the vaquéro was puzzling, but, when he didn't return after the lapse of two or three days, he imagined he had run off to Mexico with his horse, as those gentry occasionally did. As a matter of fact the man was too scared at what he had witnessed to return to the ranch, and went off at once to French's next door neighbour, a man named Simons, who owned a ranch some fifteen miles down the creek.

Now this man was not on friendly terms with French, and directly he heard the vaquéro's story concluded that, if it were true, his enemy deserved hanging. Simons repeated what he had heard to some five others of the neighbours, and they, partly because French was unpopular, and partly because murdering Mexican cattle-buyers savoured of killing the geese that laid the *silver* eggs, agreed that he ought to be hanged.

The vaquéro took the whole party over to the chaparral and showed them the remains of the Mexicans, and where their saddlery was hidden. Then, knowing his two boys were away with me, they went straight off to French's ranch, found the murdered Mexicans' dollars in his possession, and arrested him.

Simons was for hanging him then and there, but the rest overruled this, and took him into San Antonio with the intention of handing him over to the authorities. But before they could do this, the news of the capture reached the ears of Hiram Minshul, old Asa's son, and Sol Chiff, the Vice-President of the Vigilance Committee, who, with some of their friends, seized the prisoner and forthwith hanged him on a china-tree on the plaza in front of the house of Padre Sanchez, the highly respected Catholic priest of the town. The Padre, a very decent old fellow, was highly indignant at this outrage, and had the tree promptly cut down. There, for the moment, the matter ended, for of course none of the Vigilance Committee people were punished.

The sons returned home three days after their father had been carried off, and followed hard after him to San Antonio, where they arrived the day after he had been hanged. Their first impulse, as they told me afterwards, was to shoot down Hiram Minshul and as many of the gang as they could ; but these folks were on the alert, and the boys recognised that, if they tried that on, they would probably be hanged themselves before they could exact one half of the vengeance that would satisfy their wrath. So they promptly cleared out of the town, determined to bide their time, let the matter blow over, and, when it was forgotten, as it would soon be, take their enemies unawares and kill every one who was connected with their father's death.

French was hanged in the early days of November, and, to the great surprise of all who knew them, the two boys took no steps to avenge his death for nearly six months. By that time so common an occurrence as the lynching of a man was forgotten, or, if it was ever talked of, it was only because the sons had taken it so quietly, and shown so little " grit." Simons and the rest, who for some time walked warily, and kept a sharp look-out for Jim and Dick French, were now quite at their ease, for the boys appeared to be as friendly with them as ever. They were, however, destined to have a rude awakening.

By the end of May 1865, Lee's surrender was known in Texas ; the " break-up " of the Confederacy had come, and my frontier company was of course disbanded. A kind of interregnum followed, for though San Antonio and the other chief towns were held by Federal troops, who promptly established the régime of law and order, the outlying districts were left to themselves for some time, and of course every man was a law unto himself for the time being. This was the opportunity the two young fellows had waited for so patiently. Their enemies were lulled into false security, there were no frontier troops to interfere with them, and they would wipe out every man however remotely concerned in their father's death !

Hiram Minshul, Asa his father, Sol Chiff, and the rest of the leaders of the Vigilance Committee, with " an intelligent anticipation of events to come," had cleared out before the " break-up " was actually known, and had gone no one knew whither, probably into Mexico; but there were plenty left to satisfy their craving for vengeance, and every one of them they would shoot like dogs.

Directly then the company had been disbanded, Jim and Dick came down to the Leona, well mounted, and armed with a couple of six-shooters and a repeating rifle apiece. When they arrived, Simons was out cow-hunting with a friend of his named Bishop, and their camp was a few miles down the creek, not very far from the spot where French had murdered the Mexicans.

The boys followed them at once, stole into their camp just before daybreak, roused them from their sleep, and shot them down before their eyes were well open. The three Mexican vaquéros with Simons promptly bolted, and the two Frenches, leaving the bodies where they fell, set off at once for the ranch of a man named McConnel, some miles higher up the Leona than Simons' place. The vaquéros, they knew, would soon spread the news of the deed they had done, so they pushed on all that day and best part of the next night, reaching McConnel's ranch, well ahead of the news, whilst it was yet dark.

Now McConnel had two sons, handy men with their six-shooters, as was well known to the French boys, for they had served with them on the frontier. Having then, as they thought, to deal with three well-armed fighting men, they determined to run no risks, but to lie by close to the door of the ranch, shoot the first man that came out, and then rush the house for the others. It is true that the McConnel boys had had no hand in old French's death, but their father had, and they must pay the penalty too.

The watch was not a long one, for just after sun-up McConnel senior, newly awakened from sleep, came to his door, and fell across his threshold, shot through the head. Into the house dashed the murderers, only to find it empty, for the sons, as it happened, were away cow-hunting, and so escaped their father's fate. The young ruffians dragged the body into an outhouse close by, and then sat down coolly to breakfast in their victim's house ; then, their thirst for vengeance as keen as ever, set off for Hay's ranch, nearly a day's ride across the prairie. After a brief halt at midday to rest their horses, they had arrived, as the afternoon was waning, within about five miles of Hay's place when, as they topped a ridge, they saw the man they sought riding towards them.   He saw them at the same moment, instantly turned his horse's head, and galloped homewards for dear life.   The news that the French boys were " on the shoot " had reached him, and he was making his way to the settlements to escape them.

The pursuers and pursued were separated by about three hundred yards, and for a time the latter held his own.   For a couple of miles or so the grim race lasted, without change of position ; the hunted man rode for his life, and the hunters followed after, thirsting for his blood. Now the better condition and quality of the latter's horses began to tell, and, yard by yard, they began to overhaul their quarry.   Now he was only a hundred yards ahead ; now only fifty, and he drew his six-shooter to make a fight for his life.   Turning in his saddle, without pulling rein, he let drive and missed ; fired a second and third time, with the same result.   Then, in desperation, he pulled his horse sharp round to get a fair aim ; but the poor animal was done, and he and his rider came heavily to the ground.   Now his enemies were upon him, and, before he could rise, put two bullets into him where he lay, and so slew their fourth victim.

Then they caught and unsaddled his horse and turned it loose, camping on the creek hard by for the night.

One wonders how they slept ; but probably they were not troubled by dreams of what they had done.

The next man they had marked down for vengeance was one named Stokes, who lived near Atacosa Court House, and thither then they wended their way ; but whilst they were still some miles distant, they learned

from some vaquéros that Stokes and his son had started
three weeks before with a bunch of cattle for Eagle Pass,
on the Rio Grandé.   So they turned back at once, and
struck for the well-beaten trail that led there, confident
that they would encounter those they sought on their
homeward journey.

The way was long, but they kept steadily on by easy
stages, knowing they must meet their men sooner or
later ; nor, as far as I gathered from the story they told
me, did any thought of relenting enter their souls through
all the long ride.   Indeed their one thought was to
avenge their father's death, for which the blood they had
already shed was quite inadequate, so long as any one
concerned in it was still alive.

They followed the road for about a fortnight, when one
midday they came on Stokes and his son " nooning " it
under the shade of some live-oaks, hard by a water-hole.
No news of the Frenches' vendetta had reached these men,
and they had no suspicion of their impending fate.   They
greeted the newcomers, and these dismounted, apparently
to join them in their midday rest.   News was asked for
on either side, and the father and son were much interested
to hear of the Federals' doings in San Antonio.

Soon it was time to saddle up and part, each on their
own road.   The Stokeses were busy with their horses ;
the last business that would ever occupy them in this
world.   For now the prearranged signal was given, and
Jim French, whilst he gave it, whipped out his pistol and
shot the younger Stokes dead.   Dick French fumbled
with his six-shooter, and the elder Stokes ran for his life,
though he had no chance, for his arms were on his saddle.
Both the brothers fired after him, and a bullet through
his leg brought him to the ground.   Now they bound
him hand and foot, carried him back to where they had
lately sat talking and laughing together, and hanged him
on the live-oak beneath which lay the dead body of his
son.   Then they unsaddled the dead men's horses, turned

them loose as before, and departed, leaving the dollars of their victims for the first chance thief who might come along, and their corpses for the buzzards and coyotés.

This is a tale of cold-blooded, ruthless murder, it will be said, not fit to be told to decent law-abiding people ; besides, it is incredible that two young fellows, such as here described, could be so bloodthirsty and remorseless in their vengeance. But it is true nevertheless, though not quite complete yet ; for yet another death penalty had to be paid before they were satisfied, or partly so.

What these boys did was the outcome of the lawless state of society in which they lived, where only private vengeance could requite private, or as a matter of fact, public wrongs, and where human life was held as cheap as that of the " beasts that perish." Moreover, as is always the case, at least in my experience in the West and South, when men start shooting like this, the appetite grows by what it feeds on, till blood-shedding seems to become a real pleasure. I think these young fellows had reached this stage, for now they grew quite reckless, and were a mind to run "amok," not only against their father's enemies, but against any one who had held office in the State service.

In this frame of mind they rode into Atacosa Court House, a one-horse little place, though the capital of the county of the same name. Their errand there was to seek Jake Peat who, next to Simons, had been most prominent in their father's arrest, and who they heard was in the place. Jake knew well enough they would be after him at any moment, and therefore went fully armed and prepared for the meeting. He was a fighting man, and loudly declared he wasn't afraid of the French boys, but would shoot them on sight, if they ever came near him.

The town boasted one drinking and gambling saloon, and the boys, inquiring for Peat, were told he was there with several of his friends. They hitched their horses hard by, and, six-shooters in hand, rushed in, shouting " hands up ! " as they did so.

Standing at the bar, or seated at the tables, there were about a dozen men in the place, and all promptly obeyed the order, except Jake and a friend, who were standing together talking. They whipped out their six-shooters, but before they could fire the boys pulled on them, and both fell—Peat shot through the chest, and the other man through the left shoulder. Peat was mortally wounded, and never spoke again ; but his friend, who still held his pistol, sat up, and let drive at Jim French, sending a bullet through the fleshy part of his left arm. Before he could fire again, Dick French shot him through the head. Then, as coolly as though nothing had happened, they both walked out of the saloon, six-shooters in hand, no one daring to hinder them.

As it happened, business took me to the Court House that very afternoon, and as I was riding into the place, I met an acquaintance who told me what had been done. He was a good bit flurried, and said he was going to get out of the town, which didn't seem a very healthy place just then, for the French boys were on the shoot, and vowing they would kill every one who had anything to do with the defunct Vigilance Committee or the State service, adding, " If I were you, I should go too, for those boys will shoot you else to a certainty ; they're real mad, I tell you." " Nonsense," I answered, " the French boys shoot me ! Why, they served under me for months on the frontier, and we were the best of friends."

So I rode on into the town, which seemed strangely quiet and deserted, and my friend continued his journey. I can't say I felt quite easy in my mind all the same, for, as I have said, when men go " on the shoot," they are not always so particular as they ought to be as to whom they practise on. I certainly looked to my six-shooters, and put them handy for use in case of accidents, and then went on to hunt up my young friends.

As I passed the Court House, I saw them riding some hundred yards or so ahead of me, and, putting a bold front on my uneasiness, called after them by name. At once they swung their horses round, and came to meet me with their six-shooters at the ready. It was rather a nervous moment, but directly they made sure who it was, they put them up and greeted me in the most friendly way. " Why, boss," said Jim, who carried his left arm in a sling, " what brings yew here ? Anyway, I'm real glad to see yew again." " And so am I," said Dick.

I told them I had happened to come into the town on business, and had just heard of their doings. " And now, boys," I said, " I think you've done enough of this shoot-ing business, and perhaps a little too much, if you ask me. Besides, if you don't clear out, you'll have the whole country raised on you directly. I should advise you to get across into Mexico as soon as you can."

" Jist what we was figuring to do, boss," said Dick ; " your head's level, sure enough. We reckon we've about wiped out all them as we wanted to this side the Rio Grandé, and over there we're goin' to hunt round a bit for Asa and Hiram Minshul, Sol Chiff, and any of the dog-gorned gang we can find." " We reckon to work down as far as Matamoras," chimed in Jim, " for we heard say as some on 'em had skedaddled there. If we do happen on 'em, yew bet your bottom dollar, Cap., we'll hang old Asa with his own rope, and I'll count that the best day's work that ever I done."

" Well, boys," I said, " I wish you luck in that, any way. Now good-bye, for you'd best be gone." So we shook hands and parted, and I never heard any more of them.

As to their quest for Asa Minshul, it was most improb-able they would succeed in it, for the old villain was far too cute to stay in Matamoras, even if he had gone there ; it was too near the frontier of Texas to be healthy. Most likely he had gone up North straight away, and was by that time a shining light in some Methodist church in Boston, or elsewhere.

BOOK V

THE BREAK-UP, AND AFTER

CHAPTER I

MY COMPANY'S LAST INDIAN FIGHT

In this autumn of 1864 the last scenes in the awful drama of Civil War were being enacted far away from us in Texas. But though news filtered slowly down to us in our remote corner of the Confederacy, it was uniformly bad, and told of defeat and disaster without a gleam of success to lighten the despondency that reigned throughout the South. None but those who actually lived in the South during that wartime, and were regarded as true Southerners by the people, can realise what the victory of the North meant to that proud race.

The great struggle was begun by most Southerners with a light heart, and an absolute assurance of success. The Yankees wouldn't fight; but if they were rash enough to do so, we could whip them easily. Now, after three years and a half of desperate fighting, General Lee, and the remnant of his gallant army that survived the dreadful slaughter of the battles of the Wilderness, were shut up in the lines of Petersburg. The South was exhausted and drained of men, money, and munitions. No more armies could be raised to help our leader, and to all men's minds the end we dreaded seemed very near.

All the world knows now that it was only his indomitable soul and resourceful war-genius that staved it off for a few brief months. He and his shoeless, ragged, starving army covered themselves with glory, but the cause for which they had fought so gallantly was lost already.

In the towns and settlements a kind of hushed expectancy prevailed ; business and pleasure alike seemed at a standstill, and men waited and watched as before the coming of some great storm or catastrophe of nature. But on the frontier it was different, for our untiring enemies the Indians kept us always on the alert, and it was only by constant vigilance that we could keep them in check at all. It was as though they knew that the time of comparative freedom from restraint they had enjoyed for more than three years was drawing to an end, and that they must make the most of what remained.

All that autumn and winter not only we, but all the other frontier Rangers, almost lived in the saddle, and still could not efficiently protect the lives of the ranchers and their property from the ubiquitous Indians. Their ravages extended up the frontier from the lower Nueces and Frio Rivers, along the line of the Rio Grandé del Norte, and almost across to the Brazos River on the east, a country nearly 700 miles in length by 500 in breadth. All therefore that the few companies of Rangers could do was to establish their camps where best they could protect the widely scattered ranches, and follow up the raiding bands as soon as news reached them that they were in their neighbourhood. Of course many of the marauders got clear away with their plunder and the scalps of their unfortunate victims, surprised in some lonely ranch ; for they spared neither men, women, nor children if they could murder them without too much risk to themselves.

Their main object in all their raids, however, was horse-stealing ; the killing of cattle and the murder of defence-less human beings were only pleasant interludes to their chief business. Many and many a weary and fruitless ride we had that season over the endless prairies and through the difficult mountain region between the Pecos and the Rio Grandé ; but sometimes we were lucky enough to come up with the crafty thieves, and then we neither gave, nor expected, quarter. After the two Indian fights described in the last chapter but one, it may perhaps

be wearisome to tell of another ; but it was the last one
in which I ever took part, and in some respects the most
disastrous, so maybe the story is worth giving.

It was in April 1865, and my company was still in camp
on the Leona, under command of my senior Lieutenant,
Fred English, for I was away at the ranch for a spell of
leave, to look after my own business, when news was
brought there that a strong band of about eighty Comanchés was slaying, burning, and raiding on the middle
Nueces. They had met with a hot reception at the first
ranch they raided, for the two brothers who owned it,
Scotsmen of the name of Cockburn, had fought desperately
for their lives and property, and killed three of the
marauding demons before they were overpowered and
scalped. With them died the wife and three children
of one of the brothers—how, it is best perhaps not to
know ; the other brother fortunately had no family.

The sight of white men's blood had inflamed the
Comanchés' thirst for more, and the next ranch they came
to they fiercely attacked, and promptly captured. Not a
very great exploit for eighty savages to accomplish, for it
was only held by one white man and three of his vaquéros,
who usually are not much good in a fight. However,
they managed to kill a couple of the Indians before they
were killed, scalped, and mutilated in the nameless
fashion of these savages.

The unfortunate owner of this place was well known to
me, poor fellow, for he was a cousin of my junior Lieutenant Dan Williams, and no doubt it was that fact that led
Dan and English to throw away their lives in their rash
thirst for vengeance, as will be seen. By this time the
alarm had been given all along the river, and the ranchers,
not strong enough to hold their own, had taken refuge
elsewhere ; but the Indians, if they couldn't get them,
had got pretty well all their horses, and were driving off
a very big bunch, probably nearly two hundred in number. The moment English heard the tidings he mustered

all hands in camp, twenty-five all told, and with Dan Williams, his junior, set off in pursuit. At the same time he sent an express to a detachment of ten of the boys a few miles higher up the creek, with orders to join me at my ranch, and, if I were not there, to come on after him, without waiting for me.

Luckily I was at home, and, having a fresh horse just caught, we were speedily riding over the prairie to join the rest. I was anxious for my friends English and Dan Williams, especially when I heard the fate of the latter's cousin, and for my brave boys too. The odds were terribly against them, and I had reason to fear they might do something rash, for both were brave to a fault, and were apt to hold Indians and their fighting powers too cheaply. It is always foolish to do that, especially when your enemy is cornered, and must fight or die ; even a rat, when he can't bolt, will fight to the death.

Dan Williams was a great friend of mine, and we had been in many a tough Indian scrimmage together, and, so far, had always come out on top. It was he who led the attack on the rear of the Indians' position so cleverly in the Hondo fight, when we whipped them so badly and got their horses, mainly through the way he carried out his orders. And now he was going to fight his last fight against any foe !

The two Lieutenants and their party had about eight hours' start of me, but their trail, and that of the Indians, was a very plain one, leading as it did over the grassy prairie, and I rode on it as fast as I dared press the horses. When night fell I was sure from the sign that they were not far ahead of us ; and it was easy to see that they, and we, were catching up with the Comanchés.

Unfortunately it was a dark, moonless night, and I had perforce to wait for daylight, for fear of missing the trail, anxious as I was to push on and be in time for the fight. A foreboding of ill weighed on me, and, tired out as I was, I hardly closed my eyes all that weary night. An hour before daybreak I roused the boys out of their heavy sleep, and with the first streak of dawn we were on the trail again. I found afterwards that our party had camped only five or six miles ahead of us ; if we had had but half an hour's more daylight we should have caught them in time ! But it wasn't to be. Plainer and plainer grew the wide trail, and we rode on it at a fast lope.

The bright, fresh morning, and the certainty that we were now close at the heels of our friends, had dispelled my fears, and I had every hope of catching them in time. But that half hour of daylight, that had failed us overnight, still held us in its toils, and by that much we missed our opportunity.

We had ridden perhaps ten miles, and, as we topped a rise on the prairie, saw a sight that made my blood curdle. A mile or so away on the level plain, without a tree on it to hide the view, was the band of Indians, dismounted, and drawn up in their favourite " V " formation to receive the boys' attack. The latter were charging right at this, and were then, as I judged, within a few hundred yards from it. In the clear, dry air of the plains the whole scene was as clearly visible as though it was close at hand.

In frantic excitement, and forgetful of the distance that separated us, I yelled to them to halt, and then fired my rifle as we galloped on, hoping they might hear that and wait for our coming. But they heard nothing, and saw nothing but the band of murdering villains in front of them, against whom they dashed at a full gallop. The " V " closed in on the little troop of boys who were so recklessly throwing away their lives, and in a moment friend and foe were mixed in extricable confusion. On we rode to the help of our hard-pressed friends, and as we neared them the tangle unravelled itself gradually, and those of the boys who still kept their saddles came clear out of the mass of yelling Indians. But five horses galloped riderless over the plain, and one of them was Dan Williams'. Six more of the boys, and English amongst them, came out of the mêlée badly wounded, but they had accounted for twenty of the Comanchés, who never would rob or murder any more, for they lay dead in their tracks, killed by the fire from the six-shooters at very short range.

Meantime we, the latest comers, and the remnant of the attacking party were in a perilous position, for the Indians, shaken as they were by the furious onslaught we had seen, outnumbered us by nearly three to one, and, if they mounted and charged home, could pretty well ride over us. It was hopeless to attempt to rescue our fallen comrades, for they would be despatched with tomahawks the moment they fell ; all we could do was to look out for ourselves.

I halted my little party a couple of hundred yards off, and sent the horses to the rear, making the men lie down. With the survivors from that desperate charge we were twenty-eight all told, for four of the wounded were past any more fighting. Each man had his rifle and six-shooter, and if the Indians did get us, I knew we could make it pretty hot for them first.

By this time the Comanchés had got to their horses, and were ranged up in line in front of us. Evidently they meant charging, but I had good hope of stopping them, if only the boys kept steady. No time was to be lost, and from my position in the centre of the line I ordered the boys to fire alternate volleys from left to right when I gave the signal. With whoops and yells on came the savages, and it almost looked as if they meant to ride over us. As they came within a hundred yards or so they let fly their arrows, and the few who had rifles banged away at us, but without any result beyond grazing the heel of one of the boys with a bullet.

Now they were only fifty yards off, and as yet we had

fired no shot.   Then the signal was given, and the fifteen rifles on the left were emptied into " the brown " of them. A good many horses were riderless now, but the rest kept on till the volley on the right was poured into them, at very short range, whilst we on the left gave them the contents of our six-shooters.   It was too hot for any Indians to stand, and now they wheeled right and left, and bolted as hard as they could go to get out of the fire, leaving seventeen dead and wounded behind them. One of the former, evidently the chief of the band, from his feather headgear, and who led his men gallantly enough, fell almost on top of us, shot clean through the heart.   So they had got pretty close up before we turned them.

The Indians being now well on the run, it was best policy to keep them at it ; besides, there were the stolen horses to be recovered, and we were bound to have some of them at any rate.   Some five miles in front lay the Nueces River with its wide border of dense chaparral, and for that they were making as fast as they could go, driving the big mob of horses before them.   " Boot and saddle " therefore was the word now, and after them we went as hard as we could gallop.   But they had a longish start of us, and the covert the savages were bolting for seemed all too near.

Every man rode his best in that race, and our horses having the legs of the Indian ponies, we gradually drew up to them, till we were not more than two or three hundred yards behind them.   The chaparral was only about a mile ahead of them now, and how the beggars did ride to reach its shelter !   No thought of turning on their pursuers seemed to enter their heads ; their one idea was plainly enough to get to covert with as many of the horses as they could keep in front of them.   Of course a good many of these had broken back during the pursuit, and were now peacefully grazing on the prairie behind us, and could easily be gathered by and by.

26

The Comanchés kept a fairly even line, though they were rather scattered in driving the horses, which ran in bunches. Each man lay almost flat on his barebacked pony, so that it wasn't very easy to shoot them at the gallop. However, I thought a volley would help to scatter them, and so let out more of the horses. There was no time to halt and fire, so we let drive with our rifles as we went, and, by good luck more than anything else, bowled over a couple of the Indians. This so scared the rest that they seemed to forget even their precious horses, and broke in all directions, bolting into the thick chaparral like so many hunted rabbits. They carried a good many of the loose horses with them, but we got seventy they left behind.

It would have been quite useless, besides being very risky, to follow the Indians into the brush ; moreover, we had our wounded to look after, so took the back trail immediately, driving the captured horses before us. On the way we gathered forty-five more, so we did pretty well considering all things, for we had recovered one hundred and fifteen out of the two hundred they had stolen.

On the scene of his rash exploit lay my poor friend Dan, with a spear thrust right through his body, and terribly hacked by tomahawks. It was the same with the other four, and all were dead, but not scalped or mutilated ; the savages had had no time for that. Of our six wounded, four were in desperate case ; and English amongst them, suffering, poor fellow, from severe spear wounds. He was then past speaking, and evidently dying.

All we could do was to bind up the wounds as best we could, and, making litters with the Indians' spears and our own blankets, carry them as tenderly as possible to the nearest ranch, a long day's journey. Poor English never lived to reach it, but died just before sundown, still unconscious. The other three didn't live through the night, so we had to mourn the loss of nine brave souls out of our little company. Truly a grievous loss, which might so easily have been avoided. Next day we dug their graves under the shade of some giant live-oaks, hard by the creek, and I read the English Church Burial Service over them, out of a tattered Prayer-book, found by the owner of the place after much search.

Notwithstanding the whipping we had given the Comanchés, and the spoil of horses we had taken, it was a sad and mournful party that marched into camp the day after the funeral. We had lost some of our best and bravest boys, but no one was more missed than my poor friend Dan, the pluckiest, cheeriest in all the company.

Thirty-nine long years have passed since that last fight of ours with the Comanchés, and now I suppose these savages have been exterminated, or driven over the border into Mexico. Where they roamed, plundering and murdering, are now peaceful settlements and prosperous cattle-ranches, whose owners can sleep without fear of midnight raids and yelling savages.

Well, " the old order changes," and in this case it must be a change for the better.

CHAPTER II

It was on April 9, 1865, that Lee surrendered to General Grant at Appomattox Court House, but this was not officially known in Texas till more than a month after the event.

Desperately as the South had clung to the hope of victory, and confidently as she trusted in the resourceful genius of her great leader, it had been patent to all thinking men for many months past that the great struggle between such unequal forces could have but one ending. And now that the end had come, I believe the feeling of the vast majority throughout the Southern States was one of relief. We in Texas, far away from the central theatre of the war, had suffered but comparatively little, but the great slave-holding States of the Confederacy were devastated and ruined, as it seemed then, beyond recovery. Reduced to misery and despair, all men were sick of fighting, and longed for peace ; but how would the triumphant Northerners treat their fallen foes now they were at last beaten to their knees ? That was the great question for us all.

My own belief is that if we had realised that the Federal Government would behave as magnanimously as it did to those it was pleased to call " Rebels," the war would have ended much sooner. But the conduct of the war on the Federal side had given us no reason to believe in its clemency or its justice. In face of the constant remonstrances of General Lee, and the noble example he set them, when Northern property and Northern lives were at his mercy, the Federal commanders, with rare exceptions, treated the unfortunate Southerners with a harshness and a cruelty that were an everlasting disgrace to their cause.

If any proof of this is wanted, it is only necessary to recall the proclamation issued to his troops by the great Southern leader when he invaded Pennsylvania. He was incapable of maligning his bitterest enemy, and, after reminding them of their obligation, as members of a civilised Christian State, to observe certain laws, whether in an enemy's country or their own, went on as follows : " The commanding General considers that no greater disgrace could befall the army, and through it our whole people, than the perpetration of the barbarous outrages upon the innocent and defenceless, and the wanton destruction of private property that have marked the course of the enemy in our own country."

So, not only the leaders of the Secession movement, civil and military, but all those who had taken an active part in the war, had grave cause to fear for their liberty and their property. But to the surprise of all the world, and especially of the Southerners themselves, the victorious Federals behaved with a generosity and magnanimity for which no parallel can be found in history. Jefferson Davis, the President of the Confederacy, suffered a short imprisonment, and was then released ; and no other punishment was inflicted on him, except the forfeiture of his civil rights. Every one else who chose to apply for the benefits of the amnesty proclaimed was restored to his full status as a citizen of the Union, as soon as he had taken the oath of allegiance, or, as we called it in the South, the " ironclad oath." No man's property was confiscated save that of one, and he the greatest and the noblest of the Southerners.

It is a standing disgrace to the people of the North, to their Congress and to their President, that General

Lee's ancestral estates and houses in Virginia were not restored to him. Even his wife's house at Arlington was pillaged of all the mementos of Washington, whose adopted son her father was, and when she petitioned Congress for their return was rudely refused. Unfortunately Abraham Lincoln, whose greatness of soul all men have come to recognise, was dead, and Andrew Johnson, a very different man, reigned in his stead, or these things would never have been done.

So General Lee, with the quiet heroism which was his chiefest characteristic, ended his days in comparative poverty, as President of the College at Lexington, in Virginia ; and dying, left behind him an imperishable memory, enshrined in the hearts of all his people.

Down in our corner of the late Confederacy we certainly had no cause to complain of the treatment meted out to us by the Federal authorities, and for my own part I was on the most friendly terms with them from the very first.

In the closing days of May 1865, San Antonio was occupied by a Federal force of two regiments of infantry and one of cavalry, and the town was made the headquarters of the South-western District of the State.

The troops were under the command of a smart young cavalry general who had served with some distinction in the war, but whose name I have forgotten (in my diary I only refer to him as " the General "), but I remember he was killed some years after the Civil War in the last big fight with the Apaché Indians, on the north-west frontier, when many of his command also lost their lives.

The leading lawyer in San Antonio was a Mr. Cleaveland, who, though a man of strong Northern proclivities, had been popular with all parties throughout the war. Of course he was discreet enough to keep his opinions to himself, except in intercourse with friends he could trust, of whom I was one. He took no part either for or against the Southern cause, and though his leanings were pretty well known, he was never molested even when party feeling ran highest. He then, on the advent of the Federals, was at once made Mayor of the town, and they could not have chosen a better man ; for his intimate knowledge of the people, and his absolute impartiality, enabled him to bring order out of chaos in a surprisingly short time. Neither the General nor Cleaveland molested any one for his political opinions, or for any action done during the war, unless he had been guilty of some crime.

The greater criminals, such as Wasp, Dunn, and Asa Minshul, had made themselves scarce before the arrival of the Federals ; but some of the smaller fry rashly remained behind, and suffered the penalty of their crimes, after trial by courts-martial. But I can vouch for it that no one was shot, or hanged, who did not richly deserve his fate.

This leniency was the more remarkable since, as I have already told, many Unionists, notably those at Friedricksburg, were done to death most shamefully, without trial of any sort, by such ruffians as Dunn and Wasp. Indeed, as lately as the previous month of April there had been renewed trouble at this same place with the Germans, who were to a man strong Unionist sympathisers.

I was ordered from headquarters to send a detachment with the troops sent against them. Not liking the work which I guessed would be done, I did not go myself, but sent my then senior Lieutenant with twenty men. There was some little fighting, in which the Germans were easily beaten, and several prisoners were taken by our troops. These poor fellows had done nothing to exasperate their captors, for, as I have said, they made but a poor resistance, and I believe our total casualties did not exceed two, and they were only slightly wounded ; so there was no excuse for what followed.

The prisoners were confined in the lock-up of the little town; a trumpery wooden building over which a weak guard was mounted. The very first night a mob of men appeared, overpowered the guard, broke open the place, took out the ten prisoners, and hanged them on the live-oaks outside the town. Whether this was done with the connivance of the officer commanding the party I can't say, but I strongly suspect it was, though my subaltern averred that he, at any rate, knew nothing about it.

It was an infamous, barbarous crime against humanity, and why it was perpetrated is difficult to imagine, except that a taste for blood seemed to possess the ruffian elements amongst us. For this business only two men were made amenable to justice, and they were tried by court-martial and shot at San Antonio. The chief culprit, a Major Roberts, who was in command of the party, and who must have connived at the murders, bolted into Mexico, and was no more seen on our side of the Rio Grandé.

The day we marched into the town to be disarmed and disbanded, my friend the Mayor introduced me to the General in very flattering terms, and we became at once very friendly. He was a fine soldierly man, without any " side " or pretence about him, and he treated me, in a short time, as though we had been comrades in arms instead of enemies arrayed against each other in one of the bitterest civil wars ever waged.

All power, both civil and military, centred in the General in command of the district of San Antonio, which comprised the greater part of Western Texas, so that his hands, ably as he was assisted by my friend Cleaveland, were pretty full for some time. But when civil order, never very strongly established in Texas, had been in a measure restored, and Freedmen's Bureaux, to protect the negroes, and set them to work for wages, been duly formed, he had to turn his attention to the frontier and the Indian troubles thereon, which now were getting rampant. It was at this time that, knowing my pretty intimate acquaintance with my friends the Comanchés and Lepans and their ways, he consulted me a good deal about the establishment of frontier posts, the number of men required for each, etc.

Of course I was glad to give him all the information in my power ; and I suppose he found it useful, for, to my great surprise, he one day offered me a captain's commission in a corps he contemplated raising locally for frontier service. I confess I was much flattered by the offer and, at first, almost tempted to accept it ; but my own affairs claimed my attention, if they were not to go to rack and ruin. Then, to take service under the Federal flag, so soon after our debacle, seemed almost like treachery to the Southern cause. So, after a day's consideration, I refused the offer with many thanks, assuring my friend that, if I could ever render any assistance to him on the frontier, my services were always at his disposal. So we parted the best of friends, and I went off to my ranch, to look after the remnant of my cattle left me by the Indians, Mexican raiders, and other thieves. There I met my friend the General again, for he put up with me a couple of days on his way up country to visit the frontier and establish his posts.

When he left, I, at his urgent request, rode with him for a week, and acted as his guide over the country that was so new to him and so familiar to me, and we passed through the district along the Rio Grandé which had so recently been the happy hunting-grounds of the Indian marauders. We came across plenty of deserted and ruined ranches, the scalps of whose owners were then probably drying in some Indian camp, but of the Indians themselves we saw nothing. No doubt they had heard from their Mexican spies of the advent of the Federal troopers, and had made themselves scarce ; anyway, they took particular care not to show themselves.

The General was an able man, and a capital organiser ; moreover he was determined to establish order on the wild frontier under his command as soon as might be. To this end he devoted an untiring energy, and spent the best part of his first year in Texas in the saddle riding round his posts, and keeping every one on the alert and up to their duty. The result was that by that time things assumed a very different aspect. Indian raids were not of course entirely put down, but they became comparatively few and far between, so that folks who were not too " scarey " could sleep in some degree of peace, even in a lonely ranch away out in the Rio Grandé country.

But, at the time I am writing of, my friend's Indian troubles were only beginning, whilst my own, I am happy to say, were nearly over. Only one more narrow escape did I have of losing my scalp to the Comanchés ; but it was " touch and go " that time, and I got one of the worst scares the Indians ever gave me. It happened in this wise :

By this time I was heartily sick of Texas and its roughing, and was longing for a peep of the " Old Country " after six years' absence from its delights : moreover, there was a special attraction that drew me thither on which I need not further dilate. But unfortunately I had found ranching in wartime was not a remunerative business, and, to put it plainly, I was very short of hard dollars. Paper-money I had, but it was by this time almost worthless, and the wind must be raised somehow.

In Texas there was no market for cattle, and no hard cash to pay for them ; but in New Orleans it was different, for reports reached us that the demand there was brisk and the price good. To get the beeves there meant a drive of over seven hundred miles, and, after that, a steamboat journey some three days in length ; but it was my only resource, and I determined to try it.

Cattle fit for market were rather scarce on the ranch, and to make up my number I set to work to collect those that Bacon's man, Blackaller, had turned loose on the Carisa Creek the previous spring. They were all prime steers when that rascal had taken them, and, as the pasture on the creek was first-rate, they should now be in tiptop order, if only I could find them.

So, early in the month of June, with five vaquéros and spare horses, and fixed up for a month's trip, I started one lovely morning for my fifty-mile ride across the open prairie. The rains had freshened all nature ; the sun shone brightly, and the flowering cacti and acacias, then in fullest bloom, made the scene one of marvellous beauty, had one had time to enjoy it all. But, with all its brightness, the weather was treacherous, and we must push on if we were to reach the old " Mustanger's " camp at the head of the creek before nightfall.

We got there just at dark, when down came the rain in a perfect deluge, which didn't cease for twenty-four hours. This was bad for cattle-hunting, making the ground deep and holding, and hard on the horses. But I had come out for those cattle, and meant to have them if they could be found ; so there was nothing for it but to make the best of it. The day after the rain ceased I rode over to a ranch some ten miles away to let the owner, with whom I was well acquainted, know I was in the country, and my errand there ; also hoping to get some help from him. I caught sight of my friend near the house, but the moment he saw me he bolted indoors, and presently emerged with a rifle in his hand, followed by another man, also armed. Naturally I pulled up in some surprise at my reception, but soon was reassured, for when he made me out, my host shouted, " Come along, and hitch your horse ; darned if I didn't reckon it was some one else—mighty glad I didn't shoot afore I looked."

" Well, anyway," I said, " what's the fuss ? "

Then he told me that a week ago he had had a row with a man in the settlements, and had shot him, and was fully expecting a visit from his victim's friends, which was only natural. After a short stay I rode back to camp, my friend promising to send me some of his vaquéros the next day to help in the hunt ; for himself he intended going over into Mexico, to lie low for a few months, when his little affair would be forgotten.

All that day my hands were high busy, drying our fixings, which had got pretty well drenched, for the old camp leaked like a sieve. The following morning broke fine and clear, and, as the weather seemed more settled, I sent the hands out to hunt up the horses, intending to begin work in the afternoon. As soon as they were gone, I strolled down to the creek to try my hand at fishing, and presently was enjoying first-rate sport in a deep reed-fringed pool a few hundred yards from camp. The water was in splendid condition after the rain, for the flood had not yet come down from the mountain sources of the stream ; the fish were as unsophisticated as fish could be, and had no suspicion that my bait of raw beef covered a treacherous hook ; so, though I am no " fisherman " in the accepted sense of the word, I was doing as well as though I had been the most expert angler.

I had spent an hour or two in this way, and began to wonder why the hands were so long gone, when suddenly I heard the sound of horses' feet in the distance. I rolled up my line, and began to " thread " my pile of fish to carry them back to camp, and then the horsemen, whoever they were, were close at hand.

I was coming up the sloping bank, through the reeds, which were not quite as high as my head, and indeed was within a yard or two of the open ground, when it occurred to me that the horses coming on at a steady lope didn't sound as though they were loose. I had no idea, not the remotest, that Indians were in the country, but I wasn't taking any risk, and, as the thought flashed into my mind, threw myself down in the covert. Not an instant too soon, for, as I peered through the screen of reeds, which barely hid me, I saw, to my horror, a band of a dozen Comanchés ride up, driving before them two of my best saddle-horses.

I frankly confess I never was in a bluer funk in all my life, and, when the whole party suddenly pulled up just opposite me, not twenty yards away, I made sure my last hour had come ; for I had only my six-shooter on me, my rifle was in camp, and I had no chance for my life.

Their sharp ears had heard the rustle of the reeds as I threw myself down. Great heavens ! would they search for the cause ? I neither stirred nor breathed, but lay flat on the ground, watching every movement of my deadly foes.

The leader of the band rode up to the edge of the reeds, but fortunately a little to my right, and peered into them. "Surely he will see me," I thought, "for the brute has eyes like a cat ! " But he didn't.

Presently, though to me it seemed an eternity, he wheeled his pony round, saying in Spanish, "Son javalines " (" they are peccary.")

" Pienso que si," said another (" I think so "), and away they all rode.

I have had many narrow escapes of my life amongst Indians, and folks even wilder perhaps than they are, but that I think was the narrowest of all, for two yards of reeds only divided me from death by torture.

When I crawled out of my hiding-place, ten minutes later, the Indians had disappeared, and I went back to camp to wait for my vaquéros. In half an hour they turned up, having been kept so long looking for the two horses we should probably never see again, though I meant to have a try for them. They had seen nothing of the Indians, or their trail, for the two stolen horses were " half-breeds," and had strayed away from the rest, and being hobbled had been easily caught. It was bad luck to lose two good horses like that, but I was fortunate not to have lost the lot, my vaquéros, and my own life as well.

What befell on the rest of the trip, and what the Indians did after they left me, must, however, be reserved for another chapter ; and that will be the last I shall write of Indian " doings."

CHAPTER III

THERE was no time to be lost, if we were to catch up with the Indians and recover my horses ; so I at once sent one Mexican over to my ranch, to warn the boys to turn out and be ready with fresh horses, and another with a note to my friend with the little difficulty in the settlements. In this I told him what had happened, and asked him to follow the trail with all the boys he could muster, and I would meet him, with my party, on the Presidio road that evening.

Though we pushed on all we knew, it was late afternoon before the three Mexicans and I reached the ranch, and then I found that the presence of Indians in the country was known before my messenger arrived, and that my friends Lem Brown and Jack Vinton, reinforced by three boys from the neighbourhood, and taking four Mexicans with them, had already started to follow the trail. There was nothing for it then but to go after them as soon as might be ; so as soon as fresh horses were caught and a hasty meal was eaten, we were in the saddle again, steering across the deep prairie by the guidance of the stars, for the old Presidio road, near which I hoped to cut the trail. Near midnight we struck the road, and presently came to the rendezvous, where I found my friend and three others, he having kindly deferred his trip across the Rio Grandé to give me a helping hand.

When, after a few hours' rest, we hit the trail, soon after daybreak, it was plain to see we had a big job on hand, for it showed us we were following between forty and fifty Comanchés, who were heading on a bee line for the Rio Grandé, driving a big bunch of horses before them. Soon we struck the camp of my friends from my ranch, and, topping a rise on the prairie, saw them in the far distance, cutting along at a pace which it was quite evident couldn't last in that deep ground. In about an hour we overhauled them, their horses being pretty well done up, and then held a council of war.

Lem Brown and his party from the ranch were not in much condition to hunt Indians, they having foolishly pumped out their horses. All told, we were only ten white men and seven " greasers " against forty or fifty Indians, who had got into the difficult country bordering the Rio Grandé. I was very reluctant to turn back, for I had a strong hankering after the sight of those two stolen horses of mine ; moreover, I had heard at the ranch that a wagon, laden with goods for Mexico, had passed two days before, and, as its route lay by the Presidio road, there was great risk the Comanchés might come across it. If that happened, God help the owner, his son, and the two men with them !

The majority, however, voted for returning, saying it was useless to follow any farther ; and as for the folks in the wagon, if the Indians had caught them, they would be past help by that time, and would be dead and scalped. So we turned back and separated ; I going off to my camp on the Carisa, with my Mexicans and Lem, who said he would come with me, the rest going their various ways.

If only we had held on another half-dozen miles we should have spared one poor human being a day and night of terror and agony, and ourselves a long and wearisome ride ! But it was not to be.

That night I got into camp quite late, and found the one Mexican I had left behind mighty glad to see us, though he said everything had been quiet. Next morning early we were all starting out to hunt up those blessed cattle, when a messenger named Bell arrived from my ranch with the news that a poor young fellow had turned up there the previous afternoon, sorely wounded by the Indians, who had found and attacked the traders' wagon. Weak and exhausted from loss of blood, shoeless and almost naked, he had crawled in in a terrible plight, and this was the story he had told :

His father, whose name was Norman, a trader from Eastern Texas, making his way into Mexico with a heavy load of goods, had camped just off the road a few miles ahead of where we had halted the previous day. They had turned out their eight yoke of cattle, and, having finished supper, the whole party were sitting round the camp fire, which, as they had no suspicion that Indians were in the country, was blazing cheerfully. Suddenly and stealthily the Comanchés crept on them, and, as they sat round chatting and smoking in the bright firelight, poured a deadly volley of arrows into them. The father and one of the hands fell dead at once, but young Norman and a man named Lee, though badly wounded, jumped to their feet and ran off into the darkness, pursued by the yelling savages.

How he escaped he didn't know, but he bolted through the thick cactus growth, regardless of the awful prickles, for dear life, and at last lay down under one of the great plants, and there remained till all was quiet. In his hiding-place he could hear the Indians searching for him, occasionally coming quite close to where he lay. Once he made sure his last hour had come, for an Indian stopped on the other side of his covert and thrust his lance under it, the point just grazing his leg ; but he neither moved nor cried out, and the prying savage passed on. He thought the man Lee might still be alive, for he had run with him some distance, and, like himself, might have found a safe hiding-place.

Such was the young fellow's story, and of course there

was nothing for it but to postpone the cattle-hunt again, for the unfortunate man Lee must be rescued, if yet alive, the remains of the property secured, and the dead men buried.

The messenger brought word that Jack Vinton, and the other boys at the ranch, would meet me on the Presidio road that afternoon, at the place we had turned back from so unfortunately the day before. The horses were already saddled, and our other preparations were soon finished, so that in less than half an hour from young Bell's arrival, he, on a fresh horse, and Lem, the three Mexicans, and myself were off for the old Presidio road once more. We met the rest of the boys as the sun was falling low in a cloudless sky, shining brilliantly on the level plain of the prairie, covered as far as the eye could reach with the golden yellow of the dwarf cacti in full bloom. A scene of peace and of beauty indeed ; but we pressed on unheeding, for we had other business to attend to that brooked no delay.

Soon, as we topped a gentle rise on the prairie, we saw what we were in search of—the great tilted wagon, or " prairie schooner," standing in solitude on a low hill hard by the Las Olmas Creek. No smoke rose from the camp fire, and, as far as the eye could reach, no other token of human presence was visible, save only the wagon. The Indians had done their murderous work, and had gone, leaving their mutilated victims to the coyotés and the buzzards.

But Lee might be alive, though I hadn't much hope of it ; so, whilst the rest of us rode forward in open order, and with rifles unslung, as a precaution against an Indian ambush, I sent three of the boys and the same number of Mexicans away to the right to search the cactus growth. Presently a shout from one of the former and a frantic waving of his hat told us the wounded man was found. He lay hidden under the drooping, spiked leaves of a great yucca, and might never have been discovered but that he had just strength enough left to raise a feeble cry when he caught sight of the boys.

He had been struck by several arrows, all of which, except one in the shoulder, he had managed to pull out, but that was beyond his reach. I thought he was dead, poor fellow, but a little aguadiente from one of the boys' flasks revived him, and then we carried him, as gently as we could, in a blanket litter to the wagon. There a sight met our eyes little calculated to soften the heart of a frontiersman towards " the poor Indian." Close to the cold ashes of their fire, where they had been so treacherously surprised, lay the lifeless bodies of the unfortunate men, scalped and mutilated in nameless fashion, and turned face downwards on the ground.

From the sign we could read so plainly, it was clear enough both had been killed outright where they sat ; so far they were fortunate, for thus they escaped the tortures of these fiends in human shape, who luckily could only disport themselves with the poor dead bodies.

We were near the crossing of the Rio Grandé, and the light was failing rapidly, but so moved were we by the thirst for vengeance that, leaving one Mexican to look after Lee, we all set off at a lope on the broad trail, in the faint hope that we might overtake these wretches. We didn't stop to think, or we might have known it was useless to do so, as indeed it was ; for after riding on it best part of an hour, it took us over the river, and there we had to turn back.

Next morning Lee had somewhat revived, and it seemed possible he might recover, though he was in a desperate plight from his neglected wounds and loss of blood, so we resolved to get him to the ranch as soon as possible.

We found two yoke of cattle ; the rest had been killed by the Indians for their marrow-bones, delicacies so highly esteemed by them that they will often kill quite a number (belonging to other people) and leave all the meat for the coyotés. We packed such of the goods as the Indians had left, which was not a great quantity, into the wagon, making as comfortable a bed as we could for the wounded man, and taking the two bodies with us, set off for my place. Slow and tiresome was the journey, and often we had to hitch our horses on to the wagon by the lariats, to help it over the deep ground ; but by midnight we arrived, and handed over our patient to the care of Pépa, my very wise old Mexican woman, who, with her simples and her herbs, was a wonderful mistress of the healing art. At any rate she managed to cure both Lee and young Norman, both pretty bad cases ; so that in about a month's time they could crawl round again, and presently seemed little the worse for their terrible adventures.

At sunrise next day we laid the two murdered men to rest in rough shells, under the spreading shade of a great live-oak, hard by the graves of two of my vaquéros, recently killed by the Indians, and then I set off once more to resume the interrupted cattle-hunt. This time I had altogether ten hands with me—*i.e.* Lem Brown and nine vaquéros ; the latter all first-class cattle-men, as so many of these Mexicans are, and more at home in the saddle than anywhere else.

Bearing in mind the class of animals they ride, mostly wild, half-broken horses, and the wonderful way they manage them, I think they are, take them for all in all, the finest horsemen I ever saw. I don't mean they are finished masters of the art, as understood in this country, but for cutting out a steer from a bunch of wild cattle, turning and twisting like cats in the doing of it, or " roping " a charging " beef," they are, I believe, unrivalled.

I don't think I have described the way we worked a cattle-drive like this before, so perhaps it may be worth while to give some description of it. As we were many miles away from my corrals, we had to drive pretty well all the cattle we found towards the ranch, and there separate my own brand from others, for of course in an entirely open country like that they get a good deal mixed up.

Beginning about twelve miles down country from camp, we found the first herd on the prairie, not very far from the thick chaparral that lines the creek, and from which of course we had to do all we knew to keep them out. Flanking out on either side at a gallop, we soon had the most of them under control, but every now and then some of the wildest and fastest cattle would make a dash for the bush and liberty. Then was the time to watch the doings of the vaquéros ; turn and twist and charge as the steer might, the Mexicans were generally too quick for the runaway, if he hadn't too much of a start, and back he had to come, reluctant, to the herd.

They didn't often use their lariats, but sometimes, when a steer couldn't be headed off without it, they would rope him on the very edge of the chaparral. Out shot the raw-hide like lightning, over the horns went the noose, and, before he knew what had befallen him, the galloping steer was thrown heavily on to his side by a sudden dexterous twist to right or left of the active little cattle-horse, and there he lay sprawling with all the wind, and most of the fight, knocked out of him. For the time being he would be submissive enough, and could generally be driven back to the herd without much difficulty.

At the season of the year in which we were working cattle congregate very much in the chaparral along the creek-sides, since the mosquitoes are not numerous enough to drive them out into the open. A month or two later these pests, which love the shelter of the trees, swarm in such incalculable numbers, and are so vicious in their attacks, that even the tough hides of the cattle fail to protect them, and out they must come on to the prairies. We were, therefore, very lucky in our first drive to find so many beeves out in the open, for hunting in the chaparral is quite a different matter, and is about the hardest work man and horse can do.

Having then got our first herd pretty well under control, we left four of the vaquéros to keep it moving slowly along, whilst the rest of us went off to hunt up more cattle to drive to it. By noon we had collected a good bunch of about two hundred head, though of course a great many of these were not my own, and of those that were mine, only comparatively a few belonged to the wild lot I was after. Now, coming to a good water-hole, shaded by hackberry-trees, laden with ripe fruit, we called a halt, stripped the horses for an hour's grass, and refreshed ourselves on dried beef, bread and coffee, the usual prairie fare, which is not half bad, when eaten with the best of sauces.

Working again in the afternoon for an hour or so, we got another fifty head ; and then came the " cutting out "—i.e. the separating from the herd of those we wanted to drive to the ranch, the remainder being let go to wander away at their own sweet will. It is wonderful how they all hang together when you want to separate them, but at last by the free use of the lariats and by dint of much hard riding, we had singled out some forty head of first-class beeves, in which were included twenty-five of the Carisa Creek cattle. All these I dispatched to the ranch corrals, under charge of three vaquéros, and the rest of us turned back to camp, to be ready for another day's drive on the morrow.

The night was dry and warm, so after a supper, after the pattern of the midday meal, washed down by strong black coffee, we were all presently stretched on our blankets, under the star-lit canopy of heaven, and slept the sleep of the weary, lulled by the night sounds that are so plaintive and so weird in those vast solitudes.

Not that I for one wanted much lulling that night ; but often when camping out by myself on the prairies, miles from any human being, I have listened long to the voices of the night, which one soons learns to recognise. They give confidence, and a sense of security too, to the lonely watcher, for where they are heard there is but little fear of prowling foes ; when silence falls upon them, it is time to be on the alert, if you are in an Indian country especially.

The great bullfrogs, recently aroused from their dry-weather slumbers in the mud of a water-hole by the coming of the rains, commence the concert with a vigour all their own, which is somewhat disconcerting at close range, but heard afar off is soothing, and not unmusical. When the deepening dusk veils all but your immediate surroundings, come the night-jars on noiseless wings, wheeling, circling, poising, close overhead, till their feathers almost brush your upturned face—" mos-quito-hawks " the natives call them ; and all night long they are busy swallowing wholesale these and other flying enemies of poor humanity.

Now as the last gleam of light dies in the western sky, the dwarf owls from the neighbouring clumps of live-oaks begin their ceaseless queries of " Who're you, who're you ? " in low tones, " most musical, most melancholy."

Afar off, in the chaparral by the creek, the great green cicadæ, as large as locusts, begin to drum their wings, with shrill whistling ; whilst their small cousins the little brown grasshoppers in the herbage all around utter their insistent " Hist ! hist ! " below their breath, like some stage villain in a minor theatre. Of sounds not quite so pleasant as these is the curious lowing cry of the solitary bittern, bewailing the scarcity of fish, as he stands knee-deep in the shallows of the creek ; and you rejoice in your heart of hearts that he is not gregarious in his habits.

Far over the prairie comes the baying of the great grey wolves and the barking of the coyotés, hunting the deer and antelope, or possibly your own cattle, to try and cut out some of the calves. These are voices of the night that startle you at times from your slumbers ; as when once a small pack of big " lobos " came driving close past my solitary camp in hot pursuit of their prey. So near they came that, as I sat up half dazed with sleep and fumbled for my six-shooter, not well knowing what the rushing sound might mean, I saw their misty forms dart by, and heard the patter of their many feet and the snapping of their hungry jaws as they ran their quarry in view ; but so swiftly did the chase pass by that, before I could shoot, it had vanished into the darkness of the night.

But this night no lulling of soft voices was necessary to induce sleep, nor could any harsh ones break it ; we were all too tired for that, though an hour or so before day we were astir again, cooking breakfast and boiling coffee, preparatory to an early start ; for that day we were going to hunt the chaparral, and had all our work cut out. There I felt sure of finding more of my wild cattle than in the open, and was not disappointed.

Riding down the creek-side some miles before we commenced, we drove back towards camp. At that spot the chaparral was about half a mile wide, so we formed line with the inner flank thrown forward very considerably, so as gradually to edge the cattle out into the open.

But first I must try to give some idea of what chaparral is like, before I describe the driving. The main growth is " mesquite," a bushy, low tree bearing a plentiful crop of pods, of which cattle and other animals are very fond. The loftier timber is live-oak and cedar ; and the undergrowth of hackberry and other bushes, mostly provided with a full armament of thorns, is very dense. Everywhere through this run the prickly and tiger-claw bamboos, and often the vines, that cling and climb to the tops of the highest trees, make an almost impenetrable network. Here and there in this thick scrub are to be found grassy open glades, but never of any great width.

The line advances with much shouting and hallooing, in fact with all the noise that a dozen able-bodied human beings can raise, and presently a bunch of cattle is started. The din increases. Crash! bang! through the under-growth go the beasts at a surprising pace, and after them we scramble and stumble, as best we may. The inner flank man fires his six-shooter now and then to tell his position, and the rest follow in such order as they can, keeping a sharp-look out for back-breaking steers.

Across an open glade scuttles a bunch of peccary, with much grunting and snapping of tusks; and a loud and angry gobbling tells you that you have disturbed an ancient turkey and his harem at their early breakfast of hackberries.

These flutter off, or take wing across the creek, and are no more seen; and then perhaps you catch a fleeting glimpse of the brown-red coat of a deer, or antelope, as he steals on before the drive. But all these, and many other *feræ naturæ* we put up, are all unheeded, for we have as much as we can do to keep the cattle ahead of us.

This scrambling racket goes on for half an hour, perhaps an hour, and when at last we emerge into the open, with torn hands and faces, and clothes rather the worse for wear, we are lucky if we have a dozen or so cattle in front of us. No time is there for rest, or even for taking breath, for the steers we have got must be hustled and bustled far out on to the open prairie, or they will break back into covert again to a certainty. There they are left in charge of a vaquéro, and the rest of us go back for another drive.

The hunt went on, with varying success, for eight days longer, by which time both men and horses were pretty well done up. I was fairly satisfied with the result, for I had 250 prime steers, mostly from four to five years old, safely penned in the corrals.

At the ranch I found a messenger from Don Immanuel Garcia, Alcaldé of the little Mexican town of San Juan, a couple of days' ride across the Rio Grandé, with whom I had had previous dealings in the cattle line. He sent word that, owing to the war, there was a brisk demand for beeves, and that he could take fifty or a hundred, at a good price, if I had them to sell.

It was a tempting offer, so instead of starting at once on my long drive to New Orleans, I took the smaller number across the river, with what result I must tell in another chapter.

CHAPTER IV

CATTLE-DEALING IN MEXICO

THE Rio Grandé is a turbulent stream when the snows melt in the Sierras at its sources, and is then quite deserving of the name the Mexicans have given it, " El Rio Bravo," or " fierce river." But, by the way, how characteristic of their nature is that little word ! " Bravo " means brave, or angry, or fierce ; cool courage with them, as indeed with most of the South-American Spanish races, is not common.

The river was sufficiently " bravo " when we reached it with my little drove ; running strong and brown between its shelving banks at the " crossing." It took some time to force the cattle into the stream ; but once the plunge was taken, they were soon over, for they are wonderful swimmers, and fortunately not easy to drown.

The country on the other side is much like Texas, but more thickly populated, the people living either in small " pueblos," or villages, or round some large " hacienda," or farm, in patriarchal fashion. The climate is so dry that not much cultivation is carried on, and that only by the aid of irrigation, which is very primitive in character. The farms therefore are mostly grazing, and produce only enough corn for the wants of the immediate neighbourhood.

I am writing of Mexico, or rather the small part of it I knew, nearly forty years ago, and wonderful changes have taken place since then under the strong, but beneficent, sway of that born ruler of men Porfirio Diaz. In those days the various States of the Republic, separated from the seat of central government in Mexico City by hundreds of miles, without railways or even decent roads to connect them, were bound together by the slenderest of ties, and " Pronunciamentos," headed by some ambitious General or Governor of a State, were everyday occurrences.

President Diaz was elected for the first time some thirty-one years ago, and is now serving his eighth term of office, to the general satisfaction of all his people. In that comparatively short time he has evolved order out of chaos ; has opened up the country by railways and roads, and developed its marvellously rich natural resources to such an extent that to-day Mexico is one of the most prosperous and well-governed countries on the continent, while its credit stands high on the bourses of the world. To have done all this in any country in the world would have been a marvel ; but to have done it in Mexico, and to have so changed the mixed race he rules as to convert it to industry and honesty is an achievement almost unique in the history of humanity. I have no doubt his all-pervading influence has been felt even in the remote States of Nuevo Leon and Coahuila, on the distant Rio Grandé, which were best known to myself in the days of which I write, and which were then backward and uncivilised enough, goodness knows !

Two days' drive, over a dry, desolate-looking prairie, during which we passed two pretty large ranches, apparently devoted to the raising of goats, for they swarmed all around them, brought us late one evening to the Pueblo of San Juan, and a more poverty-stricken, uninviting-looking place it would be hard to conceive. Its reputation was no better than its appearance, for, if not sorely maligned by rumour, its inhabitants chiefly followed the ancient and honourable occupation of horse and cattle stealing.

Owing to the fact that their own neighbourhood didn't supply a sufficiency of these commodities, they mainly

A MEXICAN PUEBLO

exercised their talents on our side of the Rio Grandé, with much profit to themselves : of course if they were caught it was a case of a short shrift and a quick " look-up " a live-oak. We " Americanos " were therefore not so popular as we might have been with these freebooters, and, as I rode up the dirty, straggling street, the " greasers," seated at their doors enjoying the cool of the evening and the never-failing " cigarettas," cast very unfriendly glances at myself, and very hungry ones at my fine beeves. But when I inquired my way to the house of " mi amigo Don Immanuel el Alcaldé," a change came over them at once, and half a dozen jumped up to show me the way. Don Immanuel was evidently a person in authority, which was so far satisfactory, for, though I of course went well armed, with a rifle and a couple of six-shooters, San Juan was not a healthy place for an " Americano " to venture into alone. Let me try to describe it as it then was, and perhaps is still, in that outlying country ; for the Mexican changes but slowly, and not then without much pressure brought to bear upon him.

The single street, if such it can be called, went straggling up a rocky, sun-scorched slope, one of the low foothills of a distant range of mountains. The houses, of which there might be twenty or thirty, were set at all angles : some with their fronts, some with their backs, and others with their ends facing the street, through which a black and evil-smelling stream of sewage, and the like abominations, slowly trickled, being much blocked on its downward course to the prairie by rocks and accumulations of refuse. Here and there these formed sizable pools, wherein wallowed the black pigs of the pueblo, which took not only their pastime therein, but drew most of their sustenance thereout. Except for a brief period of their existence, when they were penned and fed on maize, I don't think they got any other food. Certainly they didn't look as if they did, for they more resembled half-starved greyhounds than comfortable English porkers.

This same stream, a few hundred yards above the pueblo, ran clear and bright from its limestone source, and might have supplied the inhabitants with excellent drinking water at their very doors ; but that would have involved " mucho trabajo "—too much trouble.

Next to the pigs, which pervaded the whole place, and the fowls, which roosted in every house, the most numerous inhabitants were curs of every degree, and in every stage of starvation, poor wretches ! I don't think there is any living thing in creation so hungry as a Mexican's dog.

Peep into one of the houses, which are all much like, only that some are perhaps a shade less dirty than others. The walls are of adobe, or sun-burned clay, and the roofs of palmetto thatch, which is excellent covering, except that it harbours hosts of insect plagues. The floor is of beaten clay, hard and dry, and swarms with " pulgas y chinchas "—fleas and bugs, which perforce reside there, since the only furniture the house contains consists of two or three low wooden stools, a rickety table, and hammocks slung to the rafters for sleeping accommodation. On this rickety table, set against the wall, stands the " Santo " ; a tawdry little image of the Virgin, or of the patron saint of the casa set in a glass case, decked with gawdy-coloured paper flowers, but an object of much reverence to the owner, who always doffs his sombrero to it on entering, usually crossing himself as well.

His wife, or " La Señora," if she is young, will probably be good-looking, with large dark eyes and a bright complexion, which alas ! will fade so soon, in her life of drudgery. For she is the working partner in the firm, if any work is to be done, except cattle-tending or cattle-stealing, and these her lord and master does. She rises from her knees and, in reply to our greeting, gives us a pleasant " Buenos tardes, Señor ! " She was hard at work rubbing down maize, soaked in " lye " to soften it, on a grooved stone with a rolling-pin, to convert it into paste for the " tortillas." These, something like substantial pancakes, are excellent when eaten hot, but when cold are an abomination to any self-respecting stomach. Hot or cold they are the staple of every Mexican's diet ; and not only are they eaten themselves but are also used in lieu of a spoon, to scoop up soup or gravy, or any such trifle ; and very handy tools too, in the hands of an expert, they prove to be.

While La Señora is busy, as we have described, preparing the family meal, the " family," probably a numerous one, is reclining on the earthen floor in every stage of dirt and semi-, or entire, nakedness ; the elder children possibly boasting a shirt of the briefest, but the younger being clad in nature's garb alone. La Señora herself is apparently not overdressed, for, as well as a mere man can judge, she seems only to wear one garment, and that a loose, long cotton gown, ungirt at the waist, and reaching nearly to her shapely ankles. But business must not be interrupted ; so, with a polite " adios " on both sides, we depart.

Don Immanuel's residence is somewhat different from the rest, for the worthy Alcaldé, besides dispensing justice, keeps the only " venta," or wayside public-house, in the place. There he sells " aguadiente," or aniseed brandy, which fully merits its equivalent in English of " fire-water," and accommodates passing " arrieros," or muleteers, and other travellers, if such rare victims turn up.

The Alcaldé, like the rest of the inhabitants, is taking his ease in his hammock, but rises at our approach and, with a cordial greeting, bids me welcome to San Juan. The tired horses are taken to water, *above* the village, and the cattle sent with one of his vaquéros to the same pool, and thence to my host's corral, to be penned for the night. This done I am invited to enter the house, with that polite phrase which sounds so pretty, but means so little,

though invariably used in Mexico, " La casa es suya,
Señor " (" the house is yours, sir ").

The house, in this particular instance, being both
venta and dwelling combined, is a low one-storied
building about one hundred feet long, with the usual
earthen floor. Three-fourths of its length is devoted to
the accommodation of the four-footed guests, and the
remainder, the floor of which is raised about a foot
above the other, to that of the humans ; but there is
no partition to shut off the stable from the dwelling-
place.

At the far end of the stable are six mules, with their
packs but just unloaded resting behind them, whilst a
hungry and inquisitive black pig is nuzzling at one of
them, in the hope that perchance it may contain something edible. The two arrieros, seated on low stools on
either side of a little table, are eating their frugal supper
of " gaspacho," or soup of oil, haricot beans, chili-peppers,
pimentos, and pieces of black bread, on which mixture
boiling water has been poured. If the meal is not appetising it is plentiful, for the wooden bowl into which
each man dips his tortilla, with resolve to get his fair
share, is nearly full.

With Spanish politeness they rise to greet the stranger,
and so catch sight of the marauding pig investigating
the pack. " Maldito sea el puerco ! " they cry with one
breath, and rush to the rescue. Away goes the puerco
with screams that arouse three of his friends reposing
in a corner hard by, and the hullabaloo disturbs all
the hens who had gone to roost on the rafters. The
racket is appalling for a time, but presently quiets down
and all is peace again within.

Outside, however, it is soon renewed, for La Señora,
after greetings duly given, sallies forth with some of her
offspring, on the hospitable errand of getting my supper.
" El pollo," or the chicken, destined for the sacrifice
runs for his life, with vociferous remonstrance, in which

all his friends and relatives join ; but presently is bowled over by a clever shot with the short cudgel La Señora carries.

With surprising rapidity he is plucked, split, and grilled to a turn on the hot embers, and served up with a pile of steaming tortillas, making a most excellent dish. This is followed by a bowl of " huevos y tomati," or in plain English, " scrambled eggs," cunningly mixed with finely chopped tomatoes—a first-rate compound. The supper is washed down with an abundance of good black coffee. Milk of course there is none, for, though there are plenty of cows about, no one in a Mexican pueblo would dream of taking the trouble to catch and milk them. Then comes the aguadiente, and everybody lights his, or her, cigarette, made of strong native tobacco, wrapped in " mazourka," or the leaf of the maize-cob, which is far better than any paper. Lazily we swing in our respective hammocks, and the Alcaldé and I open the deal over the cattle I have brought, though without any hope, or expectation, of concluding it that night. Lucky if we can fix it up before the next evening !

Mexico was in those days in the throes of the bitter struggle between the Liberalistas, or Republicans, under their Dictator Juarez, and the unfortunate Emperor Maximilian, supported for a time by French bayonets. My friend Don Immanuel was a strong Liberal, but was, from his own account, terribly harried by each side in turn, till he was inclined to cry, " A plague of both your Houses ! " Only a few days ago, he said, a band of Liberals had come along and requisitioned horses, arms, and cattle. It is true they gave him a receipt, which he regarded as of very doubtful value as he didn't suppose for a moment the Government would ever acknowledge it.

Next came a company of " Los Coutrarios," or Imperialists, and they took what they wanted, without even the formality of a receipt, and moreover carried off with them eight of his peons as unwilling recruits for their cause.

As long as I could keep awake I listened to the tale of my host's wrongs, but at last weariness overcame me, and I slept; but not for long. My foes had gathered thick and fast, and seemed bent on eating me alive: whether they dropped down on me from the thatch overhead, or whether they crawled down the hammock ropes, I know not, but, when I struck a light, my hammock was literally swarming with hungry " chinchas," or bugs. I turned the hammock over, shook out my enemies, and squashed as many as I could on the floor, and so back to bed again, to toss and turn till daybreak.

At the first gleam of light the whole household was astir, and whilst the early morning coffee was preparing, the Alcaldé and I strolled up to the corrals to see to the cattle and horses. Everything was all right, and we were on the point of returning, when up galloped one of his vaquéros with the startling news that a body of mounted men, some thirty strong, had been seen about two miles off, and were evidently making for the pueblo. " They'll have the half of your beeves, if they're Liberals, and the whole of them if they are ' Los Coutrarios,' amigo mio," said Don Immanuel; " but we will see if we can't be too clever for them, malditos ladrones ! " He threw down the corral bars as he spoke ; out bolted the cattle, and away they went as hard as they could pelt, with two of my men and one of the Alcaldé's at their heels, making for a deep ravine a little way off, there, it was to be hoped, to lie safely hid till the danger was overpast.

Meantime the Alcaldé and I strolled back to his house, and were beginning to sip our coffee on the piazza in front of it, when we were aware of the arrival of the Partido in the village. Down the stony street it came clattering, and, heralded by squealing pigs and yelping curs, pulled up in front of the venta. A motley crew enough to look upon, but well mounted and serviceable in appearance, all being armed with rifles and six-shooters. Uniform there was none, and the only distinguishing marks of the officer in command were the feather in his sombrero and the sword dangling by his side.

There was nothing to indicate whether they were Liberals, and so possibly friendly with mine host, or Los Coutrarios and enemies, and I was deeply pondering which they were when, to my great relief, Don Immanuel jumped up and greeted the commander as an old friend. Presently he was introduced to me as Don Manuel Gutierrez, a well-known Republican leader, who had earned for himself a somewhat evil reputation amongst the Imperialists by his ruthless deeds, and whose fame had even crossed the Rio Grande. To all appearance he was " as mild a mannered man as ever cut a throat," and we soon became quite friendly. He was informed by Don Immanuel that I was a ranchero from across the river, come to see if there was any market for cattle in Mexico, as they were unsaleable in Texas. He smiled grimly at this and remarked that the market was there, but the difficulty was to get paid ; for *they* had no money, and the Imperialists were thieves !

El Capitan, for such he was, announced he would stay in San Juan till the following morning to rest his troop, which had a long march before it to Presidio, some fifty miles higher up the river. Could his friend Don Immanuel feed his men and horses for the day ? He had no money to give him, but plenty of receipt forms ! Of course he could, " con todo el gusto del mundo " ; but when the Captain's back was turned, I caught the victim shaking his clenched fist at him, with a horrible grimace.

To make sure his friend didn't get wind of my beeves, Don Immanuel now sent an order for his men to drive them some miles farther up the valley, there to remain till the coast was clear. The fact is that stern patriot intended selling them to the Imperialists, who would pay a good price, and he had no mind to be robbed of his profit ; which was just as well for me.

Seeing there was no help for it, my host put the best face he could on it, and had one of his own cattle slaughtered, to feed his unwelcome guests. So towards evening there was great feasting in the pueblo, and especially in the venta, where the Alcaldé entertained Don Manuel, his two Sergeants, and myself with a very special dish, dear to the hearts of all frontier Mexicans. This is the head of the bullock, baked, with all the hair on, in a hole in the ground, which, when properly heated, is covered with slabs of stone and earth piled on them. When thoroughly cooked the skin and hair peel off, and you have a dish which for tenderness, juiciness and flavour, is very hard to beat.

After supper we started out to join the " fandango," or *al fresco* dance, on the hard-beaten earthen floor behind the venta. The music was discoursed by a violinist, and the dances mostly waltzes, though now and then a cotillion was called, or a " danza," the national dance, something like a very slow polka. Coffee was supplied " free gratis " by mine host, but any one who wanted aguadiente had to pay for it—as a matter of principle, I suppose. The fandango was kept up till near daybreak, though I retired early ; for the Mexican loves dancing with all his soul, and is generally a very good performer.

Their overnight dissipation notwithstanding, Don Manuel's ragged troop was early on the road, to the no small relief of myself and Don Immanuel, who speeded the parting guests with a cup of coffee and a nip of aguadiente. In an hour or two my cattle were brought back to the corral, and my friend and I set to work to complete the deal we had commenced on my arrival.

Finally, after an hour or two's haggling, I agreed to accept $12 apiece in hard cash.

Then I saddled up, and with many " adios " and a " Vaya te con Dios " from La Señora, departed with my plunder, well satisfied with the result of my trip.

CHAPTER V

DROVING TO NEW ORLEANS

AFTER my return from Mexico, business matters at the ranch claimed my attention for some two months, so that it was not until September 15, 1865, that I was ready to start on my seven-hundred-mile drive to the Chafalaya River, *en route* for New Orleans. At sunrise that morning, then, I set out with 102 splendid steers, and accompanied by my friend Jack Vinton and four vaquéros. Each of us, including the Mexicans, had a spare horse, for driving wild cattle is no child's play, and soon wears out horseflesh. Such clothing and necessaries as we took were carried in our " malletas," or saddle-bags ; so we travelled in light marching order.

The cattle were very troublesome at first, and we made but slow progress, so that it was the 18th before we reached the first creek west of San Antonio. There, the following day, we were joined by Dick Lemmons and four more vaquéros, who brought 118 additional beeves, from another part of the ranch, making my drove up to 220 head. They were all prime beasts, such as any cattle-raiser in this country might be proud to own ; indeed, I never saw a finer lot anywhere in the West, though I say it who shouldn't.

Whenever my route led near a cattle-ranch, I penned my cattle at night, if possible, for I was mortally afraid of a stampede in the darkness, especially so comparatively near home as we then were. If no corrals were available they had to be herded all night ; and if the feed was not good and water scarce, and the beeves in consequence restless, all hands had to turn out for that purpose. Well, the night after Lemmons joined us, we had to herd on the prairie a few miles east of San Antonio. The evening was close and oppressive, and the sun set with an angry glare I didn't like the look of ; but the cattle had had good water, grass was plentiful, and I dismissed care from my mind. Soon the half of us, who had the first watch in, had off-saddled and picketed our horses, and were enjoying our frugal supper of dried beef, bread and coffee. This dispatched, we rolled ourselves in our blankets and, with saddles for pillows, were presently asleep.

It seemed to me I had only just dozed off, though they told me afterwards I had been snoring for two hours, when I was rudely awakened by a deluge of rain and an awful rolling, rending clap of thunder overhead. I was on my feet in an instant, but for the moment could see nothing in the inky blackness of the night, though in the distance I could hear, above the turmoil of the storm, the shouts of the men and the galloping of the horses and the cattle. Then came a blinding flash of lightning, that for one brief moment lit up the scene and showed me my drove scattering to all the four winds of heaven. It also showed me my horse straining at his lariat to join the fray. Fortunately it was good strong rawhide and held him, so that in less time than it takes to tell, we of the watch in were mounted and in hot pursuit of the vanished cattle, guided in our search by the lightning-flashes.

What need to tell of the miseries of that dreadful night ? The wind and the rain buffeted and soaked us ; the thunder rolled overhead almost incessantly, and the cattle became wilder and more terrified the more we tried to stay their headlong flight. Fortunately for me the country was open, rolling prairie for miles and miles ; had it been brushy I should probably have lost the whole drove, at least temporarily. As it was, when day at last broke, and we rounded up the cattle about twelve miles from camp, forty of them had disappeared. The remainder by this time were pretty well done up, so with half my hands and Jack Vinton I returned to camp with them, whilst Lemmons and the others set off to hunt up the absentees, with orders not to return without them.

For ten days we waited, herding the cattle in the neighbourhood, without losing any more ; and then Lemmons came into camp, bringing only fifteen head with him. The other twenty-five no doubt had made a bee line for home and had for days been enjoying their native pastures on the Frio.

It was a bad start, but I could wait no longer for fear of losing my market, as the season was already late and the way was long. Many were my misgivings as to how many more I should lose before I reached my journey's end, but I may say at once that I only lost five head besides these, and that in the almost impenetrable brush we got into on the borders of Louisiana. So, after all, I was fairly lucky in my drive.

For the next ten days we kept steadily on our journey eastwards without any incident worth recording, passing gradually out of the purely ranching district of Western Texas into the region of cotton plantations and farms. Before the war the planters had been prosperous and, many of them, wealthy men, but now all that was changed. The ravages of war were not much in evidence till we neared the borders of Louisiana, but the planters had lost their slaves, and, with them, the bulk of their capital. Things were in a transition stage, and many of the freedmen refused to work at first, preferring to live on the produce of the " truck patches," or gardens, they cultivated as slaves, and on what they could steal. Deprived so suddenly of their labour, the masters, for the most part, sat down in dull, hopeless despair ; dig they could not, and " to beg they were ashamed " ; moreover, there were few to beg from with any hope of profit, for almost all their neighbours were reduced to the same depths of poverty.

The planters in their days of prosperity had been an open-handed, hospitable folk, spending their incomes freely. No one thought of saving; indeed, to do so would have savoured too much of the ways of the despised Northern traders; so when evil days came they had no resources to fall back upon, and families, brought up in luxury and refinement, were reduced to dire want, if not absolute starvation. To this conduct of the freed-men there were, however, honourable exceptions, and on more than one plantation I passed, the former slaves were working for their old masters just as heretofore; only now they were working for wages, or the expectation of them when better times came and "Massa" had money to pay them with.

In these cases the planters had earned the affection of their negroes by kind treatment, and chiefly by never separating families if it could possibly be avoided. These kindly folk were often overrun by slaves for whom it was difficult to find work, though they had to be fed, clothed, and housed at the owner's expense, for nothing can stop the increase of the black races. Then the only remedy they could adopt was to let out their superfluous hands to work on the neighbouring plantations, or in the towns; but they never sent them to auction at the slave-marts, or sold them to the dealers, who were always on the look-out for "likely" niggers, and would pay heavy prices for them too. So these men, when misfortune and ruin fell upon their neighbours, reaped the reward of their good deeds, and weathered the storm.

One of the most curious and interesting cases I came across of freedmen standing by their old master was that of a mulatto named Carol Jones, who owned a small cotton plantation on the Sabine River, the boundary between Texas and Louisiana. He was a man of intelligence and some education, and before the war had owned some twenty niggers, and was well-to-do. Whether he had purchased, or been given, his freedom I don't remember; but he was a strong Secessionist, and so popular with his white neighbours, though of course he had to remember his colour and not attempt to mix with them on terms of equality. This of course he would have had to do equally in the North, as in the South; indeed, notwithstanding the fuss the Yankees made about the niggers and their wrongs, many of which were very real, they held them socially in greater abhorrence than did the Southerners.

All his hands remained with him, and he and they appeared to be on the best of terms; so he must have been a good master in the vanished days of slavery. This is the more remarkable since, as the ranker who gets a commission in the army is always the severest disciplinarian, so the workman who rises to be an employer is usually the hardest taskmaster. We put up one night at his place, and received the best entertainment we had had for many a day, Jones, of course, waiting on the three white men at his own table.

There is a great gulf fixed between white and black which, I gather, is ever widening in the Southern States; and what the end of it will be, and whether it can ever be bridged over, no man can tell. The outlook, I fear, is ominous of trouble for the future, for there are already 7,000,000 negroes, mainly in the Southern States. In another twenty-five years this number will be doubled; and then, if a *modus vivendi* cannot be arranged between the races, what is to be done with them? Truly the curse of slavery has come home to roost!

When we went on our way, and bade good-bye to the friendly mulatto, I held out my hand to him. He, glancing shamefacedly at my companions, hesitated to take it, but, as I still held it out, at last grasped it, and wrung it hard, then turned away with tears in his eyes. A little scene perhaps hardly worth recalling, only it speaks volumes anent the relations between the races. Jack and Dick scowled at the " nigger " as they turned their horses away, but said never a word.

On October 8 we were nearing the Brazoo River, a wide stream 150 miles east of Austin. Here, either stupidly or maliciously, I was put on the wrong road, which took us forty miles out of our way and into the very thickest brush I ever drove cattle through. For three days and nights we floundered about in these thickets, wherein were no roads to guide us, finding little water and less grass. All this time the cattle were getting more and more restless and difficult to drive, and we had our clothes pretty well torn off us in the effort to keep them together. The fourth day things were no better, and that night my misfortunes culminated in a terrific thunderstorm and a deluge of rain. In the midst of this the cattle broke in all directions, and nothing we could do could stop them. Since there was nothing else to be done, we camped just where we were and as we were—*i.e.* hungry and cold and wet— and waited for daylight.

With the first streak of light we started out to search for the drove, though with no good hope of finding many of the cattle that day. I knew well enough the beeves wouldn't stop till they got out of the brush and found water and grass ; but how far would they have to go— and would they scatter, or bunch up together ? These things we could only guess at as we pushed on, following the widest trail through the brush, but never seeing hoof or horn all the morning.

Towards afternoon, side trails began to come in right and left, and join the main one we were on ; instinct was guiding them to what they wanted, and pretty well the whole lot were steering for it straight ! The brush began to get less dense, then vanished entirely, and at sundown we came out on a big clearing, some hundreds of acres in extent, with good grass, and a creek running through it. There were the cattle sure enough, scattered all over the place, making up for lost time, and all our troubles were over, for that day at least. When we came to round them up, all were there but three, and those I never saw again.

The day after my lucky find we travelled through brush again, and then came out on a comparatively open " piney-barren " country, through which it was easy enough to drive, and, travelling easily, reached Trinity Creek on October 18. Here was a considerable extent of rich, well-timbered river-bottom land, with good plantations at intervals, but most of them, alas ! in woful plight. The next day the track we followed led us into thick brush again, and there I lost two more of my cattle.

But now my troubles were at an end, for a time at least, for that evening we emerged at a good farm, belonging to a Mr. Gorman, where was a large pen for the beeves ; and all hands could rest that night. Here I met a Mr. Duncan, a cattle-buyer from New Orleans, who made me an offer for all my stock. The cattle showed signs of their long journey and often scanty pasture ; moreover, there were conflicting rumours as to the state of the markets, so I made up my mind to sell, if I could get my price, though we didn't come to a deal that night.

The next morning Duncan turned back with me, and having agreed the price at $4,875 for the lot, I handed over the 190 head to him at the next pen we came to, receiving $500 down, the balance to be paid in New Orleans. Having settled with my hands, I sent them back to the ranch with the horses, but of course had to go on myself with Duncan to get my cash in the city. There I intended to take steamer for Galveston, and thence make my way back to the ranch. If I had only done so, I should have saved myself from heavy loss, and much fruitless toil.

Everything went smoothly on the rest of the journey, and on November 11 my fifty-seven days' drive ended at the boat-landing on the Chafalaya River. There the next day we shipped the cattle on the ss. *Tatan*, and the afternoon of the following day landed at Jeafferson City, on the outskirts of New Orleans. There, having got my cash all right, I said good-bye to Duncan, and was going to take the cars for the city, *en route* for home, when unfortunately an acquaintance I had made on the boat introduced me to a salesman named Noel, one of the biggest dealers in the cattle-yards. He showed me a big drove of hogs he had just bought from up-country, and told me there was a splendid market for them as the stocks were very low and the demand brisk. Finally, to cut a long story short, he persuaded me there was heaps of money in the spec. ; so, instead of going to Galveston, and so back to the ranch, I took the back passage on the *Tatan* to the boat-landing, and presently turned myself into a pig-drover, which was the most heart-breaking, hateful occupation I ever followed in all my varied experience.

As we passed through the part of Eastern Texas bordering on the Sabine River, I had noticed that the farmers thereabouts were great hog-raisers, an industry I had never come across since my early days in Western Virginia. A few of the settlers in Kansas kept a small number of pigs for their own use, but the cattlemen of Western Texas held the brutes in abhorrence, and one rarely saw them on the ranches in that country. What my friends there would have said to me, had they known I had turned pig-dealer, I don't know. I certainly never bragged of my doings in that line when I got back, and I don't think they ever got wind.

We had a very pleasant run back to the cattle-landing, for I made the acquaintance of a Mr. Rabalais, a planter from Bayou de Glade, who had seen much service with the Confederate forces in those parts. We passed the scenes of many of the fights in which he had taken part, and his descriptions of them were most interesting ; but these battles are now a twice-told tale, and space will not permit to re-tell them, for I must draw to the end of this long history of my doings.

On November 16 I parted from my friend and set out on my solitary ride back to Texas, recrossing the Sabine River on November 24. Two days later I turned off the road to a place called Jonesville, a small village, where lived a man named Brown, reputed to be the king of the hog-raisers in that district.

I found he owned about 150 hogs himself, and that he was willing to sell me 100 of the best, and to help me hunt up as many more as could be got in the neighbourhood.

I therefore made my headquarters with him, and by December 10 we had collected 377, which were penned on his farm, and fed on maize, till I was ready to start. Now the hogs in those parts are mostly turned loose in the woods to get their own living on the abundant mast of the live-oaks, and it is only when that runs short that they are driven up to be fed on corn. Consequently the brutes are as wild as hawks, and wonderfully fleet of foot. Add to this a contrariness above all hogs whose acquaintance I had made before, and you may in part realise what an awful job it was to drive them, especially through a brushy country.

In the open it was bad enough, for then, after going along sedately for a time, as though reduced to discipline and order, the leaders would take it into their heads to break back, followed by the bulk of the drove, and that meant a long run before they could be turned from the error of their ways. But in brush, who can describe the dreadful scene of trouble and confusion ? They scattered in all directions, and after them we had to go, tearing through thorns and briars and thickets, in the wild endeavour to stop them, till our clothes became as rags upon us. By the time we had gathered the first drove at Brown's place, my new suit that I had bought in New Orleans would scarce decently cover my nakedness, and had it not been for the kindness of Mrs. Brown (a good motherly woman), who made me a coat and pants out of her own home-spun cloth, I don't know what I should have done.

The hogs were generally bought by weight, when the farmer owned a weighing machine; if he didn't, a guess had to be made, with the result that the bargaining was almost interminable. I paid for my hogs, either by weight or by guess, 5 cents a pound, or thereabouts, and their average weight was 140 lb., so that altogether I invested \$3,500 in hog flesh. When I left New Orleans they were fetching 9 cents per pound, so I had a good and substantial profit to look forward to, after deducting all expenses. That profit tempted me into the business, in the hope that, with the money realised by the sale of my cattle, I might have enough to carry me home to England, there to realise a longing that had been in my heart all through my stormy life in Texas. But it was not to be, and bitter was my disappointment.

On December 11, with three negroes and a hired two-horse wagon to carry corn, I started from Brown's with a drove of two hundred head, leaving an American named Scanlan and three more niggers to follow on with the remaining 177 the next day. The droves were divided for the convenience of penning and feeding.

On December 17, which was a Sunday, I picked up another lot of 133, which had been gathered for me by a Baptist preacher and his class-leader, who had adjoining farms on the Angelina River. These I remember were all black but one, and I think wilder than even their relatives in the other droves. The preacher and

his friend made some little fuss about dealing on the
" Sabbath," but when I said I couldn't stop, because of
the other droves behind me, they waived their scruples,
and made a pretty keen trade too.   Here I hired another
white man, named Davis, and three more niggers, as
well as another wagon, and leaving him in charge of my
original drove, went on with the new one myself that
afternoon.

I thought I knew by this time what running after
half wild pigs meant, but this lot taught me my ignorance.   However, I managed to drive them six miles
before dark, and then penned them at a Mrs. McAnulty's
farm.   But I was clean done up, and good Mrs. Brown's
new pants were nearly torn off me ! They were past
mending, and I must have gone practically naked, had
not Mrs. McAnulty, a kindly old Irishwoman, let me
have a pair of her husband's.

I don't propose to tell all the miseries I endured on
that trip, between December 11 and January 6, 1866,
on which latter date my troubles ended, for the time
being, at the Chafalaya landing, but one very special
one I may mention.   Towards the latter part of December we had a bad spell of rain, with bitter cold and
sharp frosts at night, and the roads became almost
impassable.   On December 24 it culminated in a perfect
deluge, that flooded all the low-lying lands.   Through
it all I had to ride backwards and forwards, as best I
might, to look after the various droves and keep them
going.

Three days after this I had ridden seventeen miles
back to the rear drove, and, catching up the leading
one, soon after dark, found it and the hands floundering
about in a swamp.   The hogs were all swimming hither
and thither in the deep water, and the men wading after
them nearly up to their necks.   Hitching my horse to
the nearest tree, I plunged into the ice-cold water ; and
it *was* cold ! Standing pretty close together in the

swamp was a thicket of Cypress-trees, each one draped from top to bottom with festoons and sheets of grey moss, that added to the difficulty of getting about. By the light of a young moon we splashed about for four hours or more, for it was nearly midnight before we got through that horrible place, and then only with the loss of twenty-six hogs. Two hours more we toiled on through the mud, and then found a hospitable farmer, who penned the hogs and took us in and fed and warmed us.

I don't think there is anything else worth noting, except that on reaching a small town called Alexandria, on the Red River, which had been partially burned by the Yankees, I found a coloured regiment quartered there, the first I had ever seen. They seemed to be having "high old times," and strutted about much pleased with their uniforms. Poor fellows! it was a new sensation to them to be *somebody*. My niggers fraternised with them, and, I remember, got so drunk that they were good for nothing next day!

At the Chafalaya landing I shipped 463 hogs on the ss. *Tatan,* and no mortal was ever more thankful than I that my pig-driving was over. I must have looked like some dilapidated tramp when I stepped on board that boat, for my clothes were in rags and tatters, and I had only the remains of boots on my feet. However, I comforted myself with the thought that all my toils were over, and that now I should reap my reward, but what that really was I must tell in another chapter.

CHAPTER VI

A TEXAN RAILWAY

THE good ship *Tatan* ran alongside the wharf at Jeafferson City at 2 p.m. on the 7th, and soon my hogs were safely penned in Noel's yard. They were a good lot and in very fair condition, notwithstanding their travels, for I had fed them well on maize *en route*.

When I came to total up all my expenses, including payments for corn, hire of hands and wagons, freight to New Orleans, etc., I found the hogs stood me in a trifle over $9 apiece. That was more than I had calculated on, but if the market had kept up, I still might reckon on a fair profit. Off I went then to my flattering friend's office to see how the land lay. I told him how many hogs I had brought, and the trouble I had had in bringing them, and we strolled out to the pens to inspect them.

" Yes," said he, " I guess they're a likely lot, but hogs is away down since you was here two months ago ; pity you couldn't ha' hurried up a bit, and got here sooner ! "

" Get here sooner ! How the blazes could I do that ? " I cried. " Why, I had to drive the brutes all across Louisiana, all through the swamps and the mud —till I wished there was no such thing as a hog in all creation ; but what do you reckon they're worth now they are here ? " Slowly he shifted his quid of tobacco from one cheek to the other and then back again, but said nothing, whilst I listened, and waited to hear my fate.

At last, just as I was going to repeat my question, he squirted a brown stream of juice into the ear of a hog peacefully basking at his feet, with such force that it jumped up as if shot and went off with a grunt. "Now for my fate," I thought. But no ; not yet was I to know it.

My friend seemed so pleased with his success that he moved further down the pen-side, his hat tilted well off his forehead, and his hands deep in the pockets of his pants, till he found another unsuspecting victim. This one, roused from his slumbers by the sound of our steps, raised his head and opened a wary eye, in which he instantly received such a charge of juice that he too jumped up and made off. Noel seemed satisfied with the execution he had wrought, for now he turned to me, and slowly said : " Waal, they're a likely lot, as I said afore, and if they'd been here two months ago, they'd ha' been worth $12.50. Now I put 'em at $7 apiece, and not a cent more."

That meant a loss of more than a thousand dollars, and the salesman saw my dismay, I suppose, for he quietly added, " But you needn't be in any darned hurry to sell. The market can't go much worse, and likely'll rise afore long ; so you hold on, and I shan't charge you nothing for penning, only for the corn." I believe the man was really disinterested and friendly, and gave me what he thought the best advice under the circumstances. Unfortunately for me I took it again, and determined to hold on for a week or two, hoping for better times.

By the end of the first week the market was worse, and the best offer I could get was $6.50. The second week brought no improvement, and the miserable animals began to die of some disease, probably swine fever. Then in despair I put my stock in the hands of a commission agent, to sell as best he could before they all died, as I fully expected they would. To cut a long story short, he got rid of the last lot by the end of the third week, and I found myself a loser of quite $2,500, or about £500. "Served me right," I kept saying to myself, for going into such a speculation, instead of going back to my ranch with nearly £1,000 in my pocket. "Why had I been such a fool ? " But blaming myself and my folly brought no relief to my grievous disappointment, for now I saw that my long-looked-for trip home, and all it meant to me, had to be put off indefinitely.

My three weeks' stay in New Orleans might, under other conditions, have been interesting enough, especially to a man like myself who had dwelt so long on the out-skirts of civilisation ; but I was too much worried about the vile hogs and my losses to enjoy myself. The " Queen of the South," as the natives call her, is a fine city, though I must confess the most malodorous I ever was in, and there was, even in those days, plenty to see as well as to smell.

Though she was said by eloquent editors to be " groaning under the hated yoke of the Yankees," the groans were not audible. The theatres, of which there were several, were crowded night after night, as were the music-halls and dancing-saloons ; whilst in the houses of the wealthy, dinner-parties and balls were the order of the day. The endless quays and wharves on the levee, beside the Mississippi, began once more to fill with goods from all parts of the world ; though still the piles of cotton-bales, which before the war crowded them in every part, were few and far between. In fact, the city was rapidly recovering from the ruin and misery of the great struggle, in which she had suffered so deeply, and preparing to reoccupy her proud position of capital and chief emporium of the South and West.

To divert my thoughts from my many worries and anxieties, my friends and acquaintances took me to vari-ous places of amusement, and I well remember hearing Artemus Ward lecture on the Mormons, at the Masonic

Hall. At that time he was quite unknown to fame on this side the Atlantic, for it was not, if I remember, till the following year that he visited England for the first and last time. His humour certainly was of the driest, and his stories, told without the ghost of a smile, were most comical. I never heard any audience laugh so heartily as his did that night. I thought his lecturing infinitely superior to his writings, which, for most people, are in a measure spoiled by the silly phonetic spelling he adopted.

Another night I saw " Macbeth " at the St. Charles' Theatre, with the Keans in it, but, though the acting was of course good, and the play well put on the stage, I didn't enjoy it as I ought to have, for, in the most thrilling scenes, my thoughts *would* turn to the hog-pens down at Jeafferson City, and my dying pigs.

Yet another night I saw Charlotte Thompson in " The Lady of Lyons," at the Varieties Theatre, and enjoyed her acting as well as my troubles would permit.

On one occasion I had an amusing rencontre with a notorious gambler in a saloon in the city, of which there were plenty ; for the Southerners in those days were much given to cards, which were played everywhere—on the steamboats, in the hotels, and in the regular saloons set apart for the purpose. In all these places professional gamblers abounded, most of whom were pretty " hard cases," and quick with their six-shooters ; this they had to be, or they wouldn't have carried on their trade long. But this fellow, though a bouncer and a bully, had no real fight in him, which perhaps was lucky for me.

With a couple of friends I strolled into one of these saloons, after the theatre, just to look on and pass the time. We called for drinks, and sat down to watch the proceedings, but without any intention of playing, for I at least never gambled. The game was " poker," than which there is none at which the really clever professional can more easily plunder his victims. The stakes were high, and the " pro." seemed to be having a very good time of it, for he raked in the dollars and notes nearly every time. At last one of the players was either cleared out or had enough of it, for he rose to go, and couldn't be persuaded to sit down again ; so probably my first surmise was correct.

The gambler, however, was doing too well to leave off without trying for another victim, and he pitched upon me to fill the billet. Maybe he took me for a " young man from the country," which indeed I was, and for a greenhorn, which, in some respects, I was too ; but not in the matter of gamblers—I had seen too many of the gentry at work. He leaned over my friend, who sat next him, and, touching me on the shoulder, said, " I guess, stranger, you'll make one, and take a hand ? "

I was just then immersed in a mental calculation of how much I had already lost by the confounded hogs, and how much more I was likely to lose before I had done with them, so I answered somewhat shortly, " No, I won't, I don't gamble " ; and then resumed my calculations. Deep in my own not very pleasant thoughts, and with my hands in my pockets, I sat tilted back in my rocking-chair, and paid no heed to what was passing, till I heard the fellow say, with a sneering laugh, " Maybe the young fellow don't know how, but I reckon we can soon teach him ! " Then some of the others laughed too, and I looked up and saw they were laughing at me. Then the man leaned over again, and, touching me once more on the shoulder, said, " I guess you look as if a lesson would do you good ; come along right now, an' I'll give it you—you can't have a better master."

Almost before he had done speaking, I jumped to my feet and clapped my six-shooter to his head. My friends jumped up too, and drew their weapons ; but no one else stirred. We had been too quick for the rowdies, of whom there were only three or four. Meanwhile my man sat pale and trembling, with all the bounce and laughter gone to terror and sheer funk. " Get out of this, you cheating rascal," I said, " or I'll shoot you like the dog you are " ; and I saw him to the door, and watched him go down the street in a hurry. His friends sat still and said never a word, so presently we departed, keeping of course a wary eye on the gamblers till we got out ; but they didn't molest us, and we thought ourselves well out of what might have been a very unpleasant adventure.

By January 28 I had settled up with the commission merchants, who I believe robbed me after their kind, and that evening engaged a passage by the ss. *Magnolia* of the Harris line sailing for Galveston and Indianola next morning. By 8 a.m., on a lovely morning, we were under weigh and steaming down the broad Mississippi. As we left the city behind us, I shook off dull care as far as I could, consoling myself with the thought that after all I was still young, the world was wide, and I couldn't always meet with bad luck in it. We passed many plantations, chiefly of sugar ; but alas ! many of them were ruined, and the fine houses of their owners nothing but heaps of blackened stones and wood ; such ravages had the dogs of war wrought in this paradise of industry !

It was three days steaming to Indianola, and there I took passage in a schooner for Lavacca, fifteen miles distant, where I hoped to catch a train for Victoria, *en route* for San Antonio. I say hoped advisedly, for I gathered from my fellow passengers that the departure of the train was very uncertain, and its arrival at its destination still more so. However, we were assured at the hotel that it would start without fail at 2 p.m. the day after our arrival, and accordingly, in simple faith, we marched up to the station at that hour. No sign of the train was to be seen, and the shed that did duty for a station was quite deserted. After waiting for an hour or so we hunted round for the station master, and at last unearthed him in a saloon, taking his ease, and his drinks, in a rocking-chair. He evidently resented our inquiries as to the missing cars, and seemed annoyed at being disturbed by such foolish questions as when they were likely to start.   At last we got him to admit that nobody knew the answer to that riddle ; it *might* be the next day, or the day after, or the day after that.   " You've jist got to wait at the hotel till she comes in ; and I reckon she's broke down somewhere, or she'd ha' bin in afore now.   You've no call to hurry any ; I'll let you know when she's ready " ; and with that we had to be content.

This was on Thursday afternoon.   All Friday there were no tidings of the missing conveyance till nearly midnight, when a message arrived from our friend the station master that she had turned up at last, and would probably start early next morning if the driver—" engineer," they called him—was sober enough !   Cheerful, to have one's train driven by a drunken man !   But anything was better than kicking one's heels in Lavacca and anathematising the railroad management.

We received notice that the cars would start at 9 a.m., but an hour before that I realised we were doomed to disappointment again, for at that time everybody connected with the railroad, station master, conductor, and driver—all were hopelessly drunk at the hotel !   And as if this were not evident enough, they announced the fact to their unhappy victims by shouting in chorus, at short intervals, " The Railroad's drunk !   Hooray ! the Railroad's on the tight ! "

Not till the following morning had they sufficiently recovered to make a start, but we did get off by 10 a.m. on the Sunday morning.

Was ever such a road dignified by the name of a railway as this ?   I never saw anything like it in all my travels. The ties were hardly within hailing distance of each other, and the rails were so bent and crooked that the engine could only keep the road with great difficulty.

However, it was comforting to think that there wasn't much risk to life and limb if we did run off, for I vow an ox-wagon could easily have beaten us in a race. For about two miles we crawled and bumped along ; then came to a halt, and presently began a retrograde movement. The " engineer " had taken in so much whiskey over night that he had forgotten to take in any water for his boiler, and we had to return for it ! Two hours were wasted by this strategic movement to the rear, and then we started once more, but not before our thirsty " engineer " had moistened himself with more whiskey.

Slowly we crept along for about twelve miles ; then came to a sudden halt, and discovered we had been left standing on the line, whilst the engine was steaming off by itself ! Many were the surmises as to the cause of this extraordinary proceeding, and most were of the opinion that it was a practical joke on the part of the drunken " engineer." Some of the more truculent passengers began to handle their six-shooters, and talk ominously of what they would do to him if, and when, he did return ; and all took a gloomy view of things in general, for we were eighteen miles from Victoria and twelve from Lavacca, and, except one man who had brought two bottles of champagne, no one had anything either eatable or drinkable with him. Moreover, between us and Victoria was nothing but open prairie, with not a single house upon it.

At last the conductor—who, by the way, was a lieutenant in a black regiment of U.S. infantry, the line being run by the Government—informed us that it was the water difficulty that was stopping us once more. The " engineer," bemused as he still was, had neglected to take in enough at Lavacca, and had now gone on six miles to a water-hole, where he *hoped* to find sufficient. " And if he didn't find it ? " we asked. " Waal, then he's got to go on to Victoria to get it, I reckon."

For two mortal hours we waited, with growing wrath and impatience, and still no sign of the engine that had so basely deserted us appeared. It was noon, and the blazing sun on the shelterless prairie beat down on those dog-boxes of cars till they were like ovens. Groups of angry passengers gathered about the conductor, whose position was far from pleasant ; we began to think we should have to walk the eighteen miles that lay between us and our goal, and it wasn't a cheerful prospect.

Then out and spake an old fellow who suffered from rheumatism, a planter from Eastern Texas. " Say ! you Mister Conductor, you're the Boss of these one-horse cars on this dog-gorned track, and if you don't put out and fetch that ingine back, and quickly too, there's going to be trouble right here." So the conductor went, and we all turned out and watched him grow smaller and smaller, until he finally disappeared in the flickering heat of that apparently endless line of rails. Then we all sat down under the lee of the cars—it was too hot inside—and waited again.

The hours sped slowly with the hungry, thirsty crowd, and it was not till dusk that those who had energy enough left to keep a look-out saw the cause of all our woes come puffing and rocking along the wretched line. Soon we all crowded into one car, and leaving all the others standing in the desert, for fear of another breakdown, steamed off with hope revived. It was 10 p.m. before we reached Victoria, and then we made a bee-line for its one hotel. When we had finished our supper I think I may say we had had our money's worth ; at any rate there wasn't much left for those who had the ill-luck to come after us.

This was my first and only experience of a Texan railway, and is perhaps worth describing. Now, I believe, the trunk line from the States to Mexico runs somewhere through the country we so painfully traversed, and San Antonio is a great railway depôt ! " The old order changeth," and it is lucky for railway travellers that it does.

It was not till Tuesday morning, February 6, that I

could continue my journey to San Antonio by stage coach, which did the trip either way once a week. We started at 9 a.m. and, with six good mules to draw us, did the forty miles to our first halting-place early in the evening, and by 2 p.m. next day reached our destination.

It was nearly five months since I had heard any news from the ranch, and I lost no time in looking up my friends to learn the tidings from the frontier. From the best of these, Dan Cleaveland, the Mayor, I learned that things were in their usual state : no adequate protection had been provided by the Government, and the Indians had killed several frontiersmen, though, as far as he knew, my ranch had not been raided.

I stayed only two days in San Antonio settling up important business, chief of which was paying most of my debts, and then, with scarce a dollar left in my pocket, set out to ride home by myself. Not in the best of spirits either, as may be imagined ; for I had lost five precious months of time, and many dollars, in my attempt to make a small pile for my homeward trip ; and now that was impossible and out of the question. But as I rode along trying to make up my mind as to what I would do, a sudden resolve came to me. I *wouldn't* give up, but have one more try for a sight of the old home.

I had met several prominent Mexicans in San Antonio, who had left their native country for reasons not altogether unconnected with the safety of their necks, and amongst them a General Ortega, who said he was *de jure* President of the Republic, only the confounded " Liberales " wouldn't let him assume office. President, or not, he was a very agreeable man, and I had had a good deal of talk with him at Jacqués' Hotel, when he told me amongst other things that cattle were selling well in Mexico, and that at Monterey, which was within reach from my ranch, there was a good market for them.

That is what I would do, then : hunt up two or three hundred good steers, if such could be found on the range, and drive them over into Mexico. With any luck, I might still see old England before the summer was over. It was seven years since I had seen its green fields and pleasant, peaceful homesteads, and the longing for a sight of them, and of some of the folks that dwelt therein, was not to be restrained.

CHAPTER VII

CATTLE IN SMALL COMPASS

IT was good to be on horseback once more, after the lumbering, jolting train and swaying stage, and I resolved that, as long as I was in Texas, I would travel no other way.

I had a touch of fever on me, which I suppose I had picked up at Indianola, which is a very feverish place, so had to make short stages, impatient as I was to get back to the ranch, and it was not until noon of the third day out from San Antonio that I rode up to the door of my own place. There I found my friend John Vinton, who had been left in charge during my absence, and his elder brother Jaque; the latter I now met for the first time, and took to him at sight, forming an opinion of him which later on he justified in every way.

Every one was surprised at my arrival, for they didn't even know I was back in Texas, and had had no news of me since my hands and I parted on the borders of Louisiana. That night the brothers and I sat long over our pipes, and I heard all the news of the frontier; who had been killed by the Indians, and whose horses had been stolen by them and by the Mexican thieves. It was a long list, but again my ranch had escaped with small loss, only one horse having been taken.

The season had been very dry on the Frio, and my cattle on the home range were in poor order; nor had Master Jack Vinton looked after them particularly well, as I found as soon as I was well enough to ride round.

Amongst my possessions I had a fine herd of goats, which should have been corralled at night; this had been neglected, and the lobos and coyotés had pretty well finished them off. Vinton hadn't taken the trouble to poison or hunt these vermin, and they were thick all over the range, enjoying themselves, no doubt, mightily at my expense.

Immediately after my return I sent word to Dan Lemmons, who was herding a big bunch of beeves for me west of the Nueces River, to bring over all that were fit for market.

After a week's rest, and a good dosing with quinine, I was fit for work once more, and with the Vintons and all the vaquéros that could be spared set out for a cattle-hunt on the Carisa Creek, to get the remnant of the fine beeves I had left behind the previous fall. If I was to have a chance of seeing old England this coming summer, there was no time to be lost; for I reckoned it would take me a month to six weeks to get together the cattle I wanted; and then Monterey was a good two hundred and fifty miles away, as the crow flies.

In a previous chapter I have fully described a cattle-drive in this very region, so do not propose to give any details of this one, which, except for a bit of a brush with a small band of Comanchés, was uneventful. This happened near the spot where they so nearly got me the year before. We had seen their sign in the neighbourhood, so were on the look-out for midnight marauders, and when they tried to stampede our horses, which were picketed close to camp, we treated them to a volley from our five rifles. It was a dark, moonless night, and we couldn't see the result, especially as the " vermin " cleared out in double-quick time, but the sign revealed by the morning light showed that one at least had been badly wounded, if not killed.

By the third week in March we had got together 280 good cattle, but it was real hard work to do it, and all hands were in need of rest before starting on the long drive into Mexico ; consequently, it was the 31st of the month before we got under weigh. Everything had been prepared overnight, and by daybreak on that day the cavalcade of five white men and six vaquéros, all mounted on fresh horses, and leading a spare one for each man, set out, steering a south-west course across the prairie for the Presidio crossing of the Rio Grandé.

We went well armed, of course, with rifles and six-shooters, for it was the season for Indian raids, or we might have trouble with Mexican guerillas over the border. But we saw no Indians, though we crossed the trail of a big band passing up country with a lot of horses ; and in Mexico no one molested us, so that we reached Monterey on April 22 without incident worth recording.

I almost forgot to mention a piece of news we heard on the Leona, where we camped *en route* to the Carisa. It was a common enough incident of the frontier in those lawless days, but it shows how uncertain life was there, and both actors in the tragedy were well known to me. John Hill was a large stockman on the Leona, and a former member of my Ranger Company. He had a long-standing feud with John Burleson, a rancher on the Espantosa, about some trifling matter which I have forgotten. Hill was a splendid shot and especially deadly with his six-shooter, and it was always thought he would kill Burleson sooner or later, if the quarrel wasn't patched up. As it turned out, it was the former who was doomed.

The two men met on the trail to San Antonio the evening before our arrival and not a mile from where we camped on the Leona. The quarrel was renewed ; hot words passed, and then both men drew their six-shooters.

Burleson was quickest with his weapon, and hit poor

Hill full in the chest, then turned his horse and fled for his life. Both men had fired together, but Hill's first shot only grazed his enemy's arm. Now, sorely wounded as he was, he steadied himself for a moment, and, taking a deliberate aim across his left arm, sent a bullet through Burleson's shoulder, high up ; then reeled from his horse, and, two hours later, was found dead on the prairie. Burleson fled into Mexico, for fear of Hill's friends, who were many, and was no more seen in Texas, at least during my stay there.

Monterey was a good-sized town in the days of which I write, and, being the capital of the State of Nuevo Leon, was a fairly busy place ; it was also occupied by a considerable body of troops of the " Liberal " faction. But, like most Mexican towns that I have seen, it had a slipshod, poverty-stricken appearance ; the streets were of course " cobble " paved, with the usual sewer running down the middle ; the shops were few and ill-furnished, and there was an air of general listlessness peculiarly characteristic of a Spanish-American town. Indeed, I think the only *really active* inhabitants of the place were the fleas and bugs in the posada at which we put up, and they certainly were energetic and un-tiring !

The deal for my cattle was a long one, but by the end of the month I had got rid of the last lot. The prices varied, of course, but the average realised was $23 a head, in hard cash, no paper ! And, with a lighter heart than I had carried for many a day, I set out, with my little retinue, on the homeward journey on the morning of May 1.

With my hard cash safely fastened on my led horse, I felt as though " home " was not so far off after all, for, after a brief halt at the ranch, I meant to start for that goal of all my hopes and longings. It was a ticklish job riding through that disturbed country with all that solid specie, and though we got through without any adventures, it was a great relief when we reached the ranch in safety on the eleventh of the month. Arrived there, another difficulty presented itself, for I had no safe, or other secure lock-up, in which to place my money. So I e'en buried it at dead of night in the chaparral at the back of the ranch!

Five days I stayed at the ranch, and then, having arranged with John Vinton to take charge of everything for me during my absence, which probably would extend over many months, started for San Antonio, *en route* for Indianola, with Lemmons and a couple of vaquéros as escort for the specie.

Vinton's remuneration was to be one-fourth of all the calves he branded, and $1 per head on all the beeves he sold; the proceeds of sales, after deducting current expenses, such as wages, etc., to be remitted to me through my agents in San Antonio. At San Antonio I changed the bulk of my specie into a draft on Messrs. Spofforth Brothers, a firm of leading merchants in New York who had large business connections in Texas, and with whom I had subsequently very pleasant relations.

It was a ride of nearly one hundred miles to Indianola, but I had had enough of lumbering stage coaches and " tight " railways, and therefore preferred to do the journey on horseback. At Indianola, after selling my horse and kit, I took passage to New Orleans; and thence, after a brief stay, for yellow fever was raging in the city, sailed in one of the Houston Line steamers for New York.

The first week in June saw me on board a fine Hamburg-American steamer, bound for Southampton, and I felt really and truly as though I was going home at last! Perhaps to a man used to club life in London or New York, a fine passage in a vessel like that may seem hardship, but to me, after my seven years of real roughing and often short commons, it appeared the very acme of luxury. Nothing to do but to eat, drink, and enjoy yourself! And what enjoyment it was to sit lazily on deck under the awning and watch the ever varying, sunlit waves, and think that every beat of the paddles was bringing me nearer " the haven where I would be " !

It was mid-June when we landed at Southampton on a perfect summer morning such as, when you get it, makes mere existence a delight, and you are content " not to be doing, but to be." I maintain that for richness, and green luxuriance, there is nothing like the dear old country in full summer. Why, the very trim, green hedges and leafy woodlands are a delight to eyes that have longed for a sight of them for years, and the banished man is almost repaid for his banishment when once he looks upon them again. So we sped through that summer scene of fairyland in the prosaic London express, whilst I sat silent and absorbed, scarcely taking my eyes off it till we rattled into London, and the spell was broken.

That evening I was at the old vicarage home once more, and in that quiet resting-place, and amongst my dearest friends, my wanderings and hardships were forgotten, and I was happy and content.

When I left Texas I had it in my mind to return by the end of the year, but it was not till the spring of 1867 that I turned my face westwards once more, and for the last time. By that time I was married, and though my wife was plucky enough to wish to go out with me, there were many good reasons why she should not. So early in April we parted, and I crossed the Atlantic again, intending to wind up my affairs and return in a few months to settle down in England for good.

In the previous August I had received rather startling news from Jaque Vinton, who wrote from my ranch to tell me that his brother John had betrayed his trust, and gone off no one knew whither ; that he thought he had been gambling, to which he was much given, and had made away with some of my property. That he (Jaque) had gone out to the Frio, as soon as he knew of his brother's absence, and was looking after things for me, and would continue to do so till he received my instructions. I had at once replied that I was much indebted to him, and should be very glad if he could see his way to remain in charge till my return. He did remain, and looked after my interests as if they had been his own ; and in all our subsequent transactions proved himself the honourable, upright man I took him to be.

Though I went out with the full intention of selling out my stock and property in Texas, the puzzle was how to do it without ruinous loss, for business there was at the lowest ebb, and no one seemed to have any money to invest, or if they had, deemed it prudent to place it where life and property were more secure.

At New York I asked my friend Mr. Spofforth's advice, and he counselled me very strongly to remain in Texas, the possibilities of which as a stock country he was well acquainted with. He even reverted to a scheme I had propounded to him on my former visit, viz. to take up a big block of land on the coast between Galveston and Matagorda, and offered to finance me in a large cattle-raising business on that spot. It certainly was an ideal one for the purpose, being a peninsula containing some twenty leagues of good grasslands, with a narrow neck at the land end that could be easily fenced. It was a most tempting offer, and if I could have seen my way to make a home in Texas, I would gladly have accepted it—but that was out of the question.

Finding I had made up my mind to clear out, my friend then advised me to drive my stock up into Missouri and Illinois, where prices were high, though he added he had heard a rumour that the State Legislatures were threatening to prohibit the import of Texan cattle, on the pretence that there was disease amongst them, but really to protect their own stockraisers, who feared competition. I thought the idea a good one, and started at once for Cairo in Illinois to see how the land lay. I soon discovered that the report was well founded, and that the Legislature had passed an act of prohibition just before I arrived. I then tried to get special permission for my own cattle, under stringent conditions of examination, but without success, and so had to wend my way back to Texas by devious railway routes, *viâ* New Orleans, and thence by steamer to Indianola, in great disappointment.

At that place I met a Doctor Hughes, who had been surgeon to the U.S. troops quartered there, after its capture by the Yankees. Though we were as far asunder as the poles in politics, I found him a very " clever " fellow, which, being interpreted, means pleasant, or genial ; moreover he was a smart, enterprising man of business, with a fair amount of capital at his command.

Though we had never met before, I believe I was known to him by reputation ; so when I propounded to him a scheme for turning my cattle into salt beef and extract of meat, which had been floating in my mind for some time, he listened very favourably, and presently agreed to join me in the venture. People do things quickly in those parts, so by the middle of May we had settled terms of partnership under which Hughes was to provide the bulk of the capital, and I the beeves ; profits to be divided equally. We had also secured premises on the outskirts of the town and had ordered hundreds of barrels, salt, and all necessary appliances for the extensive business we hoped to start as soon as I could get the first drove of cattle down to the coast.

Everything then being arranged, I started off to the

ranch to hunt up the cattle, which I hoped to drive down some time in July.

I found my friend Jaque a great improvement on his brother John, for he had looked after the stock properly, and had branded a rare lot of calves, whilst their enemies, the lobos and coyotés, had had a bad time of it. With him, and half a dozen vaquéros, I went all over the whole of the extensive district over which my cattle ranged, and found I could reckon on nearly fifteen hundred in good condition, and fit to kill.

Then we set to work to gather the first drove for Indianola, and by the middle of June had nearly two hundred first-class beeves penned in the corrals. We were just ready to start with these when I received a message from Hughes that the worst epidemic of yellow fever they had had in Indianola for many years had broken out ; that everybody who could get away, even the negroes, were leaving the place, and that business was entirely at a standstill. Under these conditions, of course the packing had to be put off till the fever abated, which probably would not be till the autumn, and I at once turned out the drove I had so laboriously collected.

Hughes wrote that he had sent his family away, but was remaining on himself, because doctors were scarce and his duty was to look after the sick. He would keep an eye on our property and stores, and as I could do no good in Indianola, I had best remain at the ranch. This I did till nearly the middle of July, and then, not having received any tidings from Indianola for some weeks, went down to see how Hughes was getting on. I can't say he was very pleased to see me, for his first greeting was, " Why in creation have *you* come to this tarnation fever hole, where· there's nothing for you to do ? "

Notwithstanding this, I believe he really was glad to see me, though he urged me to clear out as soon as possible. " I'm well used to Yellow Jack," he said,

" and it takes a powerful lot of it to kill me, but I don't want to lose my partner." I stayed only a few days, but long enough to see what a noble work he was doing amongst the scores of sick he attended with a devotion worthy of the best traditions of his profession.

In this he was ably seconded by a confrère, who had served as surgeon to a regiment of Texan cavalry, Sam Slocum by name. He was a bachelor, and lived with his mother, a good old lady who was a strong Methodist. Mother and son were devoted to each other, though it must be confessed that she ruled Master Samuel rather strictly, for his good, or. tried to do so. To this he submitted with a tolerably good grace, as a rule, though in moments of confidence he would sometimes complain to a friend, " My Ma is such an almighty Christian ! "

It was hoped that the worst of the fever would be over by the middle of September, and I returned to the ranch promising to have a drove of cattle ready by that time, Hughes undertaking to let me know how things progressed as often as he could. That month of August I spent on the Frio, where the monotony of existence was at times broken by Indian raids, of the same character I have so often previously described that it would be wearisome to give further details.

By the end of the month the news came that the epidemic was rapidly dying out, and I immediately sent off the first bunch of cattle with Dan Lemmons in charge. On September 12 Hughes wrote that he expected to begin packing in a week's time, and that he would want two hundred more beeves by October 15 ; another two hundred by November 5, and after November 20 they might come as fast as I could get them down. I had collected a large staff of vaquéros, and engaged several Texan cattlemen as well, and now all were hard at work driving up the beeves from far and near.

Having arranged with Jaque Vinton to send me

down batches of cattle as required, I went down with the next drove myself, and, except for one or two visits to the ranch, remained at Indianola all that packing season. It was disagreeable, nasty work superintending the doings of the niggers in the slaughter-houses, but it had to be done by some one, and I took care that it was well and properly carried out.

The extract-of-meat business was my friend Hughes's department, and he turned out some excellent stuff, much like that which to-day meets with such a ready sale all over the world. But in those days such preparations had not been popularised ; the demand for them was comparatively small and the market restricted, so it was not financially a success. Early in November the following entry appears in my diary : " My first droves of beeves are in barrels ; some of them are already travelling in that snug shape to New Orleans ; others visit Galveston, and again others have to-day taken berths for New York, whilst a few favoured ones will in a day or two's time start for London. It remains to be seen how they will account for themselves. Well, I trust, for the first outlay is enormous."

I may as well say at once that they did not account for themselves at all well, for when we had packed and " extracted " some twelve hundred of my best cattle, the pick of the range, we found we were losing money, and so dropped the business. Prime salt beef, such as we shipped, was worth only $9 a barrel ; salted tongues $10 per barrel, and as to the extract, the most expensive of all, we could hardly give it away ! The speculation was a failure, and, in the spring of 1868 I went back to the ranch to make arrangements for getting rid of it altogether.

How to do so, on anything like remunerative terms, was the puzzle that exercised me greatly, and it was therefore a great relief to my mind when Jaque Vinton proposed to take it off my hands, and to pay for horses, cattle, ranch, and everything I had, by instalments of so much per annum. This being settled by the end of May, I handed over everything to Jaque, and he and I rode down to San Antonio, to give and receive the legal transfer of the property.

There we spent a week together, whilst I wound up my affairs and said a last good-bye to many old friends and comrades. Then we parted, never to meet again, though we had much correspondence for some years, during which he loyally and honourably fulfilled his engagements with me.

So the page of my life that I had opened in Virginia in 1852, little dreaming of the wild scenes with which it would be inscribed, was closed for ever, and I exchanged the risk and stir of the Far West for the peace and quietness of a happy English country life.

It was in July 1868 that I finally returned home; and now, looking back through the mists of thirty-six years on the scenes I have attempted to depict, they seem almost like the phantoms of a dream. But they were real enough in the enacting, and, as I sit by my fireside and recall the memories of the past, I am filled with thankfulness that I am alive to tell the tale, which may be of interest to those who come after me; since in these latter days the world's boundaries have grown narrow, life is more or less stereotyped, and the dramas I witnessed in Virginia, Kansas, and Texas can never be re-enacted.

HISTORICAL NOTES

page 74: "Johnny Cake" was Charles Journeycake.
    75: The Leavenworth *Democrat* was really the *Kansas Weekly Herald*, the first regular newspaper published in Kansas. It was democratic and proslave in politics. It was edited by Lucian J. Eastin (not Euston) and published by Eastin and Adams. The first issue, dated 15 September 1854, was printed under a tree near the Missouri River.

   A. B. Miller was active in the proslave militia, captain of the Southern Rangers, Fourth Regiment, Northern Division, Kansas Militia, in 1856.
    77: The Potawatomi mission was located in the present town of St. Marys, Kansas.
    82: Samuel J. Jones was elected territorial sheriff of Douglas County, Kansas, by the first territorial legislature, which was proslave. He was commissioned 27 August 1855, and served until early in 1857, having tendered his resignation on 16 December 1856. His appointed but not commissioned successor, William T. Sherrard, was shot in a public meeting and died 21 February 1857.

   Sheriff Jones was wounded on 19 April 1856, but recovered. He was attempting to arrest Free-Soil advocate Samual N. Wood when he was shot.
    83: "Davy" Atchison was David Rice Atchison, who served as United States senator from Missouri from 1843 to 1855. When the administration of President Millard Fillmore ended on Saturday, 3 March

474

1853, and Franklin Pierce, president-elect could not be sworn in on Sunday, the country was in effect without a president for one day. Atchison, as president pro tempore of the Senate, was the senior official remaining and as such could claim to be president for that day.

84: The Massachusetts Emigrant Aid Company soon (spring, 1855) became the New England Emigrant Aid Company and sent several parties of settlers to Kansas.

Robinson was Charles Robinson, later to become first governor of the state of Kansas.

85: Governor Shannon was Wilson Shannon of Ohio, who served as territorial governor of Kansas from 10 August 1855 to 24 June 1856, and from 7 July to 18 August 1856.

Mount Oread is now the campus of the University of Kansas.

Williams evidently is referring to the first sack of Lawrence, which occurred on 21 May 1856. In the morning, Deputy U.S. Marshal William P. Fain entered Lawrence and arrested George W. Smith and George W. Deitzler, without resistance. He then dismissed his fifteen-hundred-man posse, telling them he had no further use for them. In the afternoon, Sheriff Samuel J. Jones appeared in Lawrence with a body of armed men. Colonel Shalor Eldridge's Free-State Hotel and the offices of the *Herald of Freedom* and the *Kansas Free State* were destroyed. Stores were broken open and pillaged, and the home of Charles Robinson was burned. The wanton destruction of property in Lawrence led to retaliation by bands of free-state men in different parts of the territory.

86: Topeka was never a proslave town; it was founded by free-state people and was always free-state. No force ever occupied Topeka.

Lone Jack was more commonly known as Black Jack. Here on June 2, 1856, John Brown captured twenty-nine proslave men after a short battle.

89: Cody was probably Isaac Cody, father of William F. "Buffalo Bill" Cody. Isaac was an ardent free-stater.

93: Auction of the Delaware trust lands commenced 17 November 1854 and continued to 13 December 1856.

98: Judge Lecompton was Judge Samuel D. Lecompte. The proslave town of Lecompton was named for him, probably causing Williams's error.

TEXAS

page 153: Edmund J. Davis (1827–83). At the time of the meeting described by Williams, Davis was a district judge whose territory covered the lower Rio Grande Valley. Davis opposed secession; fled to Mexico, where he organized a regiment of Texas Unionists; and ended the war as a brigadier general. As president of the constitutional convention (1868–69) he led the barely unsuccessful movement to divide Texas into three states. He headed the Republican party in Texas until death.

159: Charles Anderson (1814–95). In 1858 Anderson came from Ohio to San Antonio, where he bought and operated a horse ranch. He was arrested and imprisoned as a Union sympathizer in September 1861 but escaped the next month and returned to Ohio, where in February 1863 he was elected lieutenant governor. In August 1865 he became governor of Ohio on death of his predecessor. He never returned to Texas.

162: Twig is Major General David E. Twiggs (1790–1862). He was appointed commanding general, Department of Texas, with headquarters at San Antonio, in 1857. In February 1861, he surrendered, under armed compulsion, all U.S. Army forces and supplies in Texas to state authorities, the only such occurrence among all the U.S. Army officers who resigned to go with the Confederacy. General Winfield Scott once described Twiggs as unfit for command "either in the presence or the absence of the enemy." Ben McCulloch (1811–62) distinguished himself at the Battle of San Jacinto. He was a scout, Indian fighter, Texas Ranger, and congressman under the Republic of Texas. In May 1861, he was appointed brigadier general, C.S.A. He was killed in action at Pea Ridge, Arkansas, in March 1862.

173: Colonel Van Doon is Earl Van Dorn (1820–63), a nephew of Andrew Jackson. He resigned from the U.S. Army in January 1861 and was appointed colonel, C.S.A., the following March. The confrontation Williams describes occurred 9 May 1861 about sixteen miles west of San Antonio and involved approximately 400 Union troops and 1,750 Texas Confederates. On 8 May 1863 Van Dorn was killed (though not in action) at Spring Hill, Tennessee.

179: "Daddy" Greene is Thomas Green (1814–64), a veteran of the Battle of San Jacinto. On 20 May 1863 he was appointed brigadier general, C.S.A. He was killed in action at Blair's Landing, Louisiana, during the Red River Campaign in 1864. Tom Green County is named in his honor.

195: General Wasp is Hamilton P. Bee (1822–97). He fought in the Mexican War, and served (1849–59) in the Texas legislature, where he was speaker of the House from 1855 to 1857. Contrary to Williams's statement, Bee did not graduate from West Point. His brother, Barnard E. Bee, killed in action at the first Battle of Bull Run, is reputed to have given Stonewall Jackson and his Stonewall Brigade their famous nickname.

196: The "young ranger" is Bob Augustine, a known ruffian who had been convicted of murder in Eagle

Pass and pardoned. In May 1861 the drunken Augustine rode through Military Plaza in San Antonio, knocking over outdoor chili stands and dining tables. He chased some of the Mexican waitresses and cut off their hair with a knife before his arrest. The next day at his trial for disorderly conduct he threatened to kill the jury if found guilty. One juror was a local vigilance committee leader. Apparently in response to the threat, Augustine was acquitted. When he walked from the courtroom, a crowd of approximately two hundred vigilantes (which included a future associate justice of the Texas Supreme Court, a former marshal, a judge, four city aldermen, and a former Texas Ranger captain) seized Augustine and hanged him from a nearby oak tree. That same night four other local badmen were also strung up, three from the same tree as Augustine.

197: Mr. Sweets is James R. Sweet (1818–80), who moved to San Antonio from Nova Scotia in 1849. A merchant and speculator, he was elected mayor five times. On 26 May 1862 he was appointed lieutenant colonel, Thirty-third Texas Cavalry Regiment, serving in the lower Rio Grande valley. His homestead is now the campus of Incarnate Word College.

198: Asa Minshul is Asa Mitchell (1795–1865). He came to Texas in 1822 as one of the "old Three Hundred," the settlers of Stephen F. Austin's first colony. He was an early supporter of Texas independence from Mexico, and served as a sergeant at the Battle of San Jacinto. He became a rancher, merchant, and lay Methodist preacher; acquired extensive ranch properties south of San Antonio along the Medina River; and moved to Bexar County. At the start of Civil War he headed the local vigilance committee that hanged twenty-three known horse thieves in twenty-five days. Solomon Chiswell is Solomon Childress (1819–?), a member of the local vigilance committee who was on the jury that Augustine threatened.

203: Sydney Johnson is Albert Sidney Johnston (1803–62). A graduate of West Point, he served as secretary of war, Republic of Texas (1838), and fought in the Mexican War. In 1861 he resigned from the U.S. Army and was appointed general, C.S.A. He was killed in action at the Battle of Shiloh.

220: Colonel Vinton is David H. Vinton (1803–73). He was appointed by General Twiggs to the three-man military commission that arranged the disposition of federal property in Texas after Twiggs's surrender to Texas authorities. Vinton remained loyal to the Union and was repatriated to federal control. He was breveted to brigadier general, U.S. Army.

224: Mont Woodward is Montalcon Woodward (1841–?), eldest son of rancher John Woodward. Louis Oje is Louis Ogé (1832–1915). He went to Texas in the 1840s with his father, who was a member of Henri Castro's colony west of San Antonio. Upon his father's death (1847) he went to work on John Woodward's ranch south of San Antonio.

226: Dunn is James Duff (1828–88), a native of Scotland who joined the firm of Rose and McCarthy, importers, in San Antonio in 1859. He organized an irregular unit which elected him captain in 1861. As a commander of Texas Partisan Rangers, he was sent to Fredericksburg to suppress pro-Union sentiment; he declared martial law and ruled harshly. In August 1862 he sent his soldiers after some male German settlers fleeing to Mexico, an action that culminated in the Nueces Massacre later described by Williams. In March 1863 a party of Duff's men crossed into Mexico and kidnapped some Texas Unionists, including E. J. Davis; some of the captives were lynched. The diary of a British observer, Lt. Col. James A. L. Fremantle, indicates that Duff and his partner, McCarthy, profited in the wartime cotton trade from Duff's position. J. McCarthy was an antebellum San Antonio merchant. As a partner in Duff and McCarthy, he was involved in the Civil War cotton trade through Mexico.

233: General Herbert is Paul Octave Hébert (1818–80). In 1852 he was elected governor of Louisiana. In 1861 he was assigned command of the Department of Texas. The next year, he declared martial law over all Texas, a very unpopular action.

234: Henry Hopkins Sibley (1816–86) resigned from the U.S. Army in 1861 and organized Sibley's brigade of about two thousand men to take New Mexico for the Confederacy; the expedition failed.

244: Cole McCree is Colin D. McRae, a lieutenant in the Partisan Rangers who commanded the attack on the Germans at the Nueces River; he was seriously wounded.

Luck is probably Frederick Luck, who in December 1861 was appointed second lieutenant in the Alamo City Guards. Apparently he gave the order to shoot the wounded Germans captured at the Nueces.

260: Bethel Coopwood (1827–1907), who had gone to California seeking gold, returned to Texas at the start of the Civil War. An ardent secessionist, he captured a federal party that had fourteen camels, which he confiscated. He was a guide for Sibley in the unsuccessful New Mexico campaign. In March 1866 he bought at auction the remaining sixty-six camels from Jefferson Davis's antebellum experiment and sold five to Ringling Brothers' Circus, five to the International Circus, and tried using the others in caravans to Mexico.

263: Charles L. Pyron (1819–69), a freighter and rancher, had a ranch south of San Antonio near Mission San José y San Miguel de Aguayo. In 1861 he raised a company of troops and served in

Arizona under John R. Baylor. He was a major on Sibley's New Mexico campaign. In 1864 he became commander of the post of San Antonio.

264: John R. Baylor (1822–94) was a delegate to the secession convention, and was appointed lieutenant colonel, Second Texas Cavalry Regiment. From 1863 to 1865 he was a member of the Confederate Congress.

266: John M. Carolan (1821–63), a very successful businessman, was elected mayor of San Antonio in 1854. In 1862 he was a captain in Woods's Texas Cavalry Regiment.

282: José María Jesús Carbajal (d. 1874). Born in San Antonio, he represented Bexar at the legislature of Coahuila and Texas. In 1846 he was a division commander in the Mexican Army fighting the United States. He advocated an independent republic in northern Mexico. In 1862 he served in the Mexican liberal army against the French, and in 1865 he was governor of Tamaulipas and San Luis Potosí.

Colonel Locky is Philip N. Luckett (1825–69). He represented Nueces and Webb counties at the secession convention. Luckett, with Thomas J. Devine and Samuel A. Maverick, constituted the Committee of Public Safety that negotiated Twiggs's surrender of all Union forces and supplies in Texas in 1861. That September he was the colonel commanding the Third Texas Infantry Regiment stationed at Brownsville. He fled to Mexico for a brief period at war's end. Upon his return, he was arrested and indicted for high treason. In June 1867 he was pardoned.

Colonel Bushel is Augustus C. Buchel (1815–64). He was born in the Rhineland, received military schooling in Paris, served in the Turkish Army, and fought in Spain. In 1845 he emigrated to Texas. In the Mexican War he was aide-de-camp to General Zachary Taylor. In September 1861 he was commissioned lieutenant colonel, Third Texas Infantry Regiment. By May 1863 he was a colonel in the First Texas Cavalry Regiment. He died in April 1864 from wounds received in action during the Red River Campaign.

283: Major White is Edwin Fairfax Gray (1829–84). An Annapolis graduate, he accompanied Commodore Perry to Japan in 1853. During the Civil War he rose to the rank of lieutenant colonel, C.S.A.

Captain Kaupmann is John Herman Kampmann (1818–85). Born in Germany, he moved to San Antonio in 1848 and joined a contracting and building firm. In 1861 he raised a company of one hundred German Texans for the C.S.A., was elected captain, and joined the Third Texas Infantry Regiment. In August 1863 troops at Galveston under Kaupmann mutinied and were disarmed by another regiment. In 1866 he started a large steam-powered planing mill in San Antonio which became the city's largest employer. He was politically active and influential during Reconstruction as a Republican. In 1883, with Edward Hoppe, he started the Lone Star Brewery. At the time of his death he was a multimillionaire and probably the wealthiest man in San Antonio.

289: Kemp's Ranch on the San Gertrudis is the ranch of Richard King on Santa Gertrudis Creek in south Texas—popularly known as the King Ranch. King was active in the Civil War cotton trade.

Adrian J. Vidal commanded Vidal's Partisan Rangers under General Bee until 26 October 1863, when his company mutinied at Brownsville, killed several fellow Confederate soldiers and some civilians, and then fled. Vidal and others made their way to Union Army lines near the Gulf Coast, where they mustered into federal service. Vidal deserted the Union Army some months later.

290: Kennedy is Mifflin Kenedy (1818–95). At the time of Williams's account, Kenedy was a partner with

Richard King in steamboating, ranching, and the cotton trade. His Luareles Ranch eventually enclosed about a quarter of a million acres.

Dashields is D. H. Dashiell, son of Jeremiah Y. Dashiell. The senior Dashiell was a former U.S. Army paymaster at San Antonio and editor of the *San Antonio Herald*. During the Civil War he served as adjutant general, quartermaster general, and inspector general of state troops.

292: Monson is William Montgomery, a Unionist.

293: Sampson is probably Ed. Sampson, who in 1861 joined the "Mustang Greys," Company F, Fourth Texas Infantry Regiment, as fourth sergeant.

319: Governor Murrough is Pendleton Murrah, a lawyer who was elected to the Texas legislature in 1857 and elected governor of Texas in 1863. When the trans-Mississippi Confederate forces surrendered, Murrah went to Mexico, where he died of consumption in July 1865.

320: Colonel Benavides is Santos Benavides (1821–91). At the start of the Civil War he was appointed captain of state troops and soon became a major in Duff's Thirty-third Texas Cavalry Regiment. In 1863 he organized and was elected colonel of Benavides's Texas Cavalry Regiment. He was promoted to brigadier general in 1865.

329: Dan Westfall is Edward D. Westfall (1821–?). He lived on Leon Creek.

337: The Frenchman who lived with Westfall is Joseph Blanchard (1824–?).

364: Major Hunter is Sherod Hunter, who had served in Colonel G. W. Baylor's Second Cavalry Regiment, Arizona Brigade.

Colonel Franks is John Salmon "Rip" Ford (1815–97). He received his nickname during the Mexican War by starting letters notifying casualties' next of kin with "Rest in Peace." He was a member of the secession convention and was appointed colonel, Second Texas Regiment of

Mounted Rifles, stationed along the Rio Grande. On 13 May 1865 he commanded in the Battle of Palmito Ranch, the last battle of the Civil War.

377: Captain Minshul is Hiram Mitchell (1838–?), a son of Asa Mitchell.

383: Sol Chiff is Solomon Childress. See note regarding p. 198, Solomon Chiswell.

406: The "smart young cavalry general" is Major General Wesley Merritt (1834–1910), who commanded the Cavalry Corps of the Shenandoah, then the Cavalry Corps of the Potomac in the latter part of the Civil War. In both commands George Armstrong Custer was one of his subordinate division commanders. At war's end both Merritt and Custer were ordered to Texas to command cavalry divisions—whose main purpose was to disturb and make uneasy the French forces then in Mexico. Merritt went to San Antonio and Custer to Austin. Williams here appears to describe Custer, but he is in error. In a letter of 25 January 1866 Custer wrote that he had never been in San Antonio; he left Texas almost immediately thereafter.

Mr. Cleaveland is D. Cleveland. He was appointed, not elected, mayor of San Antonio by Gov. A. J. Hamilton. He served 9 October 1865–23 August 1866.

459: Jacques is William B. Jaques (1799–1870), who operated a stagecoach line in Mexico in the 1820s and 1830s. In 1838 he moved to San Antonio.

INDEX

Printed by Hazell, Watson & Viney, Ld., London and Aylesbury.